Economics of Agriculture

Second Revised and Enlarged Edition

A.A. Rane
A.C. Deorukhkar

ATLANTIC
PUBLISHERS & DISTRIBUTORS (P) LTD

ATLANTIC
PUBLISHERS & DISTRIBUTORS (P) LTD

7/22, Ansari Road, Darya Ganj, New Delhi
Tel.: +91-11-4077 5252, 2327 3880
E-mail: orders@atlanticbooks.com
Web: www.atlanticbooks.com

Published by Atlantic Publishers & Distributors (P) Ltd.

Reprinted in 2025

Printed & bound in India by Atlantic Print Services

Preface to Second Edition

The first edition of this book has been published in 1983. Since then several reprints were brought out in the market. Unfortunately, the revision of book remained pending due to my engagement in Economic Research at Regional Fruit Research Station, Vengurle. However, since October 2003 again, I joined Department of Economics, College of Agriculture, Dapoli (Maharashtra), Dr. Balasaheb Sawant Konkan Krishi Vidyapeeth, as Professor of Economics and got opportunities to teach courses to B.Sc. (Agril.), M.Sc. (Agril. Economics) and Ph.D. (Agril. Economics) students. This facilitated the inclusion of topics related to recent developments in rural finance and also in other branches of Agricultural Economics in detail in this edition. Likewise, new topic regarding Agricultural Business Management has been included in the syllabus of B.Sc. (Agril.). In addition, new colleges of Agricultural Marketing and Business Management have been started across India including Maharashtra that offer graduate and post-graduate courses in Agricultural Economics and in Agril.-Business Management. Considering these developments a new chapter on agriculture business management has been added in this revised edition. Similarly, questions and answers on various parts, along with syllabus and questions of ASRB/NET are included in this book. Thus, this book has been thoroughly revised, taking into account current market prices of inputs and outputs, recent development of the subject and changes in syllabi of different courses. Accordingly, this revised and enlarged second edition is rather more exhaustive in coverage and valuable. This book will be useful to B.A., M.A., M.Com., M.Sc. (Agril. Economics), Ph.D. (Economics), graduate and post-graduate students of Agril.-Business Management. This book is also useful to candidates appearing for competitive examinations. Besides, for Professors of Agril. Economics/Economics, it is an ideal reference source of lasting value.

We have been fortunate in receiving help and kind co-operation of a large number of persons in accomplishing this great task. We sincerely thank Dr. S.S. Magar, Vice-Chancellor of Dr. B.S. Konkan Krishi Vidyapeeth; Dr. V.B. Mehta, Dean, Faculty of Agriculture; Dr. G.D. Joshi, Associate Dean, College of Agriculture, Dapoli and Director of Extension Education, Dr. B.S. Konkan Krishi Vidyapeeth, Dapoli; Dr. T.A. More, Director of Research, Dr. B.S. Konkan Krishi Vidyapeeth, Dapoli; and Shri V.M. Pansare, Registrar, Dr. B.S. Konkan Krishi Vidyapeeth, Dapoli, for their encouragement and generous attitude.

We also thank Shri S.V. Mote, Asst. Registrar (Admin.); Shri Kokani, Asst. Registrar; Shri Mohite Ramakant, Asst. Comptroller and Shri V.D. Dinde, O.S., for their co-operation and encouragement.

We record our profound thanks to Dr. H.K. Patil, Dr. S.N. Tilekar, Dr. J.M. Talathi, Dr. V.A. Thorat, Dr. J.S. Dhekale, Dr. P.D. Veerkar, Dr. V.G. Naik, Dr. S.S. Wadkar, Dr. Shobha Vichare, Dr. S.L. Sananse and other staff members and students of the Department of Economics, College of Agriculture, Dapoli for their help and co-operation.

We record our sincere thanks to Shri S.M. Rodge, Librarian; Shri M.B. Nikam and Shri S.R. Bagade for their help, co-operation and valuable suggestions. We are extremely grateful to authors of various books, articles, data books referred while revising this book. We sincerely thank to Shri Santosh Shinde and Mrs. Bharati Shinde for typesetting of this book.

Above all, we are thankful for the constant encouragement received from students and readers of the first edition. We hope this revised edition will also be well-accepted by them.

Last but not least, we appreciate Mr. Prashant, Mrs. Pradnya, Mrs. Shalini Rane, Kumar Nikhil & Amol, and Mrs. Amruta Deorukhkar for their inspiration.

A.A. Rane
A.C. Deorukhkar

Preface to First Edition

Most of agricultural universities and non-agricultural universities in India have shifted to trimester/semester system. In these universities, agricultural economics is divided into different courses. Students have to study vast portion within a short period. While teaching to undergraduate and post-graduate students, it was observed that most of the students are not able to read through voluminous books as well as not able to purchase them because each book is useful only for a single course or so. As such there is a paucity of suitable textbooks on agricultural economics in the country. Considering this difficulty in mind, this book has been written in such a way that it will be useful to the students for all courses in agricultural economics taught at undergraduate and post-graduate level as well as in future for any competitive examination or for interview. The book will also be useful to the teaching staff. For obtaining precise knowledge of the subject, multiple choice questions, true and false statements along with their answers are given at the end of the book.

The book is also useful to B.A., M.A., M.Com., and M.Sc., students, who are studying agricultural economics. Agricultural finance officers working in banks, extension workers and those, who are associated with rural development work may find useful material in this textbook. For illustrations, examples based on Indian farm data and diagrams are given in this book. Language of the book is purposely kept simple and lucid.

I sincerely thank Dr. C.B. Mamoria and Dr. S.S. Johl, Dr. (Mrs.) Dru Shrivastava and Dr. A.S. Sirohi for their encouragement.

I am also indebted to Dr. P.V. Salvi, Vice-Chancellor, Konkan Krishi Vidyapeeth, Dr. S.B. Kadrekar, Dean, Faculty for Agriculture, K.K.V., Dr. D.S. Chaugale, Director of Research, Dr. J.G. Patil, Director of Extension Education, Shri M.D. Ambre,

Asst. Registrar, Shri R.K. Baviskar, Asst. Registrar for their encouragement and generous attitude. I also thank Prof. I.A. Bhatkar for his encouragement.

I record my profound thanks to Prof. S.G. Borude, Department of Agricultural Economics, who read through the manuscript and made valuable suggestions.

I express my deep sense of gratitude for all authors of different books, articles which I used while writing this book.

I record my sincere thanks to Shri S.M. Rodge, Asst. Librarian for his help, co-operation and valuable suggestions.

I also thank Prof. Miss S.R. Pawar, Shri J.M. Talathi, Shri E.R. Patil, Shri P.D. Veerkar and other staff members, and students of the Department of Agricultural Economics, College of Agriculture, Dapoli for their help and co-operation.

I must mention about help and co-operation received from my youngest brother Shri Laxman.

Finally, I appreciate my wife, Shalini, who inspired me for this endeavour.

A.A. Rane

26th January, 1983

Contents

1
Introduction to Agricultural Economics

Agriculture is modernizing year after year. It is changing from traditional type to commercial agriculture. It is no more remained a way of life, but it has become a profitable business. For maximizing profit of a farm, knowledge of agricultural economics is necessary. During recent years subject has acquired great importance.

Economics

Economics is defined as study of human behaviour in relation to ends and scarce means which have alternative uses. In other words, it educates people about how they can maximize their satisfaction from limited resources. At present, subject has been well-developed and provides various principles which help for maximizing satisfaction of human beings.

Agricultural Economics

Agricultural economics can be defined as application of principles of economics to the problems of agriculture. In other words, it educates man or cultivator so that he can maximize his profit from limited resources, as well as knowledge of agricultural economics is necessary to different types of agricultural specialists and to those, who are working for rural development.

Agricultural Economics and Plant Breeder

Plant breeder should possess knowledge of agricultural economics. The plant variety which he will find out should possess economic characters such as high yielding, suitable for profitable cultivation in a particular area. This is also applicable to fruit crop breeder.

Agricultural Economics and Animal Breeder

Animal breeder should try to find out a breed of milk animals which can give maximum returns per unit of feed/fodder consumption.

Agricultural Economics and Entomologist/Pathologist

He has to find out the insecticide/pesticide/fungicide which can protect the crop with minimum cost.

Agricultural Economics and Agril. Engineer

New tool or implement which engineer will invent should be such that people of the area can afford to purchase it, as well as it should complete the operation within minimum cost.

Agricultural Economics and Agronomist

Agril. Chemist should be able to find out fertilizer which is economical one as well as he should be able to suggest economical method of fertilizer application.

Thus, different agricultural specialist must know about agricultural economics.

Branches of Agricultural Economics

Agricultural economics is conveniently divided into following parts:

1. Agricultural finance,
2. Co-operation,
3. Agricultural marketing,
4. Farm management and production economics,
5. Research methodology,
6. Economic information about Indian agriculture,
7. Agricultural growth and economic development,
8. Agricultural Business Management.

Each part of agricultural economics is separately explained in a separate part. Research methodology and economic information about Indian agriculture, these two topics are also discussed in separate parts. Seventh part, *i.e.*, Agricultural Growth and Economics Development and eighth part is also added in this book. Thus, the book is divided into eight parts.

PART I
Agricultural Finance

2
Introduction to Agricultural Finance

Meaning

Agricultural finance includes agricultural credit, saving, income, investment and capital formation. It is not only agricultural credit but also it is more than agricultural credit. It can be defined as "Agricultural finance is an economic study of financing the farm business". It is that part of farm management which pertains to acquisition and use of capital. The field of agricultural finance extends beyond the usual bounds of farm management—to include institutional aspects of credit. It is concerned with the basic structure and characteristics of lending institutions as related to obtaining and using credit. Agricultural finance deals with the economics of using financial resources, a study of acquiring credit comprises a major part of the field of agril. financc. For this reason, considerable emphasis is placed upon a study of agricultural lenders, including their basic organization, objectives in making agricultural loans, loan policies, procedures and source of loan funds. Agril. finance provides the economic principles for analysing of how much it would be profitable and safe to borrow and the principles or type of information needed to select a lender which will best suit the needs of the borrower. Agricultural finance can be divided into two categories: (*i*) Micro-agril. finance, and (*ii*) Macro-agril. finance. In micro-agril. finance problems of individual farm, are studied and in macro agril. finance, government agricultural credit policy, credit policy of a bank for a particular region such problems are tackled. Thus, agricultural finance includes study of both lender and borrower.

Importance and Scope

In ancient period, agriculture was subsistence type, capital need was less for agricultural production and hence, credit need was also limited. In course of time agriculture became more capital intensive and hence credit intensive. In India about 80 per cent cultivators are small and marginal cultivators, their income level is quite low. Low income results into low saving, because of low saving one cannot make additional investment and again one has to face low income. Thus, majority of Indian cultivators are found in a vicious circle of low income, to break this circle, credit is essential. Thus, during recent years, agricultural credit and agril. finance assumed great importance. Indian agriculture is modernizing and becoming more capital intensive, modern inputs and greenhouses needs more and more capital. Hence, agril. finance will be important in future also. Agricultural finance has also a vast scope in future.

Credit

Word credit came from the word credo (Latin) means I believe. Credit is mainly based on the faith in borrower's willingness and ability to repay the amount borrowed. Meaning of term credit can be explained as follows:

1. Credit means trust in borrower's ability to repay and his willingness to repay.
2. Credit is that form of confidence reposed in a person which enables him to obtain from another the temporary use of thing of a value.
3. Credit refers to amount borrowed. Credit is a powerful agency for good in the hands of those who know how to use it but equally dangerous in the hands of those who do not know how to use it.

Credit Worthiness

Credit worthiness of a person for qualifying himself to borrow from lender. It mainly depends upon following things:

1. Character of a person,

2. Capacity to repay,
3. Capital (Asset position).

These three points are known as 3 Cs of credit.

Advantages of Credit

1. Burden on metallic money is reduced. People use credit instruments and carry out their business. They need not use metallic money often.
2. Most of the firms carry out their financial transactions through credit instruments such as cheques, etc.
3. Credit makes capital more productive. With the help of credit, idle resources can be best utilised to obtain high rate of return.
4. With the help of credit facility a person with meagre financial capacity is able to launch a big business. Some people possess idle resources and business ability; they are able to launch big business if they obtained credit. Thus, credit is advantageous.

Abuses of Credit

Credit has also some disadvantages:

1. Reckless borrowing ruins both the borrower and the lender. There are certain principles of credit use. If those principles are not followed, borrower has to face negative effect of credit.
2. Credit may encourage extravagance and waste.

Need for Credit

Credit is needed for following purposes:

1. Repayment of old debt: When persons are in urgent need they borrow from private money lenders at high interest rate. Such debt can be repaid by taking loan from institutional sources.
2. Expenditure on social customs, litigation, marriages, etc.
3. Sometimes credit for consumption expenditure is taken.
4. For productive expenditure: This kind of credit is needed in larger proportion for development of particular enterprise.

Credit Instruments

Credit instruments mean documents those enable credit transactions smoothly. It is safe to use credit instruments. It makes transaction easy and safe as well as efficiency in transacting is also achieved.

Various credit instruments are as follows:

1. Cheques,
2. Draft,
3. Hundis,
4. Promissory note,
5. Bill of exchange,
6. Debit card,
7. Credit card.

1. Cheques: It is a written order on a printed form by a depositor to his bank to pay a sum of money to himself or to somebody else whose name is entered on it or to the bearer. If there is enough money in the account who has issued the cheque, the cheque will be honoured. If there is no balance or if no credit limit or no loan granted, the cheque will not be honoured by the bank, *i.e.*, bearer will not get cash in hand.

Cheques are of following kinds:

(*i*) *Bearer cheque*: Any one can get such a cheque cashed. In this case, the bank need not worry as to who presents it, at the counter. If a bearer cheque is lost, the finder can cash it, unless the bank is notified in time to stop the payment.

(*ii*) *Order cheque*: The person who presents the cheque at the counter has to prove his identity before the proceeds of the cheque can be paid to him.

(*iii*) *Crossed cheque*: A cheque is crossed by drawing two parallel lines across its face or in a corner and writing the words "& Co" between them. It is the safest form of payment as it cannot be cashed at the bank counter. The payee cannot get proceeds of the cheque in cash. He can only get the sum transferred to his own or to somebody else's account.

(*iv*) *A post-dated cheque*: If you have to pay somebody after one month put down future date and issue the cheque, it can be cashed only after that date.

(*v*) *A blank cheque*: This is a unlimited offer because signature by a depositor is made keeping space for amount as blank. Hence, a drawee can enter any figure. Generally, nobody ordinarily signs blank cheque.

Thus, cheque is a convenient credit instrument. There is no fear of loss when the cheque is crossed. Counterfoil of the cheque serves as a receipt and therefore ensures honesty.

2. Draft: A draft is a cheque drawn by a bank on its own branch or on another bank requiring the latter to pay a specified amount to person named in it. If you want to pay ₹ 1,000 to a person in Delhi, you will obtain a draft say from State Bank and send it to a concerned person by a registered envelope. When State Bank Delhi branch will identify a concerned person, will issue the cash. Similarly, when we are on tour at that time also drafts are convenient, we can avoid the risk of getting robbed by taking cash with us.

3. Hundis: Hundis are internal bills of exchange in one of our languages and have been prevalent in India long before the dawn of civilisation elsewhere.

4. Promissory Note: The simplest form of credit instrument is the promissory note. A promissory note is a written promise from a borrower to pay a certain sum of money to the creditor. It is an acknowledgement of debt and an obligation to repay.

5. Bill of Exchange: It is an order by a seller to a buyer or by a creditor to the debtor to pay a certain sum of money to himself or to bearer or to another person named therein.

6. Debit Card: After opening a personal account in a bank and money is deposited in that new account. Concerned bank issues a debit card to concerned account holder. By using debit card person can withdraw the required cash from ATM (Any Time Money). Person can withdraw the cash from ATM which are located in other cities. He can withdraw the amount to the extent of balance available in his account. In some banks daily maximum 10,000 rupees can be withdrawn. Nowadays this is a convenient method of handling the cash.

7. Credit Card: Here concerned bank grants credit limit to the individual person to the extent of ₹ 50,000 or ₹ 1,00,000 and then person can withdraw the cash from ATM as per his requirement or he can purchase the commodities from shops and pay with the help of his credit card. Bank which has issued the credit card will charge interest on the amount utilized and concerned person has to repay that used amount along with interest within one or one and half month to the concerned bank. This card is also useful when cash is needed immediately.

Classification of Credit

Credit is classified for convenience as below:

(I) Broad categories

(*i*) *Consumption credit*: Credit is used for consumption expenditure.

(*ii*) *Production credit*: Credit is used for production purposes.

(II) According to time

(*i*) Short-term credit (up to 18 months).

(*ii*) Medium-term credit (18 months to 5 years).

(*iii*) Long-term credit (5 years to 30 years).

(III) According to purpose

(*a*) *Agricultural purposes*

(*i*) *Short-term credit*: Generally credit is used up to one year or one and half year. At the end of term, it must be repaid, *e.g.*, loan taken for seeds, manures, fertilizers as crop loan.

(*ii*) *Medium-term credit*: Within five years this type of loan must be repaid, *e.g.*, loan for purchasing implements, dairy animals, etc.

(*iii*) *Long-term credit:* This type of credit is repaid within 25 to 30 years, *e.g.*, loan for purchasing land, for reclamation of land, for pipelines, for land improvements, etc.

(*b*) *Non-farm business purposes*: This kind of credit is required for purchasing production equipments, furniture, transport equipments, repairing buildings, etc.

(*c*) *Family expenditure*: For purchasing clothes, utensils, foodgrains, etc.

(*d*) *Other purposes*: This kind of credit is required for purchasing shares of co-operative societies, purchasing shares of company, payment of old debts, etc.

Credit Agencies

Various credit agencies are engaged in rural credit.

Table 2.1 reveals certain important facts. Institutional credit increased many times during twenty years. Government took various steps to increase proportion of institutional credit in total borrowings. Particularly, co-operatives and commercial banks showed progress. However, cultivators have to depend for their credit need on private credit agencies. And hence, still certain improvement must be brought out in institutional credit agencies. With regard to private credit agencies agricultural and professional money lenders play important role.

Table 2.1: Percentage share in total borrowing by Indian cultivator

Sr. No.	Agency	Percentage share of individual credit agency in total borrowing by Indian cultivator	
		1951-52	1961-62
(I)	**Institutional agencies**	(7.3)	(18.7)
	1. Government	3.3	2.6
	2. Co-operatives	3.1	15.5
	3. Commercial banks	0.9	0.6
(II)	**Private agencies**	(92.7)	(81.3)
	4. Agricultural money-lenders	24.9	36.0
	5. Professional money-lenders	44.8	13.2
	6. Traders and commission agents	5.5	8.8
	7. Relatives	14.2	8.8
	8. Others (Landlords)	3.3	14.5
		100.00	100.00

Source: Menon, K.S.V. "Rural Development and Financial Institutions". *Issues in Indian Agriculture*, edited by K.R. Gupta, p. 248, New Delhi, 1980.

It is observed from Table 2.2 that proportion of institutional finance is increasing very fast and in 1991 cultivators received 64% finance from institutional agencies, after nationalization of commercial banks in 1969 advances by them has been increased significantly and now they have surpassed co-operative banks. Similarly, proportion of private finance has declined significantly, *i.e.*, 70.8 in 1971 to 32.7% in 1991.

Table 2.2: Percentage share in total borrowing by Indian cultivator

Sr. No.	Agencies	Percentage share of individual credit agency in total borrowing by Indian cultivator		
		1971	1981	1991
(I)	**Institutional Agencies**	(29.2)	(61.2)	(64.0)
	Co-operatives	20.1	28.6	21.6
	Commercial banks	2.2	28.0	33.7
	Others	6.9	4.6	8.7
(II)	**Private Agencies**	(70.8)	(33.8)	(32.7)
	Money lenders	36.9	16.9	17.6
	Others	33.9	16.9	15.1
	Total	100.0	100.0	100.0

Sources: 1. Ruddar Datt, *Indian Economy*, S. Chand & Co., New Delhi.
2. *Debt and Investment Survey*, 1981-82 and 1991-92.

Advantages of Private Credit Agencies

1. Intimate knowledge of local production facilities, possess knowledge of credit worthiness of borrower.
2. Cost of administration is low, because they operate locally and often without any paid staff.
3. In granting loans, collecting interest they are prompt and less costly.

Disadvantages of Private Credit Agencies

1. Cover very small number of farmers.
2. Charge very high interest rate.
3. Some cases of cheating may occur such as writing wrong amount, obtaining signatures of borrower on wrong papers, etc.

Advantages of Institutional Credit Agencies

1. Cover large number of farmers.
2. Charge low interest rate.
3. Cases of cheating do not occur.

Disadvantages of Institutional Credit Agencies

1. Time required for obtaining amount of loan is comparatively more.
2. It is rather difficult to keep personal touch with borrowers.
3. Cost of administration is comparatively high.

Government as a Credit Agency

Government is involved in agricultural credit by two ways.

(a) Direct finance

Government directly finances cultivators by advancing taccavi loan. In some states, taccavi loan is given in some other forms. Taccavi loan is sanctioned for short-term agricultural purposes as well as for long-term agricultural purposes. Taccavi loan is advantageous because of its low interest rate but the amount borrowed is insignificant as well as time required for advancing the loan is more.

(b) Indirect finance

1. Government purchases shares of co-operative organisations and helps for improving lending capacity of the co-operative organisations.
2. Government provides guarantee to apex banks to enable them to borrow from RBI.
3. Government provides subsidies to societies to enable them to employ trained personnel and also for some other purposes.

Commercial Banks

After nationalization of commercial banks, they are advancing considerable amount to cultivators, several banks opened their branches in unbanked backward areas of the country. Commercial banks finance directly to the cultivators as well as finance through co-operative societies. Before nationalization of commercial banks, they were not advancing loans satisfactorily to agriculturists. Agriculture is modernizing during recent years and credit requirement of modern agriculture is increasing. Commercial banks have to follow directives given by RBI and because of that commercial banks are taking lead in financing agriculture during recent years. In July, 1969 all commercial banks had over 1860 branches in rural and semi-urban areas; this number had increased to over 47,190 by March 2002. There are now 1.6 crores agricultural borrowing accounts with commercial banks amounting to ₹ 63,080 crores as compared to only 2 lakhs accounts with total outstanding advances to the extent of about ₹ 160 crores in June 1969. At present commercial banks are the main financers to agricultural sector.

One of the main purposes of bank nationalization in 1969 was to provide credit to the priority sectors like agriculture has been satisfied.

Lead Bank Scheme

Towards the close of 1969 the RBI accepted the scheme for 380 districts. Lead bank scheme is gaining popularity day by day. The credit plans for all 380 districts in the country have been launched for implementation. As on March 2002, the lead bank scheme covered 580 districts of the country. All commercial banks actively participate in this scheme.

Regional Rural Banks (RRBs)

Regional Rural Banks were established to satisfy the credit needs of small farmers and other weaker sections of the society. These banks are sponsored by commercial banks and by Government. RRBs are to combine the local feel of co-operative institutions and management technique of commercial banks.

At the end of December 1978, 56 RRBs covering 95 districts in 17 states had been set up. At the end of December 1977, they mobilised deposits of ₹ 33.96 crores and advanced loans of ₹ 43.19 crores. Out of this total advances, ₹ 39.55 crores were advanced to weaker sections and thus they tried to satisfy the objective. Still, there is vast scope for RRBs to expand as small farmers and marginal farmers constitute major part of the farmers community.

Financial Performance of RRBs

In 2000-01 as many as 170 RRBs (out of a total of 196) made operating profits of ₹ 790 crores. In 2001-02, 167 RRBs earned operating profit of ₹ 838 crores. The net profit of the 196 profit-making RRBs stood at ₹ 608 crores during 2001-02.

Agricultural Development Branches (ADBs): By the end of 1977, the State Bank of India (SBI) group had 314 agricultural development branches. Most of these ADBs have been opened in SFDA/MFAL districts, financing by ADB is done on an integrated area development basis. Programmes have been taken on about 100 villages, small agro-based industries are also financed. Each ADB is expected to cover 4000 to 5000 farmers over a period of three to four years.

Crop Loan

The conference of the State ministers, for co-operation held in Bombay in November 1965, recommended the introduction of crop loan system throughout the country with effect from Kharif season of 1966. Now, primary credit co-operatives, multipurpose co-operative societies mainly advance crop loans to cultivators. Commercial banks also provide crop loans.

Advantages of Crop Loan

1. Cultivators are encouraged for cultivating commercial crops.
2. It helps for increasing total agricultural production.
3. It helps for individual cultivator to raise his income level.
4. Repayment of loan becomes easy.

Limitations of Crop Loan

Some people do not recognise importance of fertilizer application, use of insecticides and do not spend the crop loan amount for growing the crop. They mis-utilize that amount, spend uneconomically on unproductive items. This makes the cultivator difficult to repay the crop loan.

3
Financial Institutions

Agricultural Finance Corporation (AFC)

As a positive response to social control which came in force from December 1967, commercial banks formed a club of banks known as Agricultural Finance Corporation on 10th April 1968. It is a limited liability company registered under the Companies Act, 1956 with an authorised capital of ₹ 100 crores and a paid up share capital of ₹ 5 crores. Basically, AFC is a consortium of commercial banks and consultancy agency of member banks in the formulation of projects for agriculture and rural development. Scheduled commercial banks numbering 37 had subscribed to the share capital of AFC.

Objectives

The main objectives of corporation are to finance by all possible ways and means to agricultural sector and bring out development. Agriculture must be modernized and hence financing for various purposes is essential. Hence, financing and helping following activities are determined:

1. Mechanization of agriculture and agricultural operations.
2. Processing of agricultural produce.
3. Growing, improving, preserving and maintaining of forests.
4. Purchase, sale, breeding and rearing of livestock's and animals.
5. Production, supply and distribution of fertilizers and insecticides.

6. Production, supply and distribution of agricultural produce.
7. Improving marketing facilities.
8. Strengthening transport facilities.
9. Construction of warehouses, godowns, etc.
10. Sinking and deepening irrigation wells and energising the same.
11. Establishment of agricultural service units, etc.

A national level consultative committee for bringing out co-ordination among the different lending agencies has already been set up by the corporation. Corporation organizes seminars, workshops and training programmes to bank staff. It's association with FAO and World Bank is also significant.

Functions

Agricultural finance corporation has two important functions to perform:

1. Financing of important priority projects contributing to agricultural development.
2. Promoting Commercial Banks advances to worthwhile agricultural projects. AFC tried to provide finance to above-mentioned agricultural activities. However, financing by AFC was not enough. AFC recognised the difficulties faced by other commercial banks in financing agriculture because commercial banks were not having expert staff to do it. AFC helped commercial banks to prepare worthwhile agricultural schemes and finance those schemes. Thus, AFC promoted total agricultural finances.

Agricultural Refinance and Development Corporation (ARDC)

Land development banks were financing long-term investment projects but certain schemes such as large land reclamation projects, development of plantation crops, development of large dairy husbandry were requiring large sums of money. Financing such schemes were beyond the resources of even state co-operative and land development banks. Government realised this problem and Agricultural Refinance Corporation was established in July 1963 to tackle such problems. After few years, name changed as Agricultural Refinance and Development Corporation.

The objective of ARDC is to provide medium and long-term credit through the refinancing activity for the development of agriculture and related industries. Some of the schemes which the corporation can assist are as follows:

(*i*) Reclamation and preparation of land so that irrigation facilities are fully utilised.

(*ii*) Development of plantation crops.

(*iii*) Development of mechanised farming.

(*iv*) Development of dairy, animal husbandry.

(*v*) Development of poultry.

(*vi*) Development of fisheries.

ARDC sanctioned 233 schemes up to 1968-69. Andhra Pradesh, Mysore, Punjab, Tamil Nadu are major beneficiaries. Central land development banks are the major beneficiaries of corporation, *i.e.*, 91 per cent drawls are by the central land development banks.

Sources of Funds

The corporation is authorised to issue share capital up to ₹ 25 crores into 25,000 fully paid-up shares of ₹ 10,000 each. Initially, shares worth ₹ 5 crores were issued, these shares are guaranteed by Govt. of India. Similarly fund of ₹ 5 crores was provided as an interest free loan by Govt. of India. By the end of June, 1970, the total amount of loan given by Govt. of India stood at over ₹ 26 crores.

Size of Loan

Corporation is designed to facilitate financing of only large schemes, the minimum size of loan has been set at ₹ 1 lakh.

Duration of Loan

Corporation provides refinancing facility for both medium and long-term loans. Medium-term refers to five years and long-term refers to fifteen years; bye-laws allow up to 20 years period.

Security

Apex Bank, Central Land Development Bank mortgage property of a borrower, same property is sub-mortgaged to the corporation. It will be interesting to know what type of schemes ARDC is handling, it will be seen from the Table 3.1.

Table 3.1: Progress of ARDC

Year	No. of schemes sanctioned	Corporations commitment in ₹ crores	Total financial outlay ₹ crores
1963-64	3	2.01	2.23
1964-65	8	9.35	11.02
1965-66	14	10.31	13.31
1966-67	13	7.36	9.18
1967-68	78	58.13	67.08
1968-69	108	69.32	79.20
1969-70	142	70.92	98.72
1972-73	230	172.30	196.60
1973-74	556	220.50	251.30

Table 3.2: Purpose-wise classification of the schemes sanctioned by ARDC during 1973-74

Sr. No.	Purpose of schemes	No. of schemes	Total financial outlay ₹ crores	Corporations commitment in ₹ crores
1.	Development of minor irrigation	317	211.3	188.5
2.	Land reclamation & soil conservation	10	2.7	2.1
3.	Development of plantation	40	8.7	6.8
4.	Farm mechanization	84	12.1	9.2
5.	Poultry farming	15	0.6	0.5
6.	Development of fisheries	3	0.8	0.7
7.	Dairy development	62	8.2	
8.	Construction of storage facilities & market yards	18	6.8	
	Total 1973-74	549	251.20	207.80

More schemes have been sanctioned in case of minor irrigation, farm mechanization, dairy development. However, corporation tackled schemes in various fields which resulted in healthy growth of agriculture.

Reserve Bank of India (RBI)

Reserve Bank of India was set up under the RBI Act, 1934 in 1935. For looking after agricultural finance, separate Agricultural Department was created in the Bank in 1935. Objectives of this Department were as follows:

1. To maintain an expert staff for studying all questions relating to agricultural credit.
2. To provide expert guidance to the governments and to co-operative institutions in matters of credit.
3. To finance the movement of crops and other agricultural operations through state co-operative banks and other suitable agencies of rural credit.
4. To co-ordinate the operations of bank in connection with agricultural credit and its relations with state co-operative banks.
5. To strengthen the agricultural credit structure, the RBI provides educational and consultation services. The Bankers Training College, which was open to employees of central and apex co-operative banks was financed by RBI. This function has now been transferred to state and national co-operative unions.
6. Each year the RBI sends out inspectors to visit co-operative banks and credit societies to review their procedures and to make recommendations for changes in their loan policies and book-keeping procedures.
7. Research into agricultural credit problems on an aggregate basis is undertaken on a continuous basis by the Reserve Bank.

Rural Credit Survey

In 1951, an expert committee was set up under the chairmanship of Shri Gorwala to plan, organise, and supervise a survey regarding facilities available in rural areas for providing agricultural credit to the agriculturists and to make necessary recommendations. The committee submitted its report in 1954. Committee found out, quantity of credit supplied to agriculturists is inadequate, is not of right type and often fails to go to the right people. Co-operative credit is playing insignificant role in the field of rural credit. Large cultivators benefited more.

Under such circumstances, committee recommended following things:

1. An integrated scheme of rural credit.
2. Suitable amendment should be made in RBI Act and the establishment of a National Co-operative Development and Ware Housing Board at all India level.
3. The establishment of three special funds under the RBI was suggested.
   (*i*) The National Agricultural Credit (long-term operations) Fund.
   (*ii*) The National Agricultural (stabilization) Fund.
   (*iii*) National Agricultural Credit (relief and guarantee) Fund.
4. A crop loan system was to be evolved.
5. The economic viability of the co-operatives at the village-level was essential. Each village society should be revitalized and reorganized and made really effective.

Afterwards, RBI has been conducting a series of annual follow-up survey of moderate scope since 1956-57.

Recommendation of Rural Credit Review Committee

To review all aspects of rural credit, committee was appointed for making certain suggestions. This committee was set up under the chairmanship of Shri B. Venkatappiah in 1969. On its recommendations, standing advisory committee of the RBI was set up. Function of committee was to issue of policy and procedure in various matters. SFDA and MFAL agencies are also suggested by Review Committee.

Small Farmers Development Agency (SFDA)

It was observed by the Rural Credit Review Committee that majority of the cultivators are small and marginal cultivators as well as there are many agricultural labourers in the country.

Since, independence agricultural development took place, but benefits are not received to these weaker sections of community. Country must plan to improve their future. Thus, with the good intention, review committee suggested SFDA and marginal farmers and agricultural labourers development agencies.

Identification of Farmers

Identification of small farmer is an important aspect. Conveniently, small farmer is a farmer having size of holding less than 2 hectare (unirrigated) or one hectare irrigated and having income less than ₹ 2,400/annum. Such farmers are identified and listed by SFDA officers and list is passed on to commercial bank branches as well as to primary credit co-operatives.

Schemes for Assistance

The agency will have to prepare different types of programmes for various categories of participants. SFDA takes up various schemes such as sinking of wells, fitting oil-engines or electric motors for lifting water, purchasing milk animals. SFDA officers advise identified cultivators and also suggest bank to provide credit facilities to these cultivators. SFDA subsidies interest rate for such cultivators and thus help cultivators for their upliftment. SFDA has identified various districts throughout the country, these districts are identified on the basis of more proportion of small cultivators exists in those districts.

Marginal Farmers and Agricultural Labourers (MFAL)

Marginal farmer is a farmer having holding less than one hectare. Agricultural labourer is a person having a homestead and earning 50 per cent or more of his income as agricultural wages.

This agency is also suggested by Rural Credit Review Committee. Area is selected as MFAL area when such people are predominant in the area. An infrastructure of institutional agencies like co-operative is available or could be developed in these areas so that the participant in the project can take advantage. The identified cultivators get subsidies in interest rate on the borrowed amount, etc. Small farmers are eligible to get subsidies, 25 per cent of total investment and marginal farmers and agricultural labourers 33.33 per cent of total investment.

Khusro Committee's Report

The Agricultural Credit Review Committee under the chairmanship of Dr. A.M. Khusro was appointed by RBI in August, 1986 and it submitted its report in August, 1989. This committee recommended ceiling for the lending rate for commercial banks towards agricultural lending was fixed at 15.5 per cent, whereas in case of PLDBs, it was 5 per cent and 8.65 per cent for RRBs. It is also suggested in areas where RRBs are not economically viable may be merged into sponsoring commercial banks. It also recommended the creation of National Co-operative Bank to function as national apex bank for all co-operative institutions in the country.

Narasimham Committee's Report

Government of India appointed a Narasimham Committee on Financial System in August, 1991. Committee's report was available in November, 1991. First set of recommendations related to the extent of directed investment and directed credit programmes. These are:

1. To cut the Statutory Liquidity Ratio (SLR) from 38.5 per cent to 25 per cent over five years.
2. To reduce Cash Reserve Ratio (CRR) progressively.
3. To bring down the priority sector credit target to 10 per cent of the total bank credit (small and marginal farmers, small business and transport operators, village industries, village artisans and other weaker sections are considered in this 10%).
4. Suggested abolition of bank branch licensing and increasing operational autonomy of the banks and financial institutions.
5. Creating three to four large banks with international character and eight to ten banks with countrywide universal banking.
6. Increasing competition between commercial banks and other financial institutions, etc.

National Bank for Agriculture and Rural Development (NABARD)

The Banking Commission 1972, National Commission on Agriculture (1976) and Committee to Review Arrangements for Institutional Credit for Agriculture and Rural Development (CRAFICARD) in 1979, under the Chairmanship of B. Sivaraman, former member of Planning Commission, recommended the setting up of a national level institution called NABARD for providing all types of production and investment credit for agriculture and rural development. The existing national level institutions such as Agricultural Refinance and Development Corporation (ARDC), Agricultural Credit Department and Rural Planning and Credit cell of Reserve Bank of India (RBI), were merged with NABARD and thus NABARD came into existing in July, 1982.

Objectives

Because of modern agriculture demand for institutional credit increased manifold, similarly rural development is also necessary for improving quality of life in rural area. Credit need for both the purposes are satisfied by NABARD as a refinancing institution. However, NABARD also provides direct credit to any institution or individual, subject to the approval of the Central Government. It has a link with RBI for guidance and assistance in financial matters.

Functions

1. NABARD provides 100 per cent refinance to pilot rainfed projects, waste land development schemes. Similarly, provides 75 per cent refinance to agro-processing units and biogas units, 70 per cent refinance to all other schemes including IRDP, 50 per cent refinance to farm mechanization.
2. It offers advice and guidance to State Government, National Co-operative Development Corporation (NCDC).
3. It imparts training, carry out consultancy and conduct research related to credit for agriculture and for rural development.

4. It extends refinance to commercial banks, co-operative banks, RRBs for term loans in relation to agriculture and rural development.
5. It provides finance to all the eligible financial institutions for conversion of production loans into term loans when farmers will face natural calamities, wars, etc.
6. It contributes to share capital of eligible institutions working for agriculture, rural development directly or through State Government.

Management Board

Management Board consists of 15 members, details are as follows:

1. Chairman.
2. Managing Director.
3. Two Directors are experts in rural economics and in rural developments.
4. Three Directors are representatives of co-operatives.
5. Three Directors are from commercial banks.
6. Three Directors are officials of Government of India.
7. Two Directors are officials of State Governments.

The Chairman and Managing Director are the two top level executives of bank and other 13 Directors work in a advisory capacity.

Sources of Funds

Auhorised share capital of NABARD – ₹ 500 crores
Issued and paid-up capital – ₹ 100 crores

Other sources are as follows:

1. Borrowing from RBI, Government of India and from any institution approved by Government of India.
2. Issue and sale of bonds by Government of India.
3. Deposits from State Governments and local authorities.
4. Gifts and grants received.

Since 1989-90 to 1991-92 NABARD has sanctioned ₹ 5,171 crores for 6706 schemes and for state and central co-operative banks. NABARD pumped ₹ 1,533 crores into agriculture and rural development in Maharashtra during 2004-05. NABARD will extend financial assistance amounting to ₹ 100 crores to set up Village Knowledge Centers (VKCs) in 10 states in the country. These VKCs will be managed by respective State Government and will be guided by Dr. M.S. Swaminathan Research Foundation, Chennai.

NABARD and Rural Infrastructure Development Fund (RIDF)

The Union Budget for 1995-96 proposed the creation of Rural Infrastructure Development Fund (RIDF) in NABARD with a corpus of ₹ 2,000 crores. This corpus was contributed by all Indian scheduled commercial banks to make up for their shortfall in agricultural lending target of 18 per cent of net bank credit. Interest on RIDF loans would be the prevailing bank rate plus 2 per cent. Apart from State Government other institutions and groups, such as Panchayati Raj Institutions, Self-Help Groups, NGO's, etc., can now implement RIDF projects. Projects may be regarding irrigation, roads, bridges and others. Total amount sanctioned under RIDF during 1995-96 to 2001-2002 was ₹ 23,430 crores.

Integrated Rural Development Programme (IRDP)

Integrated Rural Development Programme (IRDP) was launched during 1978-79 by the Ministry of Rural Reconstruction with the objective of eliminating poverty and unemployment in rural areas. The existing programmes like SFDA, MFAL, Drought Prone Area Programme (DPAP), Command Area Development Authority (CADA), National Rural Employment Programme (NREP), Training of Rural Youth for Self-Employment (TRYSEM), etc., have been merged into IRDP. IRDP is an anti-poverty programme. In this programme small and marginal farmers, agricultural labourers, landless workers, sharecroppers, artisans, scheduled castes and scheduled tribes and other living below poverty line are being covered. IRDP has covered all 5011 blocks in the country in the year 1980. The loans to the beneficiaries are granted by banks and subsidies are provided by IRDP authority. In case of small farmers, 25 per cent subsidy is granted. Similarly, for marginal farmers, agricultural labourers and non-agricultural labourers subsidy is 33.3 per cent and for scheduled tribes subsidy is 50 per cent.

During the year 1991-92 under IRDP, banks assisted 25.17 lakh beneficiaries, an amount of ₹ 1,133.27 crores were distributed as loan and ₹ 800.99 crores as subsidy.

However, up to March 1998, under IRDP, 527 lakh families have been assisted with a total investment of ₹ 30,871.79 crores. Out of this loan component was ₹ 20,352.63 crores and subsidy disbursed was ₹ 10,519.16 crore. The level of per family investment was ₹ 16,900 in 1997-98 as compared to ₹ 1,642 during 1980-81. Out of total beneficiaries 46 per cent were scheduled caste and scheduled tribes' persons.

Overall it is a poverty alleviation programme basically meant for improving the standard of living of families falling below the poverty line.

Self-Help Group (SHG)

NABARD is a pioneer in conceptualizing and implementing the concept of SHG through the pilot project on linking SHG with banks. In February 1992, the project was operationalized throughout the country. NABARD popularized the project among the bankers and NGOs through organizing a series of workshops, training programmes and seminars at different levels.

Self-Help Group is a group of people coming together voluntarily for attaining a common goal. The goal could be anything like saving habit or satisfying credit need or undertaking any subsidiary occupation like dairy, poultry, fruit processing, etc. At present 30,273 groups have bank linkage. These groups are generating employment and income to members. Similarly, habit of sowing of money in banks is also cultivated among members.

It is observed from table 3.3 that more than 10 lakhs SHGs have been started functioning out of these SHGs more than 3 lakhs SHGs obtained credit and they are using a credit of ₹ 3,900 crores.

Table 3.3: SHG-bank linkage: Cumulative progress

Sr. No.	As on March 31st	No. of SHGs cumulative	No. of SHGs financed	Bank loan disbursed (cumulative ₹ crores)
1.	1999	33,000	33,000	57
2.	2001	2,63,830	1,49,000	480
3.	2003	7,17,360	2,55,000	2050
4.	2004	10,79,090	3,61,730	3900

Sources: 1. *RBI-Trend and Progress of Banking*, 2002-03, p. 107.
2. *Indian Economic Survey*, 2003-04, p. 160.

4
Principles of Credit Management

Credit is a good tool in the hands of those who know how to use it and it is a dangerous thing to those who do not know how to use it. Now every industry uses credit and agriculture is not exception to it. Modern agriculture requires high per hectare investment and cultivators being poor cannot make additional investment from their savings and hence, they depend upon credit. After nationalization of banks, vast capital become available to agriculture, but principles involved in this regard are necessary to know both for borrower and lender. Borrower faces following questions: (*i*) How best to use the limited farm capital? (*ii*) Whether to borrow or not to borrow the additional funds? (*iii*) When to borrow? (*iv*) From whom to borrow and at what cost? Study of agril. finance and principles of credit management will provide best answers to above questions.

Similarly, credit agency should also be quite aware of principles of credit management. Credit agency faces following issues:

1. Appraising the credit worthiness of cultivator.
2. Determining repaying capacity of borrower.
3. Advising-cultivator in such a way that he will increase per hectare yield and net profit and help them to increase their repayment capacity. This will reduce the risks of non-repayment.

There are three basic principles one must consider before lending agency decides to advance a loan, the borrower decides to borrow and the extension agency advocates or recommends the loans.

Those principles are as follows:

(*i*) Returns from the investment to borrower.

(*ii*) Repaying capacity of borrower.

(*iii*) Risk-bearing ability of borrower.

These three points are known as 3 Rs of credit.

With references to every loan, answers to the following three questions must be affirmative:

1. Whether additional return will be sufficient to cover additional costs?
2. Whether borrower can repay the amount when it is due, *i.e.*, will he have adequate repaying capacity?
3. Whether the borrower is having sufficient risk-bearing ability to meet the effects of probable financial losses?

Thus, these questions both borrower and lender must consider and when answers to all three questions are affirmative then loan should be advanced. This brings soundness, minimises risk and safe way of doing the things.

Returns from the Investment

Any businessman when undertakes business he considers this point, *i.e.*, whether this act will give him sufficient profit? In a purely competitive market, if capital is limited, profit is maximum when marginal return is bigger than marginal cost at a particular production level. When capital is unlimited, *i.e.*, borrower can get sufficient amount for investment, in that case profit is maximum at a point where marginal return is equal to marginal cost. In this marginal analysis, profit from each unit is added and stage comes when total profit becomes maximum, *i.e.*, marginal cost and marginal returns are equal. This point is illustrated with the help of hypothetical example in table 4.1.

If producer is having only ₹ 100 with him then he will use five units of input and will get ₹ 300 profit, this is a case of limited capital. When producer will have 140 rupees, he will use seven units of input and will achieve maximum profit of ₹ 310, thus, marginal analysis will indicate us how much to

Table 4.1: Maximum profit level

Unit of input	Marginal cost @ ₹ 20 unit	Total cost in ₹	Marginal return @ ₹ 10 unit	Total return in ₹	Profit in ₹
0.	—	—	—	220	220
1.	20	20	20	240	220
2.	20	40	30	270	230
3.	20	60	40	310	250
4.	20	80	50	360	280
5.	20	100	40	400	300
6.	20	120	30	430	310
7.	20	140	20	450	310
8.	20	160	10	460	300
9.	20	180	0	460	280
10.	20	200	–10	450	250
11.	20	220	–20	430	210

be spent. This analysis is applicable when producer take only one activity but in reality, cultivator requires a credit for several enterprises on the farm and at that time total credit needed should be estimated. This is illustrated with the help of example based on hypothetical data in table 4.2.

From table 4.2, it is clear that cultivator should not spend all the amount on only one enterprise. He should spend first ₹ 500 on crop enterprise, second ₹ 500 on dairy and third ₹ 500 on poultry, fourth, fifth and sixth on poultry, dairy and crop enterprise, respectively. So that he gets total return of ₹ 5,200 and net profit of ₹ 2,200. If he does not have any saving he should borrow ₹ 3,000 from suitable credit agency and should obtain a profit of ₹ 2,200.

Table 4.2: Marginal returns in rupees from different enterprises

	Investment of ₹	Crop enterprise ₹	Dairy ₹	Poultry ₹
First	500	1,000 (1)	900 (2)	900 (3)
Second	500	800 (6)	800 (5)	800 (4)
Third	500	600	600	700
Fourth	500	400	500	500
Fifth	500	200	300	300
Sixth	500	100	100	100
	Total	3,200	3,300	3,100

Suppose he borrowed the amount, at an interest rate of 15% then he has to pay ₹ 450 as an interest and thus net profit he will get ₹ 1,750 (2,200–450). Thus, return should be sufficient to cover cost of production as well as cost of credit and cultivator should get some profit. Thus, return is an important principle in use of credit.

Cultivator has to take credit for a enterprise which he is going to undertake in future. He should estimate production and gross income with the help of previous year's data. From gross return and total cost, work out net return. This estimated net return should be used to decide whether to use credit or not. Estimated net returns should be greater than estimated cost of credit. This net return should be used to finalise the decision about loan.

Repaying Capacity

Repaying capacity means capacity of a borrower to repay the amount borrowed. Two cultivators having same gross or net return may have different repaying capacity.

Repaying Capacity = Gross cash income minus living expenses, working expenses (not including proposed loan), taxes, other loans and repayments due.

It can be illustrated with our previous example.

Table 4.3: Finding repaying capacity

Items	With credit of ₹ 3,000
Gross returns	5,200
Working expenses	2,000
Return over cash expenses	3,200
Living expenses	1,500
Old loans	500
Balance (Repaying capacity)	1,200

Thus, concern cultivator is having repaying capacity worth ₹ 1,200 as shown in table 4.3. He can repay interest and instalment of a loan worth ₹ 3,000 within three years.

Cultivator may get sufficient net return but if his family expenditure is heavy his repaying capacity will be poor. This can be illustrated with the help of example. Another cultivator is getting ₹ 5,200 by using ₹ 3,000 credit but his repaying capacity, is only ₹ 100 as shown in table 4.4. Under such circumstances it will be difficult for cultivator to repay interest on borrowed amount as well as instalment of principal. Thus, both the cultivators are having similar gross income, but their repaying capacity vary. Hence, only return criteria is not sufficient, both borrower and lender must estimate repaying capacity taking into consideration estimated prices and output data.

There are two approaches to estimate the repaying capacity:

1. Conventional approach.
2. Modern approach.

Table 4.4: Finding repaying capacity

Items	With credit of ₹ 3,000
Gross returns	5,200
Working expenses	1,900
Return over cash expenses	3,300
Living expenses	2,600
Old loans	600
Balance (Repaying capacity)	100

1. Conventional Approach

As per this approach, repaying capacity is worked out as one third of the total gross income including off-farm income. Two-third of the gross income is required by the family for household expenditure and for farm expenses.

There are certain defects in this approach, those are as follows:

1. For estimating gross return average data for yield, prices were used which did not account for fertility variation of land, managing ability, size of farm, etc.
2. Small and large farms differ in their marketable surplus, home consumption, farm expenses and hence taking one-third as a repaying capacity is not justified.

2. Modern Approach

Here in this case one has to estimate yield, prices and obtain a gross income. From this gross income estimated farm expenses, estimated family consumption expenditure and previous year's dues are deducted and remaining is a balance or repaying capacity. This approach is more scientific which takes into account various factors.

Conventional approach also does not take into account whether loan is self-liquidating or non-liquidating or partially liquidating loan, use of loan, provides sufficient income from which we can repay the loan, *i.e.*, it is used in a production process only once *e.g.*, loan for fertilizer, seeds, etc., and in this case repaying capacity is worked out as below. Example is given in table 4.5.

Repaying Capacity. Gross cash income less living expenses, working expenses (not including proposed loans), taxes, other loans and repayments dues.

Table 4.5: Finding repaying capacity

Items	Without credit ₹	With credit of ₹ 1,200
Gross returns	3,000	5,000
Working expenses	1,000	1,000
Return over cash	2,000	4,000
Living expenses	1,500	1,500
	500	2,500
Other loans due	400	400
Repaying capacity	100	2,100

Thus, because of self-liquidating loan sufficient repaying capacity has been increased, as it is shown in table 4.5.

In case of non-liquidating or partially liquidating loan repaying capacity is worked out as below:

Repaying Capacity. Gross cash income less working expenses (including season loan), living expenses taxes, other payments due.

Example: Suppose some cultivator decided to take a loan of ₹ 4,000 for electric motor for lifting water from a well and repay the loan amount in eight instalments, each instalment of ₹ 500.

As shown in table 4.6, his repaying capacity is ₹ 1,800. He can very well repay an instalment of ₹ 500 and thus it is quite sound to take a loan for electric motor.

Table 4.6: Finding out repaying capacity

Items	Without credit ₹	With credit of ₹ 1,200
Gross returns	3,000	6,000
Working expenses	1,000	2,200
Return over cash	2,000	3,800
Living expenses	1,500	1,600
	500	2,200
Other loans due	400	400
Balance (Repaying capacity)	100	1,800

Maximum Credit Limit (MCL)

For short-term loan MCL is ₹ 2,100 (Refer to table 4.5). Here repaying capacity is treated as MCL. Hence loan worth ₹ 1,200 should be granted because MCL is quite high. Hence considering MCL and loan requirement based on production requirement, loan should be granted. For electric motor MCL is ₹ 14,400 (1,800 × 8), ₹ 1,800 is repaying capacity as shown in table 4.6 and duration of repayment is eight years, and hence, there should not be any difficulty in granting ₹ 4,000 for electric motor. Instalment of ₹ 500, cultivator can easily repay from his net income or repaying capacity of ₹ 1,800 per annum.

Strengthening Repaying Capacity

Repaying capacity is very important while granting the loan and hence, cultivator must try to strengthen his repaying capacity. Following are some of the important points:

1. Period of loan,
2. Type of loan,
3. Resource imbalance,
4. Resource use planning,
5. Improved technology,
6. Equity,
7. Marketing of produce,
8. Management factors.

1. Period of loan: Period of loan is very important to adjust the repayments to the repaying capacity of the borrower, *e.g.*, the cultivator under study has a 1,800 rupees repaying capacity.

Instead in addition to electric motor he started thinking about purchasing a land. For purchasing land, he has to borrow one lakh rupees. He will improve his repaying capacity by ₹ 6,200 per year. Thus, total repaying capacity will be (₹ 6,200 + ₹ 1,800) ₹ 8,000. If he has to repay the loan taken for purchasing land within 10 years then every year he has to repay about ₹ 10,500 (10,000 + 500). This is beyond his repaying capacity. However, if he is permitted to repay the loan within 20 years with an instalment of ₹ 5,000 + interest on capital + ₹ 500 instalment of electric motor. This will be less than his repaying capacity or ₹ 8,000 and he can easily pay the amount. Thus, by adjusting period of loan, repayment capacity will be improved.

2. Type of loan: Self-liquidating loans are easy to repay than non or partially liquidating loans. Hence, preference should be given to self-liquidating loans.

3. Resource imbalance: For achieving maximum return, resources must be available in balanced condition. For example, if irrigation or labour is a limiting factor maximum returns may not be achieved and automatically repaying capacity will be poor. Hence, attempt must be made to obtain all the resources in balanced condition, it will improve repaying capacity.

4. Resource use planning: Judicious planning or best use of resources will improve net income and repaying capacity also.

5. Improved technology: Better crop variety, better method of cultivation will improve the yield, gross return and repaying capacity also. Hence, cultivator must use improved technology.

6. Equity: Equity means total assets minus total liabilities. Equity can be increased by higher saving and repaying debts. When equity will improve automatically repayment capacity will also improve.

7. Marketing of produce: Cultivator should sell his produce in a better market at higher prices. This will increase net return and repaying capacity.

8. Management factors: Management decisions are very important if he took best decisions, the net income and repayment capacity will increase automatically.

Risk-bearing Ability

Risk-bearing ability is a ability to withstand shocks of probable financial losses. This is a third and final test of the soundness of a loan to be advanced. Returns and repayment capacity is worked out on the basis of average estimated prices, yields. Agriculture business is subject to the vagaries of nature and is exposed to many other hazards such as pest attack, disease attack and price fluctuations. Under such circumstances, cultivator will not get average yield also. He has to face such circumstances. How far his repayment capacity will be hampered by natural calamities is estimated. For working out repaying capacity, taking into consideration risk factors. One has to work out variability in returns. Sum of variability amount in each crop throughout the year will constitute a total variability in total or gross returns. If we considered our previous cultivator, his gross return is ₹ 6,000 and it is assumed that total variability amount, *i.e.* loss due to natural calamities in the same year is ₹ 1,500, *i.e.*, 15 per cent. Then we have to find out deflated gross income which is ₹ 4,500 (6,000–1,500) and his repaying capacity will be as follows:

Items	With credit of ₹ 4,000
Gross return	6,000
Total variability amount	1,500
Deflated gross return	4,500
Working expenses	2,200
Return over expenses	2,300
Living expenses	1,600
Balance amount	700
Other loan dues	400
Balance (Repaying capacity)	300

This deflated repayment capacity may be termed as risk-bearing ability of cultivator. Now, cultivator will not be able to repay an instalment of ₹ 500 plus interest on capital and thus he cannot borrow for electric motor. Final decision depends upon lending institution. Thus, repayment capacity is affected by risky factors, such type of analysis may not be possible for every cultivator but variability in returns can be worked out for an area and those figures may be used for individual cultivator.

Maximum credit limit may be worked out taking into account deflated repayment capacity or risk-bearing ability.

However, some arrangement is made in co-operative societies to tackle problems of natural calamities. Government may help cultivators and thus problem of risk factors is minimised. Similarly, credit guarantee corporation of India also helps to banks, if loan is not repaid by borrower cultivator. Crop insurance company is another agency to tackle the problem of risk. Thus, intensity of risk factor is minimised.

Factors Strengthening Risk-bearing Ability

1. Cultivating saving habits and reduction in expenditure.
2. Building up personal credit during bad period.
3. Taking more stable enterprises.
4. Diversification of production.
5. Flexibility in farm planning.
6. Taking better plant protection measures.
7. Development of irrigation facilities.
8. Insuring crop where it is possible.
9. Seeking non-agricultural employment for some family members.
10. Developing ability to adjust adverse conditions. These factors will strengthen risk-bearing ability of cultivators.

Other Seven Principles of Credit

There are other seven principles of credit which are useful in bringing commercial gains to the bankers but also social benefits. These principles are as follows:

1. Principle of productive purpose: The principle of productive purpose says that loan disbursed to any borrower should be capable of generating additional income. Short-term loans of small and marginal farmers can be made more productive, if they are provided with loans of having other income augmenting assets through medium-term loans. For example, loans granted for dairy, poultry, goat and sheep keeping help in increasing returns from crop loans.

2. Principle of productivity: While sanctioning loan, lender should advise the borrower cultivator that he should use the credit for best variety of crop or best animal breed. Not only total production should increase but also per hectare yield, *i.e.*, productivity of variety should be highest. For example, farmer should prefer variety Sahyadry hybrid rice which gives 60 q/ha rather than other high yielding varieties of rice like Jaya, Ratna which yield 40 to 45 q/ha. Productivity of variety should be highest.

3. Principle of personality: There are several rich farmers they are capable of repaying the loan but they have no will to repay it. They became willful defaulters and lending institution in trouble under such circumstances. Lending institution should see the character of person, *i.e.*, his reputation in the society, whether the borrower is honest or dishonest person.

4. Principle of proper utilization: Proper utilization means utilizing the borrowed amount for the purpose for which it has been sanctioned. This enables farmer to repay the loan easily. However, if the loan is sanctioned for application of fertilizer to a particular crop and if it is properly utilized. Farmer will get higher yield of crop and repayment of loan will be easy. However, if the loan is used for marriage of a daughter, then repayment will be difficult. Therefore, principle of proper utilization is quite useful to both borrower and lender.

5. Principle of phased disbursement: Loan amount should be disbursed in phases. In case of sugarcane loan amount is utilized throughout the year for different operations. Therefore, amount should be disbursed in phases, *i.e.*, first instalment at the time of sowing, then second instalment for weeding and application of second dose of fertilizers. This ensures proper utilization of loan otherwise if loan disbursed in one instalment at beginning then it is likely loan amount may be misutilised. Therefore, principle of phased disbursement helps in proper utilization of loan.

6. Principle of payment: As per this principle repayment schedule should be fixed by following mutual discussion among borrower and lender.

7. Principle of protection: Whatever amount of loan has been taken, then that amount should be insured. Similarly, credit should be linked with marketing. This will protect the loan amount. Institutional agencies resort to safety measures, *viz.*, insurance coverage, linking credit with marketing, provision of finance on production of warehouse receipt, covering credit under small loan guarantee scheme of deposit insurance and Credit Guarantee Corporation of India.

Repayment Plan

Good repayment plan is necessary to improve the repaying capacity. Repayment also depends upon nature of loan and when it star't generating income. Repayment should start when the loan will generate income. If suppose cultivator purchased electric motor and he is growing sugarcane crop; he will be able to start repaying only after harvest of sugarcane crop after one year. Repayment plan should be finalised taking into consideration at what time loan will generate income or at what time money will be available to repay the debt. Particular repayment plan will be best suited to particular cultivator and not to other. Various repayment plans are as follows:

1. Amortised even repayment plan.
2. Amortised decreasing repayment plan.
3. Variable or Quasi variable repayment plan.
4. Lumpsum repayment plan.

1. Amortised even repayment plan: When cultivator has a regular income, he will repay as per this plan. This plan will be convenient to him. For example, dairy farmer, or poultry farmer start getting regular income and for them this repayment plan will be convenient. In this repayment plan, amount of instalment is same for all instalments. Each instalment consists of principal component and interest component. At advance stages, principal component goes on increasing and interest component goes on decreasing.

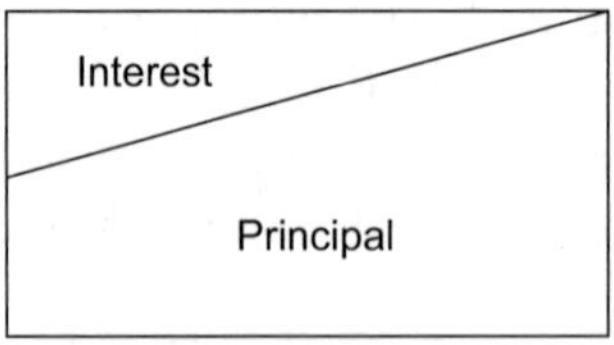

Fig. 4.1: Even repayment plan

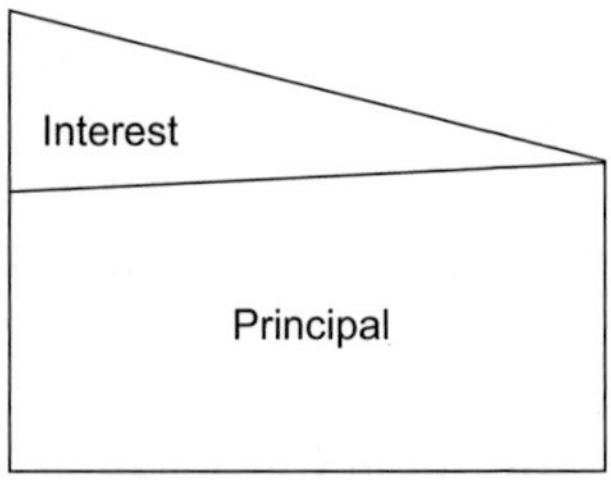

Fig. 4.2: Decreasing repayment plan

Example:

Loan amount : ₹ 10,000
Time period : 5 years
Rate of interest : 10%

Formula for working out instalment under even repayment plan:

$$I = P\frac{i}{1-(1+i)^{-n}}$$

where I = Yearly instalment
P = Principal amount
i = Rate of interest
n = Number of years

Putting values in formula

$$I = 10,000 \times \frac{0.1}{1-\frac{1}{(1-0.1)^5}}$$

$$I = 10,000 \times \frac{0.1}{1-\frac{1}{(1.6105)}}$$

$$= 10,000 \times \frac{0.1}{1-0.6209}$$

$$= 10,000 \times 0.2638$$

$$I = ₹\ 2,638$$

Table 4.7: Amortised even repayment plan

Year	Principal amount (₹)	Interest amount (₹)	Balance principal amount	Instalment amount ₹
1	(2 = 5 – 3)	(3)	(4 = 4 – 2)	(5 = 2 + 3)
–	–	–	10,000	–
1.	1,638	1,000*	8,362	2,638
2.	1,802	836	6,560	2,638
3.	1,982	656	4,578	2,638
4.	2,180	458	2,398	2,638
5.	2,398	240	0	2,638
Total	10,000	3,190		13,190

* Interest of first year @ ₹ 10 per cent for ₹ 10,000.

2. Amortised decreasing repayment plan: When cultivator wants to repay loan as early as possible and when he gets bigger incomes at initial period of loan. In such cases this repayment plan is convenient.

In this repayment plan, instalment of principal component remains constant and total interest amount goes on decreasing and hence, total instalment goes on decreasing, *e.g.*, loan taken for a crop which gives more income initially and goes on decreasing later on, *e.g.*, cotton picking is more intensive during early period and goes on decreasing later on. Same thing for grape garden.

Example: Loan amount

i.e., Principal : ₹ 10,000
Rate of interest : 10%
Repayment period : 5 years

Table 4.8: Amortised decreasing repayment plan

Year	Principal (₹)	Interest (₹)	Instalment (₹)	Balance Principal amount
1	2	3	4 = 2+3	₹ 5 = 5−2
	–	–	–	10,000
1.	2,000	1,000	3,000	8,000
2.	2,000	800	2,800	6,000
3.	2,000	600	2,600	4,000
4.	2,000	400	2,400	2,000
5.	2,000	200	2,200	Nil
Total	10,000	3,000	13,000	

3. Variable or quasi variable repayment plan: Agricultural business has to face several uncertainties. Some years are better and some are worse. Cultivator would like to pay more when he will get a good yields and will like to repay less amount during bad year. Thus, repayment plan is flexible and such repayment plan is called as variable or quasi variable repayment plan.

4. Lumpsum repayment plan: Lumpsum repayment plan means paying all the amount of principal and interest at the end of period of a loan. Cultivator gets sufficient time to adjust with risk and uncertainties and pays all the amount at the end. Similarly, he goes on investing instead of repaying thus achieves a high level of capital formation.

Thus, particular repayment plan will be suitable to particular cultivator in a particular situation.

5

Economic Feasibility of Project, Loan Proposals and Credit Policy

(A) Crop Loan

Cultivator invests in his land either from his own savings or he has to borrow from other financing agencies. Private credit agencies do not ask for many documents while giving loan, but their interest rate is very high. Institutional credit is the main source of credit to the cultivators. Co-operatives and commercial banks provide various kinds of credit to cultivators.

Crop loan is a short-term credit and is generally obtained from primary credit co-operative society of the village or from commercial bank. Loan is sanctioned to the extent of one-third of the gross value of the produce. Total cost of cultivation is considered while granting loan. Money is repaid after the harvest of the crop.

Loan Procedure

For obtaining a crop loan from primary co-operative society, cultivator has to become member of the society by paying entrance fee and by purchasing shares of the society. Then he has to fill up the application form for obtaining loan. While submitting loan application cultivator has to submit certain documents, particularly, document for providing land for security and few no objection certificates. Cultivator should also obtain signatures of two surety. If he is obtaining loan from primary credit co-operative, he should submit his application to the secretary of the society and if he is obtaining loan from commercial bank, he has to submit his application at nearest branch of the particular commercial bank. Agricultural finance officer of the bank will examine loan proposal, if necessary, he will pay personal visit and will give his recommendation for sanction of the loan. Finally, loan is sanctioned by appropriate authority of the bank.

Details of the Loan Proposal are given below:

1. One-third of the gross value approach:

(*i*)	Yield of Sahyadri hybrid rice	60 Q/ha
(*ii*)	Price	₹ 400/Q.
(*iii*)	Gross value	₹ 24,000
(*iv*)	One-third of the gross value	₹ 8,000

Bank will sanction ₹ 8,000/ha, for hybrid rice crop and remaining money cultivator should manage from some other source or from his own savings.

2. Cost of cultivation approach: Per hectare cost of cultivation of Rabi groundnut is as follows:

(*i*)	Seed	₹ 3,500
(*ii*)	Fertilizers	₹ 1,800
(*iii*)	Pesticides	₹ 450
(*iv*)	Hired human labour	₹ 3,283
(*v*)	Other expenses	₹ 5,141
	Total cost	₹ 14,174

Thus, bank will grant ₹ 14,174 per hectare.

Economic Feasibility of Agricultural Projects

Long-term Loan

Investment in agriculture is of two types. The first type involves operating investment, such as seed, feed, fertilizers, etc., and the second one is concerned with long-term investment in capital assets such as land, machines, projects, etc. Analysis of investment is different for these categories of investment owing to differences in timing of expenses and their associated returns. Investment on operating inputs occur within one production cycle of a year or sometimes less but investment on capital assets entails a longer time period. Capital investment made in agricultural projects are made in different time periods and the returns are also spread over a period of time.

Components of a Project

A project necessarily involves five important components, they are:

1. Investment: There is some amount of money which has to be spent at the beginning of the project. Usually this is referred to as Initial Investment. This investment is utilized for creation of capacity to produce goods or services, which is marketed to earn revenue for the project. The investment helps the project to generate income for the length of time, which is referred to as the life of the project.

2. Gestation period: Any project has some gestation period. Gestation period is the time period between the investment and the time when project starts yielding returns. The length of the gestation period cannot be defined as it depends upon the nature of investment/business. For example, a coconut plantation has a gestation period of seven years while a mango orchard has five years. Thus one has to look into the nature of the business to define the gestation period of the project.

3. Cash flows: Every project has a series of cash flows over a period of time. Cash flows are of two types, *viz.*, cash outflows and cash inflows. The difference between the two is the net cash flow.

Cash outflows occur in the business because of purchase of raw material, purchase of assets and repayment of loans. Cash inflows occur because of sale of produce, sale of assets and borrowing. One has to ensure that the net cash flows are positive in the business. Cash outflows refer to investment expenditure and inflows refer to income/returns received from project.

4. Life of the project: Every project has a defined life period based on the life of the most crucial assets on which investment is made. For example, a mango orchard has a life of 50 years while an irrigation pump set has a life of about 10 years. The life of a project is important to determine the benefits from or costs of a project. However, decision-making cannot be based just on the life of a project.

5. Junk value/salvage value: The value of the unspent assets remaining after the life of a project is referred to as Junk value. Though the most crucial asset has spent its life span. Some money can be recovered from the project. This also helps in determining whether the project can be continued with minimum additional investment.

Decision criteria for appraisal of a project is based primarily on three techniques, namely: Net Present Value (NPV), Benefit Cost Ratio (BCR) and Internal Rate of Return (IRR).

(i) Net Present Value (NPV)

This refers to the value of the project in financial terms. The initial investment made is deducted from the discounted net cash flow series. However, if initial investment included in first year then it is not necessary to deduct initial investment at the end.

$$\text{NPV} = \sum_{i=1}^{n} V_i (\text{I}+r)^{-n} - 1$$

Where V_i = Net cash flow in ith period

r = Discount rate

n = Time period

I = Initial investment.

Decision Criteria:

$$\text{NPV} \geq 1$$

i.e., if a project has NPV which is zero or positive, project is feasible.

In case an entrepreneur has number of alternative projects for investment, the projects shall be arranged in the descending order of NPV and selection for investment shall start from the project with highest NPV.

(ii) Benefit Cost Ratio (BCR)

BC Ratio is ratio of discounted benefits and discounted costs.

$$\frac{\sum_{t=1}^{n} \text{B}(\text{I}+r)^{-n}}{\sum_{t=1}^{n} \text{C}(\text{I}+r)^{-n}}$$

Where B = Benefit

C = Costs

n = Time period.

Decision Criteria:

BCR ≥ 1

Relationship between NPV and BCR

BCR = 1, NPV = 0

BCR < 1, NPV –ve

BCR > 1, NPV +ve

Projects shall be arranged in the descending orders of BCR for prioritization of investment.

(iii) Payback Period

This refers to the time taken by the project to recover initial investment. It is estimated by adding the net cash flows in the project until the cumulative net cash flows equal to initial investment. Select the project which has the least payback period. If investor has a number of alternatives, then one has to arrange the project in the ascending order of payback periods and start selecting one by one. The payback period depends upon the capacity utilization in the business. Higher the capacity utilization, lower the payback period and *vice-versa*.

(iv) Internal Rate of Return (IRR)

It is rate of return generated in the project. It is also defined as the discount rate which makes the NPV in the project zero. In calculating the NPV, we independently choose a discount rate between discounted benefits and cost. IRR calculation reverse the procedure instead of selecting the discount rate, we set the NPV at zero and try to identify for the discount rate which gives results. Since higher the discount rate reduce the present value of future cash flows, hence, the lower will be the NPV. The process of finding IRR involves trials and error. An arbitrary discount rate is used to find out NPV. If the result is positive, a higher rate is used to find out the NPV. If negative, a lower rate is used. The process is repeated till NPV = 0.

Decision Criteria: IRR > Ruling Rate of Interest

$$\text{IRR} = \begin{pmatrix}\text{Lower} \\ \text{discount} \\ \text{rate}\end{pmatrix} + \begin{pmatrix}\text{Difference} \\ \text{between two} \\ \text{discount rates}\end{pmatrix} \times \left(\frac{\text{Present value of net income at the lower discount rate}}{\text{Difference between the present value of net income at lower discount rate and present value of net income at higher discount rate}} \right)$$

Solved problem

Table 5.1: Details about one hectare sericulture. Initial investment is ₹ 40,000 (Hypothetical data)

Year	Outflow (expenditure) in ₹	Inflow (Returns) in ₹	Net returns in ₹	Discounting factor @ 12%	Net present value in ₹
1	2	3	(4 = 3 – 2)	5	6 = 5 × 4
1.	40,000	—	– 40,000	0.89	–35,600
2.	9,000	30,000	21,000	0.79	16,590
3.	10,000	32,000	22,000	0.71	15,620
4.	12,000	35,000	23,000	0.64	14,720
5.	13,000	40,000	27,000	0.57	15,390
Total	84,000	1,37,000	53,000		26,720

Net present worth/net present value should be positive for carrying out the project.

Benefit Cost Ratio (BCR)

$$\text{BCR} = \frac{\text{Present value of returns in ₹}}{\text{Present value of costs in ₹}}$$

In our sericulture project details are given in table 5.2.

Table 5.2: Estimation of benefit cost ratio in case of sericulture

Year	Costs in ₹	Gross returns ₹	Discounting factor at 12%	Present value of costs	Present value of gross returns
1	2	3	4	5 = 2 × 4	6 = 3 × 4
1.	40,000	—	0.89	35,600	—
2.	9,000	30,000	0.79	7,110	23,700
3.	10,000	32,000	0.71	7,100	22,720
4.	12,000	35,000	0.64	7,680	22,400
5.	13,000	40,000	0.57	7,410	22,800
Total	84,000	1,37,000	—	64,900	91,620

$$BCR = \frac{91{,}620}{64{,}900} = 1.41$$

Internal Rate of Return (IRR)

$$IRR = \begin{pmatrix}\text{Lower}\\ \text{discount}\\ \text{rate}\end{pmatrix} + \begin{pmatrix}\text{Difference}\\ \text{between two}\\ \text{discount rates}\end{pmatrix} \times \left(\frac{\text{Present value of net income at the lower discount rate}}{\text{Difference between the present value of net income at lower discount rate and present value of net income at higher discount rate}} \right)$$

Table 5.3: Estimation of IRR for sericulture

Year	Net returns in ₹	Discounting factor (40%)	Net present worth in ₹	Discounting factor (43%)	Net present worth in ₹
1	2	3	4 = 2 × 3	5	6 = 2 × 5
1.	–40,000	0.71	– 28,400	0.70	– 28,000
2.	21,000	0.51	10,710	0.49	10,290
3.	22,000	0.36	7,920	0.34	7,480
4.	23,000	0.26	5,980	0.24	5,520
5.	27,000	0.19	5,130	0.17	4,590
Total	53,000		1,340		–120

$$\text{IRR} = 40 + 3 \times \frac{1340}{1340-(-120)}$$

$$\text{IRR} = 40 + 3 \times \frac{1340}{1340+120}$$

$$= 40 + 3\,(0.92) = 40 + 2.76 = 42.76$$

For finding out IRR arbitrary discount rate is assumed, and its corresponding net present value is calculated. The positive NPV indicates still higher discount rate should be tried and this should be continued until net present value becomes negative. Then by interpolation method the exact IRR is found out by using the equation given above.

Procedure for Obtaining Loan from Commercial Banks

The application form prescribed by the commercial bank includes information of the borrower, broadly on the points such as information on wise use of loan, personal information of the borrower and his family members, the amount of loan required, its purpose and duration, the nature of securities offered and the repayment plan. Besides, it contains information on following points:

1. Financial or net-worth statement containing information about assets and liabilities.
2. Past three years cropping pattern, production record, income statement and profit and loss record.
3. Particulars of fixed and working assets owned.
4. Particulars of all loans or debts outstanding or 6-D form.
5. The crop plan for next three years.
6. 7-12 extract of his own land.
7. 8-A extract of the land.
8. Details of proposed proposal for loan.

The procedure to be adopted in filling all these documents should be clearly explained to the borrower.

Procedure for Obtaining Loan from Primary Co-operative Agricultural & Rural Development Bank

Maharashtra State Co-operative Agricultural and Rural Development Banks [MSCARDBs].

There is a specific and prescribed application form to be filled-in by the borrower for obtaining long-term loan from Land Development Bank. Along with this application form following documents need to be provided by the borrower:

1. 7-12 extract of the land possessed by the borrower,
2. 8-A extract of owned land,
3. Two guarantors,
4. 6-D form,
5. No objection certificate of:
   (*a*) Primary Agricultural Credit Society.
   (*b*) Village Revenue Record Officer/Tahsildar for Government loans.
   (*c*) Block Development Officer.
6. Quotations from the dealer for the material to be purchased by the borrower out of the loan asked for.
7. Land record abstracts for additional security if any.
8. Map of the mortgaged land on which development is proposed.

After submission of the proposal by the borrower to the bank, the bank officers make an appraisal of the proposal. The loan is granted to the extent of 75 to 95 per cent of the estimated amount of the proposal. From the sanctioned amount of loan 10 per cent is deducted for shares to make an eligible member of Primary Co-operative Agricultural and Rural Development Bank (PCARDB) since the PCARDBs provide loans only to member borrowers. Thus, the borrower receives loan to the extent of 65 to 85 per cent of the estimated amount of the proposal. Remaining 35 to 15 per cent of the loan amount is to be borne by the borrower himself.

Following economic indicators are needed to be study while preparing loan proposals:

1. Net worth statement: This statement should contain information of previous year of submission of the loan application. In the first part, it carries information on current assets; working assets and fixed assets as well as current and fixed liabilities. The difference of the two should give an idea of net worth.

(*a*) **Current assets:** It includes cash in hand, cash deposited in bank, notes receivable, grain and fodder, livestock, stores, spare parts and other current assets if any.

(*b*) **Working assets:** It includes tractors and pumps, machinery and equipments, trucks, bullocks and other working cattle.

(*c*) **Fixed assets:** It includes land and buildings. The totaling up of current, working and fixed assets and investment would give an idea about the value of total assets.

(*d*) **Liabilities:** Outstanding liabilities; amount in cash or kind, unpaid taxes, notes payable and amounts payable to other sundry creditors are included in current liabilities. Mortgage of lands by bank gives other liabilities. The excess of total assets over total liabilities is the net worth of the debtor.

2. Income statement or record of past enterprise: An income statement is the record of the receipt and gains during a specified period, usually a year, less the expenses and losses during the same period with a net income or net loss as a result. It is thus a statement of all crops raised during the previous year, total yield of crops and the total value of the produce less cost incurred on various inputs. This information if available may be compiled at least for 2-3 years.

3. Particulars of all loans or debts outstanding: In this statement nature of loan or debt, nature of security, original amount, unpaid balance, etc.

4. Future crop plan: Usually the 'Future crop plan' statement of the next year's crops is attached to the application form meant for 'working capital loan'. While the statement in relating to the 'technical feasibility and economical viability' of the project should be attached to the application form which meant for the fixed capital loan.

5. Rules for wise use of loan: Along with the loan application the lender should provide to the borrower some set rules for the wise use of loans. These are:

1. Obtain loan for running a profitable enterprise.
2. Keep loan at lowest point.
3. Confine the use of loans to income generating purposes.
4. Chalk-out a definite repayment programme.
5. Behave in a business-like manner with the lending agency.
6. Loan should not surpass total assets.
7. Get insurable items insured.

8. Maintain proper record and accounts of the business for which loan has been taken.

(B) Bank Proposal for Plantation of Alphonso Mango Fruit Crop and its Economic Feasibility

Alphonso mango is a perennial rainfed plantation crop with a normal life of about 60 years.

Fig. 5.1: Alphonso mango tree

The Alphonso mango tree starts bearing fruits after five years from the date of plantation by sufficient bearing when orchard becomes 10 years old. The mango growers have to invest considerable amount in the form of inputs for establishing the mango orchards till its bearing stage. Inputs are: (*a*) Labour services for cleaning of land, marking and digging pits. Transporting FYM, filling pits, application of fertilizers, preparation of rings and mulching, irrigation, providing support and shades to seedlings, application of pesticides, fencing, repairs, etc., (*b*) FYM, (*c*) Planting material, (*d*) Fertilizers, (*e*) Pesticides and insecticides, etc. In gestation period, the mango growers do not get any returns from the orchard. Therefore, the investment made by the farmers for establishing mango orchard during the period from planting to age of first flowering is regarded as capital investment for establishment of orchard. The details are given in tables 5.4 and 5.5.

Table 5.4: Per hectare cost of establishment of mango orchard in rupees from planting to age of first flowering

State of orchard development	Cost (₹)
1st Year	37,608
2nd Year	13,076
3rd Year	12,284
4th Year	10,432
5th Year	12,780
6th Year	14,118
7th Year	16,218
Total	1,16,516

Amount of loan available : 1,16,516 × 75/100

(*i.e.*, 75% of total cost) *i.e.*, rounded to : 87,387 say 87,000

Amount of farmers contribution is 25% : 29,516

Total : 1,16,516

It is observed from tables 5.4 and 5.5 that for one hectare mango orchard total amount required is ₹ 1,16,516, out of the total amount 25 per cent has to be contributed by farmer and 75 per cent, *i.e.* 87,000 will be a bank loan.

Table 5.5: Per hectare item-wise cost of establishment of mango orchard up to seven years

Sr. No.	Particulars	1st year	2nd year	3rd year	4th year	5th year	6th year	7th year	Total cost
1.	Labour								
	(*a*) Human (₹)	19,530	7,560	5,670	2,800	3,850	4,130	5,320	48,860
	(Days)	(279)	(108)	(81)	(40)	(55)	(59)	(76)	(698)
	(*b*) Bullock (₹)	560	280	560	560	840	840	840	4480
	(Days)	(4)	(2)	(4)	(4)	(6)	(6)	(6)	(32)
2.	FYM (₹)	1950	900	1350	1800	2250	2700	3150	14100
	(Cart load)	(13)	(6)	(9)	(12)	(15)	(18)	(21)	(94)
3.	Fertilizers								
	(*a*) Urea (₹)	114	228	342	456	570	684	798	3192
	(kg)	(30)	(60)	(90)	(120)	(150)	(180)	(210)	(840)
	(*b*) Single Super Phosphate (₹) (kg)	1150 (230)	300 (60)	450 (90)	600 (120)	750 (150)	900 (180)	1050 (210)	5200 (1040)
	(*c*) Murriate of potash (₹) (kg)	40 (10)	80 (20)	120 (30)	160 (40)	200 (50)	240 (60)	300 (75)	1180 (285)
4.	Planting (₹)	2000	200	-	-	-	-	-	2200
	Material (Nos.)	(100)	(10)						(110)

(*Contd.*)

Sr. No.	Particulars	1st year	2nd year	3rd year	4th year	5th year	6th year	7th year	Total cost
5.	Plant protection								
	(*a*) Carbaryl (₹)	120	240	360	480	600	720	800	3320
	(kgs)	(1.5)	(3)	(4.5)	(6)	(7.5)	(9)	(10)	(41.5)
	(*b*) Wettable sulphur	144	288	432	576	720	864	960	3984
	(₹) (kgs.)	(1.5)	(3)	(4.5)	(6)	(7.5)	(9)	(10)	(41.5)
6.	Cost of fencing (100 × 100 mt)	12,000	3,000	3,000	3,000	3,000	3,000	3,000	30,000
	Total Cost	37608	13076	12284	10432	12780	14118	16218	116516

Note: Figures in the parentheses indicate quantity of inputs.
Source: Records from experimental data of Dr. B.S. Konkan Krishi Vidyapeeth, Dapoli.

Table 5.6: Statement showing cash outflow (Returns) from one hectare mango orchard (Figures in rupees)

Sr. No.	Particulars	8th year	9th year	10th year	11th year	12th year	13th year	14th year	15th year	16th year
1.	No. of fruits/ tree	60	75	100	125	150	175	200	250	250
2.	No. of fruits/ha	6,000	7,500	10,000	12,500	15,000	17,500	20,000	25,000	25,000
3.	Yield in kg/ha (@ 5 fruits/ kg) (3=2+5 fruits)	1,200	1,500	2,000	2,500	3,000	3,500	4,000	5,000	5,000
4.	Gross Returns (₹)(@ ₹ 15/kg) (4 = 3 × 15 ₹)	18,000	22,500	30,000	37,500	45,000	52,500	60,000	75,000	75,000
5.	(Annual maintenance cost) (₹)	10,000	10,000	10,000	12,000	12,000	12,000	12,000	15,000	15,000
6.	Net returns (₹) (Available for repayment) in ₹ 6=4−5	8,000	12,500	20,000	25,500	33,000	40,500	48,000	60,000	60,000

Note: Annual maintenance cost includes cost of labour (both human and bullock) cost of manures, fertilizers and plant protection, etc.

It is observed from table 5.6 that the amount available for repayment from 8th year is ₹ 8,000 which increases to 60,000 in 15th year and remains more or less constant for future years to come.

If the farmers are repaying total loan amount of ₹ 87,000 in a period of five years, his repayment plan will be as under (Rate of interest per annum is 8 per cent).

Table 5.7: Repayment plan

Sr. No.	Age of orchard	Total loan (Principal)	Interest (₹ 8%)	Total dues in ₹	Instalment in ₹	Dues remained ₹
1.	9th year	87,000	6,990	93,990	11,310	82,650
2.	10th year	82,650	6,612	89,262	15,312	73,950
3.	11th year	73,950	5,916	79,866	25,056	54,810
4.	12th year	54,810	4,384	59,194	30,484	28,710
5.	13th year	28,710	2,296	31,006	31,006	Nil

Table 5.7 reveals that repayment instalment starts from 9th year and ends in 13th year. The rate of interest is assumed ₹ 8 per cent per annum. The all-loan amount will be repaid within five years, by following variable repayment plan while preparing any long-term loan scheme this proposal will be useful.

It can be concluded from above analysis that the farmer is able to repay his loan with interest leaving sufficient amount for meeting his family expenses by establishing mango orchard.

(C) Bank Proposal for Obtaining Loan for Poultry Enterprise

Poultry farming is a developing industry in our country, and it has a great scope in future. During recent years, demand for eggs and meat has increased considerably and has encouraged the development of poultry industry. Nowadays poultry production is undertaken on a massive scale in most of the states. India ranks sixth among the world's top egg producing countries and is only next to the USA, USSR, Japan, West Germany and UK. However, per capita availability of eggs per annum is only 17 in India as against 276 in USA and 208 in USSR. It indicates that there is enormous scope for further development and expansion of poultry enterprise in our country.

Nowadays poultry is a paying enterprise. It provides additional employment to cultivators. Cultivators get continuous income and compost from this enterprise. Various financing agencies give loan for poultry. Cultivators have to contribute to the extent of 35 per cent of the total investment and remaining amount can be borrowed from bank. While taking loan, cultivator has to hypothecate the assets which he will create as well as if necessary, land can be provided as security. In addition to above, signatures of two sureties are necessary. Details of the loan proposal are given below:

The poultry business involves the following activities:

1. To raise the layers for egg production.
2. To rear broilers for meat production.
3. To rear birds for breeding purpose (hatchery or breeding farm).
4. For supporting activities like plants for processing of eggs and birds and providing cold storage facility.

Financing layer farm

The borrower is required to contribute 25% of the capital cost as margin. Banks as a matter of policy have significantly reduced the margin amount in case of small farmers and agricultural labourers (*i.e.*, up to 15%).

Scale of finance

A poultry farmer needs two types of financial assistance, *viz.*, (*i*) Loan for construction of poultry building, *i.e.*, broilers' house, layers' house and purchase of equipments, (*ii*) Loan as working capital by way of cash credit for purchase of chicks, feeds, medicine, paying electricity charges, paying labour, water charges and other day-to-day expenses.

The quantum of finance for fixed assets is determined keeping in view the total investment margin to be contributed by the borrower and profitability aspect. Proforma invoice of equipments and estimates of cost of construction of building, etc., should be called.

The working capital should be provided for a period till the birds reach laying stage. Thereafter, there is no need to provide working capital as returns from eggs will be available for incurring expenditure.

Security

1. Hypothecation of poultry birds, feed, medicines, equipments and other farm assets.
2. Mortgage of land on which a poultry farm is set up.
3. Guarantee of two respectable persons acceptable to the bank.

Repayment

The repayment period is decided keeping in view the quantum of loan and the net income. Normally, it does not exceed five years. Instalments are fixed on monthly basis and a startup period of six months in case of new units is necessary. Startup period is necessary for the existing farms where the facility is sought for expansion of business.

Loan proposal for 1000 layers

A. *Fixed cost*

Rearing shed for 1000 birds, *i.e.*, 2,500 sq. ft. space @ ₹ 150 sq ft.	3,75,000
Cost of equipments	
(*i*) @ ₹ 5 per bird for 1000 birds (feeder, waters, feed/egg, trolleys, vaccination equipment etc.)	5,000
(*ii*) Water supply and electricity connections @ ₹ 2 per bird	2,000
Total fixed cost	**3,82,000**

B. *Variable costs*

Rearing cost up to laying stage	
(*i*) Cost of 1100 one day chicks @ ₹ 16 per bird (10% added on account of mortality)	17,600
(*ii*) Cost of feeding up to laying stage for 1050 birds @ 10 kg. feed/chick @ ₹ 9	94,500
(*iii*) Electricity charges, litter, labour charges for 1050 chicks @ ₹ 2 per chick	2,100
Total variable cost	**1,14,200**
Total capital requirement = Fixed cost + Variable cost = 3,82,000 + 1,14,200	4,96,200
Availability of loan (*i.e.*, 75% of total capital requirement)	3,72,150
Say	**3,72,000**

C. *Production expenses*

(*i*) Feeding cost for 1000 layers @ 40 kg per layer/12 months @ ₹ 9 per kg (laying stage)	3,60,000

(*ii*)	Cost of litter, medicine, etc. @ ₹ 2 per layer	2,000
(*iii*)	Labour charges for 12 months for 1 labour @ ₹ 2,000 per month	24,000
(*iv*)	Depreciation on fixed capital @ 5% (Considering the life span of building and equipments 20 years)	19,100
(*v*)	Interest on fixed capital @ 10% for one year	38,200
(*vi*)	Interest on working capital @ 13% (while calculating interest on working capital interest for period of six months is calculated)	7,423
	Total production expense	**4,50,723**

D. *Production and receipts*

1.	Sale of 275,000 eggs @ ₹ 1.70 per egg (Production of eggs 275 eggs per bird/year)	467,500
2.	Sale of manures @ ₹ 7,000 per tonne for 5 tonnes	35,000
3.	Sale of 950 old birds @ ₹ 60 per bird	57,000
4.	Sale of gunny bags @ ₹ 12 per bag for 500 bags	6,000
	Total receipt	**565,500**
	Net profit = Total receipts – Total production cost = 565,500 – 450,723	114,777

Repayment plan

If the borrower is repaying the loan amount of ₹ 3,72,000 in equal instalments of principal + interest, his repayment plan will be as follows:

Table 5.8: Repayment plan

Sr. No.	Age of orchard	Total loan (Principal)	Interest (₹10%)	Total dues in ₹	Instalment in ₹	Dues remained ₹
1.	1st Year	3,72,000	37,200	4,09,200	1,11,600	2,97,600
2.	2nd year	2,97,600	29,760	3,27,360	1,04,160	2,23,200
3.	3rd year	2,23,200	22,320	2,45,520	96,720	1,48,800
4.	4th year	1,48,800	14,880	1,63,680	89,280	74,400
5.	5th year	74,400	7,440	81,840	81,840	Nil

Thus, it can be said that the borrower will be free from his loan at the end of the 5th year.

Cost and Profit Ratios

1. Per bird per month cost of production
   = Total production cost/No. of birds/No. of months
   = 4,50,723/1,000/12 = ₹ 37.56
2. Per egg cost of production
   = Total production cost – (Value of by-products, *i.e.*, value of manures + value of old birds)/Total no. of eggs
   = 4,50,723 – 92,000/2,75,000 = 3,58,723/2,75,000
   = ₹ 1.30
3. Net profit per bird per month
   = Total profit/No. of birds/12 = 1,14,777/1,000/12
   = ₹ 9.56
4. Net profit per egg
   = Total Profit/No. of eggs produced = 1,14,777/2,75,000
   = ₹ 0.41
5. Benefit cost ratio = $\frac{\text{Total revenue}}{\text{Total cost}} = \frac{5,65,500}{4,50,723} = 1.25$

4. Proposal for Obtaining Finance for Dairy (2 Buffaloes)

Mixed farming which is the most common system of farming in India. Dairy is a good subsidiary occupation particularly to marginal and small farmers, who have limited holding and surplus labour force. Dairying provides gainful employment to idle family labour and supplement the income. In following dairy proposal ₹ 25,000 per buffalo, *i.e.*, ₹ 50,000 for two buffaloes is a bank loan component. The other expenses are made by the farmer himself.

Preparation of Bank proposal for obtaining finance for Dairy enterprise as a subsidiary occupation (Unit of 2 buffaloes)

Financial aspects

1. **Assumptions**
   (*a*) Average cost of buffalo (one) ₹ 25,000
   (*b*) Average lactation period 250 days
   (*c*) Average dry period 110 days

(*d*) Average milk production per lactation animal	2,500 lit.
(*e*) Average milk retained for home consumption	500 lit.
(*f*) Average milk available for sale/ lactation/animal	2,000 lit.
(*g*) Average sale price of milk/litre	₹15 lit.
(*h*) For rearing of two buffaloes unit no separate byre is constructed but a part of house is used.	

2. Feeding expenses for two buffaloes

(A) During lactation period of 250 days	
(*i*) Green fodder @ 15 kg/animal/day (@ ₹ 0.50 per kg)	3,750
(*ii*) Day fodder @ 6 kg/animal/day (@ ₹ 1.00 per kg)	3,000
(*iii*) Concentrate @ 3.5 kg/animal/day (@ ₹ 9 per kg)	15,750
Total expenses/during location period	**22,500**
(B) During dry period of 110 days	
(*i*) Green fodder @ 10 kg/cattle/day (@ ₹ 0.50 per kg)	1,100
(*ii*) Dry fodder @ 2 kg/cattle/day (@ ₹ 1.00 per kg)	440
(*iii*) Concentrate @ 1 kg/cattle/day (@ ₹ 9 per kg)	1,980
Total expenses during dry period	**3,520**
Total feeding cost (A + B) (₹ 22,500 + 3,520)	**26,020**

3. Other costs (for two buffaloes)

(*a*) Insurance per annum (@ 4 per cent value of cattle)	2,000
(*b*) Expenses on veterinary aids (@ ₹ 3% value of animal)	1,500
(*c*) Maintenance of 2 calves @ ₹ 1,000 per calf	2,000

(*d*) Management (labour) charges @ ¼ labours per animal 12,600
(@ 70 per day) for one year (₹ 35 × 360)

(*e*) Interest on fixed capital @ 10% considering fixed capital of ₹ 5,000 is ₹ 500
(Water trays, milk cans, and other daily required instrument).

(*f*) Depreciation

(*i*) Buffaloes @ 10%	₹	3,000
(*ii*) Buildings @ 15%	₹	7,500
(*iii*) Equipments @ 15%	₹	500
Total	**₹**	**11,000**

Total other cost 29,600 (2,000 + 1,500 + 2,000 + 12,600 + 500 + 11,000)

Total cost = Total feeding cost + other cost
i.e., ₹ 26,020 + 29,600 = ₹ 55,620

4. **Gross income/annum**

1. Sale of milk (5000 lit × 15)	75,000
2. Sale of manure @ 800/year/animal	1,600
3. Sale of calves @ ₹1,200/calf	2,400
4. Sale of empty gunny bags @ ₹12 per bag (50 bags)	600

Gross income 79,600

5. **Net income and repaying capacity**

Net income = Gross returns – Total cost
= 79,600 – 55,620 = 23,980

Thus, a farmer is getting a net income of ₹ 23,980 per lactation.

If we assume the one-fourth amount (₹ 5,995) will be required for his family maintenance then his repaying capacity will be ₹ 17,985.

Table 5.9: Repayment plan

Sr. No.	Year	Total loan (Principal)	Interest (₹10%)	Total dues in ₹	Instalment in ₹	Dues remained ₹
1.	1st year	50,000	5,000	55,000	17,500	37,500
2.	2nd year	37,500	3,750	41,250	16,250	25,000
3.	3rd year	25,000	2,500	27,500	15,000	12,500
4.	4th year	12,500	1,250	13,750	13,750	Nil

Thus, by availing loan for two buffaloes farmer can get a good subsidiary occupation. He can repay loan within 4 years as shown in table 5.9. By having this business as a subsidiary occupation farmer can fulfil his family requirement of milk, can generate employment and also FYM is available for agriculture. Thus, it is a very good subsidiary occupation for farmers.

(E) Loan Proposal for a 35-H.P. Tractor

Mechanization of agriculture is necessary to complete various operations in time and economically. Similarly, intensive cultivation is also possible. Use of tractor has reduced the cost of cultivation and added the profit margin. However, cultivator should be able to employ the tractor at least 1000 hours per annum. Otherwise, tractor cultivation becomes uneconomic. These 1000 hours may be distributed as partly employing tractor on own farm and partly working on hire. Nowadays, various co-operative societies employ tractors for carrying sugarcane from field to factory as well as some contractors also employs tractor. Similarly, other cultivators can also use tractor on hire basis.

Cost of Operation and Maintenance of 35-H.P. Tractor

Average cost price of 35-H.P. tractor is ₹ 4,00,000. Average cost price of three common implements is ₹ 70,000.

		₹
1. Operational cost per hour		
(*a*) Consumption of fuel @ 3 litres per hour @ ₹ 42 per litre		126.00
(*b*) Lubricants @ 25 per cent of fuel cost		31.50
Total		**157.50**
2. Overhead costs (on the basis of 1000 hours per year)	**Per year**	**Per hour**
(*a*) Insurance, registration and other charges @ 2 per cent per year	8000	8.00
(*b*) Major repairs @ 50 per cent of the depreciation of tractor and minor repairs @ 20 per cent of depreciation	28000	28.00
(*c*) Repairs @ 20 per cent on the cost of implements	14000	14.00
(*d*) Depreciation on tractor (₹ 40,000 and on implements 7000)	47000	47.00
(*e*) Average interest on loan amount @ 9 per cent	31725	31.72
Sub Total	128725	128.72

Total operational cost per hour is ₹ 286.22 (157.50 + 128.72). If we assumed a cultivator is having a 4-hectare farm, he will require 300 tractor hours for carrying out various farm operations and tractor works on hire for 700 hours/annum.

Net income from 4-hectare farm is ₹ 40,000 and tractor works for 700 hours on hire (₹ 300/hour)

Total amount received	2,10,000
Total amount required	4,70,000
Margin fund (25 per cent of total amount)	1,17,500
Loan amount required	3,52,500

Repaying Capacity

Net income (2,10,000 + 40,000 = ₹ 2,50,000)

If we deduct ₹ 1,20,000 as family living expenses from net income then ₹ 1,30,000 is his repaying capacity.

Table 5.10: Repayment plan

Sr. No.	Year	Total loan (Principal)	Interest (₹10%)	Total dues in ₹	Instalment in ₹	Dues remained ₹
1.	1st year	3,52,500	35,250	3,87,750	1,30,000	2,57,750
2.	2nd year	2,57,750	25,775	2,83,525	1,30,000	1,53,525
3.	3rd year	1,53,525	15,352	1,68,877	1,30,000	38,877
4.	4th year	38,877	3,887	76,864	42,764	Nil

Repayment: Thus, within four years cultivator can repay the borrowed amount as shown in table 5.10. The repayment plan is an amortised even repayment plan.

Phases of Agricultural Credit Policy in India

As time passed agricultural credit acquired more and more significant position and its importance remained constant for agricultural development. Agricultural credit policy passed through different phases. During early period, it was relief-oriented. Then production-oriented and now development-cum-welfare-oriented.

Credit Need

Credit is required by all categories of farmers for their agricultural production as it is an important input. In ancient time, agriculture was subsistence type, capital need was less for agricultural production and hence, credit need was also limited. In course of time, agriculture became more capital intensive and hence credit intensive. As credit need was limited initially, farmers were borrowing from money-lenders and relatives as a ready source of credit. This borrowing from money-lenders increased over a period of time which led to rural indebtedness. Agricultural credit policy plays a significant role in demand and supply of credit. Hence, attempt is made to study agricultural credit policy during different period and outcome of this study is discussed under different headings.

Required data for this study were collected from secondary sources such as all India rural credit survey committee report, all India rural credit review committee report, etc. The results are discussed below by giving suitable tables.

Government Awakes

Deccan witnessed agrarian disturbances in 1875. Peasants of Poona and Ahmednagar districts of Maharashtra united against the money-lending classes, who were charging exorbitant interest rates, keeping the peasants in perpetual indebtedness. It became clear to government that some substantial action must be taken to avoid recurrences of such acts of violence. Therefore, government adopted two types of measures and passed three important acts, *i.e.*, first Deccan Agricultural Relief Act (1879), second, Land Improvement Loans Act (1884). All these made the beginning of our credit policy, which was initially mainly relief-oriented.

First type of measure was the Money Lending Legislation. The basic objectives underlying the various legislative enactments on regulation of money-lending can be broadly stated as follows:

(*a*) To bring out an improvement in the terms on which private credit was available to the agriculturists and place legal restrictions on the unreasonable exploitation of the borrowing peasant class.

(*b*) To enable the civil courts to do greater justice between the lenders and the borrowers, that was not possible in the prevailing circumstances under the ordinary code of civil procedure.

Although legislation for the regulation of money-lending has been enacted and enforced in most of the states, practically none of them has any adequate machinery for the specific purpose of ensuring an effective implementation of the various acts.

Second measure was Debt Relief Legislation. Here again two types: (*i*) Voluntary reduction of debt and for this purpose legislation was passed in many states to set up "Debt Conciliation boards", a machinery through which debtors could be assisted to get the permission of their creditors to reduction of debt and its repayment in convenient instalments, (*ii*) Compulsory reduction of debt.

According to the above-mentioned Land Improvement Loans Act (1883), and Agriculturists Loans Act (1884), Taccavi system for institutional credit supply by government came into existence. The basic purpose of Taccavi is to give relief to farmers in famine and in distress condition. But unfortunately, it would not be far from the truth to say that the record of Taccavi is a record of inadequacies. These may be considered, in their different aspects, which are: (*i*) inadequacy of amount, (*ii*) inequality in distribution and inappropriateness of basis of security, (*iii*) inconvenience of timing, and (*iv*) inefficiency of supervision and incompleteness of co-ordination.

Table 5.11: Inequality of distribution of the Taccavi

Type of cultivator	Amount borrowed from government by this group as percentage of the total borrowing from all agencies by this group	Amount borrowed from government by this group of cultivators as percentage of total borrowing of all cultivators from government
Big	4.5	34.5
Large	3.8	58.1
Medium	3.2	32.1
Small	2.0	9.8

Table 5.11 shows 58.1% of the Taccavi was shared by the large farmers, 32.1% of the Taccavi credit was shared by medium farmers and small farmers only accounted for rest 9.8%. In fact, small farmers are in real need of such type of credit facility but the above figure shows that they were not given their proper share.

Birth of Co-operatives

Due to various deficiencies of Taccavi system and previously analysed problems of money-lending and debt-relief legislation, all these measures are described as partial and incomplete to fulfil the increasing need of agricultural credit.

In 1892, the Madras Government placed Sir Fredric Nicholson on special duty to study the theory and practice of agricultural and other land banks in Europe and to suggest means by which similar movement might be popularized in India. Based on Nicholson's recommendations and report of the Famine Commission (1901) Co-operative Credit Societies Act of 1904 was passed. Thus, Co-operative movement was introduced in India mainly to give relief to the Indian peasants from clutches of the money-lenders. However, this also turned out to be relief-oriented agricultural credit policy.

Again in 1912, Act of 1904 was revised to make co-operatives more reliable credit institutions.

Initially, co-operative credit was granted both for production and for consumption purposes. Government of India in its famous resolution of 1914 explained that it was not possible for the societies to insist on loans being only for productive purposes, but loans for purposes other than productive purposes could be granted within certain limits. Maclagan Committee also recommended that consumption credit should be granted when it is inevitable, but it should not be excessive.

Table 5.12: Purpose-wise analysis of borrowing (1951-52)

Sr. No.	Purpose	Cultivators in percentage			
		Large	Medium	Small	All rural families
1.	Capital expenditure on farm	34.7	30.5	23.2	27.8
2.	Current expenditure on farm	12.1	10.1	6.8	9.3
3.	Family expenditure	41.2	49.5	59.8	50.2
4.	Non-farm business expenditure	4.9	3.4	6.0	6.6
5.	Other expenditure	6.6	6.0	3.9	5.7
6.	More than one purpose	0.5	0.5	0.3	0.4
		100.0	100.0	100.0	100.0

Table 5.12 reveals that if we considered all rural families together then only 37.1% of the total borrowings by all rural families were spent on the farm and large portion, *i.e.*, 58.8% of the borrowings were spent on family expenditure and non-farm business expenditure. This supports that credit policy was taking into account the consumption credit too.

Another Post Independence Development feature of credit policy is that it is based on size of holding, *i.e.*, those who own, more land get more credit because basis for loan security is land, the efficiency of farmer as well as tenant cultivators are ignored by lending institutions. Therefore, to make the institutional credit facilities more wide some new things must be introduced. On this background Rural Credit Survey Committee (1954) recommended that the provision of short-term credit should be based on the crop loan system. So that the loans would be for productive purposes. In 1959, the committee on co-operative credit was appointed under the Chairmanship of Late Shri V.L. Mehta to go into the question of how adequate production credit might be provided. With recommendations of this committee in 1963 crop loan system acquired great emphasis in Action Programme. However, the conference of the state ministers for co-operation held in Bombay in November, 1965, recommended the introduction of crop loan throughout the country with effect from Kharif season of 1966. However, this type of lending did not prove popular with the farmers mainly due to administrative inefficiency. The farmers do not get the credit in time as well as credit limit preparation and recommendations for crop loans by supervisors are largely guided by vested interests.

Another, landmark in credit policy is "Developmental or Growth Oriented Credit Policy". Table 5.12 reveals the fact that larger the cultivator more proportion of borrowed fund was spent on farm expenses compared to small and marginal farmers. Large, Medium and Small farmers spent 46.8%, 40.6%, 30.0% on farm out of total borrowings, respectively. This also shows that cultivators with strong resource base are able to undertake investment in land. In other words, this segment of cultivators was identified as a source of growth and obviously the credit policy also tilted in their favour. The major attempt in this direction was the launching of Intensive Agricultural District

Programme (IADP) popularly known as 'package programme' in 16 selected districts spread over 15 states during 1960-62. The districts were selected having regard to maximum availability of irrigation and minimum natural hazards and provision has been made to provide the credit. The selection of districts for this programme clearly indicated the bias of our credit policy towards resourceful areas neglecting the others.

Another development which indicates development-oriented credit policy is that Government realized the importance of medium and long-term investment for rapid development of agriculture, Government of India and Reserve Bank of India took a step in establishing Agricultural Refinance Corporation (ARC) by passing the act in 1963 and corporation came into being on first July, 1963, agricultural financing agency provides medium and long-term finance to eligible institutions for promoting the development of agriculture. Agriculture Refinance Corporation sanctioned 233 schemes up to 1968-69, Andhra, Punjab, and Tamil Nadu are major beneficiaries.

With regard to ARC, one important point to be noted is that central land development banks are the major beneficiaries of Corporation (ARC) as 91% of the withdrawals are by the central land development banks. The history of co-operative movement has already recorded that any co-operative institution is more favourable to the better off sections of the farm community and so indirectly benefits of ARC are also snatched by this particular section.

Another development in agricultural credit was the establishment of Agricultural Credit Corporation. It was recognized by the rural credit survey committee that uneven growth of co-operatives as in Assam, Bihar, Orissa, West Bengal, Rajasthan was due to their backwardness as compared to Gujarat and Maharashtra which are comparatively advanced states. Commercial bank also neglected these states and so these states were recognized as areas of retarded growth.

It is observed from table 5.13 that loan for productive purposes increased from 50.1 per cent in 1971 to 69.2 per cent in 1981 but it declined to 22.5 per cent in 1991. This might be due to increasing amount of overdue in agricultural sector.

Table 5.13: Purpose-wise distribution of borrowing

(Percentages)

Sr. No.	Purpose of loan	1971	1981	1991
1.	Farm business	44.7	60.1	14.7
2.	Non-farm business	5.4	9.1	7.8
	(*a*) Productive Expenditure (1+2)	50.1	69.2	22.5
	(*b*) Household expenditure	40.9	22.3	40.1
	(*c*) Others	9.0	8.5	37.4
	All purposes	100.0	100.0	100.0

Source: *Indian Economy by Ruddar Datt and Sundaram*, 50th edition, p. 608.

However, in 1991 percentage under household expenditure category in rural area has increased to 40.1 per cent which is quite significant. This phenomenon may be due to increase in per capita income might have resulted in purchase of luxury items like car, fridge, etc.

Informal group on institutional arrangements for agricultural credit recommended establishment of Agricultural Credit Corporation (ACC) which would make loans broadly on the basis of the crop loan system to cultivators or group of cultivators, who should be encouraged gradually to form co-operatives. Corporations (ACC) were to raise Share Capital from central and state government, Food Corporation of India and Reserve Bank of India. In April 1966, proposal for establishment of the corporation (ACC) received general endorsement and Parliament passed the concerned legislation. Some states expressed that it would hamper the progress of co-operative movement but more recently some of these states have taken a step to establish proposed corporation. This establishment of Agricultural Credit Corporation indicated that Indian government paid attention towards areas of retarded growth and partly tried to shift the credit policy in their favour.

Due to recent breakthrough in Agricultural production because of advancement in agricultural technology, government felt the credit gap in meeting the large requirements of agricultural credit. Co-operatives even where they attempted to expand strengthen and improve could not have covered even 40% of farmers requirements by March 1974. Therefore, it was necessary that additional agencies should enter in this field so as to provide adequate, timely and cheap institutional finance for agriculture. Similarly, it was observed that commercial banking business is a well-developed banking business in the country and so far it has neglected the agricultural sector. It is seen that the percentage share of commercial banks in total borrowings by the farmers in 1951-52 and in 1961-62 was 0.9% and 0.6% respectively. So government amended the Banking Regulation Act of 1949, under this amendment every banking company is required to reconstitute its board of directors (and thus social control came in force from December, 1967). So that the majority of the members of the board should have special knowledge or practical experience in Agriculture, rural economy, small scale industries, Co-operation, banking and do not have substantial interest in business undertakings. Due to this several of the leading commercial banks have chosen to enter in the field of Farm Credit.

As a positive response to the above government action, commercial banks formed a club of banks known as Agricultural Finance Corporation (AFC) in April, 1968. It gives direct and indirect finance. Corporation (AFC) helped the member banks for energization of irrigation wells in Andhra area, development in Kosi region of Bihar, reclamation of sandy soil, etc.

But weakness of social control system, were felt in many respects, *viz.*, persons controlling the policies of banks continued to exercise their influence over the banks in one way or the other, while quick channelizing of the funds into the desired avenues of priority areas was not assured. As well as progress made by the banks in the following programmes and policy directions under the social control scheme was found to be too slow. Due to these reasons government felt that to make a banking system as a instrument of economic growth, with special emphasis on neglected sectors such as agriculture. Nationalization of major commercial Banks is necessary. So, Government of India nationalized fourteen major commercial banks in July, 1969.

If we examine the progress made by these nationalized banks. We will find that loan advances to agriculture including plantation. Outstanding at the end of June, 1968 was 44.58 crores; it increased to 392.96 crores in March, 1972. This is a significant increment in loan advances, but still general complaint is made that major beneficiaries are the farmers having sound resource base. This is because; it is difficult to prove credit worthiness for small farmers.

Neglect of small man; out of total operational holdings under Indian Union, 40.7% were small holdings (below 2.5 acres), 34.1% holdings between 2.5 and 7.5 acres. In other words, 74.8% farmers were having operational holding below 7.5 acres. This indicated large proportion of the small holdings in the country. On the other hand, it is well-known fact that most of the credit institutions failed to serve the purpose of the small farmers. It is also accepted by Government and according to recent national objectives, *i.e.*, growth with social justice, government designed a programme for weaker sections of the rural population which shows shift in our credit policy which we may call as development- cum-welfare-oriented credit policy.

On this background, Small Farmers Development Agency (SFDA) and Marginal Farmers and Agricultural Labourers (MFAL) development agency came into existence in 1969, based on the recommendations of All India Rural Credit Review Committee as a institutional agency to help small and marginal farmers. But it was critically pointed out that at present our social structure and infrastructure for agricultural development is such that any programme designed for weaker section, at implementation level it fails, and its benefits are snatched by the strong section of the society. In other words, there are large leakages in these programmes in favour of rich farmers.

Another effort of central government to help the weaker sections of society, Regional Rural Banks (RRBs) were set up in 1975. The objectives of these banks is to provide credit and other facilities particularly to the small and marginal farmers, agricultural labourers, artisans and small entrepreneurs, so as to develop agriculture, trade, commerce, industry and other productive activities in the rural areas. Thus, these efforts were leading towards "Agricultural Development", however, there is little shift took place in credit policy from Agricultural Development-oriented to Rural Development-oriented and therefore for paying more attention towards rural development NABARD, *i.e.*, National Bank for Agriculture and Rural Development was set up in July, 1982 by the act of Parliament to take over functions of ARDC and functions of Agricultural credit department of RBI. The NABARD is helping both for agricultural and for rural development. Recent development in agricultural credit is to forming the Self-Help Groups (SHGs) and linking them with bank credit. NABARD took initiative in this case. And at the end of March 2004 about 10.8 lakh SHGs are linked with banks and cumulative disbursements of bank loans to SHGs stood at ₹ 3,900 crores. However, only 30 per cent of poor families have been covered and yet 70 per cent poor families are to be covered in due course of time.

Selected References

1. Agrawal, G.D., and Bansil, P.C, *Economic Theory as Applied to Agriculture,* Vikas Publications, Delhi, 1969.
2. Agricultural Finance Corporation Ltd., *Guidelines for Formulating Scheme and Projects,* Agricultural Finance Corporation Ltd., Bombay.
3. Chauhan and Dev, "Problems of Rural Credit Rural India," p. 37, Feb.-March, 1980.
4. Datey, C.D., "Agricultural Development and Co-operative Credit," *Financing Agriculture Annual,* p. 1, 1975.
5. Dhaliwal, J.S., "Natural Calamities and Financial Institutions," *Financing Agriculture,* Vol. XI, No. 3 and 4, p. 20, January-March, 1980.
6. Johl, S.S. and Moore, C.V., *Farm Financing Management Today and Tomorrow,* New Delhi, 1970.
7. Kathuria, G. and Chandrasekharan, K., *Elements of Agricultural Finance,* Progressive Corporation Pvt. Ltd., Bombay, 1933.
8. Kohli, P.S., "Study of Commercial Banks Financing in Small Farmers Development Agency - Patna," *Financing Agriculture,* Vol. VI, No. 3, October, 1970.
9. Murray, W.C., and Nelson, A.C., *Agricultural Finance,* The Iowa State University Press, Fifth ed., 1967.
10. Nair, K.R., "Capital Growth in Indian Agriculture," *Indian Journal of Agricultural Economics,* pp. 155-162, 1965.
11. Narasimhan, V.S., and Kappini, M., "Impact of Bank Nationalization on Co-operative Credit," *Financing Agriculture,* Vol. VI, No. 4, p. 261, January, 1975.
12. Pandya, K.C., "Bank Agricultural Officer Farmer's Friend, Philosopher, and Guide," *Rural India,* p. 18, January, 1979.
13. Pandey, H.K., "Institutional Credit and HYV Programme," *Financing Agriculture,* Vol. VI, No. 1, p. 23, April, 1974.

14. Patel, A.R., "Fundamentals of Farm Financing," *Financing Agriculture,* Vol. VI, No. 2, p. 4, July, 1974.
15. Rane, A.A., "Phases of Agricultural Credit Policy in India," *Rural India,* p. 3, January, 1980.
16. Ruddar Datt and Sundharam, *Indian Economy,* 52nd revised edition, 2006, S. Chand and Co. Ltd., New Delhi.
17. Salunke, V.G., "Performance of Small Farmers Development Agency as perceived by the Beneficiary Small Farmers," *Financing Agriculture,* Vol. X, No. 4, p. 26, January-March, 1979.
18. Shastri, C.P., "Investment on Farm and Capital Formation in Agricultural with Particular Reference to Bihar," *Indian Journal of Agricultural Economics,* pp. 174-183, 1956.
19. Shukla, B.D., and Mishra S.D., "Impact of Co-operative Finance," *Financing Agriculture,* Vol. VI, No. 2, p. 26, July 1974.
20. Shukla, Tara, " Regional Analysis of Institutional Finance for Agriculture," *Indian Journal of Agricultural Economics,* Vol. 26, No. 3, 1971.
21. Sisodia, J.S., and Agarkar, V.L., "Income, Saving and Expenditure in Rural Areas of Malwa Region of Madhya Pradesh," *Indian Journal of Agricultural Economics,* p. 131, 1970.
22. Tewari, S.K., and Sharma, J.S., "A Critical Appraisal of Nature of Flow of Bank Credit to Agriculture," *Financing Agriculture,* Vol. XI, No. 1, p. 8, April-June, 1979.
23. Thingalaya, N.K., "Rural Credit: Structure and Flows," *Indian Journal of Agricultural Economics,* Vol. XXXIV, No. 1, p. 21, January-March, 1979.

PART II
Co-operation

6
Introduction to Co-operation

Co-operation originated in Europe and now it is spread all over the world. It is a boon to a common man. It has covered most of the human activities. Everybody must know about co-operation because it has become a part of life. In agriculture, it has been used extensively.

Meaning of Co-operation

Co-operation is derived from the Latin word 'co-operari'. 'Co' means with and 'operari' means to work. In other words, Co-operation means working together with others for a common purpose. For example, group of cultivators wanted to irrigate their fields. They will unite together, manage the capital and they will irrigate their field by digging a well and by purchasing an electric motor for lifting water. Thus, it means system of people voluntarily associated, working together on terms of equality to satisfy economic interests.

Definitions of Co-operation

Some of the definitions are as follows:

1. Mr. Calvert defines it as "A form of organisation wherein the persons voluntarily associate together as human beings on a basis of equality, for the promotion of economic interests of themselves."
2. Dr. C.R. Fay describes the co-operative society as "an association for purposes of joint trading, originally among the weak, and conducted always in an unselfish

spirit on such terms that all who are prepared to assume the duties of membership may share its reward in proportion to the degree in which they make use of the organization."

3. Seligman observes that "Co-operation in its technical sense means the abandonment of competition in distribution and production and the elimination of the middlemen of all kinds."
4. Mr. M.T. Herrick defined co-operation as "The act of persons, voluntarily united, for utilizing reciprocally their own forces, resources or both under their arrangement to their common profit or loss."
5. The Maclagan Committee on Co-operation defined co-operation as "The theory of co-operation is, very briefly, that an isolated and powerless man can, by association with others and by moral development and mutual support obtain, in his own degree, the material advantage available to wealthy or powerful persons and thereby develop himself to the fullest extent of his natural abilities. By the union of forces material advancement is secured and by united action self-reliance is fostered, and it forms the interaction of these influences that it is hoped to attain the effective realisation of the higher and more prosperous standard of living which has been characterised as better business, better farming and better living.

Various aspects of co-operation are clear from above definitions. Co-operation may be redefined, as "Co-operation is a voluntary organisation of people meant for satisfying their economic interests".

Sociological Ideas of Co-operation

Two basic sociological ideas were involved in co-operation:

1. People desire to have personal relationship rather than impersonal relationships involved in modern business dealings.
2. People would like to join with others in a mutual effort and to live in peace rather than to compete against each other.

Religious Idea about Co-operation

Some church people thought the co-operation is Christianity, applied to business. Each has to work for all, and all have to work for each. There, should not be selfish motive which Christ do not like.

Economic Philosophy of Co-operation

A philosophy that tries to explain the nature and purpose of co-operation as a way of conducting business is an economic philosophy of co-operation. The economic philosophies or co-operation fall roughly under two headings:

1. *Reformistic and revolutionary philosophies:* Co-operation is, considered as a means of redistribution of income and wealth. Eliminating or harmonizing conflicts of interests between labour and management, conflicts between producers and consumers. Pioneers in the field of co-operation were of the view that workers must gain possession of means of production and use them for their mutual benefit.
2. *Evolutionary philosophy:* As per evolutionary philosophy, co-operation is considered as a evolutionary development within capitalism. According to this view, the co-operative is a type of business organization by means of which small units are enabled to gain some, if not most advantage of large-scale operation. Horizontal combinations and vertical integration, at the same time retain a maximum of independence in their individual pursuits.

Importance of Co-operation

Co-operation provided several economic, social and educational benefits to people. Poor people satisfied their some of desires through co-operation. It is a golden mean between socialism and capitalism. Underdeveloped countries can very well make best use of their resources with the help of co-operatives. In India, growth of co-operative movement is not even and, hence there is wide scope for co-operatives. Importance of co-operation for improving quality of life has been proved and hence co-operation continues to be important one. Prosperity of Indian economy, depends upon progress in agriculture and progress in agriculture depends upon strengthening and expanding co-operative movement.

Co-operation and Socialism

Socialism as an economic system would vest the ownership and control of capital and consumption goods in the state. Socialism does not recognize private property. Important industries such as railways, other public utility concerns are owned by the state, and services are rendered to people at low cost. Co-operation aims to satisfy economic interest of members, try to provide services to members at low cost. Some fundamental principles of co-operation and socialism are the same. Both the systems emphasize human and social welfare. However, socialism and co-operation differ from each other, *i.e.*, co-operative economy recognizes individual ownership of property but socialism does not. In recent years, a number of socialists consider co-operation as an integral and important part of the movement towards the socialistic society.

Co-operation and Communism

Like socialism, communism as an economic system would; vest the ownership and control of all capital and consumption goods in the state. Private property and private business do not prevail in this system. Main aim of both the systems is to provide services to the community at lowest cost but the methods adopted under communism to achieve these objectives are entirely different from socialism. Under socialism the ownership and control of the economy is acquired gradually and through legislation. They are more or less evolutionary in their methods and aim. But the methods adopted under communism are entirely revolutionary. They believe in radical changes. Communism suggests poor people should pull down the rich people and capitalistic class from their dignified and secured positions and should take up the means of production in their own hands.

Thus, there are some fundamental differences between co-operation and communism. Co-operation suggests to the people to raise themselves to a dignified position in the society through self-help and mutual-help. Methods of co-operation are evolutionary while communism is revolutionary. Radical changes have no place in a co-operative organization. Final aim of serving the people at low cost is same in both, but methods are different.

Co-operation and Capitalism

Sometimes co-operation and capitalism have been considered similar. This is because:

1. Both accept the right of private property.
2. Each use capital and pays interest for it.

However, there are some glaring differences, those are as follows:

1. Capitalism is based on principle of survival of the fittest, *i.e.*, competition. Co-operation is based on the principle of self-help through mutual-help.
2. Capitalism believes in exploitation of man with the help of money, whereas co-operation fights against exploitation of man by man with money.
3. Capitalism is devoid of morality whereas co-operation stands on moral grounds and honesty.
4. One man, one vote is a rule in co-operation but in capitalism extent of the holding of the share capital will determine the strength of a person.

State Undertaking (Enterprise) and Co-operation

State or municipal enterprise is a form of business organization. Here the government or local body like a municipality runs a business. This is generally done in the case of public utility services like electricity, fertilizer industry, water supply, etc. The aim of state undertaking and co-operative society is same to provide services to people at low cost. However, state undertakings are generally larger than co-operatives. Co-operatives have to seek help of government for their development.

It can be concluded that co-operation comprises desirable principles and concepts from socialism, communism and capitalism. Recognizing private property is same as in capitalism. Democratic control by members is similar to state control as in communism, socialism. Like communism co-operative movement is also devoted to common welfare of members.

Principles of Co-operation

Co-operative principles are guidelines and rules required for running co-operative organization successfully. These principles are based on several years' experience of different co-operators from all over the world. Principles are revised from time to time in order to make co-operatives most reliable in the changing world. International Co-operative Alliance (ICA) appointed a commission in 1964 under the chairmanship of Prof. D.G. Karve of India. This commission laid down the following basic principles in its report, published in 1964. These are known as ICA principles of co-operation. ICA commission has also stated that these principles may be modified to some extent in the interest of success of particular co-operative organization. These principles are as follows:

1. Voluntary and open membership;
2. Democratic control;
3. Limited interest on capital;
4. Equitable distribution of surplus or patronage dividend;
5. Co-operative education; and
6. Co-operation among co-operatives.

1. Principle of Voluntary and Open Membership

"Membership of a co-operative society shall be voluntary and available without artificial restriction or any social, political, racial or religious discrimination to all persons who can make use of its services and are willing to accept the responsibilities of membership".

Voluntary Membership

Individuals are free to join or not to join the co-operative organization. Such freedom helps to develop true co-operative spirit amongst the members. All who join the society must be loyal to it.

However, under certain circumstances co-operation can be imposed upon persons who are anti-social elements. For instance, if 60 per cent or more people are ready to become member of co-operative marketing society remaining may be compelled to join it. Similarly, membership of co-operative sugar factory may be imposed in the interest of majority.

Open Membership

Open membership means following three things:

1. There will not be any artificial restriction on the admission of members. Artificial restrictions include high initial shareholding or entrance fee, and restriction of membership for exploiting non-members.

   Open membership does not mean that anybody can demand, as of right, admission to any co-operative society; it only means that a society formed with certain definite objects shall keep its door open for all people who share, those objectives. Sometimes anti-social elements are denied membership. Similarly, membership also denied to persons living in the area of operation of another society of same type.
2. Membership should be available without any social, political, racial or religious discrimination against persons who wish to join it.
3. Membership should be available to all persons who need and can make use of the services of society and are willing to accept the responsibilities of membership.

Similarly, some restrictions can be imposed on a person with drawing from membership. Though member is free to withdraw, he cannot free himself from his liability or losses that may have arisen during the period of his membership.

2. Democratic Control

In co-operative organization, each member has only one vote and distinction is not made according to the amount of wealth any member may contribute to the organization. Majority rule in all matters related to society. After paying for minimum number of shares of a society, person is equally important.

3. The Principle of Interest on Capital

The ICA principle is as follows, "share capital shall only receive a strictly limited rate of interest if any."

Payment of interest is not obligatory. The ICA commission has made this point clear. There is no co-operative principle which obliges interest to be paid. The principle is that if interest is paid on share capital the rate should be limited and fixed on the ground that the supplier of capital is not equitably entitled to share in savings, surplus or profit. In a commercial enterprise, net surplus is distributed in proportion to the share held by a person. This increases gap between poor and rich. Rich dominates poor. So as to avoid this situation, rate of interest on capital is kept limited.

4. Principle of Equitable Distribution of Surplus or Patronage Dividend

The ICA rule is as follows:

> "The economic results, arising out of the operations of a society belong to the members of that society and shall be distributed in such manner as should avoid one member gaining at the expense of others."

Surplus or profit of the co-operative organization generally utilized to strengthen the organization as well as for providing common services to the members. Some amount of profit is distributed to members in proportion to their transactions with the society. More the transactions of a person, more he contributes towards profit and hence he must get back in the form of profit in the same proportion as he transacts with the society. This is also called as patronage dividend. For example, Mr. Mohan's transaction with society is of ₹ 1,000 per annum while Mr. Ram's transaction per annum is of ₹ 500 only. At the end of the year, Mohan got double the amount of profit that Ram got from a society.

5. Principle of Co-operation Education

The ICA rule is as follows:

> "All Co-operative societies shall make provision for the education of their members, officers, employees and the general public, in the principles and techniques of co-operation both economic and democratic."

Objective behind educating members, officers and employees of co-operative organization is to develop true co-operative spirit in them. So that they will act honestly without any selfish interests. Educating the public in principles of co-operation, will help for strengthening and for expansion of co-operative movement. Many people will take advantage of co-operation.

6. Principle of Co-operation among Co-operatives or the Principle of Growth

The ICA rule is as follows:

> "All co-operative organizations, in order to best serve the interests of their members and their communities, shall actively co-operate in every practical way with other co-operatives at local, national and international levels, having as their aim of achievement of unity of action by co-operators throughout the world."

Main objective of co-operation is to serve the people in best manner. This principle helps to avoid competition within co-operatives. Co-operatives should not compete with each other, they should co-operate among themselves. This will bring more benefits to members. State co-operative bank can organize national co-operative bank and later on international co-operative bank. This will help to solve the problems at different levels. This will also strengthen co-operative movement throughout the world. International Co-operative Petroleum Association and the International Co-operative Alliance are the examples of co-operations among co-operatives.

These six principles should be observed in their entirety by all co-operatives if they claim to belong to the co-operative movement.

Other Principles

There are some other general principles of co-operation. Those are as follows:

1. Self-help and mutual-help: This principle implies self-financing and self-management by the co-operatives. Members should associate together with a view to promote the economic interest of their own. Their motto is "Each for all and all for each", working on this motto members help each other.

2. A spirit of service or profit motive: The main objective is to protect the members at the hands of the middlemen and to improve the economic status of its members. Poor co-operate each other with a view to solve their problems and satisfy economic interest. Their main aim is not profit but to serve the members at low cost. For example, co-operative credit societies.

3. Principle of thrift: Thrift or habit of saving is very basis of self-help. Without saving or without credit facility we cannot invest. Without investment no further progress. Thrift must precede credit.

4. Principle of publicity: For educating people wide publicity should be given to principles of co-operation. List showing the loans issued to every member, the names of his sureties and amount of the loan still unpaid and such matters should be known to members. This help for effective running of co-operative society.

5. Honest trading: Co-operative should sell pure and unadulterated goods and give correct weight and measure. Co-operative is not mainly meant for earning profit, best service to members is the main objective. Hence, co-operative should carry out honest trading.

7
Co-operative Credit Structure

Co-operative credit structure mainly divided into two broad categories:

1. Short-and medium-term credit structure which is known as three-tier system, and
2. Long-term credit structure which is known as two-tier system.

Co-operative Agricultural Credit Structure

Agricultural Credit

Short-term and Medium-term
(Three-tier system)

1. State Co-operative Banks
2. Central Co-operative Banks
3. Primary credit societies

Long-term
(Two-tier system)

1. State Co-operative agriculture and rural development banks (Central Land Development Banks)
2. Primary Co-operative agriculture and rural development banks (Primary Land Development)

1. Short-and medium-term credit structure (Three-tier system)

Three-tier credit system is just like a pyramid. State Co-operative Bank or apex bank is at state level, Central Co-operative Banks are at districts level and primary credit societies are at village level. Numbers of central co-operative banks depend upon number of district in the state and numbers of primary credit societies depend upon number of villages in the district. There is only one apex bank in a state, few central co-operatives banks and many primary credit societies in a state.

Primary Agricultural Credit Societies

Primary credit societies form the base of co-operative movement. They are maximum in number as compared with other societies. Success of co-operative movements depends upon success of these societies. The organisation of these societies dates back to 1904, when (the first co-operative societies were started with the object of providing cheap credit to agriculturists in order to free them from the clutches of private money-lenders. In 1974-75, there were 1.53 lakh primary societies covering 95 per cent of villages under Indian Union. Total membership was 361.83 lakhs in the same year. Total working capital of these societies was ₹ 1,646.38 crores and they had advanced total loan amount of ₹ 843.54 crores in 1974-75. However, in 1994-95 there were 0.66 lakh societies covering 97 per cent of villages. They have advanced loan during the year was ₹ 8,300 crores. The per cent overdue to loans outstanding was 40.

Functions of Primary Agricultural Credit Societies

The main function of primary credit co-operative society is to provide short- and medium-term credit to members. The society should supervise use of credit. Society should supply certain consumer goods also. Society should associate itself with programmes of economic and social welfare, for village. Saving habit should be developed. However, certain other functions must be carried out by society, and this leads to origin of multipurpose societies.

Management

Management of society is democratic and honorary. It is based on the principle of one man, one vote. General body consisted of members is a supreme authority. Managing committee of five to nine members chosen from general body, this management committee looks after day to day function of society. Secretary carries executive work. Management committee admits new members, supervises credit, and raises funds for the society. Accounts are maintained by secretary. The management is honorary and only secretary is paid small remuneration for clerical work. Most of the members are not only illiterate but also are indifferent and this leads to mismanagement. When society functions unsatisfactorily, Registrars for co-operatives supersede management committee until society start normal functioning.

Audit

Auditing is very important for avoiding mismanagement and increasing efficiency of society. Audit work is carried out by a person of Registrar for Co-operatives.

Supervision

Supervision and inspection are vested in one body. Practice varies from state to state. In Tamil Nadu and in Maharashtra, it is carried out by supervision union under the control of district central bank in the area.

Membership

Personal relation is essential in society and hence, membership must not be too large, and area of operation should be compact. The N.D.C. Resolution of 9th Nov., 1958, laid down the pattern of organization at primary level, *viz.*, society for each village. If villages are small, two or more of them can join to form one society, provided the population covered, does not exceed about 1000. Membership is open for agriculturists, artisans and small traders in villages. The minimum initial membership is 10. The average membership per society was 236 in 1973-74 as against 80 in 1960-61; and 45 in 1950-51. The average membership per society in 1994-95 was 1458.

Liability

During early period of co-operative movement, liability of society was unlimited, but shift has taken place from unlimited to limited liability. In 1973-74, 75 per cent societies were with limited liability as against, 70 per cent in 1965-66 and 60 per cent in 1960-61.

Raising Fund

There are two sources of fund:

1. Internal sources:
   (*a*) Share capital,
   (*b*) Entrance fees,
   (*c*) Reserve funds,
   (*d*) Deposits from members.
2. External sources:
   (*a*) Deposits from non-members
   (*b*) Loans from central financing bodies
   (*c*) Government
   (*d*) Loans from commercial banks.

The working capital of all primary credit societies in India increased from ₹ 37.25 crores in 1950-51 to 1,646.38 crores in 1974-75 and to ₹ 15,809 crores in 1994-95.

Deposits

One of the objectives of society is to develop saving habit among members. Deposits of primary co-operative societies increased from ₹ 4.26 crores in 1950-51 to ₹ 99.30 crores in 1974-75 and to ₹ 2,868 crores in 1994-95.

Reserve Fund

The reserve fund, maintained by the society can be utilized for meeting unforeseen losses.

Borrowings

Major portion of the fund which society lend to member comes from district central co-operative bank. Criterion of giving loan to society by central bank varies from state to state. In Maharashtra; the borrowing limit is 8 times the paid up share capital and accumulated losses. In Tamil Nadu and Andhra Pradesh, it ranges from 8 to 10 times of the owned funds of society.

Loan Advanced

Primary agricultural credit society grants short and medium-term loan to members. Short-term loan is given for the purchase of seeds, fertilizers, pesticides, manures, payment of wages to workers and for paying land revenue. Crop loans are most popular.

Medium-term loans are given for purchase of cattle, implements, equipments, construction of small irrigation facilities, repair of wells, construction of bunds and improvement of land.

Total loan given by these societies increased from ₹ 22.90 crores in 1950-51 to 202.75 crores in 1960-61 and to ₹ 1,023.45* crores in 1975-76 and ₹ 8,300 crores in 1994-95. The loan per member also increased from ₹ 44 in 1950-51 to ₹ 119 in 1960-61, ₹ 222 in 1973-74 and ₹ 86 in 1994-95.

Security

In most of the states fixed property is insisted upon for security. However, loans are also given on the security of movable property and against personal security. Repaying capacity is also taken into consideration while granting loan to members.

Rate of Interest

As co-operative societies initiated in India to save cultivators from exorbitant interest rates of the money-lenders. Hence, as far as possible the credit should be cheap. The rates of interest charged by primary agricultural credit societies on advances to members varied from 6.75 per cent to 9.38 per cent per annum. State government may subsidies the rate of interest to any extent depending upon type of cultivator.

Period of Repayment

It is expected by the society that short-term loans will be repaid as soon as produce is sold. Normally 18 months is a maximum period for short-term loans and five to seven years medium-term loans.

Overdues

Amount of loan becomes overdue if the loan amount is not repaid within prescribed time limit. Overdue is a serious

* Statistical statements relating to Co-operative Movement in India.

problem for these societies. The amount of overdues rose from ₹ 6 crores in 1950-51 to ₹ 44 crores in 1960-61 and ₹ 379 crores in 1973-74. The percentage of overdues to outstanding (loans plus overdues) has gone up from 22 in 1950-51 to 36 in 1973-74 and 40 per cent in 1994-95. It was 81 per cent in Assam, 20 per cent in Gujarat, 25 per cent in Maharashtra and 20 per cent in Tamil Nadu.

There are two types of defaulters: 1. Willful defaulters. 2. Genuine defaulters. These willful defaulters do not follow principle of co-operation and do great harm to co-operative movement. Sometimes state government declares concessions to defaulters. As it is recently declared by Maharashtra Government.

The objective of government is genuine one, but borrower may take a view that we may get concessions in repayment in future and it will lead towards non-repayment of loans. Hence, it will be worthwhile to set easy terms and conditions before granting the loan and not after granting the loan. Societies should supervise use of credit and avoid misutilization of credit. Problem of overdues must be tackled tactfully so that it will not hamper growth of co-operative movement.

Multipurpose Co-operative Society

Along with credit facility cultivator need several other services for his farm development and hence, primary agricultural credit societies are converted into multipurpose co-operative societies. Number of multipurpose co-operatives increased from 18,162 in 1947-48 to 75,000 in 1957-58. The total membership of these societies increased from 5,77,386 in 1947-48 to 43,00,000 in 1954-55 and declined to 22,00,000 in 1955-56. Because of multipurpose society, farmer is in constant touch with the society and this creates a real spirit of co-operation amongst farmers.

Definition: The multipurpose co-operative society is an association for the purpose of joint trading and conducted always in unselfish manner on such terms that those who are prepared to assume the duties of membership may share its reward in proportion to the degree on which they make use of an association.

Objects

1. To create funds for lending to the member for useful and productive purposes.
2. To undertake the purchase and sale of agricultural requisites like seeds, fertilizers, insecticides, pesticides, etc.
3. To provide to the members the educational facilities.
4. To promote and encourage among members the practice of thrift, self-help and mutual-help.
5. To make arrangement for marketing and storage of agricultural produce of the members.
6. To undertake measures to spread knowledge of co-operative principles and practices.

Jurisdiction or Area of Operation

To know the members, each other for their financial position, assets and liabilities and the moral characters, the area of operation of society is kept restricted to one village.

Membership

The four conditions of membership are as follows:

(*i*) The prospective member should be a normal adult.

(*ii*) He should not have bad debts or declared to be a bankrupt.

(*iii*) He is of good moral character and has not been sentenced for any offence.

(*iv*) He resides and operates in the jurisdiction of the society.

For admission to membership entrance fee of ₹ 1 is collected and a new members required to purchase at least one capital share. The value of which ranges from ₹ 5 to ₹ 50 depending upon the particular society. If a person applies for membership and if it is denied by the society, an appeal can be made to the Registrar of the Co-operatives.

The member of the Executive Committee including Chairman and Vice-Chairman serves honorarily. While other staff such as Secretary, accountant, etc., are paid staff. All the business of the society and day to day conduct of the society is in the hands of executive committee.

Sources of Funds

To grant loans to the members and to make capital available for conducting the business of the society, the funds are collected by the society from the following sources:

1. Deposits from members and non-members,
2. Share capital,
3. Reserve funds,
4. Loan from central co-operative banks, commercial banks and Government,
5. Grants and subsidies from the Government.

Loan Operation of the Society

(*a*) **Types of Loans:** There are three types of loans namely short, medium and long-term loans, multipurpose co-operative societies grant short and medium-term loans. As societies raise their funds mainly through short-term deposits, they do not advance long-term loans.

(*i*) Short-term loans. Short-term loans are advanced for meeting the expenses of crop production such as purchase of seeds, manures and fertilizers, insecticides, pesticides, payment of irrigation charges and labour charges. The length of loan period is 12 to 15 months and even up to 18 months in certain cases, depending upon the type of crop. These loans are recovered after the harvest of the crops, from the sale of produce. To avoid the misuse of credit, some societies advance loans partly in cash and partly in-kind form, short-term loans are also given to cover the cost of harvesting and marketing, to avoid forcing the farmer to sell his period of immediately after the harvest other crop during the period of market glut and low prices.

(*ii*) Medium-term loans. The medium-term loans are advanced for a period of five to seven years for purchase of livestock and machinery, etc. These loans are recovered in instalments and then the interest is charged only on the paid capital.

(*b*) **Security:** The loans are generally advanced on co-lateral security on personal promise of the cultivator to repay the loan.

In certain cases, the pledge of another member to repay the loan is taken into consideration, when there is fear of default by the borrower. However several multipurpose co-operative societies use land and other property for security.

(*c*) **Limits of loans:** The MCL (Maximum Credit Limit) is fixed by the general body. The loans are advanced up to 20 times the land revenue paid by the member. Another method nowadays, used by some societies to set MCL is one-third of the expected gross income from the crops under consideration. Nowadays, repaying capacity of borrower member is also taken into consideration while granting loan.

(*d*) **Rate of interest:** The rate of interest charged by society depends upon the rate of interest paid by the society to the other higher financing institutions. Since society must cover the administrative cost, generally 3% more rate of interest cover the interest rate of other financing institution charged for the society.

In Case of Defaulters

Sometimes cultivators either purposively or due to circumstances beyond their control do not repay the loan. Most societies charge higher rate of interest for overdues (loans) as penalty for late repayment. On the other hand, provision is also made by some societies in their laws to grant concessions in repaying the loan in case crop fails or floods or any other unfavourable condition for the crop growth exists.

However, it is observed that these societies do not take up non-credit activities on large scale and concentrate more only on credit supply to cultivators. Progress of these societies is a good hope for development of agriculture.

Service Co-operatives

It was observed that Primary agricultural credit societies and even multipurpose societies also emphasize more only on supplying credit facility to members. For increasing agricultural production several services such as technical guidance, marketing facility are very important. Hence, Nagpur session of the National Congress in 1959 emphasized for starting service co-operatives. Several, primary credit societies and multipurpose societies were converted into service co-operatives by amending their bye-laws or by adopting model bye-laws of service co-operative societies drawn by each state. In 1974 there were 1,53,808 such service co-operatives in the country. It is clear from above discussion that service co-operatives are not altogether different from primary credit societies and from multipurpose societies but these societies emphasize more on providing various services to members other than credit facility. These societies help cultivators for increasing their agricultural production by adopting modern agricultural technology.

Central Banks

Central bank stands second 'in a pyramid like structure of short and medium-term credit'. They are above the primary credit societies and below the state co-operative or apex bank. There are now (2001-02) 369 district central co-operative banks in the country.

Objective of Central Bank

It is essential to supervise and inspect the primary credit societies. Similarly, development of primary credit societies should be even throughout the district. Sometimes some primary credit societies possess excess funds and these funds must be provided to deficit societies. These various functions are carried out by central bank. Mainly, financial support to primary credit societies is obtained from these banks. These banks also carry out regular banking business.

Overdues

The overdues in central banks increased from ₹ 27 crores in 1960-61 to 375.5 crores in 1974. Percentage of overdues to the total outstanding loans increased from 20 in 1966 to 32.3 in 1974.

These overdues are due to willful defaulters and due to lack of proper supervision of primary credit societies linking of credit and marketing is not successful to the desired extent.

Management

The central bank is administered by board of management and by executive committee. Societies, individual shareholders are represented on the board of management. Some persons, who have served co-operative movement are also co-opted by the central bank on its board of directors. The number of board of directors consists of 12 to 15 members.

Now, major commercial banks have been nationalised and particular bank is decided as lead bank and it should organise all credit supply of the district. Central bank should co-operate with lead bank and should work out healthy credit plan for the district.

State Co-operative Bank

State Co-operative Bank is at state level and only one for whole state. It is at apex level in three-tier short and medium-term credit structure. There were only 16 state co-operative banks, but number increased to 26 in 1973-74 and 30 in 2001-02.

Functions

1. The chief function is to co-ordinate and guides the working of central banks and to arrange financial accommodation to them.
2. They form connecting link between the money market, Reserve Bank and the co-operative movement.
3. They bring out uniformity of banking policy as between the different central banks in the areas of their jurisdiction.

Membership

Membership is open to central banks, and to other societies those having dealings with it. In some states only co-operative institutions become members of apex bank, *e.g.*, in Punjab, Andhra, Mysore, etc. In some other states membership is also given to individuals, *e.g.*, in Maharashtra, Tamil Nadu, Madhya Pradesh, etc. Their membership as on 30th June, 1975 consisted of 11,623 banks and other societies and 7,198 individuals and institutions other than co-operatives.

Management

Administration of these banks is carried out on the line of central bank, administrative structure. General body consists of members and is a highest administrative body. Day-to-day working is entrusted to the Board of Directors. General body meets once in a year to decide about how to utilise surplus, etc. A general body also elects the board of directors and receives and approves the report of the year's work. The constitution of apex bank varies from state to state. The state government being the shareholder also nominates some of the directors. In 2001-02, the 30 state co-operative banks had lent about ₹ 34,220 crores to central co-operative banks and primary co-operative banks.

Sources of Capital

Working capital of apex banks consists of share capital, reserve funds, deposits from members and borrowings and the direct state contribution.

Table 7.1: Working capital of all apex banks as on 30th June, 1975

(Amount is in ₹ crores)

Sr. No.	Item	Amount	Percentage of working capital
1.	Owned funds	142.5	12
2.	Deposits	546.4	46.1
3.	Borrowings from		
	Government	34.3	2.8
	RBI	376.9	31.8
	Other sources	34.6	2.9
	Others liabilities, etc.	51.8	4.4
	Total	1,186.5	100.0

Source: Statistical statements relating to Co-operative Movement in India 1974-75.

Total working capital was ₹ 1,186.5 crores in 1975.

Deposits

Deposits constitute major portion of working capital. In 1975, deposits constituted 46 per cent of total working capital. Apex banks get deposits from members as well as non-members. The central banks also deposit their surplus funds and a part of their working capital with the state co-operative bank. Deposits increased from ₹ 21.18 crores in 1951-52 to ₹ 546.4 crores in 1975.

Borrowings

Apex banks mainly borrow from state government, Reserve Bank and from State Bank of India. Borrowings constitute 37.5 per cent of working capital of apex banks. Borrowings increased from ₹ 11.23 crores in 1951-52 to ₹ 445.8 crores in 1975.

Loans and Advances

The apex banks advance short-term loans for seasonal agricultural operations and marketing of crops. Medium-term loans are advanced for purchase of cattle and machinery etc. Short-term loans increased from ₹ 280.87 crores in 1962-63 to ₹ 1,244.34 crores in 1974-75. Medium-term loans increased from ₹ 13.96 crores in 1962-63 to ₹ 137.82 crores in 1974-75.

There is a steady increase in total co-operative credit, *i.e.*, ₹ 3,440 crores in 1984-85 to ₹ 3,970 crores in 1990-91 and nearly ₹ 20,660 crores in 1999-2000.

It is observed from table 7.3 that primary co-operative societies have covered most of the villages, but number of co-operative societies is decreasing. This might be due to recently commercial banks having increased their advances to agricultural sector. It is also observed that 37 per cent of loans outstanding are overdues and therefore this overdue problem is a serious matter in co-operative credit. It is estimated that there are nearly one lakh primary agricultural co-operatives at the end of March 2001, with membership of 10 crore farmers.

Central Co-operative Banks

In 2001-02, there were 369 district central co-operative banks. The loan outstanding of ₹ 56,650 crores, NABARD is contributing to the share capital of the weak central co-operative banks.

State Co-operative Banks

There are now 30 state co-operative banks (SCBs) in the country. It is a link between NABARD and district central co-operative banks. In 2001-02, all SCBs lent about ₹ 34,220 crores to central co-operative banks.

Table 7.2: Co-operative credit (short and medium-term) in India (1974-75)

(Figures at a glance)

Sr. No.	Item	Primary agril. credit societies	Central banks	Apex banks
1.	Total number	1,52,572	341	26
2.	Total membership (in thousands)	36,442	717	34
3.	Total working capital (in ₹ crores)	1,801.47	1,842.83	1,186.53
4.	Deposits (in ₹ crores)	99.30	805.3	546.4
5.	Advances			
	(*a*) Short-term (in ₹ crores)	782.60	1,348.04	1,244.34
	(*b*) Medium-term (in ₹ crores)	118.23	176.46	137.82
6.	Overdues (in ₹ crores)			
	(*a*) Short-term	407.64	358.78	36.45
	(*b*) Medium-term	95.75	75.66	7.92
7.	Outstandings (in ₹ crores)			
	(*a*) Short-term	903.78	1,015.78	707.31
	(*b*) Medium-term	272.85	331.82	212.65
8.	Percentage of overdues to outstandings	43	32	5

Source: Statistical statements relating to the Co-operative Movement in India 1974-75.

Table 7.3: Primary agricultural credit co-operatives (short-and-medium-term loans) salient features

Sr. No.	Item	1980-81	1990-91	1993-94
1.	No. of societies (lakhs)	0.94	0.70	0.66
2.	Percentage villages covered	97	97	97
3.	Membership (lakhs)	576.53	593	920
4.	Paid up share capital (₹ crores)	571.09	1,110	1,451
5.	Deposits (₹ crores)	290.58	1,466.67	2,722
6.	Working capital (₹ crores)	4,035.98	9,984.84	14,089
7.	Loan advanced during the year (₹ crores)	1,763.59	4,797.92	9,301
8.	Percentage loans overdue to loans outstanding	42	39	37

Source: *Agriculture Research Data Book*—2004.

Problem of Overdues

The unhappy fact about co-operative credit is the heavy overdues of co-operative credit institutions, now estimated to be ₹ 9,000 to 10,000 crores. The overdues are mainly due to lack of will to repay. Borrowers expect Govt. will waive the debt or will give concessions in repayment. Because of heavy overdues co-operative structure is becoming weak.

Commercial Banks and Rural Credit

All commercial banks had 1,860 branches in rural and semi-rural areas in July 1969 which increased to 47,190 branches in March 2002. Commercial banks advances term loans to farmer which account for 35.37 per cent of total disbursement. Southern region had disbursed 52 per cent of total disbursement to farmers. Now share of commercial banks in total borrowing by an average farmer is more than co-operative or any other agency. Commercial banks are also facing problems of overdues.

Overdues

Overdues are increasing year after year. Overdues increased from ₹ 9.3 crores in 1966 to ₹ 44.37 crores in 1975. The percentage of overdues to outstanding loans which was only three as on 30th June 1966 increased to nine in 1974. At present overdues of co-operative institutions in India estimated to ₹ 9,000 to 10,000 crores.

Stabilization Fund

As per recommendations of Rural Credit Survey Committee, RBI created such fund. Some apex banks also created such fund it was ₹ 29 lakhs as on June 1962, it increased to ₹ 38.73 crores in 1973-74. This fund was created to enable apex banks for converting short-term loans into medium-term loans if short-term loans are not repaid on account of natural calamities.

National Federation

All apex banks formed national federation in 1964. The main objective of this federation is to discuss commonly technical, financial problems and find out solution for them.

Federation also tries to establish contact with central and state governments, the RBI, the State Bank of India, industrial and agricultural finance corporations for taking advantage of them.

Apex banks shown remarkable progress in various fields. However, they face a problem of overdues. In light of bank nationalization and their performance in agricultural finance, it is necessary to give thorough consideration to functioning of apex banks.

8

Co-operative Agricultural and Rural Development Banks (Land Development Banks)

Long-term credit needs of cultivators are satisfied by land development banks. Recently, land development banks have been renamed as co-operative agricultural and rural development banks. Primary Land Development Banks are renamed as Primary Co-operative Agricultural and Rural Development Banks (PCARDBs) and Central Land Development Banks are renamed as State Co-operative Agricultural and Rural Development Banks (SCARDBs). The number of PCARDBs increased from 286 in 1950-51 to 739 in 2001-02, while that of SCARDBs increased from 5 to 20 during the same period. The loan advanced by PCARDBs during 2001 02 wcrc ₹ 1,930 crores and the loan outstanding stood at ₹ 8,960 crores, whereas SCARDBs had sanctioned loan worth ₹ 2,690 crores in 2001-02 and amount of loan outstanding was ₹ 12,380 crores.

Long-term investment is very important for development of agriculture. As savings of Indian cultivators are meagre and hence, they are not able to invest from their own income.

A long-term investment in agriculture requires larger amounts. Hence, terms, conditions and criteria's of advancing loans differ from short-term loans. Therefore, long-term credit is dealt by a two-tier credit system, central land development bank is at state level and primary land development banks are at taluka level. The loans are given for a period of five to 25 years. These loans are needed for purchasing costly implements, making permanent land improvements, sinking of wells, purchasing land etc. Previously land development banks were known as land mortgage banks because land was mortgaged while granting loan to individual. Existing land development banks in India belongs to co-operative movement. Principles and practices of co-operation are followed in them. First land development bank was registered on 30th June, 1920 at Jhang in Punjab. There were 19 central land development banks and 872 primary land development banks in the country in the year 1975.

Primary Co-operative Agricultural and Rural Development Banks (PCARDBs) (Primary Land Development Banks)

Primary land development bank is a lower link of a two-tier system and in most of the states they are established at taluka level. Main function of this bank is to provide, long-term loans to agriculturists and to supervise their use as well as to recover the amount of credit given to them.

Area of Operation

In those states where primary land development bank is at each taluka, area of operation is the whole taluka. It varies from state to state.

Sources of Capital

Following are main sources of capital:

1. Share capital
2. Deposits
3. Loans from central land development bank
4. Grants and subsidies from government
5. Borrowing from other agencies.

Loaning Policy

Previously loans were given for redemption of old debt but now loans are mainly given for productive purposes. The rate of interest should be low so that cultivators can take advantage of these banks. Gadgil Committee and Saraiya Committee had recommended to government for giving subsidies so that interest rate can be kept low.

Loan Procedure

Primary land development bank gets applications, scrutinises them and sends them to central land development bank. Person of the central land development bank visits the land of applicant, determines its value and examines all other aspects and finally sanction the loan. Finally, amount of loan is obtained by the applicant from primary land development banks. Primary land development bank charges slightly higher interest rate than what they will require to pay to central land development bank. Similarly, loan amount is recovered by the primary land development bank from borrower. If the amount of loan mentioned in the application is less than ₹ 4,000, final decision is taken by primary land development bank; otherwise applications of bigger amounts are sent to central land development bank. Following documents are necessary to attach with the application:

1. Copy of the survey number of the record of rights.
2. Encumbrance certificate.

State Co-operative Agricultural and Rural Development Banks (SCARDBs) (Central Land Development Banks)

Primary co-operative agriculture and rural development banks are federated into the SCARDBs at the state level. Thus, it is a two-tier system. In most of the states this two-tier system is followed but in some states and union territories instead of PCARDBs, SCARDBs have opened their branches.

Functions

Main function of SCARDBs (central land development bank) is to supervise and guide PCARDBS (primary land development banks) in the state. As well as they provide credit facility to primary land development banks.

Raising Fund

SCARDBs raise their working capital from the following sources:

1. Share capital,
2. Issue of debentures,
3. Loans from the state bank,
4. Admission and other fees,
5. Deposits,
6. Grants and subsidies,
7. Other funds.

Debentures

A debenture is a bond conveying and acknowledgement of a debt also containing provisions as to payment of interest and repayment of principal.

As land development bank requires fund for a longer duration debentures are very convenient. Debentures constitute major portion of working capital.

Land development banks first grant loans to cultivators by mortgaging their land. This mortgaged land constitutes security for issue of debentures. Permission for issue of debentures is obtained from Reserve Bank. Reserve Bank of India decides extent of the issue and determines interest rate. State Government is requested to provide guarantee of repayment to the respective debenture holders. State Government appoints trustee to look after the interest of the debenture holders. Generally, the Registrars of Co-operatives are appointed as trustees. After completion of above formalities, debentures are floated by the bank. The period of debentures ranges from 7 to 15 years. Debenture holders can transfer their debentures to any person they like. Such transfers are duly recorded in the registers of the bank.

These debentures mostly purchased by big financial institutions such as Life Insurance Corporations, Commercial banks, Co-operative banks and state governments. Central land development banks floated debentures worth ₹ 58.3 crores in 1973-74.

Rural Debentures

Rural population is mainly benefited by these banks and hence, special rural debentures are issued. These are issued in two sets one for short-term duration of seven years for individuals residing in rural areas and other for the longer duration of 15 years to be purchased by RBI. However, response to these debentures is not encouraging. Various central land development banks issued rural debenture worth ₹ 2.40 crores in 1965-66 and ₹ 1.60 crores in 1973-74.

Special Development Debentures

Special development debentures are also issued to obtain fund for financing special land development projects. Recently, Agricultural Refinance and Development Corporation purchased about 90 per cent of such debentures and remaining 10 per cent is purchased by public or by the state government. Like any other co-operative organization land development banks also get certain concessions from state government. These concessions vary from state to state.

Table 8.1: Progress of Land Development Banks in India

Sr. No.	Item	(Figures at a glance)			Amounts in crores of rupees		
		Primary land development banks			Central land development banks		
		1951-52	1974-75	2001-02	1951-52	1974-75	2001-02
1.	Number	289	872	739	6	19	20
2.	Membership (in lakhs)	2.1400	44.19	—	0.349	30.17	—
3.	Working capital	7.60	616.16	—	10.17	1,502.19	—
4.	Advances	1.30	111.18	1,930	2.51	183.84	2,690
5.	Loans outstanding	6.96	518.10	8,960	8.5	992.54	12,380
6.	Overdues	NA	518.10	—	8.5	992.54	—
7.	Percentage of overdues to loan outstanding	NA	5	—	NA	6	—

Sources: 1. Statistical statements relating to the Co-operative Movement in India.
2. *Indian Economy*, Ruddar Datt & Sundharam, p. 589.

It is observed from table 8.1 that land development bank shown good progress during last fifty years. Working capital, total membership, number of banks, advances shown manifold increase.

However, land development bank provided meager amount for investment in agriculture as agriculture plays important role in Indian economy. If we compare these banks with short and medium-term credit structure, we find land development banks handle small business. Total advances made by primary agricultural credit societies in 1974-75 were ₹ 901 crores. While primary land development banks advanced only ₹ 111 crores in the same year. This indicated land development banks must increase their business and satisfy growing demand of long-term credit. Increased long-term investment in Indian agriculture will accelerate growth of agriculture. Still co-operatives are not able to satisfy growing need of agricultural credit and hence, they have to improve and expand their activities.

9
Agricultural Non-credit Co-operatives

Co-operation was introduced in India to solve problem of agricultural credit in a better manner but because of its suitability in various fields, co-operation spread in various other areas of human activity. If, it is examined with reference to agriculture, following co-operatives progressed in India:

1. Irrigation societies,
2. Land reclamation societies,
3. Co-operative milk supply societies,
4. Fisheries co-operatives,
5. Co-operative marketing,
6. Co-operative processing,
7. Co-operative farming,
8. Labour co-operative societies,
9. Housing co-operative societies,
10. Co-operative education & training,
11. Fertilizers co-operative,
12. Sugar co-operatives,
13. Consumers' co-operatives,
14. Co-operative spinning mills,
15. Dairy co-operatives,
16. Poultry co-operatives.

In 1998-99, there were total 3,61,485 primary non-credit co-operatives in India.

1. Irrigation societies: Irrigation plays very crucial role in modern agriculture. This fact is recognized by Indian cultivators and therefore, they started several irrigation projects on co-operative line. In 1968, such irrigation societies with total membership of 87,380 and there is significant increase during recent years. Such societies are more popular in Maharashtra, Gujarat, U.P., Punjab, West Bengal. However, only 28 per cent gross sown area is irrigated in 1978 and hence, there is wide scope for co-operative irrigation societies.

2. Land reclamation societies: India is having very vast coast-line and cultivators from sea-shore area face problem of land reclamation. There are several such societies in West Bengal. However, vast area remained to be covered by such societies. Land reclamation societies will be very suitable in Konkan area of Maharashtra state.

3. Co-operative milk supply societies: Co-operatives had achieved a grand success in European countries. In India also co-operative dairies are gaining importance year after year. Number of primary milk societies increased from 3,200 in 1960-61 to 19,365 in 1975. Value of sales increased from ₹ 5.44 crores in 1960-61 to ₹ 87.0 crores in 1975. Nutrition Advisory Committee of Indian Council of Medical Research recommended that balanced diet for adult Indian should include about 10 ounces of milk per day but availability of milk in the country per day per adult is only 4.93 ounces in 1960-61. This makes the point clear that to obtain recommended level of milk, India has to double its milk production. Along with government efforts people should help themselves by organizing more co-operative dairy societies.

4. Fisheries co-operatives: For utilising modern techniques in fishing business, it also requires big investment in trollies and other accessories. In 1980, there were 5,400 fisheries co-operatives with a membership of about six lakhs fishermen. It is necessary to organise more fisheries co-operatives in the country.

5. Co-operative marketing: Marketing of agricultural produce involve several marketing functions. Capital is very essential for efficient marketing. Co-operative marketing though handles marketing activities, progress is not satisfactory. There were

809 marketing co-operatives dealing with sales of agricultural produce in 1973-74 and co-operative marketing dealing with sales of agricultural requisites was 614 in the same year. Still, progress is needed in these types of co-operatives in India.

6. Co-operative processing: Most of the agricultural commodities require processing before its final consumption. Most of the commodities are processed by processing co-operatives.

Table 9.1: Processing co-operatives in India (1974-75)

1. Sugar factories	—	—	126
2. Cotton ginning and processing factories	—	—	214
3. Groundnut decorticators	—	—	57
4. Copra oil mills	—	—	27
5. Oil mills	—	—	146
6. Cold storages	—	—	89
7. Rice mills	—	—	717
8. Spinning mills	—	—	23
9. Jute bailing units	—	—	61
10. Tea	—	—	13
11. Others	—	—	79
Total	—	—	1,552

Sugarcane Factories: India is an important sugar producing country. Maharashtra is having 142 co-operative sugar factories and 156 total sugar factories. These co-operative sugarcane factories have increased income of cultivators as well as provided jobs to many. Because of this, standard of living of cultivators has been increased to considerable extent. However, significant portion of sugarcane production is used for jaggery production. This is an important agro-based industry and provides jobs to many. Similarly, other processing co-operatives are also playing important role in India's development.

7. Co-operative farming: Application of the principles of co-operation in the cultivation of land is called as co-operative farming. Co-operative farming society is a voluntary association of cultivators for better utilisation of resources including man-power and lands. The majority of members participate in farm operations with a view to increasing agricultural production, employment and income.

Recent information about non-credit co-operatives

Table 9.2: Processing and other non-credit co-operatives in Maharashtra, 2002-2003

1. Co-operative sugar factories in Maharashtra	142
2. Co-operative sugar factories in India	269
3. Total sugar factories in Maharashtra	156
4. Total sugar factories in India	453
5. Cotton ginning and processing factories in Maharashtra	260
6. Rice mills in Maharashtra	88
7. Oil mills in Maharashtra	12
8. Other processing co-operatives in Maharashtra	240
9. Consumers primary co-operative stores in Maharashtra	3,449
10. Co-operative marketing societies in Maharashtra	1,252
11. Primary consumer co-operative stores in India	25,759
12. Consumers retail outlets in India	37,226
13. Primary housing co-operatives in India	92,000
14. State level apex co-operative housing federations	25
15. National co-operative housing federation	1

Types of Co-operative Farming Society

Co-operative farming societies have been classified into four categories by the co-operative planning committee:

1. Co-operative joint farming society;
2. Co-operative collective farming society;
3. Co-operative better farming society; and
4. Co-operative tenant farming society.

1. Co-operative joint farming society: In this type of co-operative farming, land is pooled together but ownership is maintained with the original land holder. The elected committee takes various decisions. Remuneration is given for work carried out by member. A member is also entitled to receive a return for ownership of land pooled by him according to its fertility, location and production capacity.

2. Co-operative collective farming society: This type of society has all the features of a joint co-operative farming society except that in the co-operation collective society, the lands belong to the society as freehold or leasehold, while in the latter, the land is held by the members as owners or tenants. Such societies are generally formed on government land and land newly-brought under cultivation.

3. Co-operative better farming society: This society acts as a service co-operative. In this form the agricultural land is not pooled but each member owns his land and cultivates it independently. He agrees to follow a plan of cultivation laid down by society and obtains from it all facilities. Improved seeds are used, and better techniques are followed. Marketing, land development, irrigation; all such important activities are carried out jointly.

4. Co-operative tenant farming society: In this type, society holds the land and entire land is divided into smaller plots and each plot is leased to tenant cultivator. There is no joint cultivation but common services like the distribution of improved seeds, implements, fertilizers and insecticides are provided by the society.

In India, cultivators are closely attached with piece of land and hence progress in co-operative farming is not satisfactory.

10
Development of Co-operative Movement in India

Before beginning of modern co-operative movement, chit funds and nidhis in South India, bunda system in Vidarbha, the phad system in Kolhapur and gonchi in Andhra were prevailing in India.

Cultivators were exploited by money-lenders. They used to charge exorbitant interest rates as well as cheating was also a common phenomenon. Disturbance of 1875 in Poona and Ahmednagar district of Maharashtra against money-lenders made then Government to think agril. credit problem seriously. In 1892, Government deputed Fredric Nicholson to Europe for studying land banks and suggesting suitable system of agril. credit in India. Nicholson submitted his report as well as in 1901 famine commission also submitted its report. After studying these reports Government passed first co-operative societies Act in 1904.

The history of co-operative movement may be studied under the following heads:

1. Period from 1904 to 1918.
2. Period from 1918 to 1939.
3. Period from 1939 to 1948.
4. Period of planned development (1951 to date).

1. First stage (1904 to 1918)

The Co-operative Societies Act was passed on 25th March 1904. Features of the Act were as follows:

1. A society can be formed by any ten persons for self-help and for co-operation among agriculturists, artisans and persons of limited means.
2. The control of co-operative credit society in each province were put under the charge of Registrar of Co-operative Credit Society.
3. Accounts of every society were to be audited by the Registrar or by his staff free of charge.
4. Co-operative societies were classified as rural and urban.
5. The liability of the members of a rural society was to be unlimited. Liability of the urban society members might be either limited or unlimited.
6. Loans could be given only to members on personal or real security although ornaments might be legally accepted as security. By the end of 1911-12, there were 8,177 societies in the country and working capital was ₹ 3.4 crores.

However, the 1904 Act found inadequate and hence, Co-operative Societies Act of 1912 was passed. The distinctive features of the Act were as follows:

1. It was decided, liabilities of central societies shall limited and the liability of the rural societies was unlimited.
2. The societies were granted exemption from compulsory registration and the state government may grant exemption from the payment of income tax, stamp duties and registration fees.

The defects of the Act of 1904 were remedied by this new Act which gave a great stimulus to the co-operative movement. It legalised many co-operative societies which had hitherto no legal recognition. Societies were now classified as limited and unlimited.

In 1914, Government of India appointed Maclagan Committee to examine whether the movement was progressing on sound lines or not. Committee submitted its report in 1915.

Recommendation of Maclagan Committee

1. Knowledge of co-operative principle and proper selection of members.
2. Honesty is the chief basis of credit.

3. Loans not to be granted for speculative purposes.
4. Proper scrutiny before advancing loan and supervision of credit after advancing loans.
5. Encouragement of thrift and the constitution of an adequate reserve fund.
6. Only one vote for one member and maximum publicity within the society.
7. Punctual repayment of loans.
8. The area of operation of primary society should be restricted to a village and it should build its own capital by compelling members to purchase shares by persuading them to offer deposits.
9. The size of the society should not be large.
10. Repayment of loan should be strictly enforced according to the instalments fixed.
11. Non-credit societies should be encouraged.
12. Societies should be properly audited, regularly supervised.
13. All co-operative societies should build up a reserve fund.

2. Period from 1918 to 1939

On the passing of the Government of India Act of 1919, co-operation become state subject and was administered by provincial governments. Several state governments passed their own Acts. During this period co-operation received sufficient encouragement under popular ministries. However, great depression of 1930 gave a tremendous set back to co-operative activity. Fall in prices of agricultural goods and of land threatened the very existence of some societies and violently disturbed the economic stability of others. Recovery of loans becomes extremely difficult. There was a serious contraction of co-operative credit. The Royal Commission on Agriculture (1928) stated, "If co-operation fails there will fail the best hopes of rural India" and suggested certain measures for its development.

3. Period from 1939 to 1948

The abnormal conditions created by World War II lead to some far-reaching development in the co-operative movement. However, due to improvement in prices, movement expanded to some extent. The war stimulated the growth of consumer's stores and marketing societies. Various kinds of co-operative societies progressed.

An important development during this period was the appointment of the co-operative planning committee in 1945, under the chairmanship of Shri R.G. Saraiya. This committee recommended that primary societies should be converted into multipurpose societies. Committee also urged that the Reserve Bank should provide greater assistance to co-operatives. Agricultural Finance sub-committee under the chairmanship of Dr. D.R. Gadgil also stated that "the spread of co-operation would provide the best and the more lasting solution for most problems of rural economy in general and for the problems of agricultural credit in particular."

4. Period of planned development

The important development in the co-operative field since independence was the appointment of the Rural Credit Survey Committee in 1951 by Reserve Bank of India. This committee submitted its report in 1954. Committee has mentioned in its report that "Co-operation has failed but co-operation must succeed". Committee agreed that co-operatives can solve most of the rural problems and hence, co-operatives must be encouraged. Committee recommended an Integrated Scheme of Rural Credit involving three important points: (1) State participation at different levels, (2) Co-ordination of credit with other economic activities specially processing and marketing, and (3) Administration through trained and efficient personnel responsible to the needs of the rural population. Other recommendations are as follows:

1. Existing village societies should be revitalised and reorganised and made really effective.
2. Loans should be given on the basis of anticipated crops and not on the security of land and tangible assets. A crop loan system should be started.
3. Producers should market their produce through marketing co-operatives so that recovery of crop loan will be easy.
4. Storage and warehousing facilities should be provided through the state partnership organization.

5. A co-operative development and warehousing board should be constituted at an all India level.
6. A national stabilization fund should be constituted in the Reserve Bank, apex and central banks throughout the country.
7. A long-term operations fund should be constituted in the Reserve Bank of India. This fund may be used for providing long-term loans as well as for providing financial assistance to co-operative organizations.
8. Relief and guarantee fund should be created at the national and state level to assist in writing off irrecoverable debts arising out of natural calamities over a number of years consecutively.

Co-operation during First Plan

Co-operation was recognised as an "instrument of planned economic action in democracy". During the Plan period, the number of primary agril. credit societies increased from 1.15 lakhs to 1.59 Lakhs. Membership increased from 51.54 lakhs to 77.91 lakhs; loans issued from 22.90 crores of rupees to ₹ 50.16 crores but the percentage of overdue to loan outstanding increased from 21.9 to 25.0.

Co-operation under Second Plan

Second Plan was drawn up on the basis of accepted recommendations of the All India Rural Credit Survey Committee Co-operative societies of all types increased from 2.4 lakhs to 3.32 lakhs. Membership increased from 176 lakhs to 342 lakhs. Working capital increased from ₹ 469 crores to ₹ 1,312 crores.

Co-operation during Third Plan

In this Plan, co-operation should become progressively the principal basis of organization in many branches of economic life, notably in agriculture and minor irrigation, small industry, processing and marketing etc.

By the end of Third Plan primary agricultural credit societies covered about 89 per cent of the villages. More emphasis was laid on making the societies viable than on their expansion.

Co-operatives handled food grain worth ₹ 136.75 crores. In the field of co-operative processing, 582 units were established.

Co-operation during Fourth Five-year Plan

Important development during this Plan was, setting up of All India Rural Credit Review Committee (1969) under the chairmanship of Shri B. Venkatappiah. Main objective of this committee was to suggest measures for the reorganisation of rural credit.

Committee suggested following points:

1. The establishment of Agricultural Credit Board.
2. Setting up of a Small Farmers Development Agency.
3. Creation of Electrification Corporation for the benefit of underdeveloped areas.
4. Formulation of a more active and much bigger role for ARDC.
5. Adoption of various measures for ensuring the timely and adequate flow of credit for agriculture through co-operatives and through commercial banks.

As per recommendations, small farmers development agencies were set up in selected districts. Rural Electrification Corporation was also set up in 1969. Sugar factories showed good progress during this plan period. Between 1950-51 and 1972-73 the membership of primary societies increased by more than four times, the share capital of all types of co-operatives increased by more than 23 times and the working capital by more than 31 times.

Co-operation in Fifth Plan

The major objective of the Fifth Plan should be to build up a strong and viable co-operative sector with special emphasis on the needs of cultivators, workers, consumers. Under the Twenty Point Economic Programme, launched in July 1975, co-operative institutions are being encouraged to provide alternative sources of credit to weaker sections of societies. Regional rural banks, nationalised banks are also playing important role for development of Indian agriculture.

11
Co-operative Movement in Foreign Countries

Germany

Germany is the birthplace of co-operative movement in the world. Mr. Fredrick Nicholson, who was sent to Europe to study the working of agricultural banks and to suggest measures for the introduction of co-operative movement in India, suggested Raiffeisen system of credit which was prevailing in Germany.

In the middle of nineteenth century, people of Germany were exploited by money-lenders and most of the people were leading miserable life. When such was the condition around, two pioneers, Herr F.W. Raiffeisen and Herr. Franz Schulze (1808-1883) started trying various methods of relief.

***Raiffeisen Societies and Schulze Banks*:** Raiffeisen was a Mayor of Weyerbusch and formed a society which is called as Raiffeisen society. Similarly, Schulze was a judge and mayor of Delitzsch started a bank which is known as Schulze Bank. Mainly cultivators were members of Raiffeisen Society (RS). Whereas artisans and industrial workers were members of Schulze Bank (SB). Area of operation in RS was smaller than SB recoveries in case of RS were spread over a long period as compared to SB's recoveries. Profiteering was never the motive in case of RS, while SBs were run for profit. Most of the RS fund was carried to reserve, funds but in case of SB's, banks did not keep any reserve fund. In RS management was honorary while in SB's management was well-paid. Thus, there were fundamental differences in the ideology behind these two systems of co-operative credit.

During Hitler regime the movement got a good fillip. In 1940, there were 38,843 societies. Further, Rural Societies, Urban Societies, Housing Societies, Consumers' Societies were progressed in this country. All above-mentioned four groups of co-operatives have their own federal organisation. At present, these societies undertake multiple activities.

England

Robert Owen was one of the important people, who devoted for welfare of mankind. He tried various ways for improving employer-employee relationship. Owen's life created a fund of experience, made people wiser and set them thinking about new ideas.

On August 15, 1844, 28 weavers started "The Rochdale Equitable Pioneers Society," registered under the Friendly Societies Act. This society made a good progress in the field of co-operation. For advising their members they developed certain principles, those are as below:

1. Open membership,
2. Democratic government,
3. Dividend in proportion to purchases,
4. Limited interest on share capital,
5. Market prices to be charged,
6. Pure and unadulterated goods to be supplied,
7. Portion of profits to be set-aside for education.

From these various points, some points are most useful at present also. International Co-operative Alliance has accepted certain points which are called as principles of co-operation. This is an important contribution by Rochdale Pioneers.

In 1850, the Christian socialists organised the "Society for promoting workman's association" by spreading the ideas of co-operation. The main and practical contribution of Christian societies to the co-operative movement was their efforts for getting passed a separate act for co-operatives. Consumers retail societies are the most important in the British co-operative movement. At the beginning of 1966 there were 680 co-operative retail consumers' societies with a 10 million members. Retail societies employed 2,30,672 workers in 1966 and had a wage bill of 140 million pounds.

Co-operative wholesale societies, co-operative retail services, Scotish co-operative wholesale society, production societies. These societies were functioning in England.

It is interesting to know, British farmers have never been in debt, nor did they have any difficulty in the marketing of their produce. They, however, felt some difficulty in procuring farming requirements such as fertilizers, seeds, and feed stuff. Co-operation among farmers thus started with what is called as "Requirement Societies". Requirement societies and marketing societies constitute the agricultural societies.

There is no co-operative department in Britain, societies are registered with the Chief Registrar of friendly societies, who also registers trade Unions and other associations. The movement neither receives any government loans nor any government grants except for a limited subsidy for educational purposes. Absence of state assistance which explains independence of the movement from Government interference.

Denmark

Denmark is a small country with 46 lakhs population. The country is rather poor in natural resources but possesses fertile land. Rainfall ranges between 25 to 30 inches and is evenly spread throughout the year. Co-operative movement plays important role in the economy and often country is called as "Co-operative Denmark". Co-operative movement in Denmark was introduced by H.C. Sonne, a social worker. Mr. Sonne was impressed by performance of consumers co-operatives started in England by Rochdale Pioneers. He founded Thirsted Workers Society which achieved a grand success within a short span of time.

The problem of credit was solved by the credit associations which began to be organised in the year 1850.

Dairy co-operatives played important role in the economy of Denmark. The first co-operative dairy was set up in Hjedding with the effort of a young dairy man named, Stilling Andersen in 1852. There were 828 dairy co-operatives in 1964. A co-operative dairy consists of number of milk producers associated to process and dispose of their milk and milk products as a joint enterprise. Co-operative dairies at the primary level are federated into the Federation of Danish Dairy Associations; private dairies are also affiliated to the co-operative federations.

In 1895, the Egg Export Association was organised. It introduced the system of grading and stamping of eggs to ensure that only eggs of good quality reached British market. In 1960, there were seven egg export societies which were affiliated of the Danish Co-operative Egg Export Association. There are some other co-operatives are also functioning in Denmark, such as butter export societies, co-operative bacon factories, cattle export societies, fruit marketing societies, fish marketing societies.

Danish Government neither supported nor hampered co-operative movement. Denmark has no law concerning co-operative societies not even a public registration of them. However, maximum benefit of co-operative movement is achieved by Denmark.

Canada

Canada has a total area of about 4 million sq. miles, which makes it the world's second largest country in size and three times as big as India. The co-operative movement in Canada plays an important part in the agricultural economy.

The first co-operative institution developed among the farmers and organised in 1877. Afterwards co-operative organizations were established in Ontario and Manitoba.

The first growers association was registered in 1906, under the name of Grain Growers Association. Marketing co-operatives achieved success. Farmers in Canada have built up strong co-operatives in all provinces for obtaining supplies for production, such as feed, fertilizers, seeds, farm machinery and various consumer goods. These societies are making steady progress. There were 795 societies in 1932, whereas there were 1,357 societies in 1967. Membership of the marketing and purchasing societies is 1.4 millions. The percentage of the farm produce marketed by these co-operatives in 1968, was about 66 of the total value of farm products marketed in the country. Fishermen's co-operatives are also prevailing in this country. Number of such societies was 86, with membership of 10,000. The credit unions were introduced in Canada by Alphonse Desjardins of Quebec. He studied the credit movement in

Europe, and suggested it, as remedy against the usury practiced in Montreal. The province of Quebec was the first in Canada to pass a credit union law in 1907. Similar laws were passed in other states and by about 1936 all the provinces had such special laws. The credit unions in each state has set up federal credit societies at provincial level. Recently, the Canadian credit co-operative society has been organised at national level to act as a balancing centre for the whole of Canada.

Israel

In 1923, a society was registered under the Co-operative Societies Act. This society is called as Hevrat Ovdim. Hevrat Ovdim is said to be the roof organization under which about 80% of the societies in the country work. Hevrat Ovdim helped the members in settling on land, develops fishing, industries and transport system, founds banks and credit associations.

In the beginning of 1970, there were 1,963 co-operative societies in Israel, out of which 1,051 were agricultural co-operatives. Agricultural co-operatives are mainly of three types:

(*i*) Kibbutz (collective villages)

(*ii*) Moshav Ovdim (worker's settlement)

(*iii*) Moshav Shitufi (co-operative settlement).

(*i*) Kibbutz (collective villages): Kibbutz is a voluntary commune established on national land, each member works for Kibbutz. All means of production, consumption, education, health are owned and maintained collectively on the basis of equality.

(*ii*) Moshav Ovdim (workers settlement): Some people do not like complete socialization in the Kibbutz and hence, they form Moshav Ovdim. The First Moshav Ovdim was founded in 1921 at Nahal. At present there are 300 such societies. Each society get land from government on lease divides it into small holdings and allots the holdings to members for cultivation. Moshav Ovdim supplies production requirement to each member, arranges marketing of produce. Health and sanitation, education is commonly managed. If there is any profit it is distributed to members. Banking duties are also carried out by Moshav Ovdim.

(*iii*) Moshav Shitufi (collective small holders settlement): Moshav Shitufi has been defined as "an agricultural settlement in which members conduct farm and allied operations jointly with pooling of land, equipment, etc. While the individual members have separate homes and live separately their own private lives." In this type also land is obtained from government or from Jewish National Fund. There were 22 such settlements in 1970.

During the last 10 years, agricultural production has increased three-fold, and the annual rate of growth is about 8 to 10 per cent.

Japan

Co-operative movement in Japan was introduced in the form of consumer's co-operatives, the first of which was organised in 1879 with the object of checking the soaring prices.

At present, the more developed types of co-operatives societies are the following:

1. Agricultural Co-operative association;
2. Fisheries Co-operative association;
3. Forestry Co-operative association;
4. Consumers Co-operatives; and
5. Industrial Co-operatives.

In 1971, there were 6,049 agricultural co-operatives covering 100 per cent villages, these societies have 5.9 million regular members (farmers) and 1.1 million associates (non-farmer). On an average each society employs about 40 employees.

Other types of co-operatives also play important role in Japan's economy.

12
General Aspects of Co-operation

Role of Reserve Bank of India in Co-operative Movement

In the interest of country's development, following functions were important and Reserve Bank is a most suitable agency to carry out them. Those functions are as follows:

1. To study the problems relating to agricultural credit.
2. To give expert advice to the Central and State Governments and to banking organisations in this respect.
3. To co-ordinate and guide the rural credit agencies such as the co-operative organisations, bankers and to provide them seasonal and emergency finance.

For carrying out above functions special department was created in RBI. This department is known as Agricultural Credit Department. For the purpose of internal administration, the Department is divided into three sections: (*i*) the agricultural credit; (*ii*) the banking and statistical; (*iii*) research section. Department carried out certain duties those are grouped under two heads: (*i*) Pre-independence period, (*ii*) After independence period.

(*i*) **Pre-independence period:** During this period, the department collected a great deal of material pertaining to agricultural finance in India as well as abroad. It issued number of bulletins and two reports in which the special features of agricultural finance were described. It gave number of suggestions in its reports for the regulation of money-lending and for reorganization of the co-operative movement so as to make it suitable for providing agricultural credit to the agriculturists.

(*ii*) **After independence period:** After independence, most important development took place, *i.e.*, Expert committee was set up under the chairmanship of Shri Gorwala to plan, organise and supervise a survey regarding facilities available in rural areas for providing agricultural credit to the agriculturists and to make necessary recommendations. The committee submitted its report in 1954. It recommended an integrated scheme of rural credit. This scheme was accepted as the basis for national policy in the sphere of rural credit. The RBI took many steps to implement the recommendations of the rural credit survey committee. Other contribution of RBI:

1. **Provision of cheap remittance facilities for the benefit of co-operative banks:** The remittance facility is available to the co-operative banks three times per week.
2. **Advisory and co-ordination function:** The RBI not only provides financial facilities to co-operative organization but also advises registrars of co-operatives on various matters.
3. **Training of co-operative personnel:** The RBI has been rendering useful services in the training of co-operative personnel since 1953.
4. **Inspection of co-operative societies:** The RBI also carries out periodical inspection of various co-operative organisations at secondary and state levels for ensuring that funds provided by it being properly utilised.

RBI also carries out certain rehabilitation of weak banks, regulatory functions. Thus, RBI provided a strong support to co-operative movement in past and will continue for many more years in future.

Government Aid to Co-operatives

Co-operative movement started in India by passing the Act of 1904 and government helped co-operatives throughout its development. Indian farmers are found in a vicious circle of low income, low saving and under such circumstances Government help is necessary for proper growth of co-operatives. However, because of government aid co-operatives become dependent on others and remain weak.

Form of State Aid

I. Legislative
   1. Law
   2. Rules and regulations of co-operatives.

II. Fiscal
   Exemption from payment of taxes, stamp duty, registration fees.

III. Financial
   1. Contribution to share capital
   2. Grant-in-aid for contribution of warehouse/appointment of staff
   3. Loans
   4. Guarantees.

IV. State partnership
   In credit and non-credit societies

V. Other aids
   1. Supply of developmental personnel
   2. Technical assistance
   3. Measures to rehabilitate and recognise societies
   4. Co-operative training facilities.

These are the various ways of government aid to co-operatives.

Co-operative Education and Training

Two essential features of successful co-operatives are:

(*i*) Informed and royal membership

(*ii*) Growing and efficient business.

In absence of informed and royal membership, a co-operative enterprise will soon lose its co-operative character and become an instrument in the hands of vested interests. Therefore, education of members for ensuring efficiency is an important pre-requisite for co-operative development. As well as officials must be trained and qualified people.

In consequence of the recommendations of the various committees, training facilities were provided in some states. In 1947, a co-operative training college was established at Poona.

In November 1953, the Government of India and the Reserve Bank of India jointly constituted the Central Committee for Co-operative Training as a high-level agency for promoting co-operative education and training in the country. The central committee classified trainees into higher, intermediate and subordinate categories. For giving training to the higher officers, in charge of direction and control at district level or above and also the executives in co-operative institutions at district level or above, the Poona College is expanded. For training of intermediate staff-five regional training centres were established at Madras, Pune, Ranchi, Meerut and Indore. Apart from this, the central committee established eight block level co-operative officers training centres at Gopalpur, Bhavnagar, Kalyani, Kota, Faizabad, Hyderabad, Tirupati and Patiala. The capacity of each training centre was to train about 100 candidates in one course of 11 months. For the training of subordinate co-operative personnel, such as junior auditors, supervisors, salesmen, various state governments in consultation with the central committee, started junior training centres at suitable places.

Recently, responsibility of co-operative training was transferred to the National Co-operative Union of India. In June 1973, the Government of India constituted an informal Expert Group on Co-operative Education, Training and Research under the chairmanship of Dr. M.S. Swaminathan to examine the adequacy of the existing structure in the sphere of co-operative education and training and to suggest measures for improving it. As a result, following important reforms have been brought about:

(*i*) The committee for co-operative training has been renamed as national council for co-operative training.

(*ii*) The chief executive of NCCT will be the Director General of NCCT. He will also be in charge of the Vaikunth Mehta Institute.

(*iii*) The NCCT will expand its training programmes by seeking financial assistance not only from the Govt.

of India, but also from bodies like NCDC, RBI, LIC, ARDC, SBI, etc.

Committee also stated standard of Teaching should also improve in various training centres.

Member's Education

Member education programme was taken up in January 1956. There were six pilot projects in three states to educate the members of the co-operative societies. The object of the programme was to train office-bearers, managing committee members and potential members in their function, duties, and responsibilities. Up to the end of June 1963, 63,750 secretaries and office-bearers, 2.6 lakhs managing committee members and 19.4 lakhs members and potential members had been trained.

Co-operation and Community Development

Community development is defined as "Community development is designed to promote better living for the whole community with an active participation, and if possible, on the initiative of community. United Nations has defined community development as "the process by which the effort of the people themselves is united with those of government authorities to improve that: economic, social and cultural conditions of the communities, to integrate these communities into the life of the nation and to enable them to contribute fully to national progress. "From these definitions, it is understood, to what extent community development is similar to co-operation. Co-operation is considered such an important part of community development. Co-operation is the soul of community development. Co-operation aims at arranging better farming, better living and better business for the people and as such its objectives are identical with those of community development. Some of the principles of co-operation namely voluntary association, self-help and mutual-help, equality etc., can also be identified with the aims of extension of education in community development. Co-operation is thus a means to the same end which community development aims at and is rather an instrument for the effective execution of many of its major programmes.

C.D. programme can also help co-operative societies in better performance of their functions. For example, co-operatives have since long been making unsuccessful efforts to ensure proper utilization of the loan they provide. Community development programme can very well assist the farmers in using credit for productive purpose and enable even the so-called non-credit worthy members to secure loans from the co-operatives for their credit worthy needs. Thus, both co-operation and community development are related.

Administration, Supervision, Inspection and Audit

Administration

Under the present administrative set-up of co-operative departments in various states, the Registrar occupies the key position. He is the chief executive head of the department and is the statutory authority for registering co-operative societies and administering the law governing them. He is the Brahma, Vishnu and Mahesh of the co-operative movement, *i.e.*, he is sole agency and ultimate authority for the guidance, supervision and control of the co-operative societies. Co-operative department has to carry out supervision, inspection and audit of societies and general administration.

Supervision

Supervision is necessary under Indian conditions for proper development of co-operative movement. Supervision involves constant administrative assistance in work, advice in financial matters and general guidance both from the business and co-operative aspects. We find the different systems of supervision in different states.

In certain states like Maharashtra and Punjab, the machinery for supervision is partly official and partly non-official. There is a State Board of supervision at the apex level, District supervising committees at the intermediate level, and Taluka supervising unions at the primary level. The supervising union has one or two supervisors attached to it and it's area of operation extends over a Taluka. Each society is inspected under this arrangement at least once in a quarter. Workload for each supervisor is heavy.

Inspection

The inspection of a co-operative society is as important as an audit or supervision. This is a function of the co-operative department. Particularly in all the states it is taken up by the Registrar with the help of a separate staff especially employed for this purpose. Inspection should be regular as well as constructive. Inspection is a systematic scrutiny of all aspects of the working of the institutions, it would be equally important to strengthen the departmental staff at all levels.

Audit

Auditing may be defined as "an examination of accounts of an organization finally prepared by the organization concerned, with reference to its receipts, vouchers and documents supporting the transactions and entries in the books of account in a just appropriate and realistic manner."

The primary aim of the co-operative audit was to improve the performance of the co-operatives themselves and to safeguard the interest of their members, public and outside persons who had business dealings with the co-operatives. The auditor has to be a friend, a guide and an educator of the co-operative society and not a hostile critic.

To audit all societies once a year is a statutory duty of Registrar. In Maharashtra the co-operative department employs a staff of special auditors, auditors and sub-auditors. The special auditors take up audit work of higher organizations, *i.e.*, of apex bank, central bank, etc., while auditors and sub-auditors take up the audit work of the smaller societies.

Societies are classified into four categories, *a*, *b*, *c* and *d*, it is called as audit classification.

(*a*) Such societies have paid the loans of the financing agencies in time and fully; they have made efforts to improve resources through deposits and by increasing share capital.

(*b*) societies are those which fulfil the above-mentioned requirements partially. The overdues percentage of such a society is within 25.

(*c*) societies are relatively ineffective. They are financially weak and do not act according to the provision of law. Their accounts are not up to date and the percentage of overdues is as high as 40.

(*d*) societies are badly managed. They are burdened with overdue payment, continuously increasing losses and inefficient management. Overdue percentage is above 40. If the auditor feels that such a society cannot be revived, he can recommend for its dissolution.

Selected References

Anonymous, "Land Development Banks and Agricultural Development," *Sahkari Viswa,* January-February, 1980.

Bedi, R.D., *Theory, History and Practice of Co-operation,* International Publishing House, Meerut, 1977.

Dadhich, C.L., *Overdues in Farm Co-operative Credit*, Popular Prakashan, Bombay, 1977.

Dubhashi, P.R., "Agricultural Marketing through Co-operatives," *Sahkari Viswa*, March, 1979.

Haquel, T. and Maji, C.C., "Structure and Flows of Agricultural Co-operative Credit in India," *Indian J. of Agril. Econ.,* Vol. XXXIII, No. 4, p. 72, October-December, 1978.

Joshi, V.R., and Vasava, K.D., *Superiority of Co-operatives in Farm Financing,* Vol. XVI, No. 2, p. 178, January, 1979.

Jayaraman, T.K., "An Analysis of Overdues of Primary Agricultural Co-operative Societies: A Case Study of Mahikadana Project in Gujarat State," *Indian J. of Agril. Econ.,* Vol. XXXIII, No. 3, p. 21, July-September, 1978.

Kulkarni, K.R., *Theory and Practice of Co-operation in India and Abroad*, Vol. 1, Co-operator's Book Depot, Bombay, 1968.

Mamoria, C.B., and Saksena, R.D., *Co-operation in India*, Fifth Edition, Kitab Mahal, Allahabad, 1977.

Muralidhar Rao, N.K., "Personnel Management in the District Co-operative Central Banks," *Indian Co-operative Review*, Vol. XVI, No. 2, p. 123, January, 1979.

Padki, M.B., and Gajarajan, C.S., "Some Basic Conflicts in Rural Credit (with reference to Farmer's Service Co-operative Societies)," *Indian Journal of Agril. Econ.*, Vol. XXXIII, No. 4, p. 84, October-December, 1978.

Pandya, V.N., "Education of Co-operative Leaders Need, Scope and Approach," *The Maharashtra Co-operative Quarterly*, Vol. LXIII, No. 3, p. 166, January, 1980.

Pandey, U.K., and Murlidharan, M.A., "Extent of Willful Default in the Repayment of Co-operative Credit," *Indian Co-operative Review,* Vol. XVI, No. 3, p. 286, April, 1979.

Shirodkar, S.L., "Seventy-Five Years of our Co-operative Movement," *Sahkari Viswa,* April-May, 1979.

Shukla, B.D., and Mishra, S.D., "Impact of Co-operative Finance," *Financing Agriculture,* Vol. VI, No. 2, p. 26, July, 1974.

Siddique, M.I., "Co-operative Sugar Mills in India," *The Maharashtra Co-operative Quarterly*, Vol. LXII, No. 2, p. 77, October, 1979.

Singh, G.N., and Pandey, K.N., "Changing Structure and Flow of Rural Credit with Special Reference to Co-ops. in District Kanpur," *Indian Co-operative Review,* Vol. XVI, No. 4, p. 326, July, 1979.

Tewari, S.C., Bhatt, J.P., and Sharma, J.S., "Socio-Economic Factors and Co-operatives Credit Borrowing Behaviour," *Financing Agriculture,* Vol. VI, No. 1, p. 1, April, 1974.

Vishwanathan B.S., "Development of Fisheries Through Co-operatives", *The Maharashtra Co-operative Quarterly,* Vol. LXII, No. 2, p. 73, October, 1979.

Xavior, G.F., "Development of Positive Attitude Towards Co-operatives", *The Maharashtra Co-operative Quarterly*, Vol. LIX, No. 2, p. 93, October, 1975.

PART III
Agricultural Marketing

13
Market and Marketing

Agricultural Marketing is one of the important branches of Agricultural Economics. During ancient period, wants of the people were limited and they use to satisfy them in their own locality. Cultivators use to produce; what they were requiring and use to exchange produce for other commodities which are produced by village artisans. Thus, they were satisfying most of their needs in the village itself.

However, in the modern era wants of the cultivators increased many times and are not able to satisfy their needs within the village only. They wanted to educate their children in cities, wanted medical treatment. They wanted to enjoy modern amenities such as motor car, refrigerator, television set, etc. For all these things they want money and hence they changed their attitude towards production. They started producing those commodities which will give them maximum money. These phenomena, increased importance of marketing in modern world.

Another simple example will illustrate importance of marketing. Assuming that you are a student, you will get up early in the morning, you will need a toothpaste, if you don't have, you have to purchase it from shop. Again at the time of lunch you have to go to lunch home. If you don't have stationery, you have to purchase it from shop. Finally before going to bed, you will require blanket and that too, you have to purchase from cloth merchant. On the other hand, if you observed shopkeeper, when he wants to drink a cup of tea, he has to purchase milk from milkman, he has to purchase vegetables from vegetable merchant. Thus, in the modern era everybody has to deal with purchase and sell transactions several times in a day or a week. Thus, marketing is important to everybody all the time.

Particularly, because of modernization of agriculture and increase in the wants, agricultural marketing has acquired great importance.

Market

Meaning of market is explained in various ways:

1. Market means an open place or large building where actual buying and selling takes place.
2. The market may extend to a locality, village, town, region or a country according to the demand of a commodity.
3. Economists understand by the term market, not any particular place in which things are bought and sold but the whole of any region in which buyers and sellers are in such a free intercourse with one another that the price of the same goods tends to equality, easily and quickly.
4. Market includes both place and region in which buyers and sellers are in free intercourse with one another (Pyle J.P., *Marketing Principles,* 1936).

Thus, in one sense market is a place where buyers and sellers come together carry out buying and selling activity. In other sense, market is a area where buyers and sellers are in such a free intercourse with one another that the price of the same goods at different places (in the same area) tends to equality easily and quickly.

Marketing

There are following definitions of marketing:

1. *Legal definition:* Marketing includes all activities which are concerned with effecting changes in the ownership and possession of goods and services.
2. *Economics:* Marketing is that part of economics which deals with the creation of time, place and possession utilities.
3. Marketing includes those business activities that direct the flow of goods and services from producer to consumer. Thus, important aspects of definition of marketing are as follows:

(*i*) Ownership of goods is changed.

(*ii*) Includes all activities which take the goods from producer to consumer.

Agricultural Marketing

Agricultural marketing in its widest sense comprises all the operations involved in the movement of goods and raw materials from the farm to the final consumer. It includes the handling of the product at the farm, initial processing, grading and packing in order to maintain and enhance quality and avoid wastage. Storage is another feature of agricultural marketing together with methods of packing and presenting the product to suit the requirements of final consumers.

Marketing System

The marketing system of a small Indian village consists of a small market area, traders, bullock carts for transportation and some storage facilities. This type of market system remained in operation for several years. There may be some minor changes according to region, *i.e.*, if it is a Rajasthan village, means of transportation may be different. But this is a marketing system prevailing in Indian villages.

In case of highly developed country-marketing system may consists, of huge, complex network of marketing organisation and facilities engaged in developing, promoting and distributing of goods and services worth crores of rupees. Thus, term marketing systems includes all the middlemen marketing environment, customers and marketing tasks performed by the marketing system.

Marketing Organization Structure

A large company must have some formal organizational structure. The organizational structure should be such that it should satisfy objectives of the company. That is, maximisation of profit and serving the customers. The company's organisation may be on the basis of functions, products, territory, types of customers or combination of these. Thus, there may be:

1. Functional organisation,
2. Products organisation,

3. Territory or area organisation,
4. Customers type organization,
5. Combined type organization.

1. Functional organization: Different duties are divided in such a way that those can be carried out in best manner.

The most common type is as below:

Managing Director or Market Executive

Financial manager	Production manager	Marketing research manager	Sales promotion manager	Marketing services manager	Personnel manager

Types of Markets

Markets are classified on the basis of various criteria such as on area basis, goods basis, etc. The detail classification is as below:

1. On the basis of competition
   (*i*) Perfect market (pure competition)
   (*ii*) Imperfect market
      (*a*) Monopoly market
      (*b*) Duopoly market
      (*c*) Oligopoly market
2. On the basis of operation
   (*i*) Primary market
   (*ii*) Secondary market
   (*iii*) Terminal market
3. On the basis of area
   (*i*) Local market
   (*ii*) National market
   (*iii*) International market
4. On the basis of time
   (*i*) Very short period market
   (*ii*) Short period market
   (*iii*) Long period market
5. On the basis of business
   (*i*) Wholesale market
   (*ii*) Retail market

6. On the basis of goods dealt in
   (*i*) Commodity market
      (*a*) Produce exchange
      (*b*) Manufactured and semi-manufactured goods market
      (*c*) Bullion market
   (*ii*) Capital market
      (*a*) Money market
      (*b*) Stock exchange market
      (*c*) Foreign exchange market.

1. On the basis of competition

(*i*) *Perfect market*: When buyers and sellers are aware of prevailing market prices and market fulfil the condition of pure competition, *i.e.*, (*i*) large number of buyers and sellers in the market, (*ii*) product is homogeneous, (*iii*) no restriction on the movement of goods.

(*ii*) *Imperfect market*: In absence of free competition, buyers do not know the price demanded by the different sellers and as a result of that the sellers may charge any price for a commodity to different buyers. When there is only one seller in the market then market is called as monopoly market. When there are two sellers, market is called as duopoly and when there are few sellers exist in the market, market is called as oligopolistic market.

Types of Agricultural Market in India

Market for agricultural produce may broadly be divided into three categories:

1. Wholesale markets,
2. Retail markets,
3. Fairs.

1. Wholesale Markets: These markets are sub-divided into:

(*i*) *Primary wholesale markets:* These markets are periodically held, either once or twice a week. Agricultural produce comes from neighbouring villages. Cultivators bring their produce with the help of bullock carts. These markets deal in sale of fruits, vegetables, food grains, glass bangles, all household requisites, cloth, etc. Generally, 2000 to 3000 people gather.

(*ii*) *Secondary wholesale markets:* These are also known as mandis. These are situated generally at district or taluka headquarters. Small merchants purchase from primary wholesale market and sell in these markets. Some cultivators directly sell their produce in these markets. Produce is also sent from these markets to terminal markets. Each market comprises area with a 10 to 20 miles radius.

(*iii*) *Terminal markets:* Terminal markets are those in which the produce is either finally disposed of, direct to consumers or processors or assembled for shipment to foreign countries or for redistribution in surrounding areas. These markets are located where warehouses and storages are available, cover a wide area, may be state, *e.g.*, Bombay terminal market.

2. Retail Markets: These markets are spread all over the city or town subject to municipal control. They generally deal in all types of produce and serve the needs of the city people as well as of the surrounding villages. Particular type of market is located in particular locality. Cloth market is in one locality and grain, vegetable, etc., are in different localities. Selling, directly to the consumer or to shopkeepers.

3. Fairs: These are held on religious occasions, at pilgrim centres. These markets deal in livestock, agricultural produce etc. There are certain fairs where only livestock markets exist, *e.g.*, Magh Mela at Allahabad, Magh Pournima at Jejuri in Pune district.

Characteristics of Farm Produce

Agricultural produce has certain peculiar characteristics:

1. Perishability: Fruits and vegetables must be consumed quickly, otherwise they would lose their quality. Grains can be stored for considerable time but must be consumed before arrival of new production. If agricultural produce stores for longer time, quality of produce deteriorates, such things do not happen in case of industrial production.

2. Raw material: Most of the agricultural produce is to be processed before final consumption, *e.g.*, Sugar is to be extracted from sugarcane; cloth is to be prepared from cotton etc. Industrial production is directly utilised.

3. Bulkiness: Agricultural produce is bulky *e.g.*, cotton, grains, sugarcane. The bulkiness increases transport cost, handling charges and storage charges.

4. Size of the product: Most of the agricultural produce vary in size, *e.g.*, big size mango, small size mango. Long staple cotton fetches higher prices, large sized egg fetches higher price. The product is not uniform.

5. Colour, palatability and nutritive value: Several agricultural products vary in colour, palatability and nutritive value and accordingly price changes.

6. Substitutability: Wheat is substituted by Jowar or Bajra grains, similarly mutton is substituted by fishes. Sugar is substituted by jaggery. The substitution plays important role in pricing.

14
Marketing Functions

Marketing is as important as production. If wheat is produced by Punjabi cultivator but is not brought to a place in Madhya Pradesh, where, people wanted to purchase it, then that wheat is of no use to these people. Hence, marketing functions and services are important. Marketing functions and services create time utility, place utility and possession utility.

A marketing function is an act, operation or service by which the original producer and the final consumer are linked together. Mainly there are two types of function, *i.e.*, concentrating functions and dispersing functions.

Classification of Marketing Functions

All marketing functions are classified by various persons, Pyle's Classification:*

The Marketing Process

Concentrating Functions	Dispersing Functions
1. Buying or Assembling	1. Selling
2. Transporting	2. Transporting
3. Storing	3. Storing
4. Grading	4. Grading
5. Financing	5. Financing
6. Risk-bearing	6. Risk-bearing
	7. Dividing

* Littlefield, J.E., and Kirkpatrick, C.A., *Advertising Mass Communication in Marketing,* 1971, p. 160

These marketing functions may be classified for our purpose as below:

Marketing Functions

Concentrating	**Dispersing**
1. Assembling	1. Grading
2. Transportation	2. Storing
3. Buying	3. Packing
4. Processing	4. Advertising
5. Storing	5. Selling
6. Standardization and Grading	6. Transporting
7. Financing	7. Financing
8. Risk-bearing	8. Risk-bearing

Concentrating Functions

Since, produce is produced at field, several marketing functions must be carried out till it reaches to the consumer. Initially, it is concentrated at wholesaler's place and then slowly and slowly it is dispersed. Thus, marketing functions are divided into two categories, *i.e.*, concentrating functions and dispersing functions.

1. Assembling

Agricultural commodities are produced by many cultivators in their small fields that must be assembled. Assembly means the seeking out of sources of supply, buying wisely as to quality, quantity, variety and making commodities available when and where they are wanted. Village merchants collect the produce and take it to arhtia. Itinerant dealers also purchase the produce and finally take it to the Arhtia. Cultivators need money as soon as their produce is ready, as well as their contribution or production is in a small quantity, so it is not economical to spend more on its transport, etc. That is why, they sell their produce to village merchants. Sometimes cultivators themselves collect the produce at one place, hire a truck and take it to arhtia.

Advantages of Assembling

(*i*) *Economy in transportation*: Because of large quantity, motor truck or railways can also be used for transportation. Thus, per unit cost of transportation is less.

(*ii*) *Availability of goods in large quantity*. Manufacturers need large quantity and place their order to arhtia and arhtia can manage to supply large quantities to manufacturer.

(*iii*) *Wide markets*: From assembling centre it can be possible to take the produce to a place where it can fetch better price. Thus, markets are wide.

(*iv*) *Grading*: Because of large quantity grading is also possible.

(*v*) *Processing*: Processing can also be possible because of larger quantity assembled at one place.

There are some difficulties also such as, transportation means are not well-developed. No regulated markets are available at short distance, etc.

2. *Transportation*

Village merchant has to hire a motor truck or cultivators have to hire a motor truck to carry their produce to Arhtia. In India, transportation means are not well-developed but due to nationalization of banks it is easy to obtain credit for motor truck. Many people are starting motor truck business. However, total road length must be increased. Similarly, number of railway routes must be increased.

3. *Buying*

Buying and selling, these are the two important activities in marketing. There are two types of buying, *viz.*, buying for consumption, and buying for resale, village merchants buy the commodities and sell them to the arhtia. Various merchants buy at regulated market and sell at distant places. Buyers who purchase for resale should first estimate quantity demanded as well as he should note seasonal variation in demand. He should purchase in a market where he will get at lowest prices.

4. *Processing*

Most of the agricultural produce requires processing before its final consumption. Sugarcane juice must be extracted from sugarcane and must be converted into sugar or jaggery. Cotton, jute, paddy requires processing before its final consumption. Arhtia manages to process, *e.g.*, cotton is ginned before using it for manufacturing cloth. Paddy is de-husked by millers. Most of the processing units are looked after by co-operatives. Processing adds value in agril. produce. Processing is one of the important marketing functions.

5. *Storing*

Agricultural produce is seasonal. It is produced at a particular point of time. However, demand for agricultural produce is constant throughout the years, *e.g.*, food grains are needed throughout the year. This particular characteristics increased importance of storing.

Storage is an exercise of human foresight by means of which commodities are protected from deterioration and surplus supplies are carried over for future consumption in seasons of scarcity. Sometimes, producer himself stores the produce in anticipation of better price. Sometimes, village merchants, some other merchants store to obtain better price in future. Now government has its own warehouses and government store some of the commodities like food grains in large quantity for maintaining particular price level as well as to use in the period of scarcity.

Storing furnishes protection of physical characteristics. Some produce is stored to enable the product to ripen, necessary loans can be raised on the collateral security of stored goods, adjustments of demand and supply can be possible with the help of storages. Warehouse also plays important role in storing the agril. produce.

6. *Standardization and Grading*

Standardisation is the determining of classes or grades of a product or service that have fixed limits.

Agricultural produce differs in the size, colour, quality and nutritive value. To take into consideration these aspects, agril. produce is standardised. Food grains are graded as coarse and fine. Mangoes are graded according to their size and quality.

Grading is the process of sorting individual specimens of a given product to the standard grades or classes to which they belong.

Before taking to market, cultivator himself grades his produce so that he gets better price, similarly, grading is done by some of the other marketing agencies whenever it is necessary.

7. Financing

Money or credit is important means to carry out various marketing functions. All market agents carry out various marketing functions for sake of earning money. This increases the importance of financing. When cultivator sells his produce to village merchant, he obtains money from him. Village merchant will get fund from big merchant or from bank. When produce is stored in a store or in a warehouse on the strength of that produce, concerned merchant obtains bank finance and will pay to the cultivator who has sold his produce to him.

8. Risk-bearing

Risk in marketing may be defined as uncertainty in regard to cost, loss or damage. In other words, risk-bearing ability means ability to withstand losses or adverse conditions faced. While carrying out various marketing functions. Cultivator worries about losses from fire, flood, storm, famine. Merchant worries about deterioration of quality of a produce as well as whether he will be able to sell all the produce which he has bought from cultivators.

Dispersing Functions

Some of the concentrating and dispersing functions are same but are carried out by different marketing agencies. Produce is concentrated with wholesale merchant, who will grade the product. He will grade in such a way that total returns from sale of produce will be more. He will require storing the product for sometimes and when there will be demand from retailers at that time, he will sell that produce. He will pack the produce. Packing help in retaining the same form of produce and material remain intact after transportation. Advertising is another marketing function which motivates people to purchase the product. Advertising means to turn people's attention to a specific thing. In other words, "Advertising is mass communication of information intended to persuade buyers so as to maximise profits." Advertising leads to cheaper prices because other people, those are doing the same business compete with each other. Advertisement acquaints public with features of the goods.

Similarly, advertisements increase the demand. Thus, advertising function is useful in creating demand.

Selling

This is one of the dispersing functions. Selling in business would mean the transfer of ownership of goods or services to a buyer in exchange for money. Selling occurs at various stages, initially farmer sells to village merchant or to a merchant in a regulated market again. Wholesale merchant sells produce to retailer and retailer sells to consumer.

Method of Selling

1. *By open auction*: This is a popular method of selling and also used in regulated markets. In this method, Arhtia or broker invites bids for produce and the highest bidder is sold the produce. Here superior quality produce fetches better price.

2. *Close tender system*: Here in this method each produce is given a lot number. Then bidders are asked to record a price against each lot number and each lot is sold to a highest bidder with the consent of the seller.

3. *Under cover*: In this method, buyer indicates the price, he is prepared to pay by clasping the hand of the arhtia or seller's agent under cover of cloth and pressing or manipulating the fingers. The name and offer of the highest bidder are then publicly announced. Here, cultivators may be cheated. Because he does not understand the language of finger manipulation.

4. *By private agreement*: Here buyer comes to seller and indicates the quantity he wants and by the end of the day decision is finalised.

5. *By quoting on samples*: Here in this method, arhtia collects the sample from produce which is in cart and on the basis of sample, price is decided, and produce is sold but here in this case there are disputes over the quality of the sample and that of produce and deductions are made by buyer if there is difference in quality.

6. *Dara sale*: In this method of selling, same price is given to many heaps of grains but in this method large number of sales can be effected. If produce does not vary in quality this method

is alright. However, there is a variation in quality, but all are paid the same price.

7. *Moghum sale*: When cultivators borrow from the merchant on the condition that he will sell his produce to merchant. Under such situation, cultivator assumes that merchant will give him prevailing market price and there are no much verbal discussions.

In dispersing functions also produce is transported from regulated market to wholesale merchant's place and again from wholesaler's place to retailer's place. Retailer has to pay when he will buy from wholesaler and thus financing also conies into picture. Wholesaler and retailer also bear a great risk of price and deterioration of quality as well as whether they will be able to dispose all the produce in time or not.

Thus, various concentrating and dispersing marketing functions are carried out.

15
Channels of Distribution

Agricultural commodities are produced by various cultivators in their farms. But the produce is consumed by people throughout the country at various places. What is the path followed by these commodities till they reach to final consumer is examined in this chapter. Distribution is concerned with various activities such as the movements of goods from producer to consumer, changing the ownership from producer to consumer. A channel of distribution for a product is the route taken by the ownership of goods as they move from the producer to the ultimate consumer or industrial user.

A marketing channel, or channel of distribution, may be defined as "a path traced in the direct or indirect transfer of title to a product, as it moves from a producer to ultimate consumers or industrial users".

Factors Affecting the Choice of Distribution Channel

There are several channels of distribution; the choice of particular channel depends upon following things:

1. **Perishable nature**: Particular channel of distribution of a particular commodity depends upon its durability. Some commodities like vegetables and fruits are perishable and must be distributed through shorter channels otherwise quality of the produce will be deteriorated before it reaches to consumers.

2. **Bulk and weight:** If product is bulky and if weight is very heavy then transportation cost becomes significant; one has to reduce this cost, for that reason distribution channels should be such that transportation cost should be minimum.

3. Financial position: Financially, sound organizations grant credit for a long period while financially weak organizations have to take help of other middlemen and thus distribution channel is affected.

4. Desire for control of channel: If the producer or Co-operative society of consumers has strong desire to control the existing channel, they can do so by avoiding some of the middlemen.

5. Storage facilities: If producers don't have good storing facilities then they take help of some middlemen because they possess storage facilities and additional middlemen are involved in the channel of distribution.

6. Marketing cost: The particular channel is better if per unit marketing cost is lower than other channel.

7. If a particular channel offered easy terms of payment of price of a commodity, consumers prefer that channel than other which do not give any concession in paying the price of that commodity.

8. If number of consumers are many then producers have to employ some middlemen. If consumers are not many then normal sale force of company will do the job.

Channels of Distribution

Generally, following channels of distribution are followed:

(*i*) Producer-consumer,
(*ii*) Producer-retailer-consumer,
(*iii*) Producer-wholesaler-retailer-consumer,
(*iv*) Producer-agent-retailer-consumer,
(*v*) Producer-agent-wholesaler-retailer-consumer.

Distribution Channels of Paddy

1. Producer-commission Agent-miller-wholesaler-retailer-consumer.
2. Producer-itinerant merchant-miller-wholesaler-retailer.
3. Producer-miller-wholesaler- retailer-consumer.
4. Producer-miller-consumer.
5. Producer-primary wholesaler-miller-wholesaler-retailer-consumer.
6. Producer-government-miller-government-fair price shop-consumer.

Distribution Channels of Wheat

1. Producer-consumer.
2. Producer-village shopkeeper-wholesaler-retailer-consumer.
3. Producer-itinerant merchant-wholesaler-consumer.
4. Producer-primary wholesaler-secondary wholesaler-retailer-consumer.
5. Producer-primary wholesaler-miller-retailer-consumer.
6. Producer-primary wholesaler-government procurement agency-roller flour mill-fair price shop-consumer.

Distribution Channels of Cotton

1. Grower-village dealer-wholesaler or ginning factory-Bombay markets or other terminal markets-textile mills.
2. Grower-itinerant trader-wholesaler-commission agent of exporting firm-exporting firm.
3. Grower-co-operative sale society-exporter or mill buyer or merchant.
4. Grower-government-exporter or mill buyer.

Distribution Channels of Mango

1. Growers-pre-harvest contractors-consumers.
2. Growers-contractors-commission agents-consumers.
3. Growers-contractors-commission agents-hawkers-consumers.
4. Growers-wholesaler-commission agents-cum retailers-consumers.
5. Growers-contractors-commission agents-stall holders and shopkeepers-consumers.
6. Grower (member of co-operative society)-co-operative sale society-consumer.

Distribution Channels of Vegetables

1. Grower-commission agent or brokers-consumers.
2. Grower-itinerant merchant-wholesaler-retailer-consumer.
3. Grower-itinerant merchant or commission agent-wholesaler-retailer-consumer.

16
Defects of Agricultural Marketing

Agricultural market deals with commodities which are very important. Food grains and other daily requirements are obtained from agricultural markets. These markets have many defects, those are as below:

1. Superfluous Middlemen: Most of the cultivators are illiterate and sell their produce at village level. There are many middlemen involved in between producer and final consumer. If we examined producer's share in consumer's rupee, we would find that it is very low. In case of mango crop in Konkan region, producer's share in consumer's rupee was estimated 31% and remaining 69% were shared by middlemen. The number of middlemen must be reduced, so that producer's share in consumer's rupee will be increased.

2. Malpractices in Markets: Most of the agril. markets are unregulated. Several malpractices are followed in such markets. There are no standard weights and measures. Similarly, arbitrary deductions are made for religious and charitable purposes. When there is any dispute, cultivator has no means of safeguarding his interest.

3. Standardisation and Grading: Many times, agricultural produce is not graded and brought to market as it is. This creates problems while pricing.

4. Multiplicity of Weights and Measures: If we observe value of seer, it varies from place to place. A seer may range from 31 tolas to 102 tolas. Such things provide good opportunity for cheating the ignorant cultivators. Similarly, multiplicity of weight and measure makes supervision difficult.

5. Lower Price to Cultivators: Many times arhtia or commission agent collude with merchant and cultivators do not get proper price. He has to accept low price.

6. Market Information: Cultivators do not have any information about market price. There is no suitable agency for this purpose. Due to lack of market price information, cultivators sell to village merchant at very low price.

7. Producer's Organization: There is no proper organization of producer and this creates many problems. They cannot reduce transportation cost as well as their bargaining power is also poor.

8. Forced Sale: Most of the cultivators are poor cultivators and they have urgent need of money. Similarly, these cultivators borrow in advance from merchants or arhtia and hence, their bargaining power is very poor. They accept the price given by these merchants and sell their produce to them.

9. Inadequate Storage Facilities: At present, we do not have sufficient storage facilities in villages and even in cities. Cultivators store the produce unscientifically which result into heavy losses.

10. Transportation Means are not Well-developed: Cultivators have to sell at lower prices at inconvenient market as well as have to spend more for transportation. There are no railway routes in some part of the country as well as pacca roads are also inadequate. Motor truck prices are also very high. Thus, transportation is one of the problems for agril. marketing.

11. Adulteration: Adulteration is also found in agril. markets, *e.g.*, in case of cotton, short staple cotton is usually mixed with large staple. Similarly, pebbles are also found in food grains.

12. Financial Facilities: Financial facilities are also inadequate in India.

Lines of Improvement

For giving justice to small and marginal cultivators in country above-mentioned defects must be removed from agril. marketing in India. Improvements must be made to secure for the cultivator, a larger proportion of consumer's price. Some measures for improvement have been discussed below:

1. *Establishment of regulated markets*: Several defects can be removed by establishing a regulated market and hence, it is suggested that regulated markets should be established.
2. *Co-operative marketing*: It should be developed so that several problems such as lack of organization of producers, etc., can be solved.
3. *Use of standard weights and measures*: Several cultivators are cheated by wrong weights, and this should be given attention.
4. *Provision of marketing news*: Because of not getting proper market news cultivators sell their produce in villages at low prices and hence supplying market news is also important.
5. *Increasing facility of storage and warehousing*: Sufficient fund must be allotted to establish storage facilities.
6. Improvement of transport facility is also an important way to improve agril. marketing.
7. Improvement in grading and standardisation is also necessary to improve agril. marketing.
8. Guarding against adulteration.
9. Auction sale method of selling should be followed so that superior quality goods will get reasonably high price.
10. Market research must be carried out so that information can be obtained about marketing.
11. Appointment of expert marketing officers on the staff of the agricultural departments is also necessary.

17
Regulated Market and Co-operative Marketing

Agricultural marketing is one of the varied problems that are to be decided the destiny, prosperity and progress of the poor and desperate cultivators. An acceptable marketing system is one that maximises the welfare of the society in the long run. An efficient marketing system is responsible for waging war against wastages and slashing down the costs so that the producer gets a fair share in the price paid by consumer. In India, particularly in the field of agriculture, the tiller of the soil is not getting these benefits. It is the middlemen, who are enjoying the cream of the cake at the cost of Indian farmers. With the intention of safeguarding the interest of farmers in India, it was in 1897 that for the first-time regulation of markets was brought out by passing Berar Cotton and Grains Market Act. The regulation movement received impetus only from the year 1927 when Bombay Cotton Market Act was passed. Then it covered only Bombay province. Later, similar Acts were passed by other provinces like Madras, Mysore and Punjab.

What is a Regulated Market?

Regulated Market is a wholesale market where dealings, or buying and selling are regulated and controlled by the State Government through a "Market Committee" that consists of representatives of farmers, traders, agents, local bodies, co-operatives and Government. In other words, it is a market where the activities are to take place under the set rules and regulations and malpractices like incorrect weighment, unauthorized deductions are curbed and settlement of disputes on amicable grounds is provided.

The establishment of such regulated markets has two objectives, *viz.*, (*i*) to safeguard the interests of both farmers and traders, and (*ii*) to create the conditions of fair competition.

Salient Features of a Regulated Market

A typical regulated market to better serve the objectives mentioned above, has the following features:

1. Market committee: A "Market committee" is to be constituted as needed by the Act, comprising representatives from different sections of society, *viz.*, farmers, agents, traders, government, local bodies and co-operatives. These representatives may either be elected or nominated by the Government concerned. The market committee enjoys certain powers. It can prescribe the conditions of 'Fair dealing' bring about improvements in methods of marketing, penalize those, who contravene the framed rules and regulations, arrange for the strict supervision of weighment. The noteworthy feature of such a representation is the farmers have 50% or more of the total membership.

2. Area of operation: The concerned State government notifies its intention to regulate the trade practices in specified area. Such an area of operation is laid down either as a municipal limit, or district or even it may be a region. However, separate market yards are necessary for effective regulation which many of the regulated market do not have in India.

3. Methods of sale: A regulated market provides for 'open auction', 'tender' and 'open agreement' sale methods to curb the ills of unorganized markets. Private negotiations are discouraged.

4. Licensing of functionaries: Those, who work in the 'market yard' should have valid licences from market committee. The functionaries operating in a market are traders, farmers, weighmen and other labourers like cleaners, etc., separate licences are issued to deal in different functions. Under the terms and conditions of licence the jurisdiction of operation of each license is restricted. It is an offence under the Act if the functionaries operate without any valid licence. The Act provides for the rate of commission, allowances and other charges payable for the services of functionaries in the regulated market.

5. Market fees: Growers and the traders or dealers have to pay market 'cess' or 'fees' which are calculated on the basis of value or volumes of the goods bought and sold in the market yard. Sometimes, it may, be based on 'load' or 'cart load' or 'truck load'. The licence fees and market cesses are the major sources of income to meet administrative expenses of a regulated market.

6. Settlement of disputes: Regulated markets provide separate machinery for settling the disputes. The usual disputes that arise in the usual course of business, mostly relate to prices, allowances, quality and quantity of goods dealt in. To settle any such disputes, there is a 'Disputes Committee' or 'Arbitration Committee' that helps in expediting settlement of disputes at least cost without resorting to courts.

Advantages of Regulated Market

Regulated Markets have been instrumental in safeguarding the interests particularly of farmers. To what extent our farmers are benefited will depend on the benefits of regulated market. There are many benefits that the class of tillers gets by entering the arena of regulated markets. Those significant benefits are as follows:

1. Reduction in village sales: Grower sellers are fully aware of the fair play of competition and other amenities. With the lapse of time, greater part of their produce enters the regulated market, thus slashing down forced village sales. For instance, in 1950 more than 40% of the total output was sold outside the regulated markets. Today the selling in regulated market has gone to the extent of 95%.

2. Reduction in market charges: In regulated markets, the market charges received by various functionaries are prescribed by the market committee and making recovery of unauthorized deduction is prohibited. Though it is not possible to estimate exactly in monetary terms the actual benefit accruing to the producer, seller on this accounts, an attempt is made by the Directorate of Marketing and Inspection to assess the extent of reduction in market charges. At present, a farmer gives ₹ 1.80 for every produce sold worth rupees ₹ 100, as against ₹ 3.50 in 1966. The net saving over the period is ₹ 1.70.

3. Better prices: The sweat of a tiller of soil is properly rewarded as the prices are the outcome of interplay of fair competition. In the past, supply side was crushed. Today, the farmers get better prices because of changes in methods of sale, correct weighment, and reduction in market charges. It is said, on an average, farmer is benefited to the extent of ₹ 4 to 7 for sale of ₹ 100 worth produce. Further there is a quicker payment, which is an additional benefit.

4. Correct weighment: Weighment of the produce by licensed weighment with standard Metric weights and measures that resulted in uprooting manipulation. In most of the markets 'beam balance' and weigh bridges are installed. This correct weighment itself is a greater justice done in favour of farmers.

5. Market services and facilities: As a rule, these regulated markets are expected to provide the services and facilities. Government of India, has been generous enough to provide grading facilities to major regulated markets. "Agmarking" is a special feature, of agriculture produce. Grading decides quality and quality fetches higher prices to the farmers.

In addition, different market amenities such as drinking water for cultivators, water tubs for animals, parking space, cattle shed, rest house, canteens, and sanitary blocks. Warehouses and cold storages, etc., are provided by the market committee.

6. Market news: In all regulated markets, appreciable arrangements are made for the collection and dissemination of market prices for the benefits of member-farmers. Besides exhibiting prices on the notice boards, the information is disseminated over loud-speakers. Radio sets are installed to get latest information from leading markets all over the country. Daily market information is supplied to village panchayats. Further, the said information is broadcasted on All India Radio on regional basis. Such an effort keeps the farmers to take decisions in their favour.

7. Settlements of disputes: Another major benefit of regulated market is the provision of machinery for settling of disputes between the producers, buyers, and sellers or their agent that may arise in the normal course of transactions relating to quality, quantity, weight, payment, etc. There is separate sub-committee referred as Disputes Committee that helps in quick settlement of disputes at least cost without having any recourse to the courts of law.

8. Reliable statistics of arrivals, stocks, prices is maintained.

Co-operative Marketing

When producers form a society with an object of carrying out marketing activities for their produce. Such society is called as co-operative marketing society. The need for co-operative marketing arises from a number of reasons, *viz.*,

(*i*) Various malpractices prevail in the system of agricultural marketing such as arbitrary deduction from the produce, manipulation of weights and collusion between the broker and the buyers. The effect is further aggravated by the circumstances that a large number of cultivators are indebted to the trader-money-lender. In such circumstances, co-operative marketing of agricultural products can largely help to reduce the malpractices in the marketing structure.

(*ii*) There exist a large number of middlemen, who take part in collection, storage, financing, insuring, grading, sale and transportation of agricultural produce. Their charges are heavy for the services, with the result that the producers do not get their due share of the price paid by the ultimate consumers. Co-operative marketing, if efficiently organised, can help reduce the market costs. Thereby assisting in giving a fair return to the producer without adversely affecting the legitimate interests of the consumer.

(*iii*) Co-operative marketing societies are expected to ensure a better return to the farmer on the produce raised by him with the assistance of loans from co-operative sources. Besides, they can act as agents for the recovery of loans advanced by the co-operative credit societies.

(*iv*) In all these circumstances, the need for co-operative marketing of agricultural produce on a substantial scale becomes urgent so that it can help in stabilising prices.

Organization

Under the system of co-operative marketing, the whole responsibility of marketing of agricultural produce is undertaken by the farmers themselves, organised on a co-operative basis. The area of operation of marketing society is usually fixed with reference to local conditions. The area may be different according to the type of produce to be dealt with. As such, a paddy marketing society may have an area of whole taluka, whereas a marketing society dealing with commercial crops like cotton, jute or sugarcane may extend to a whole district or whole area growing the crop.

Membership

Membership of the marketing society is open to individual agriculturists, large-sized credit societies, service co-operatives, or other rural credit co-operative societies and multipurpose societies.

Resources

The sources of capital are usually shares, deposits, loans from central financing agencies up to 8 to 10 times the value of paid up share capital. Reserve Bank of India or Governments grant or subsidy from Government for construction of godowns, borrowings from State Bank of India against security of warehouse receipts or pledge of goods in the society's godown and reserves created out of profit.

The marketing societies require short-term, medium-term and long-term capital: (*i*) Short-term capital is needed for financing advances for production, advances against pledge of produce and for meeting contingent and establishment expenses, it is repayable within a year, (*ii*) Medium-term capital is required for purchasing motor trucks if produce is to be delivered to a distant market or members' produce is to be collected, (*iii*) Long-term loan is needed for installation of machinery, construction of building especially where a society proceed to alter the produce or process it in any way, *e.g.*, crush oil seeds, turn milk into butter or grade a product.

Objectives and Functions of Co-operative Marketing Society

The co-operative marketing societies play an important part in the following spheres:

1. They arrange for sale of members' produce to the best possible advantage by enabling them to obtain better price, because of the sale in bulk and consequent economy in the cost of marketing.
2. They undertake activities in connection with grading, pooling, and procuring of produce of members.
3. Co-operatives provide storage facilities to their members by renting or owning godowns and thereby facilitate grant of advances against pledge or produce.
4. They protect members from several malpractices like unauthorised deduction, incorrect weighments, etc. They also eliminate the long chain of middlemen and connect the producer with consumer.
5. Co-operative marketing reduces waste and stands for fair trading practices and uses its influence against rings and manipulation of prices.
6. Co-operative marketing teaches to the farmers business methods and serves them as agency for supplying market information.
7. Marketing societies stabilize prices over long periods by adjusting the supply according to market demand. In this way, seasonal fluctuation of price or their effect can be eliminated.
8. Co-operative marketing societies are also being encouraged to participate in the export trade of the country so that the actual grower might get a better price for his produce.

18
Price Spread

Marketable Surplus and Marketed Surplus

Marketable surplus refers to the residential quantity left with the producer after meeting his requirements for family consumption, farm needs, and payments in kind to casual and permanent labourers, the landlord, artisans and others, *e.g.*, owner cultivator produced 25 quintals of wheat. His annual family consumption need is 10 quintals plus seed requirement one quintal plus four quintals payments for labourers and artisans, etc. Thus, total 15 quintals is his annual requirements and hence, his marketable surplus is 10 quintals (25-15). The term Marketed Surplus refers to the quantity of produce that is actually sold in the market by the producer irrespective of his home consumption and other requirements. Suppose, cultivator sold six quintals in the market then his marketed surplus is six quintals. Thus, marketed surplus may be less than, equal to or more than marketable surplus. Sometimes, cultivator is forced to sell more quantity than his desire because of demand for money and if he sold 15 quintals then his marketed surplus is greater than marketable surplus. If the same cultivator sold 10 quintals, then marketed surplus is equal to marketable surplus.

Marketable Surplus and Size of Holding

There are mainly three sizes of holding, below two hectares those are called as small holders. These cultivators carryout subsistence agriculture and whatever they will produce, particularly food grains, consume themselves. However, there are some forced sales. Some of the cultivators work in other's fields and those, who adopt modern technology able to satisfy their need. Mainly large cultivators *i.e.*, cultivator having holding more than four hectares able to save some grains and they sell their marketable surplus when the price will be sufficiently high. They are price conscious. Major portion, *i.e.*, about 60 per cent marketable surplus is contributed by these cultivators. In case of medium cultivators, (size of holding is in between two to four hectares) they are self-sufficient, those adopt modern technology able to produce more and contribute towards marketable surplus.

Cause for Tardy Growth of Marketable Surplus

Following are some of the reasons for tardy growth of marketable surplus:

1. The majority of our cultivators are small and marginal cultivators and in their cases, there is no real marketable surplus. They sell because of monetary pressure. In case of medium and large cultivators, if there is an increase in agril. production there is also increase in consumption of agril. production and hence there is no increase in marketable surplus in proportion to increase in agril. production.
2. At the time of rising prices, farmer need not sell more to satisfy his minimum cash needs and because of this, due to rise in production marketed surplus may not increase.
3. Because of improved financial condition, some cultivators are not forced to sell as soon as harvest is over. They hoard and sell when prices will be high.
4. Previously, superior quality grains of rice and wheat were not consumed by cultivators and were sent to cities but due to improved financial condition of cultivators they themselves consume better quality grains.

Importance of Marketable Surplus for Country's Development

Generation of adequate agriculture surplus would lead to saving of foreign exchange, promote capital formation in agril. and non-agril. sectors.

Market Costs and Price Spread

Marketing costs are the actual expenses incurred for bringing goods and services from the producer to the consumer.

The difference between the final price paid by the consumer for a commodity or a product and the price received by a grower of a crop or a primary producer, may be taken roughly to represent the costs of marketing of that commodity. Marketing costs would normally include: (*i*) handling charges at local points, (*ii*) assembling charges, (*iii*) transport and storage, financing, risk taking, market intelligence, and (*iv*) profit margin taken out by different agencies.

Objectives of Studying Marketing Costs

The objects of studying the marketing costs are:

1. To ascertain as to what intermediate agencies intervene between the producer and the final consumer of a commodity, the services they render and the remuneration they get for such services and to examine whether such services are necessary.
2. To ascertain the total costs of the marketing process of a commodity.
3. Estimate producer's share in consumer's rupee.
4. To see whether there is any alternative to reduce the cost of marketing.

The cost-studies or investigations made so far with regard to many commodities in our country revealed that greater proportion of the price paid by consumers is absorbed by the intermediate agencies in marketing of certain agricultural products. Such studies would be useful in ascertaining whether the functions performed by some of the agencies employed and the cost involved and for coming to a conclusion as to how best such integration could be brought about.

Price Spread

The price which the farmer gets for his produce is known as producer's price and the price which the consumer pays is known as consumer's price. The difference between the consumer's price and producer's price is called as market costs. The price spread includes distribution of market cost on various items of cost. It is called as price spread. The price spread includes the costs taken away by the middlemen, traders, transporters, brokers, and other functionaries. The price-spread varies from place to place and commodity to commodity.

The study of price spread also involves ascertainment of actual prices at various stages of marketing channels and the margin of various intermediaries.

Market Margin

Margin refers to the difference between the price paid and received by a specific marketing agency such as a single retailer.

Table 18.1: Market cost and price spread for vegetable (tomato) and fruit (apple)

Sr. No.	Item	Vegetable (Tomato)		Fruit (Apple)	
		₹	% of Consumer price	₹	% of Consumer price
1.	Net price received by the producer	40.54	61.42	33.25	44.33
2.	Commission agent's commission	3.06	4.64	3.48	4.64
3.	Marketing charges borne by producer's	6.40	9.70	15.00	20.00
4.	Price paid by wholesaler	–	–	51.73	68.97
5.	Wholesaler's marketing charges*	–	–	4.00	5.33
6.	Wholesaler's profit	–	–	6.64	8.85
7.	Price paid by the retailer	50.00	75.76	62.37	83.16
8.	Retailer's marketing charges*	6.00	9.09	3.50	4.67
9.	Retailer's profit	10.00	15.15	9.13	12.17
10.	Total market cost	25.46	38.58	41.75	55.66
11.	Price paid by the consumer	66.00	100.00	75.00	100.00

Notes: Figures for vegetable are per quintal and pertain to Bangalore market. Figures for Apple are per box of 16.28 kg. apples and pertain to Chennai market.

* Marketing charges include transport, loading, unloading, preparation of the produce for the market and other miscellaneous charges.

Source: *Indian Journal of Marketing*—"Marketing of fruits and vegetables around Bangalore" Dr. K.V. Subramanyam.

From the table 18.1, it is seen that in case of tomato, out of ₹ 66 per quintal paid by consumer ₹ 40.54 (61.42 p.c.) is received by producer and the total marketing margin is ₹ 25.46 (38.58 p.c.). In case of apple out of 75 rupees per box ₹ 33.25 (44.33 p.c.) is received by producer. Total marketing margin is ₹ 41.75 (55.66 p.c.).

Table 18.2: Price spread and net returns to mango growers by different methods of sale in Ratnagiri district (For one crate of six dozen fruits)

Sr. No.	Particulars	Group I		Group II		Group III	
		₹	%	₹	%	₹	%
1.	Net price realized by the producer	15.73	12.61	29.68	25.49	38.71	30.63
2.	Margin to pre-harvest contractor	22.78	18.03	9.03	7.15	–	–
3.	Expenses incurred by producer or pre-harvest contractor	20.85	16.50	20.85	16.50	20.85	16.50
4.	Price paid by wholesaler	59.56	–	59.56	–	59.56	–
5.	Margin to wholesaler	28.26	22.36	28.26	22.36	28.26	22.36
6.	Price paid by retailer	87.82	–	87.82	–	87.82	–
7.	Margin to retailer	38.54	30.50	38.54	30.50	38.54	30.50
8.	Price paid by consumer	126.36	100.00	126.00	100.36	126.36	100.00

(Based on the study undertaken by a post-graduate student from Dapoli Agricultural College in the year 1975).

Group I = Giving orchards to pre-harvest contractors on long lease.

Group II = Selling orchards to pre-harvest contractors on annual basis.

Group III = Selling fruits in the wholesale market at Bombay after harvest by the growers.

From the above table 18.2, it is seen that mango growers, giving their orchards to pre-harvest contractor on long lease received only 12.61 per cent of the price paid by the consumer. Growers, selling the orchards to pre-harvest contractor on annual basis received 25.49 per cent of the consumer's price while growers, who sell fruits in the wholesale market in Bombay themselves receive 30.6 per cent of the consumer's price. This shows that selling fruits directly in wholesale market is more profitable than giving orchards to pre-harvest contractors.

If fruit growers sold the produce directly in the market instead of giving it to the pre-harvest contractors, they will receive bigger share in consumers rupee. Price spread varies from place to place and from commodity to commodity. The marketing cost depends upon the marketing system and method of sale.

Table 18.3: Price spread and net returns to wheat growers in regulated market

Sr. No.	Particulars	Per cent share in consumer's rupee
1.	Grower	85.48
2.	Commission agent	3.65
3.	Wholesaler	1.11
4.	Retailer	3.87
5.	Processing agencies	4.80
6.	(*i*) Transportation	0.50
	(*ii*) Labour	0.34
	(*iii*) Bagging	0.25
	(*iv*) Storage losses and others	–
7.	Other agencies	–
	Total	100.00

By selling produce in the regulated market wheat grower receives 85.48 per cent of the consumer's price is observed from table 18.3.

Marketing Efficiency

1. Marketing efficiency may be defined as the effectiveness or competence with which a marketing structure performs it's designed functions.
2. Marketing efficiency can be defined as the maximization of consumer's satisfaction with the least cost incurred

in providing that satisfaction through the system of marketing.

Type or marketing efficiency:

(*i*) Technical efficiency.

(*ii*) Economic efficiency.

(*i*) Technical efficiency: Technical efficiency refers to improvement of marketing structure, the utilisation of the best method available for every marketing job and use of these methods with maximum effectiveness, *e.g.*, use of motor trucks instead of bullock carts, use of phone instead of sending messenger.

(*ii*) Economic efficiency: It refers to minimization of marketing cost per unit produce handled in market. The measurement of economic efficiency can be done as follows:

$$\text{Efficiency} = \frac{f\begin{pmatrix}\text{value-added by}\\ \text{marketing organization}\end{pmatrix}}{\text{cost of marketing services}} \times 100$$

Thus, if in a market the total marketing cost incurred by all participants (producer, middlemen and consumers) were ₹ 3,000 and the value-added by marketing were ₹ 4,500. Then marketing

$$\text{efficiency} = \frac{4{,}500 \times 100}{3{,}000} = 150$$

In other market if, marketing cost is ₹ 4,000 then marketing

$$\text{efficiency} = \frac{4{,}500 \times 100}{4{,}000} = 112.5$$

The efficiency index in second market is only 112.5 which is lower than first market and thus if market cost increased it will lower the efficiency index.

However, marketing efficiency index is based on "value-added by marketing organization," and value addition is estimated by deducting price received by producer from price paid by final consumer, which is rather a difficult task. Therefore, Shepherd suggested that the ratio of the total value of goods marketed to the marketing cost may be used as a measure of marketing efficiency. The higher the ratio, higher the efficiency and *vice versa*. Shepherd's method eliminates the problem of measurement of value-added. However, Shepherd's method does not explicitly take into account the net margins retained by the intermediaries and net price received by the farmers in assessing the marketing efficiency. Therefore, Acharya suggested following equation for estimation of efficiency indicator as follows:

$$MME = FP/(MC + MM)$$

Where MME is the measure of marketing efficiency and MC and MM are marketing costs and marketing margins, respectively. FP means prices received by the farmer. Acharya's measure of marketing efficiency can also be stated as follows:

$$MME = [RP + (MC + MM)] - 1$$

Because, $RP = FP + MC + MM$

Here, RP means price paid by the consumer. These indicators are illustrated in table 18.4.

Table 18.4: Measurement of marketing efficiency different approaches

Sr. No.	Particulars	Unit	Market 1 or channel 1	Market 2 or channel 2	Market 3 or channel 3
1.	Retailers sale price or consumers purchase price (RP)	Price of tomato/Q	741.12	820.21	820.21
2.	Total marketing cost (MC)	₹/Q	42.60	64.36	85.38
3.	Total net market margins of intermediaries (MM)	₹/Q	Nil	79.61	152.27
4.	Net price received by farmers (FP)	₹/Q	698.52	676.24	582.56
5.	Value added (1-4) Index of marketing efficiency	₹/Q	42.60	143.97	237.65
(*i*)	Conventional method 5÷2 (E)	Ratio	1	2.24	2.78
(*ii*)	Shepherd's method 1÷2 (ME)	Ratio	17.40	12.74	9.61
(*iii*)	Acharya's method 4÷2+3 (MME)	Ratio	16.40	4.70	2.45

Source: Neeta Borate, "Marketing of Vegetables in College Development Block," approved M.Sc. thesis, Dr. BSKKV, Dapoli.

It is observed from table 18.4 that as per conventional method, third channel is more efficient than second and first channel whereas second channel is more efficient than first channel. However, price received by farmer in third channels is lowest and therefore third channel cannot be considered as most efficient channel and therefore this method is not suitable under Indian condition. Shepherd's method concludes channel one is most efficient channel and second channel is efficient than third channel. However, this method is not based on what price producer has received. Acharya's method is based on the price which producer receives and also market margins are taken into account while working out efficiency index. In other words, channel where farmers get maximum producers share in consumer's rupee is considered as most efficient channel under Indian condition. Therefore, after finding out producers share in consumers rupee one can understand about efficiency of a channel which is further confirmed by Acharya's method of finding out efficiency indicator. If priority is given to value addition through marketing system which is maximum in third market. Therefore, third market is considered as most efficient market and this is indicated by conventional method. In third market more value addition has taken place and hence, as per as conventional method concludes that third market is most efficient market. Hence, which method has to be utilized depends upon objectives set by the concerned.

Objectives of the efficient marketing organisation

1. Keeping the prices down.
2. Structure of marketing should be developed on technical and economic lines.
3. By fixing prices properly, risk can be reduced.
4. Timely distribution of commodities.

Market Intelligence

Market intelligence is a businessman's greatest tool in making policy and executive decisions. It is a continuous study of market behaviour and price situation and takes into account following enquiries:

(*i*) What happens inside the market and why it happens?
(*ii*) What is the price situation?
(*iii*) What is the impact of government policies, floods, droughts on market?
(*iv*) When prices will be low and when they will be high?
(*v*) From where goods are moving into the market and what are their volumes?

Market information is published by trader's organization or by individual firm in the form of publication of daily, weekly market reports, news bulletins, monthly journals etc. Prevailing market situation will be critically studied, and various decisions are made. Businessman will get a clear picture of situation and will take decision about his policy.

Market Price Integration

Market price integration refers to the movement of prevailing market prices of a commodity at two different markets in a particular direction. If price of a commodity at two different markets show increasing or decreasing trends during a particular period, it is said that both the markets are integrated. However, price of a commodity in a given period increased at one market while it decreased at other market in such case, it is said that markets are not well-integrated. If there is an increase in price of a commodity in one market, same increase in price may percolate to nearby market. Because of this reason, supplier at both the markets is benefited and it is not necessary for a supplier to run to a nearby market where price is high for the same commodity. Similarly, buyers need not run to nearby market for purchasing a commodity at low price. Thus, in well-integrated markets increase or decrease in price percolates to nearby or distantly located markets due to better communication facilities as well as due to tendency of a human mind for maximizing profit. Prices of a commodity in two different markets equalizes gradually. This depends upon, if these two markets are well-connected with road or rail as well as other communication facilities such as telephone, telegraph facilities at both the markets exist.

If two markets are not well-connected with rail or road and or communication between two markets are lacking-then chances of movement of a commodity from one market to another market are negligible and prices in two different markets do not move in the same direction. When product is differentiated chances of market integration are weak. When product is homogeneous, higher degree of integration of markets is observed. Under Indian condition, producers enjoy lot of freedom to sell their produce in any market in the country, various markets are well-connected with road and rail and hence high degree of market integration is expected. However, sometimes certain states put ban on movement of a particular agricultural commodity from home state to nearby or any other state and farmers have to sell their produce in home state only. Under such circumstances, movement of prices for a particular commodity may not be in the same direction.

Measurement of Paddy Market Price Integration in Raigad and Thane Districts of Maharashtra

Market price integration is measured by working out correlation coefficient between prices of commodity prevailing in two different markets. Correlation coefficients were worked out for average annual prices of paddy. Average annual prices of paddy were estimated from data collected from farmers and results are presented in table 18.5. Period referred to is 1983-84 to 1989-90.

It is observed from table 18.5 that all three paddy markets, *i.e.*, Karjat, Panvel and Kalyan are highly integrated paddy markets. Correlation co-efficients are positive and significant at

Table 18.5: Paddy market price integration (average annual price data, 1983-1994)

Name of market centre	Values of correlation co-efficients		
	Karjat	Panvel	Kalyan
Karjat	1.0	0.95***	0.99***
Panvel		1.0	0.89***
Kalyan			1.0

Note: Significant at 1% level of significance.

Source: A.A. Rane, "Marketing Efficiency of Agriculture in Konkan Region of Maharashtra State, India". Ph.D. thesis approved by Pune University, p. 123.

1 per cent level of significance. Positive sign of correlation co-efficient indicates prices in both the markets move in one direction and negative sign indicates that prices move in two different directions, that is if price of paddy increased in one market price of paddy in other market decreases and *vice versa*. It means both the markets are not well-integrated. Similarly, higher the value of correlation co-efficient higher degree of integration and lower value of correlation co-efficient indicates low degree of integration. Here paddy markets are well-integrated, because these markets are well-connected by rail and road as well as telephone facilities are also available in all markets.

19
Agricultural Price Analysis and World Trade Organization

Price Determination Under Perfect Competition

Before Marshall there was dispute about which is important, in determining the price whether it is a demand or it is a supply. But Marshall gave equal importance to both demand and supply. He compared demand and supply with two blades of a scissor. Both the blades are equally important in cutting the paper. Similarly, both demand and supply are equally important in determining the price. Under perfect competition demand and supply both interact and price is determined. It can be shown with a simple example.

Table 19.1: Equilibrium price

Price in ₹ per crate (6-dozen) of Alphonso Mango	Quantity demanded (thousand per month)	Quantity supplied (thousand per month)	Pressure on price
536	9	18	Falling
530	10	16	Falling
526	12	12	Neutral (equilibrium)
500	15	7	Rising
250	20	3	Rising

It is observed from the table 19.1 that when price is ₹ 536, quantity demanded is only 9 thousand crates, these forces the seller to decrease the price, because there is no demand for mangoes and thus price decreases. If price is ₹ 250 then quantity demanded is more than-quantity supplied and hence seller will increase price. Thus, at ₹ 526 per crate both quantities demanded equals quantity supplied and that is an equilibrium price. Thus, market price is determined due to forces of demand and supply and is also shown in figure 19.1.

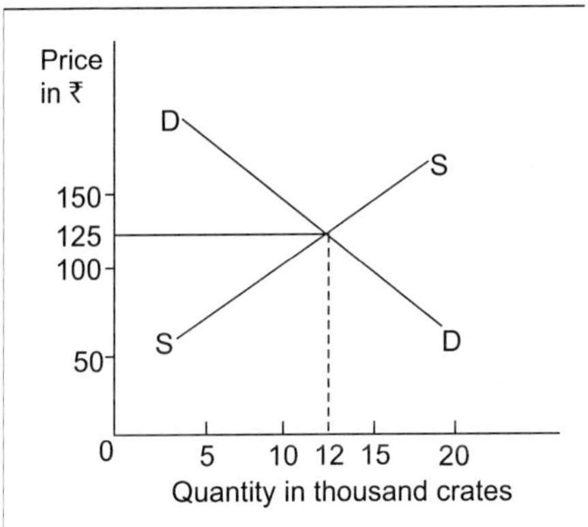

Fig. 19.1: Equilibrium price of mango crate

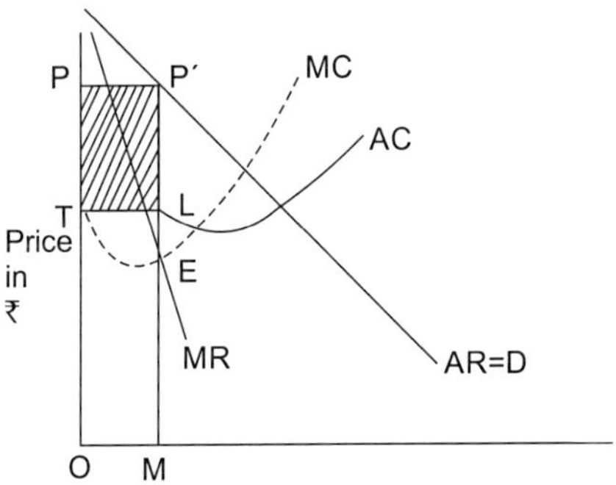

Fig. 19.2: Price determination under monopoly

Monopoly is that market form in which a single producer controls the whole supply of a single commodity which has no close substitute.

Price is determined on the basis of marginal return and marginal cost.

It is observed from figure 19.2 that marginal revenue curve and marginal cost curve crosses each other at point E. Line joining PM cuts average cost curve (AC) at L and demand curve at P. Hence, price will be OP where monopolist will get maximum profit. Monopolist will obtain a maximum profit which is indicated by a rectangle PP' LT. Thus, under monopoly per unit cost and return will determine price. However, pure competitive and pure monopoly markets rarely exist. Equilibrium price under imperfect competitive market varies in between these two extremes.

Fluctuation in Agricultural Prices

Before fixing prices, fluctuation in agricultural prices was wide. These fluctuations in prices occur due to fluctuation in supply of agril. produce, supply of agril. produce is affected by several things: (*i*) weather conditions vary from year to year which affect agril. production, (*ii*) some producers hoard, and it affect market supply, (*iii*) nature plays important role in agril. production, *e.g.*, famines, floods, etc., (*iv*) cost of marketing is very much affected by peculiar characteristics of agril. produce and changes in cost of marketing affect the price of the produce, (*v*) market intelligence relating to either supply or demand is lacking which affect price policy of businessmen and thus price fluctuates.

Price Stabilization

Price stabilization means prevention of violent fluctuations in the prices on both the sides. Prices should not be too high or too low. The government has to maintain this stability in prices. The government measures consist of buying all that is offered for sale at the predetermined minimum support prices in a bid to prevent undue fall in prices and selling the reserve stocks at control rates to check a rise in prices beyond what is considered a fair level. Thus, government protects both producers and consumers.

Need for Stabilization

It is expected cultivator should get certain fair return. This will not only lead to agricultural development, but also it will lead to general prosperity. If there are wide fluctuations in agril. prices in particular, they create imbalance in the whole economy of the country since they affect the income of more than 65 per cent of the population. Thereby affecting demand for all types of commodities. Thus, for prosperity of country; agril. prices must be stabilised. The price Sub-committee on agricultural prices under Shri Krishnamachari recognised the need of stabilization of agricultural prices.

Stabilization of Prices Achieved

Stable prices do not mean rigid and unchanging prices. Minimum and maximum prices for different commodities for specific periods are generally fixed and enforced. Through regulatory measures prices are not allowed to fall below a certain minimum level in order to protect the farmers from undergoing losses. Price rise above a certain maximum level is also not allowed in order to safeguard the interest of the consumers. From the producer's point of view, the minimum price should cover the cost of production and provide a fair margin of profit to producer. From the consumers point of view, the maximum price should not be too severe and should give rise to a demand for the maximum quantity produced. For this purpose, government has built up storages and has to buy when there will be fall in prices below certain minimum price. Government has to sell some quantity from store, when prices will rise more than certain fixed maximum price. The minimum and maximum prices are announced in advance of the crop planning period. Under special circumstances consumption is regulated by controlling supply and starting rationing. Sometimes licensing of traders asking for declaration of stock by traders and keeping statutory limit on stocks held by them, compulsory levy on the farmers on procurement from them at fixed prices. Thus, Government tries to keep the price stable.

Trends in Agricultural Prices before Independence

Because of declaration of Second World War prices began to rise. Price index increased from 100.03 in August 1939 to 137.8 in December 1939. It was 108.4 in August 1940. After, 1940 onwards the prices continuously increased.

After Independence

After the partition of the country, there developed an acute shortage of food grains in the country. This is because many fertile tracts producing rice and wheat were fallen to the share of Pakistan. The prices therefore showed sharp rise.

It is observed from the figures given in table 19.2 that there was decline in prices since 1952-53 to 1954-55 but again since 1956 the prices started increasing.

Table 19.2: Index number of wholesale prices (Base 1952-53 = 100)

Year	W. Price index	Year	W. Price index
1950-51	—	1981-82	100.0
51-52	118.8	1990-91	182.7
52-53	100.0	1991-92	207.8
53-54	—	1992-93	228.7
54-55	—	1993-94	247.8
55-56	88.0	1994-95	112.6
56-57	104.5	1995-96	121.6
57-58	107.4	1996-97	127.2
58-59	114.0	1997-98	132.8
59-60	116.5	1998-99	140.7
60-61	123.8	1999-2000	145.3
61-62	122.8	2000-2001	155.7
62-63	123.3	2001-2002	161.3
63-64	132.0	2002-2003	166.8
64-65	156.0	2003-2004	175.9
65-66	163.0		
66-67	199.0		
67-68	242.2		
68-69	234.9		

Source: Economic Survey 2003-04, Govt. of India.

The increase was even till 1962-63. From 1963 to 1967, a serious rise in prices was noticed. In 1962, the support prices for rice and wheat were fixed and arrangement were also made for the purchase at support prices in case market prices tended to decline unduly. In December 1962, procurement of rice was intensified.

Commission on Agricultural Costs and Prices

As per Jha committee's recommendation, Commission on Agril. Costs and Prices was set up in 1965 to advise Government on the price policy of agricultural commodities particularly Wheat, Rice, Jowar, Bajra, Maize, Gram and other pulses, Sugarcane, Oil seeds, Cotton and Jute.

Objects of the Commission

(*i*) To review studies relating to the price policy and collection of information regarding agricultural commodities.

(*ii*) To review the existing price situation and recommend suitable price for a commodity.

(*iii*) To suggest measures to reduce the cost of marketing.

Since 1965, the Commission has been advising on continuous basis on minimum and procurement prices of both kharif and rabi cereals.

Price Fixation

State government price fixation committee recommended certain price taking into consideration cost of production of crop. Agricultural Price Commission finally concludes from various state data and finally recommends to central government.

Central government then finally announces the procurement price. The procurement price for wheat in 1970-71 was fixed at ₹ 76 per quintal. In 1974-75, procurement price for wheat was 105 per quintal. In 1978-79, it was ₹ 115 which increased to ₹ 117 in 1979-80. At present, procurement price for rice is ₹ 570 in 2005.

World Trade Organization

The World Trade Organization (WTO) came into force on January 1, 1995, replacing the previous GATT secretariat as the organization responsible for administering the international trade regime. The WTO presently has 148 members, accounting for over 97 per cent of world trade. It is head quartered at Geneva, Switzerland.

The Structure of WTO

The WTO's top level decision-making body is the Ministerial Conference, which meet at least once in every two years and is composed of International Trade Ministers from all member countries. Below this body, is the General Council. Normally, ambassadors and heads of delegation in Geneva, but sometimes officials are also sent from each country. General Council is a Trade Policy Review Body and the Dispute Settlement Body. Next to General Council there is a Council for Trade in Services and a Council for Trade Related Aspects of Intellectual Property Rights (TRIPS). These three Councils operate under General Council. At the lowest levels, numerous specialized committees, working groups and working parties deal with individual agreements.

Role of General Council

General Council is responsible for overseeing the day-to-day business and management of the WTO and is based at the WTO headquarters in Geneva. This is a trade policy reviewing body as well as Dispute Settlement Body.

WTO Secretariat

WTO secretariat is based in Geneva, has around 600 staff members and is headed by a Director General (DG). Its annual budget is around 160 million Swiss Francs. There are four Deputy Director Generals to assist the D.G. The secretariat's main duties are to supply technical support for the various councils and committees and the ministerial conferences. Present D.G. Dr. Supachai Panitchpakdi comes to an end on 31st August, 2005. Since 1st September 2005 Frenchman Pascal Lamy succeeded Dr. Supachai.

Impact of WTO on Konkan Agriculture of India

Konkan is a narrow strip running north to south along with the western coast of Maharashtra to the west Arabian sea and to the east Sahyadri hills. Coastal agro-ecosystem possesses two types of production systems, *i.e.*, Agri-Horticulture and fishery-livestock. Similarly, eastern hilly area consists Agri-Horti-Livestock production system. Mainly crops are grown as rainfed crops. About 4 per cent net sown area is irrigated. However, area under irrigation is increasing year after year. There are four districts in Konkan, *i.e.*, Thane, Raigad, Ratnagiri and Sindhudurg. Annual rainfall is about 3000 mm and rainfall start from June and ends in October. Rice is a main crop in Konkan region. Next to rice fruits and vegetable crops are grown in Konkan.

Due to globalization and liberalization, farmers have to face international competition for selling their agricultural produce. Efforts are made in this paper to throw some light on strategies which farmers and State Government can undertake for reaping the benefits of present world trade liberalization.

1. Land utilization in Konkan region

The total geographical area of Konkan region is 29.79 lakhs hectares. Out of this only 7.97 lakhs hectares is net sown area, which is only 27 per cent of geographical area. The other cultivable and fallow land is 8.97 lakhs hectares which is 30 per cent of geographical area is lying idle. In other words, net sown area in Konkan can be doubled. This will approximately double the agricultural production and will enhance bargaining power of cultivators in International market.

2. Irrigation facilities

The Konkan region receives about 3000 mm rainfall annually but in summer season, region faces a serious problem of even drinking water. Only 27 per cent net sown area is sown more than once in a year, 4 per cent net sown area is irrigated and thus there is a vast scope for increasing area under irrigation. This will significantly increase agricultural production and will improve bargaining power of farmers.

3. Low productivity

The average per hectare yield of different crops grown in Konkan is low. In case of rice crop, the average per hectare yield is in Konkan region is 22 Quintal. However, varieties like Sahyadri and pro-agro give more than 60 q/ha. Similarly, other improved rice varieties like Ratnagiri 1, Ratnagiri 2, Ratnagiri

3, Palghar 1, Phondaghat 1 give more than 40 q/ha. Similarly, in case of mango crop, average yield per hectare is 3 tonnes, which can easily be doubled by using Paclobutrazol chemical along with double dose of recommended fertilizers. In case of cashew per hectare average yield is 1.5 tonnes; this can be doubled by planting high yielding varieties, applying protective irrigation and by using recommended dose of fertilizers. In case of coconut at present per tree per annum on an average only 65 nuts are obtained. However, about 120 nuts per tree per annum can be obtained by using suitable available technology for coconut cultivation. Recently, due to liberalization in trade, coconut fruits were imported from other countries and prices had gone down. Due to low productivity, Konkan farmers were not able to recover the costs. Thus, henceforth farmers have to make maximum efforts for increasing productivity which will decrease per quintal cost of production and Konkan farmers can thrive well in international competition.

4. Future planning in agricultural research

Due to increase in world trade in agricultural commodities, it is necessary to develop crop varieties which are liked by consumers of importing countries. The market research is needed to identify what color of mango fruit is liked in different countries, whether they like high sugar content of pulp or medium sugar content is liked most. Similarly, in case of cashew kernel what should be the weight of cashew kernel. Similarly, which fruit, vegetable or flower is in great demand in different countries and accordingly our plant breeders should evolve the varieties for export purpose.

5. Monopoly benefits

Konkan has a monopoly in certain fruits like Kokum (*Garcinia indica* C.). During recent years, this fruit crop is popular in foreign countries due to identification of its food, cosmetic and medicinal value. The area under this crop has to be increased. Similarly, research has to be undertaken in this crop. Fruit like Jamun (*Syzygium cuminii*) has better nutritive value as well as its seeds are useful for diabetic patients, this crop has to be popularized in foreign countries. Similarly, at present both the crops are neglected crops but due to WTO Konkan region enjoys monopoly in its production and hence more attention has to be paid for these crops.

6. Incidence of pests and diseases

Foreigners have denied to purchase our several agril. commodities as they are affected by pests/diseases or contain high level of harmful chemicals in it. Therefore it is necessary to take care of these agril. commodities since sowing/planting the seeds.

7. Adjustment in time of harvest

It is necessary to supply the agril. commodity when other countries have not harvested. This will help in fetching better price. In case of Alphonso mango, time of harvest can be changed by using Paclobutrazol. Normally, the mangoes were ready for sell during April-May but due to use of Paclobutrazol mangoes can be harvested in the month of March when there is no mango fruits in Indian market. Similarly, it is necessary to study the harvest period of different fruits and vegetables in other countries and then we can plan our production of fruits/vegetables. This will give better returns to farmers.

8. Value addition

Instead of selling ripe fruits/vegetables, its value can be increased by proper processing. Durability of fruits and vegetables will also be increased by processing fruits and vegetables. The transport cost will also be minimized by exporting only processed product and it will help farmers to earn more profit from international market.

Above mentioned considerations will be useful under the present situation of world trade liberalization.

Selected References

Acharya, S.S., & Agarwal, N. L., *Agricultural Marketing in India*, 4th edition, Oxford & IBH Publishing Co. Pvt. Ltd., New Delhi, 2004.

Anonymous, *Marketing of Mangoes in India*, Directorate of Marketing and Inspection, Nagpur, 1965.

Dewett, K.K., *Modern Economic Theory*, Shyamlal Charitable Trust, New Delhi, 1976.

George, M.V., and Singh, A.J., "Structure, Conduct and Performance of Wholesale Vegetable Market in Punjab," *Journal of Agricultural Marketing*, April, 1970.

Gupta, A.P., *Marketing of Agricultural Produce in India,* Vora & Co., Bombay, 1975.

Hanumantha Rao, C.H., and Subbarao, K., "Marketing of Rice in India," *Indian Journal of Agricultural Economics,* April-June, 1976.

Jain, S.C., *Principles and Practice of Agricultural Marketing & Prices,* Vora & Co., Bombay, 1971.

Karam Singh and Gurtej Singh, "Determinants of Marketing Margins and their Economic Significance," *Journal of Agricultural Marketing,* July, 1971.

Kohls, Richard C., *Marketing of Agricultural Products,* The Macmillan Co., New York, 1961.

Kulkarni, K.R., *Agricultural Marketing in India,* The Co-operator's Book Depot, Bombay, 1950.

Mamoria, C.B. and Joshi, R.L., *Principles and Practices of Marketing in India,* Kitab Mahal, Allahabad, 1975.

Moore, J.R., Johl, S.S., and Khusro, A.M., *Indian Foodgrain Marketing,* Prentice-Hall of India Private Ltd., New Delhi, 1973.

Randive, K.R., *Lectures on Prices Theory,* (Mimeographed), Indian Society of Agricultural Economics, Bombay, 1968.

Rowe, K.L., and Jimerson, H.C., *Communications in Marketing,* McGraw Hill Book Company, New Delhi.

Ruddar Datt & Sundharam, K.P.M., *Indian Economy,* 52nd revised two-colour edition 2006, S. Chand, New Delhi.

Satyal, M.R., and Gill, K.S., "Marketable Surplus and Disposal of Paddy by Bara District Farmers of Nepal," *Journal of Agricultural Marketing,* April, 1977.

Sontakki, C.N., "Role of Regulated Markets in Agricultural Marketing in India," *Indian Journal of Marketing,* Vol. VIII, June, 1978.

Stigler, George J., *The Price Theory,* Macmillan Co., New York, 1966.

Subbarao, K., "Rice Price Behaviour and Public Procurement, An Analysis of the Experience of Andhra Pradesh," *Indian Journal of Agricultural Economics,* July-September, 1978.

Thakur, D.S. and Singh, Nirphal, "Market Supply and Prices of Onion in Ludhiana and Panipat Markets of Punjab and Haryana," *Journal of Agricultural Marketing*, January, 1971.

Tiwari, S.C., "Financing Methods and Practices in Grain Markets of Punjab and Haryana," *Journal of Agricultural Marketing*, January, 1970.

PART IV
Farm Management and Production Economics

20
Introduction to Farm Management

Farm

A farm is the area cultivated by farmer or a group of farmers in common. Size of holding and farm, these terms are used as synonyms. Legally, a farm generally means an area of land under single ownership and devoted to agriculture either to raising crops or for pasture. It may be a one field or many fields.

Management

Management refers to the function of implementing the production plan and making necessary adjustments in the business of farming so that farm business will yield maximum economic returns.

Farm Management

Some eminent farm management authorities defined farm management as follows:

1. **Efferson:** As the science which considers the organization and operation of the farm from the point of view of efficiency and continuous profit.

2. **Warren:** Farm management is the study of the business principles in farming. It may be defined as the science of organization and the management of the farm enterprise for the purpose of securing the greatest continuous profits.

3. Adam: Farm management the subject is the presentation of business and scientific findings in their application to farming for the purpose of indicating the way to greatest continuous profit.

Farm Management: The method of the utilization of sound principles in selection, organization and conduct of an individual farm business for purpose of obtaining the greatest possible profit.

4. Black: These questions can best be considered under the heads of organization, operation, buying and selling and financing. The term farm management is commonly understood to include all four of these.

5. Heady and Jensen: Farm management as the sub-division of economics which considers the allocation of limited resources within the individual farm, is a science of choice and decision-making and thus is a field requiring studied judgement.

From our viewpoints, farm management can be defined as "study of application of business principles in farming for obtaining greatest continuous profit".

Due to modernization of agriculture, farming has become a business and hence business principles must be applied to farming. Similarly, cultivator needs a continuous income which can be obtained from farm if fertility status of the soil is maintained. Fertility status of farm can be maintained through management practices. Thus, cultivator should manage farm in such a way that he will get greatest continuous profit.

Objective of Farm Management

The main objective of modern farmer is to maximise net profit of the farm. Now modern cultivator has several wants which can be satisfied with the help of money, so he tries to obtain maximum cash returns from his farm. For satisfying this main objective various studies are undertaken, as given below:

1. To know which enterprise gives maximum profit.
2. To find out ways and means for increasing the efficiency of farm business so that maximum profit can be achieved.
3. To determine most profitable crop production and livestock raising methods.

4. To study the input-output relationships in agriculture and determine most profitable input-output combination.
5. To study the cost per hectare and per quintal.
6. To evaluate the farm resources and land use.
7. To determine the size of farm this gives maximum per hectare net profit and maximum per hectare return.
8. To examine impact of changes in argil. technology on farm income.
9. To examine relative performance of different kinds of machineries in carrying out different farm operations.
10. To find out ways and means to face risky and uncertainty conditions.

Types of Farming

According to land utilization and farming practices followed, types of farms are as follows:

1. Specialised farm: Specialised farm is one, on which 50 per cent or more receipts are derived from one enterprise, e.g., Sugarcane farms near sugar factories or in canal-irrigated area.

2. Diversified farm: Farm on which no single enterprise contributes more than 50 per cent of the total receipts is called diversified farm. Diversification helps for minimizing risk.

3. Mixed farm: A farm is to be categorised as of the mixed type, at least 10 per cent of its gross income must be contributed by the livestock activities, the upper limit being 49 per cent.

4. Dry farming: Farming in a area where rainfall is 20-25 inches. Yields are very low, such farming is called as dry farming.

System of Farming

The term system of farming is generally referred to the method of agriculture and the type of ownership to land.

1. Co-operative farming: Co-operative farming means a system under which all agricultural operations or part of them are carried out jointly by the farmers on a voluntary basis, each farmer retaining right in his own land. The farmers would pool their land, labour, capital. The land would be treated as one unit and cultivated jointly under the direction of an elected management. A part of the profit would be distributed in proportion to the land contributed by each farmer and the rest of the profit would be distributed in proportion to the wages earned by each farmer.

2. Collective farming: In collective farming, the members of collective surrender their land, livestock and dead stock to the society. The members work together under a management committee elected by them. Such farmers are known as 'kolkhoz' in Russia. Main source of income is 'kolkhoz' and subsidiary income is obtained from owned plot.

3. Capitalistic farming: In such farming land-owner is a capitalist and uses high amount of capital for farming.

4. State farming: Farms are managed by officials of state government. Agricultural workers are paid wages on weekly or monthly basis.

5. Peasant farming: In peasant farming, farmers follow agricultural practices in their own way and are managers and organizers of their farm business.

Scope of Farm Management

Farm management is relatively younger discipline but becoming popular year after year. Agriculture is modernizing and to carry out modern agriculture successfully, knowledge of farm management is useful. The subject of farm management includes:

- (*i*) Farm management research,
- (*ii*) Farm management teaching,
- (*iii*) Farm management extension.

(***i***) **Farm management research:** Year after year new implements are manufactured, new input substitutes are coming in the market, as well as to satisfy desire of cultivator for more income, and farm management research must be continued. It is necessary to develop suitable cropping pattern plan. Thus, farm management research is essential.

(***ii***) **Teaching:** Most of the agricultural graduates directly or indirectly concerned with farm management and hence agril. graduates must be well-trained in farm management. Higher education must be provided to those who are interested.

(***iii***) **Extension:** It is necessary to organise various training camps for farmers, so that they will understand various aspects of farm management. These camps must be continued year after year, because fast developments are taking place in the subject.

Thus, in India scope for farm management is wide and increasing.

Relationship of Farm Management with other Sciences

Social Sciences

Farm management is dependent on several social sciences. Various economic principles are used in farm management, *e.g.*, law of diminishing return, principle of substitution, marginal analysis, etc. Similarly, farm management also depends upon various government decisions such as various ceiling enactments, fixing minimum, and maximum price, etc., and thus politics comes into picture. Certain enterprises are though economic, particular class of cultivator hesitates to cultivate them because of certain psychological and social problems, *e.g.*, maintaining piggery.

Physical and Biological Sciences

Farm management depends upon other branches of agril. science, agricultural chemistry, agril. botany, animal husbandry, agril. engineering, plant pathology, agril. entomology, agronomy. Farm manager must know these subjects as well as should be able to make use of these branches for taking better decisions.

Thus, farm management is related with various subjects.

History of Farm Management

It is observed from various historic records that first man was living as a hunter. Transition took place from hunting stage to keeping animals for milk and mutton purpose. Then stage of crop cultivation with the help of various ordinary tools and implements started. Further man started using various modern tools and implements and started desired production. He started taking various enterprises in combination and now we observe modern agriculture.

However, USA is a pioneer country in the field of scientific farm management. G.A. Pond, Hays, Bross, G.F. Warren, H.C. Taylor these are the pioneer workers in the field of farm management. In India, Prof. P.C. Patil from College of Agriculture, Pune, Punjab Board of Economic Enquiry did pioneering work. Now fast development has been taken place, there are several Universities offering MSc and PhD degree programmes in the subject of farm management.

21
Principles Applied to Farm Management

Several economic and business management principles are applied to farm management. Farm management requires to take several decisions and these various principles help the farm manager to take right decisions. Those principles are as follows:

1. Laws of returns.
   (*a*) diminishing return,
   (*b*) constant return,
   (*c*) increasing return.
2. Law of substitution or principle of least cost combination.
3. Principle of comparative advantage.
4. Principle of equimarginal return or principle of opportunity cost.
5. Principle of combing enterprises.
6. Time decisions in making investments.

1. Laws of Returns

Cultivator uses various inputs for crop production. Returns to these inputs are governed by some principles. These principles can be explained by following example:

Fertilizer is used for getting better crop produce. The input-output relationship given in the table 21.1.

(*a*) **Increasing return:** It is observed from the table 21.1 that total return is increasing at increasing rate from first dose of fertilizer to third dose. Marginal return is also increasing. Such situation prevails at initial level of application of input.

Table 21.1: Relationship between input and output
(Hypothetical data)

Sr. No.	Units of fertilizer (x)	Total product T.P.(y)	Average product A.P.	Profit in ₹ Px = ₹ 10 Py = ₹ 5	Marginal product M.P.	Remarks
1.	1	2.5	2.5	2.5	2.5	Increasing return
2.	2	6	3	10.0	3.5	
3.	3	10	3.3	20.0	4	
4.	4	15	3.8	35.0	5	Constant return
5.	5	20	4	50	5	
6.	6	24	4.0	60	4	Diminishing return
7.	7	27	3.9	65	3	
8.	8	29	3.6	65	2	
9.	9	30	3.3	60	1	
10.	10	30	3.0	50	0	
11.	11	29	2.6	35	–1	Negative return
12.	12	27	2.3	15	–2	

(*b*) **Constant return:** Fourth and fifth doses add same amount of output and this is the situation of constant return. Constant return is frequently observed when no resources are fixed and all are increased together in the same proportion, *e.g.*, if fertility status of five acre farm is same then yield from each acre will be more or less equal. Under, constant return case, each additional input is equally profitable.

(*c*) **Diminishing return:** If other factors of production kept constant and particular factor of production increased, stage comes when each additional dose or input adds less than previous one. It is observed from the table 21.1 that 6th unit of fertilizer add 4 units of output while 7th, 8th, 9th units added 3, 2 and 1 unit of output to the total production respectively. Thus, total output increased but at diminishing rate and hence it is a diminishing return case.

In agriculture this phenomenon is often observed, in case of fertilizer application, yield per acre, milk per cow or weight per poultry bird.

This law is useful in deciding particular level of input use. In case of above example, if prices of output and input are not taken into consideration then that level of input is used where physical production is maximum, *i.e.*, 9th unit of input gives 30 units of output and that is a maximum output. However, cultivator possesses limited capital and he is interested in maximum profit. Assume the price of fertilizer is ₹ 10 per unit and price per unit of output is ₹ 5 then cultivator will get maximum profit by using 8 units of input. Here added cost is equal to added return or in other words, marginal cost is equal to marginal return. Thus, this law is useful in determining level of input use.

2. Law of Substitution

Any produce can be produced by various combinations of inputs. Producer is interested in minimizing the cost for a given level of output. In agriculture: (*i*) bullocks are substituted by tractor, (*ii*) particular quantity of milk can be produced by feeding various feeds. Here cultivator has to decide how; two inputs should be combined to get particular quantity of output. This can be illustrated with the help of example given in table 21.2.

Table 21.2: Least cost combination of input for given output of 50 Qtls. per ha (Hypothetical data)

Combination of inputs for a given output of 50 Q./ha		Changes in doses of inputs		Marginal rate of substitution	Cost of producing 50 Q. of output			
					₹	Price ratio	₹	Price ratio
X_1	X_2	ΔX_1	ΔX_2	$\Delta X_2/\Delta X_1$	$Px_1 = 11$ $Px_2 = 1$	Px_1/Px_2	$Px_1=8$ $Px_2=2$	Px_1/Px_2
(1)	(2)	(3)	(4)	(5)	(6)	(7)	(8)	(9)
0.	40	–	–	–	40	11	80	4
1.	25	1	15	15	36	11	58	4
2.	14	1	11	11	36	11	44	4
3.	8	1	6	6	41	11	40	4
4.	4	1	4	4	48	11	40	4
5.	0	1	4	4	55	11	40	4

Marginal Rate of Substitution

One input substitutes other at different rates. It is observed from the column nos. 3 and 4 that addition of X_1 reduces the use of X_2 in a decreasing rate. Ratio of change in X_2 to change in X_1 is called as marginal rate of substitution, which is given in column no. 5. When cost of using these inputs is worked out, it is observed that ratio of price of X_1 and price of X_2, *i.e.*, Px_1

and Px_2 is called as price ratio (Px_1/Px_2). Under first set of prices, cost is minimum where substitution ratio is equal to the price ratio and this is a minimum or least cost. Thus, under first set of prices cultivator should use 2 units of X_1 and 14 units of X_2 so that cost will be least to produce 50 Qtls. of output.

Under second set of prices, price ratio and substitution ratio are equal at 4 units of X_1 and 4 units of X_2 combination. At this point cost is also minimum.

Thus, principle of least cost combination or factor substitution is useful to cultivators for deciding combination of two inputs which are substitutes for each other, but their market prices are different.

3. Principle of Comparative Advantage

Particular region is more suitable for a particular crop than other crop. Soil, climate varies from region to region and it is more suited to one crop than other crop.

Absolute Advantage

The absolute advantage refers to the regional comparisons and comparative advantage refers to the comparison between crops. Example given in table 21.3 will clarify this principle.

Table 21.3: Wheat grown in two regions

	Region A ₹	Region B ₹
Total income	200.00	150.0
Total expenses	170.00	140.0
Net return	30.00	10.0
Return per rupee	1.18	1.07
Per cent return	118	107

It is observed from the table 21.3 that region A has absolute advantage in wheat because return per rupee is higher in region A than region B.

It is observed from the table 21.4 that region B has absolute advantage in sugarcane. If wheat and sugarcane are compared in region B, then it is observed, that sugarcane pays more than wheat and thus comparatively sugarcane is advantageous than wheat in region B. Thus, whole region B should be specialised in sugarcane crop. Thus, particular region is specialised in a particular crop, because of absolute and comparative advantage.

Table 21.4: Crop—Sugarcane grown in two regions

	Region A ₹	Region B ₹
Total income	400.0	600.0
Total expenses	190.0	200.0
Net return	210.0	400.0
Return per rupee	2.10	3.0
Per cent return	210	300

4. Principle of Equimarginal Return or Principle of Opportunity Cost

Cultivator has limited capital and his main objective is to maximise net profit. He is having several alternatives for investing this amount. He should spend the amount, in such a way that he will get maximum profit. This can be achieved by using the principle of equimarginal returns. This principle can be illustrated with the help of following example. Suppose, farmer is having ₹ 50,000 for investment. His locality is favourable to take crop enterprise, dairy enterprise and poultry enterprise.

It is observed from table 21.5 that, when all amount was invested in anyone enterprise net profit from crop enterprise, dairy enterprise and poultry enterprise is obtained as ₹ 26,000, ₹ 22,000, and ₹ 28,000 respectively. However, if the same amount is spent according to principle of equimarginal returns, total net profit will be as shown in table 21.6.

Table 21.5: Marginal return to capital on three enterprises

	Amount of capital used in ₹	Marginal return in ₹		
		Crop	Dairy	Poultry
First	10,000	20,000	19,000	21,000
Second	10,000	19,000	18,000	19,000
Third	10,000	15,000	15,000	15,000
Fourth	10,000	12,000	11,000	12,000
Fifth	10,000	10,000	9,000	11,000
Total returns from ₹	50,000	76,000	72,000	78,000
Net profit ₹		26,000	22,000	28,000

Table 21.6: Investment according to principle of equimarginal return

	Amount	Enterprise	Marginal Return
First	10,000	Poultry	21,000
Second	10,000	Crop	20,000
Third	10,000	Crop	19,000
Fourth	10,000	Dairy	19,000
Fifth	10,000	Poultry	19,000
Total returns from ₹	50,000		98,000
Net profit ₹			48,000

It is observed from table 21.6, cultivator is getting total net profit of ₹ 48,000 which is quite more than profit from any single enterprise. Thus, for maximum net profit cultivator should invest ₹ 20,000 in crop enterprise, ₹ 20,000 in poultry enterprise, and ₹ 10,000 in dairy enterprise.

It is observed from table 21.6 that marginal returns from all the three enterprises are equal, *i.e.*, ₹ 19,000. Thus, it can be stated that amount should be invested in such a way that marginal returns should be more or less equal in all the alternatives.

Opportunity Cost

In agriculture, resources are limited and have alternative uses. When resource is put to one use opportunities of other alternatives are lost. Opportunity cost refers to the value of the next best alternative foregone. It can be explained from example which is given in table 21.5. First 10,000 were invested in poultry losing ₹ 20,000 from crop enterprise as a next best alternative to first ₹ 10,000. In another example, cultivator is getting ₹ 300 by spending ₹ 100 for feeding poultry feed to poultry birds. If he spent same ₹ 100 for feeding concentrates to dairy cows he will get additional ₹ 200. Now, cultivator will forgo ₹ 200 and will spend ₹ 100 for poultry feed and will obtain ₹ 300. Thus, opportunity cost of feeding poultry birds and obtaining ₹ 300 or spending ₹ 100 for poultry is ₹ 200.

5. Principle of Combining Enterprises

Farmer is always confronted with a problem of selection of enterprises and deciding about level of combination of these enterprises. For taking this decision, this principle is useful. Enterprises have anyone or combinations of the following relationships:

(*i*) Independent enterprises,
(*ii*) Complementary enterprises,
(*iii*) Supplementary enterprises,
(*iv*) Competitive enterprises,
(*v*) Joint enterprises.

(*i*) **Independent enterprises:** Here each enterprise is independent. Increase or decrease of anyone enterprise does not affect the other enterprises, *e.g.*, Dairy and Beekeeping or nursery raising.

(*ii*) **Complementary enterprises:** Here two enterprises help for the development of each other. Expansion of one enterprise helps for another enterprise. This is known as complementarity of enterprises. Dairy enterprise and crop enterprise are complementary to each other. By-product of dairy enterprise, *i.e.*, compost is useful for crop enterprise and fodder produced in crop enterprise is useful for dairy. Thus, both the enterprises help each other. Initially, they are complementary, but later on they became competitive. When they are complementary producer need not worry about prices and should go on producing but when they will become competitive decision should be taken like that in competitive enterprises.

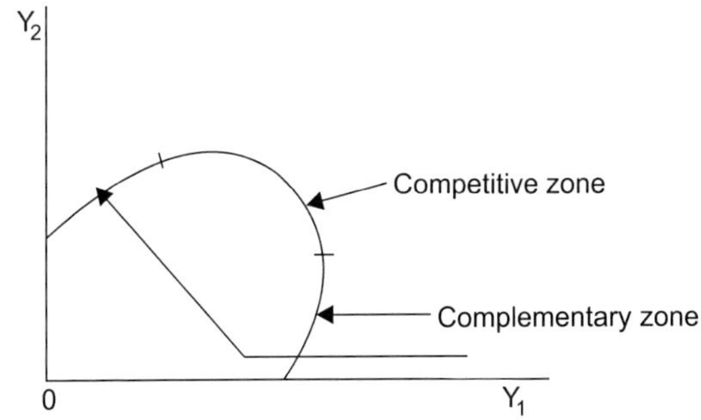

Fig. 21.1: Complementary enterprises

(*iii*) **Supplementary enterprises:** Two enterprises are said to be supplementary when an increase in the level of one does not adversely affect the production of the other but adds to the total income of the farm, *e.g.*, poultry enterprise and crop enterprise. Supplementary enterprises also become competitive at advanced stage and then decision should be taken like that in competitive enterprises. Supplementary enterprises should be developed till resources allow.

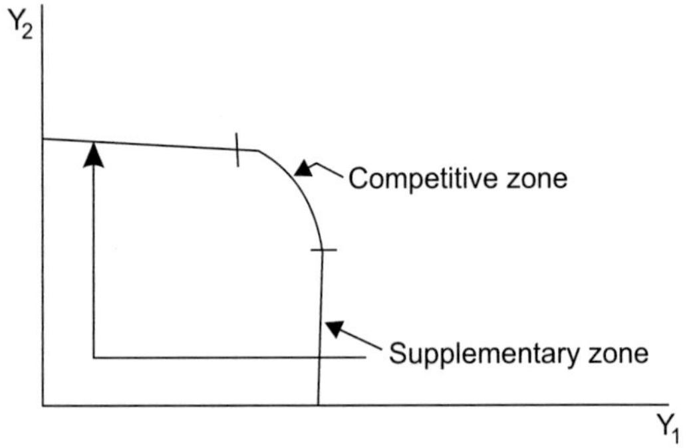

Fig. 21.2: Supplementary enterprises

(*iv*) **Competitive enterprises:** There are several enterprises competing for the resources and hence those enterprises are called as competitive enterprises. Under such situation profit will be maximum when price ratio is equal to substitution ratio and this has been explained under the principle of substitution.

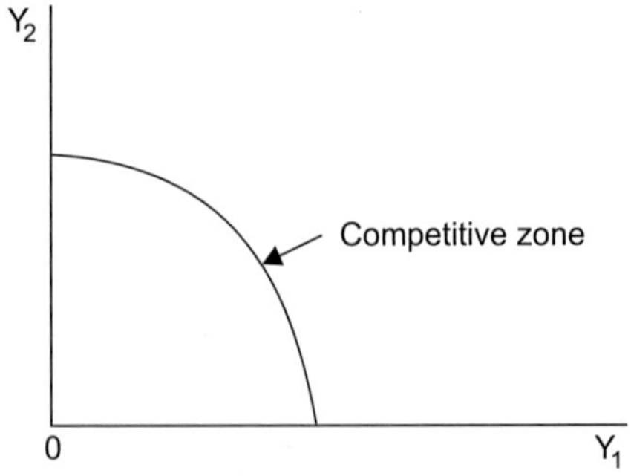

Fig. 21.3: Competitive enterprises

Thus, combining two or more enterprises depend upon the type of relationship they possess. If they have complementary or supplementary relationship one should go on expanding the enterprises till they become competitive and in case of competitive enterprises decision should be taken as price ratio should be equal to substitution ratio.

5. Joint enterprises: Joint enterprises or joint products are those which are produced together *e.g.*, cotton and cotton seeds, beef and hides, wheat and straw, mutton and wool, cattle and manure, etc. The quantity of one product produced decides the quantity of other product. Both the product should treat as one. When one becomes more costly than the other, *e.g.*, more cotton is needed than cotton seed. Such varieties can be developed with the help of research and after developing a desired variety, proportion of the two joint products again becomes constant.

6. Time Decisions in Making Investments

To do a particular thing at a particular time it is self-advantageous. Cultivator many times, faces a problem whether to invest a large sum of money now or should be invested smaller sums in future. Basically, capital cannot be obtained freely one has to pay interest for it. Following examples will illustrate this principle.

Cultivator has to construct a shed for electric motor. He has a choice to construct one, which can last for 20 years, costing ₹ 10,000 and another that would last for five years, costing ₹ 3,000 and another one lasting for 15 years costing ₹ 8,000. What type of electric motor shed he should construct? Here, he can construct two sheds one after another which will cost ₹ 3,000 and ₹ 8,000. Suppose, he constructed first for five years by spending ₹ 5,000 and for another 15 years, he has to spend ₹ 5,000 at the end of 5th year. It is necessary to work out present value of ₹ 8,000 if interest rate is ₹ 10 per cent.

$$\text{Present value (PV)} = \frac{8{,}000}{\left(1+\frac{10}{100}\right)^5}$$

$$= \frac{8{,}000}{(1.1)^5}$$

$$= 8{,}000 \times \left(\frac{10}{11}\right)^5$$

$$\begin{aligned}\log PV &= \log 8{,}000 + 5\ (\log 10 - \log 11)\\ &= 3.9031 + 5(1.0 - 1.0414)\\ &= 3.9031 - 0.2070\\ &= 3.6961\\ \text{Antilog} &= 4{,}967\end{aligned}$$

Present value of ₹ 8,000 is ₹ 4,967 and initial ₹ 3,000. Thus, total requirement is ₹ 7,967. Another alternative is, if he constructed shed by spending ₹ 8,000 then present value of ₹ 3,000 should be found out.

$$PV = \frac{3{,}000}{\left(1+\frac{10}{100}\right)^5}$$

$$\begin{aligned}\text{Log } PV &= \log 3{,}000 + 15 \log (1.0 - 1.0414)\\ &= 3.4771 - 0.6225\\ &= 2.8546\\ \text{Antilog} &= 715.5\end{aligned}$$

Thus, he has to spend ₹ 8,716 (8,000 + 716) second alternative is costlier than first one. Hence, cultivator should first construct an electric motor shed first for five years and then another shed at the end of 5th year by spending ₹ 8,000. This is a right thing to do. Thus, cultivator has to take investment decision carefully taking into consideration rate of interest and time of investment.

22
Costs

Cost in general refers to the expenses incurred on inputs. Costs are important to decide about production level. There are two approaches: (*i*) Maximization of returns, (*ii*) Maximization of costs. Various costs are considered in relation with planning period. Planning period refers to period in which decisions regarding production are made.

1. Short period: It is a period of time which is long enough to permit desired changes in output without altering or changing the size of the plant or size of the farm. During a short period, it is not possible to change the size of farm and hence, output level can be changed by manipulating some other inputs, *e.g.*, use of fertilizer can be changed during short run but size of farm cannot be changed during short run.

2. Long period: The long period is generally the period which is sufficiently long for output level to be altered or changed by varying even the size of the plant, *e.g.*, for producing more wheat in long run more area can be brought under cultivation. There are two categories of costs:

(*a*) *Fixed costs*: A cost referred to fixed resource is a fixed cost. Fixed resource means a resource which can be utilised in a production process again and again. There are two types of fixed resources cash and non-cash, *e.g.*, land taxes, interest, insurance premiums, annually hired labourer, these are the examples of fixed cash costs and depreciation on buildings, machinery, equipment are the non-cash costs.

(*b*) *Variable costs:* Variable costs refer to cost of inputs which are completely exhausted in production process, *e.g.*, fertilizers, insecticides, fuel consumption, etc.

Table 22.1: Production and cost relationships

Inputs units x	Total output units y	Average product units AP	Marginal product units MP	Total variable cost TVC (₹ 10 per unit)	Total fixed cost TFC in ₹	Total cost TVC + TFC in ₹	Average variable cost TVC/Y	Average fixed cost TFC/Y	Average total cost TC/Y	Change in output ΔY	Change in costs ΔTVC	Marginal cost Δ TVC/Δ
1	2	3	4	5	6	7	8	9	10	11	12	13
0.	—	—	—	—	20	20	—	—	—	—	—	—
1.	2.5	2.5	2.5	10	20	30	4.0	8.0	12.0	2.5	10	4.0
2.	6	3.0	3.5	20	20	40	3.3	3.3	6.7	3.5	10	2.9
3.	10	3.3	4	30	20	50	3.0	3.0	5.0	4.0	10	2.5
4.	15	3.8	5	40	20	60	2.7	1.3	4.0	5	10	2.0
5.	20	4.0	5	50	20	70	2.5	1.0	3.5	5	10	2.0
6.	24	4.0	4	60	20	80	2.5	0.8	3.3	4	10	2.5
7.	27	3.9	3	70	20	90	2.6	0.7	3.3	3	10	3.3
8.	29	3.6	2	80	20	100	3.0	0.7	3.5	2	10	5.0
9.	30	3.3	1	90	20	110	3.0	0.7	3.7	1	10	10.0
10.	30	3.0	0	100	20	120	3.3	0.7	4.0	0	10	—
11.	29	2.6	-1	110	20	130	3.8	0.7	4.5	-1	10	—
12.	27	2.3	-2	120	20	140	4.4	0.7	5.2	-2	10	—

Cost Function

Costs and production are functionally related, C = f (Y). We understand that what will happen to costs at different levels of production. These cost functions or curves can also be presented in three ways: (*i*) Arithmetically (tabular form), (*ii*) Geometrically (graphic form), (*iii*) Algebraically (in equation form).

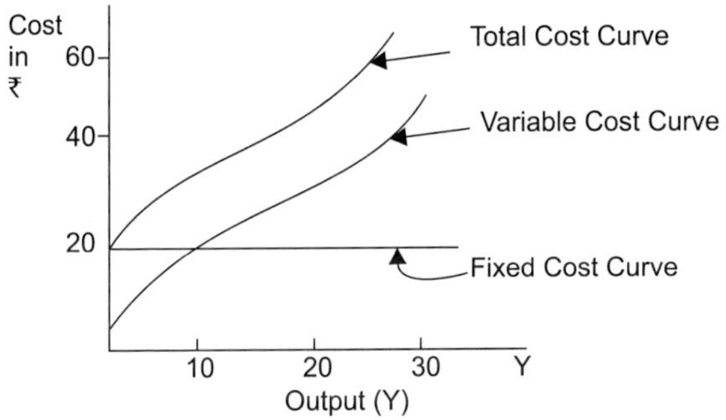

Fig. 22.1: Total cost curves

In figure 22.1 total cost curve, total variable cost curve and total fixed cost curve are indicated.

Costs are classified as follows:

Fixed cost, variable cost, total costs, average variable cost, average fixed cost, average total costs and marginal cost.

Total Cost

Total costs are the sum of total variable costs and total fixed costs. They are presented in column 7 of the table 22.1 and obtained by adding TFC and TVC. Total cost goes on increasing according to production level.

Average Variable Costs

Average variable cost is shown in column 8 of the table 22.1, it goes on decreasing and crosses to marginal cost curve at the end of the first stage. Average cost is reduced initially because of economy due to large scale production and increases at advance stage, because of law of diminishing returns.

Average Fixed Cost

Average fixed cost is indicated in column 9. At initial level of production, it is quite high and later on decreases because of its distribution on more units of output. In case of fixed cost, producer has to bear it even if production is stopped.

Average Total Cost

Average total cost is a sum of average fixed cost and average variable cost and gives idea about total expenses incurred for producing a one unit of output. For finding out profit from total return, it is necessary to know total cost of production and it can be worked out by multiplying total production units by average total cost.

Marginal Cost and Profit Maximization

It is necessary to know marginal cost at various production levels. It is shown in the column 13. Marginal cost means cost incurred for producing additional unit of output. Initially, marginal cost goes on diminishing and at advance stage goes on increasing. This happens because of economics of large-scale production and at advanced stage law of diminishing return operates. Marginal cost and marginal return are indicators to show at what level profit will be maximum. Profit will be maximum when marginal return is a price of output which is ₹ 5 and marginal cost is ₹ 5 at 8th unit of input where production is 29 units. At this level of input use, he will get maximum profit. Marginal cost and average variable cost curves cross each other at the end of first stage of production. As well as marginal cost is highest at the end of second stage of production. This is observed in figure 22.2, Marginal cost curve and average revenue line (existing price) cross each other at point B. Rectangular ABDE shows total return. Rectangle FCDE shows total cost and rectangle ABCF shows profit.

Minimum Loss Principle

In agriculture several occasions come when cultivator faces a problem whether to continue farm business or not, *e.g.*, Prices of crop are so low that profit is not possible. Under such situation

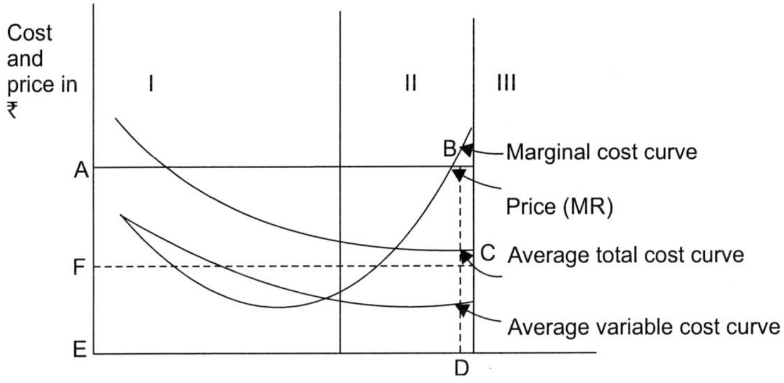

Fig. 22.2: Average cost curves and profit maximization

cultivator has to decide whether to continue farming or not. This will be clear from figure 22.3.

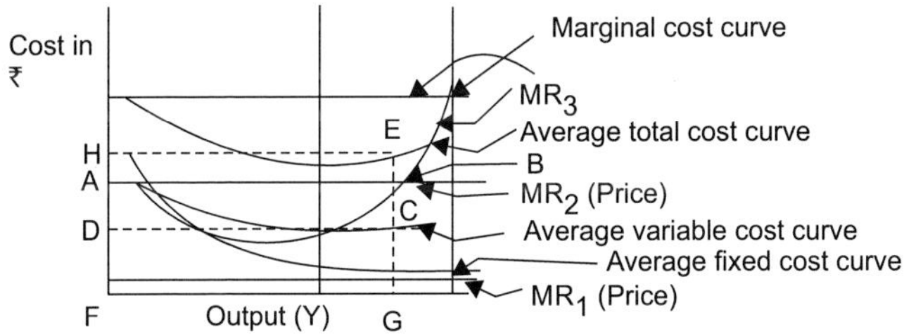

Fig. 22.3: Minimizations of loss

When price of output is at MR_3, cultivator will get profit and he needs not worry about stopping the production. When price is at MR_2, cultivator is getting total return ABGF and total cost at this point is HEGF. This means cultivator is in loss, but he is recovering part of fixed cost. Total fixed cost is HECD but he is recovering ABCD by continuing production and thus he is minimising his loss by continuing production. Cultivator is getting variable cost and part of fixed cost and that is why he should continue production for minimizing loss. If price is at MR_1 then he is not able to get variable cost also and under such situation it is wise to stop production. When prices are low this principle will guide cultivator whether to continue production or not.

Cost of Cultivation of a Crop

Government wanted to know what is the cost of cultivation of a particular crop for fixing the procurement price. Recently, various state governments appointed personnel to collect data on cost of cultivation of important crops by cost accounting method. The concepts for working out cost of cultivation have been fairly-standardized and those are as below:

Cost A

Cost A includes expenses on following items: (*i*) Hired labour, male, female, bullock, (*ii*) Seeds, (*iii*) Manures, (*iv*) Fertilizers, (*v*) Pesticides, (*vi*) Depreciation, (*vii*) Land revenue and other cesses, (*viii*) Interest on working capital, (*ix*) Rent paid on leased land, (*x*) Irrigation charges, (*xi*) Artisan's charges if any.

Cost B

Cost B includes cost A plus interest on fixed capital, plus rental value of land, amortization value.

Cost C

Cost C includes Cost B, plus imputed value of family labour (male and female), supervision charges, *i.e.*, 10 per cent of cost A.

This cost concepts are explained with the help of example which is given in table 22.2.

It is observed from table 22.2 that cost per quintal is ₹ 1,452.86 and prevailing market price is ₹ 1,600 per Qtl. The net returns at cost A, B and C are ₹ 17,006.75, ₹ 8,969 and ₹ 2,708.92. Benefit cost ratio is worked out at cost C level is 1.10, this indicates farmers get 10 per cent return on his all types of investment in groundnut crop, supervision charges which are 10% of cost A are also included.

Per hectare cost A is ₹ 13,968.25, cost B is ₹ 22,012.00 and Cost C is ₹ 28,266.08. Profit at cost C level indicates returns to farmer as an owner of a farm for his risk-bearing, *i.e.*, for his management. Profit at cost B level is a returns to family labourers and to farmer. Profit at cost A level is a returns to farmer, family labourers, fixed capital and to land.

Table 22.2: Per hectare cost of cultivation of Rabi groundnut in Sindhudurg district (2003-2004)
Variety: *Konkan Gourav*

Item of cost	Quantity/Unit	Rate (₹)	Amount (₹)
Hired human labour			
(*i*) Male	35.20 days	55.00	1,936.00
(*ii*) Female	38.45 days	30.00	1,153.50
Bullock labour	18.00 pair/days	100.00	1,800.00
Seed material	100.00 kg	40.00	4,000.00
FYM/Compost	15.00 C.L.	120.00	1,800.00
Fertilizers			
Urea	55.00 kg	4.76	261.80
SSP	313.00 kg	2.98	932.74
MOP	—	—	—
Irrigation charges	—	—	500.00
Pesticides	—	—	450.00
Total			**12,834.04**
Depreciation on implements and Machines		—	250.00
Land revenue and other cesses	—	—	50.00
Interest on working capital @ 13% for 6 months	—	—	834.21
Cost A			**13,968.25**
Interest on fixed capital @ 10%	—	—	300.00
Rental value of land (1/4th of the gross value of produce)	—	—	7743.75
Cost B			**22,012.00**
Family labour			
(*i*) Male	48.25 days	55.00	2,653.75
(*ii*) Female	73.45 days	30.00	2,203.50
Supervision charges	—	—	1,396.83
Cost C			**28,266.08**
Yield and value of			
(*i*) Main product (pods)	18.41 Qt.	1600.00	29,456.00
(*ii*) By product (Stover)	30.38 Qt.	50.00	1,519.00
Total			**30,975.00**
Net returns at			
(*i*) Cost A			17,006.75
(*ii*) Cost B			8,963.00
(*iii*) Cost C			2,708.92
Cost benefit ratio			1.10
Cost per Quintal			1,452.86

Estimation and Apportionment of Cost

Farmer spends in general for a whole farm. When he wanted to work profitability of each crop, he has to apportion these costs for all crops. Most of the expenditure is carried out separately but there are few items on which expenditure is made jointly and problem of apportionment arises. In case of hired labour prevailing hiring rates are taken into consideration. For seeds, manures, fertilizers and pesticides actual quantity used for particular crop and actual amount spent is taken into account. In case of depreciation, total depreciation for a farm in a year is estimated generally by straight line method. Then it is found out for a hectare and finally duration of crop is taken into consideration while finalising amount of per hectare depreciation for a particular crop. In case of land value and other cesses, per hectare amount is found out and then for a particular crop; duration of crop is taken into account. For finding out interest on working capital, depreciation should be deducted from cost A and on remaining amount interest should be worked out as per bank interest rate. Interest on working capital is to be worked out at bank interest rate and should be apportioned taking into account area under crop and duration of the crop. In case of rental value of land some research worker takes of the gross value of produce (yield) or prevailing rental charges can be taken into account. For finding out imputed value of family labour, prevailing labour wage rate should be taken into account. Yield is evaluated at prevailing market prices.

23
Farm Planning and Budgeting

All businessmen plan their business, whether it is a small shop of a big firm, they plan their businesses. Their financial success depends upon their careful planning. Farming has been modernised during recent years. It has become as good as business. Success of the farming depends upon its planning.

Farm Planning

Farm planning includes the adoption of business methods in every phase of farm activity. Farmer has to make proper adjustment of his capital. It is conscientious effort on the part of the farmer to think about the farm programmes in advance and adjust them according to the new knowledge on technological developments, changes in physical and economic situations and prices. Thus, farmer takes advantage of technological development, changes in prices, natural resources such as rainfall etc., and takes best decision to achieve maximum profit. Improved planning comprises careful decisions based on logical considerations and hence those decisions must be written down in a simple but in a organised way.

Advantages of Farm Planning

1. *Increase in income*: Because of making desirable changes in resource use, income can be increased. It has been practically observed, that careful farm plans have increased the farm income.

2. *Viable unit*: Farm planning increases viability of the farm. Some fixed resources are also developed, *e.g.*, well for irrigation,

land improvement helps the farmers to develop a viable farm unit.

3. Farm planning demand that cultivator should collect information regarding various alternative methods and practices which might be useful to him in his farming business.

4. Farm planning helps cultivator to find out his credit needs so that cultivator can arrange in advance for credit.

Characteristics of Good Farm Plan

What characteristics of good farm plan should possess depends upon conditions under which that plan can be used for execution. Under Indian conditions good farm plan should possess following characteristics:

1. Plan should utilise knowledge, training and experience of farmer his likes and dislikes should be ignored.
2. Plan should take into account available marketing facilities.
3. Plan should give consideration for credit facilities programme should be made for use of credit as well as for its repayment.
4. Plan should provide flexibility, so that changes can be made according to sudden changes in climate and prices.
5. Plan should not include many enterprises involving greater risks. Risks should be minimized.
6. Plan should be such that it should give maximum profit to cultivator from his available resources.

Long-term Farm Planning

Long-term investment plays important role in agricultural development. Hence, cultivator should provide sufficient attention for long-term planning. Long-term Refers to a period more than a year. Several decisions are long-term decisions. Generally, farmer requires taking long-term decisions in following cases:

1. Land improvement,
2. Irrigation facilities,
3. Farm steads,

4. Livestock development,
5. Purchasing machineries.

1. Land improvement: Planning for land improvement involved long-term investment and hence farmer has to take credit from land development bank or from commercial bank. He should estimate probable future yields after land improvement and should plan repaying of credit. Depending upon past experience and expected future income, he has to decide about his own saving for long-term expenditure. Changes may be made in decision depending upon changing circumstances.

2. Irrigation facilities: For achieving full benefits of modern agriculture well-developed irrigation facilities are essential. For creating irrigation facility, farmer can dig a well or tube well. Farmer has to consider how much land can be irrigated by digging a well. Whether it will be economical to dig a well? How much income can be increased due to well irrigation? Such questions require considerations. Cultivator has to decide repayment of loan also. If location for digging a well is scientifically selected, then risk of non-availability of water after digging is minimized.

3. Farm steads: Farm steads (houses on farm) are important on the point of view of protecting farm produce and also farm inputs. However, cultivator does not get direct income from them and hence only necessary building should be constructed. Excess expenditure in farm steads is not desirable.

4. Livestock development: Dairy enterprise is a complementary enterprise to crop enterprise as well as provides additional income to cultivator. Returns are spread over for number of years and large investment is necessary. However, finance is available from commercial and co-operative banks. Cultivator should plan for development of his dairy enterprise for next few years.

5. Purchasing machineries: Several farm operations have become cheaper because of use of modern machines. Machines can be useful for number of years and cultivator should give consideration in advance for purchasing machines. Cultivator can get finance from bank for purchasing machinery.

Short-term Farm Planning

Short-term planning refers to period required for growing crop. Generally, one agricultural year is taken into consideration. Short-term decisions are important because cultivator has to bear its consequences immediately. He requires planning several things:

1. Allocation of land under different crops,
2. Labour use planning,
3. Satisfying immediate credit needs of farm and arranging for its repayment.

Several tools are available for farm planning:

1. Farm budgeting technique,
2. Linear programming,
3. Non-linear programming,
4. Operational research technique,
5. Dynamic programming,
6. Integer programming,
7. Recursive programming,
8. Production function models, and
9. Game theory models. We will examine few of them.

Farm Budgeting

Farm budgeting is a process of estimating costs, returns and net profit on farm. How much resource should be used for a particular enterprise is governed by marginal analysis. First farm plan is prepared and when such farm plan is expressed in monetary terms by estimating costs, returns and net profit. It is called as farm budgeting.

There are two types of budgeting, several cultivators use this technique, which is simple one.

1. Partial Budgeting: Partial budgeting refers to estimating the returns for a part of business, *i.e.*, one or few activities. When farmer wants to introduce new activity on farm he tries to see its profitability over existing activity and this can be done by partial budgeting. Following example will clarify the meaning of partial budgeting. Cultivator wants to decide whether it will be profitable to shift from local paddy variety to improved variety.

Table 23.1: Comparative study of local and improved paddy variety

Item	Local variety		Improved variety	
	Quantity	Value in ₹	Quantity	Value in ₹
Seed	10 kg.	100	10 kg.	120
Fertilizers				
N	25 kg.	104	40 kg.	1,664
P	16 kg.	54	25 kg.	85
Plant protection	—	100	—	120
Labour (day)	95	4,465	113	5,311
Total		4,723		7,300
Interest on Working capital		236		365
		4,959		7,665
Production	10 Qtl.	6,000 (@ 600 ₹ per Qtl.)	20 Qtl.	11,600 (@580 per Qtl.)
Gross profit		1,041		3,935

If cultivator cultivated improved variety, he will get additional ₹ 2,894 (3,935 – 1,041). It is profitable to grow improved variety of paddy. Thus, partial budgeting helps cultivator to understand superiority of improved technique.

2. Complete Budgeting: Above we have seen consideration of only one activity. When farmer workout alternative plan for all activities on farm and reorganizes his resource utilization for maximum profit. It is called as complete budgeting. Complete budgeting considers all the crops livestock producing methods, and estimates costs and returns are found out for the farm as a whole.

24
Valuation and Depreciation

To know the total value of the resources, valuation is necessary. Different resources are valued by different methods.

1. Land

Several times land transactions occur as well as cultivator requires to know what is the value of his land for providing it as a security for obtaining credit. Land is evaluated by following methods:

1. Income capitalization method
2. Rent capitalization method
3. Prevailing market price.

1. Income capitalization method: Income is capitalised to know the value of land. Suppose cultivator is getting net income of ₹ 5,000 per acre and prevailing interest rate is 10% then value of land will be worked out as follows:

$$V = \frac{5{,}000 \times 100}{10} = ₹\ 50{,}000$$

Here, income is treated as total interest amount and to get total interest of ₹ 5,000, cultivator will require capital of ₹ 50,000, thus, per acre land value is ₹ 50,000.

2. Rent capitalization method: Rent of land depends upon soil fertility, availability of other inputs and labourers in the vicinity of land, *i.e.*, capacity of land to provide income. The land which gives better income will be having more rent. Following example will illustrate the meaning. If per acre rent of land is ₹ 6,000 and rate of interest is ₹ 10%. Then land value will be worked out as follows:

$$V = \frac{6{,}000 \times 100}{10} = ₹\ 60{,}000$$

the land value is ₹ 60,000 per acre.

3. **Prevailing market price:** Land transaction always occurs in locality and the prevailing market price is taken for evaluating the land. Thus, there are various methods exist for evaluating the land.

2. Land Improvement

The land improvement is reflected in the land value but if separately land improvement is required to be evaluated. Then actual cost required is taken into consideration.

3. Farm Building, Fencing, Wells

If farm buildings, fences, wells are not taken into consideration while evaluating land, then those are evaluated at market value. A part of dwelling house used for agricultural purpose, be considered in farm buildings. Farm building, *i.e.*, cattle shed, grain stores, wells, etc., are evaluated as per market rate.

4. Livestock

Farm animals are evaluated as per current market prices. For newly-purchased animal, same price is taken into consideration.

5. Implements (Wooden and Iron)

The present market value of similar type of new implement is ascertained as if constructed or purchased and from this value the depreciation calculated for number of years of the age of the implement will be deducted to find out value of the implement.

6. Machinery

The valuation of machinery like oil engines, etc., will be done at original value less the depreciation calculated for the years of the age of machinery.

7. Stock of Farm Produce

Stock of farm produce is evaluated at harvest prices (three months from harvest). Prevailing price of produce and of by product at the time of harvest is taken into consideration.

8. Standing Crops

Valued at cost of raising the crop to its present stage.

9. Farm Requisites Purchased

To be evaluated at purchase price and transport charges should be added.

Depreciation

Depreciation means decline the value of a given asset as a result of the use, wear and tear or due to any other cause, certain inputs are used only once but some capital assets are used again and again in the production process. Because of use its value is diminished. There are various methods of calculating depreciation.

1. Straight Line Method

In this method uniform amount is deducted, every year from the value of assets, till its value reaches to zero, *e.g.*, implement is purchased for ₹ 200, its life span is 10 years, then every year $\frac{200}{10}$ = ₹ 20 are deducted from ₹ 200. Thus, within 10 years its value will be zero.

However, some assets always possess some value at the end of expected life, such value is called as junk value. Junk value is deducted from original value. While finding out per year depreciation value, *e.g.*, value of the tractor is ₹ 50,000 its junk value is ₹ 5,000, expected life is 10 years then depreciation will be worked out as follows:

$$\text{Depreciation} = \frac{50{,}000 - 5{,}000}{10} = \frac{45{,}000}{10}$$

$$= ₹\ 4{,}500$$

2. Diminishing Value Method

Sometimes it is logical to depreciate the asset in larger proportion during initial years and in such cases this method is used. For example, if an asset is worth ₹ 2,000 and expected life is 10 years then at the end of first year value will be (2,000 – 200) = ₹ 1,800. Then again 10 per cent depreciation in second year, *i.e.*, 10 per cent of 1,800. Value at the end of second year will be ₹ 1,620 (1,800 – 180) and this will be continued till that particular asset is in use.

3. Revaluation Method

In this method, asset is valued at the end of each year and this value is used to decide depreciation or appreciation. If current year's value is more than previous year's value then it is an appreciation and if it is less, it is a depreciation. This method is useful for evaluating animals. Animals are appreciated during initial years and later on straight line method should be used, *e.g.*, the total age of draught animal is assumed 13 years. Its value is appreciated during initial three years in proportion to 1 : 3 : 5 and is constant up to five years. Then depreciated thereafter up to the age of 13 years at the rate of 12 per cent per animal in a straight line method. The appreciation and depreciation calculated on this basis is illustrated below for different ages.

Age in years	₹
1	1,000
2	3,000
3	5,000
4	5,000
5	5,000
6	4,400
7	3,872
8	3,407
9	2,998
10	2,638
11	2,321
12	2,042
13	1,797

Straight line method is easy to understand and calculations are easy. Hence, this method is widely used. Below we will examine how depreciation is worked out in various cases.

1. Land: There is no depreciation on land, but land improvement such as buildings, drainage is subject to depreciation, 7 per cent depreciation may be charged on embankments.

2. Buildings:

(*a*) Pucca buildings (substantial) 2 per cent

(*b*) Less substantial 5 per cent

(*c*) Temporary buildings. 10 per cent

Similar rate of depreciation should also be charged for wells.

3. Implements:

(*a*) *Wooden*: The rate of depreciation to be applied to old implements which are evaluated at the time of inventory will be calculated by dividing the value of similar new implements by the estimated life of the implements.

(*b*) The annual depreciation will be calculated as original value less junk value divided by life of implement.

(*c*) *Machinery*: The annual depreciation will be calculated as original value minus junk value divided by the expected life period, (*i.e.*, 10 years in case of oil engines and seven years in case of tractors).

Sickles, baskets, ropes, etc., which wear out completely in about a year, their complete cost should be included in first year.

Depreciation rate on the value of implements:

1.	Bullock cart	10 per cent
2.	Fodder cutter	20 per cent
3.	Cane crusher	10 per cent
4.	Jaggery boiling pan	10 per cent
5.	Improved plough	10 per cent

25
Efficiency Indicators

Objective of the farmer is to maximise net profit. The objective can be fulfilled if all factors of production are used efficiently. To know in what way different factors of production are used, efficiency indicators are developed. Method of production is said to be more efficient than the other when it yields a greater valuable output per unit of a valuable input. Those inputs which not efficiently used may be used efficiently so that maximum profit is obtained. There are following types of efficiency indicators:

1. Land or production efficiency indicators,
2. Labour efficiency indicators,
3. Capital efficiency indicators,
4. Farm income and profit efficiency indicators.

1. Land or Production Efficiency Indicators

It is necessary to know whether land is efficiently used or not. It can be known by studying following indicators:

(*i*) **Intensity of cropping:** This is a widely used measure. It measures the extent of the use of land for cropping purposes during a given year. It is expressed as below:

$$\text{Cropping intensity} = \frac{\text{Area cropped}}{\text{Total cultivated area}} \times 100$$

More the cropping intensity better it is. When cropping intensity is 200 that means two crops are grown in a year.

(*ii*) **Yield per acre:** It is also a production efficiency indicator. If yield per acre is more on a particular land that land is more efficient than low yielding land. Average yield of locality is also taken into consideration.

Paddy yield per acre of a farm is 35 Q. per hectare.

Average yield of locality is 25 Q. per hectare.

Production efficiency of a farm 'Y'

$$= \frac{35 \times 100}{25} = 140\%$$

(*iii*) **Crop yield index:** This index is worked out for all crops for comparison of the yields of all crops on a given farm with the average yields of these crops in the locality.

Table 25.1: Crops Yield Index

Crop	Per hectare yield in quintals		Area under crop	Crop yield on farm as % of locality yields	Per cent multiplied by acres	Crop yield index
	Locality	Farm Y				
(1)	(2)	(3)	(4)	(5)*	(6)*	
Paddy	25	35	2	140	280	
Vegetables	10	15	1	150	150	143%
Total			3		430	

$$^{*}\text{Col. } 5 = \frac{\text{Col. } 3}{\text{Col. } 2} \times \frac{100}{1}$$

*Col. 6 = Col. 5 × Col. 4

$$\text{Crop yield index} = \frac{430}{3} = 143\%$$

2. Labour Efficiency Indicators

Labour efficiency in farm business refers to the amount of productive work completed per man on the farm per unit of time. If labourers are efficient, farm business can be profitable one. Efficiency of labour depends upon following things:

(*i*) Physical condition of labour, healthy labourer can contribute more than unhealthy labourer.

(*ii*) Interest with which he works. If labour takes interest in his work, he can do well otherwise there will be many errors in his work.

(*iii*) Climatic condition under which he works.

Labour Efficiency Indicators are as follows:

(*i*) Return per family labour day:

If return per family Labour Day is to be worked out following formula can be used.

(*ii*) Return per worker:

Output minus cost of input

$$= \frac{\text{Factors other than human labour}}{\text{Total number of workers}}$$

(*iii*) In USA and in other countries where labour is scarce factor, the efficiency of labour is judged by:

(*a*) Number of hectares of crop per labour.

(*b*) Number of cows per man or the amount of milk produced or sold per man.

(*c*) The number of egg laying hens per man.

(*d*) Number of hectares of fruit crop per man.

Increasing Labour Efficiency

For increasing labour efficiency output of the farm must be increased and for that purpose following measures must be undertaken:

(*i*) Farm manager should see that all tools and implements are in good condition few days before they required.

(*ii*) Farm manager should assign duties according to interest of the labourers.

(*iii*) Facilities for lunch, rest should be near to the spot of work.

(*iv*) Where trained labourers are required, training should be provided to labourers.

(*v*) Payment should be made according to skill, capacity to work, honesty, length of continuous service of the labourer.

(*vi*) Housing facilities, medical facility, educational facility to children of labourers, recreation facility should be provided to labourers. This increases efficiency of labourers.

3. Capital Efficiency Indicators

There are various indicators to know efficiency of capital, those are as below:

(*i*) **Overhead charges:** An overhead charge refers to fixed costs such as depreciation, yearly insurance premium, interest on total investment, land revenue, water taxes miscellaneous taxes, etc.

$$\text{Overhead charges ratio} = \frac{\text{Total fixed cost per year}}{\text{Gross income}}$$

This ratio can be reduced by increasing production. Smaller the ratio more efficient is the fixed capital use.

(*ii*) **Operating ratio:** Operating ratio refers to operating cost required for agril. production. Operating ratio can be worked out for a year or separately for a season, so as to know in which season capital is efficiently used.

$$\text{Operating ratio} = \frac{\text{Total operating cost}}{\text{Total profit}}$$

If this ratio is smaller, better it is or it means, the particular capital is efficiently used.

(*iii*) **Capital per unit of gross income:** The unit of gross income may be rupees.

$$\text{Capital per unit of gross income} = \frac{\text{Total capital invested}}{\text{Gross income}}$$

Smaller ratio indicates efficient use of capital. Little capital is able to produce sufficient income.

(*iv*) **Rate of capital turnover:** This is not only used in agriculture but also used in industrial sector.

$$\text{Rate of capital turnover} = \frac{\text{Gross income}}{\text{Total farm assets}} \times \frac{100}{1}$$

Higher turnover rate is a good sign of farm business.

(v) Farm income or profit efficiency indicators

There are several measures or indicators of farm income or profit. Those are as follows:

(*a*) *Net farm cash income*: Total cash receipts from production minus total cash operating expenses.

(*b*) *Net farm income*: Net cash income plus change in inventory.

(*c*) *Farm earnings*: Net farm income plus value of farm produce used in home.

(*d*) *Family labour earnings*: Farm earnings minus interest charged on farm capital.

(*e*) *Returns to management*: Family labour earnings minus imputed value of family labour.

These farm income measures can be explained with the help of hypothetical data as below:

1. Net cash income from production — ₹ 10,000
2. Cash expenses for production — ₹ 6,000
3. Changes in inventory — ₹ 1,000
4. Farm produce consumed — ₹ 2,000
5. Interest charged on farm capital @ 10% — ₹ 300
6. Imputed value of family labour — ₹ 3,000.

(I) Net cash income (1 – 2) = ₹ 4,000

(II) Net farm income (I + 3) = ₹ 5,000

(III) Farm earnings (II + 4) = ₹ 7,000

(IV) Family labour earnings (III – 5) = ₹ 6,700

(V) Returns to management (IV – 6) = ₹ 3,700.

For knowing efficiency of a particular factor of production these measures may be used. Profit of the farm can be increased by organising efficient use of different factors of production.

Break Even Analysis

This analysis is useful for a crop season, *i.e.*, for short period. In this analysis factor prices, selling prices and technology is considered constant. The point at which total cost curve and total revenue curve intersects is called the break even point (BEP). This point indicates the level of production at which fixed costs are covered. After covering the fixed costs farmer gets the profit. The production level which is less than BEP production, that farm is considered in loss and the farm where production level is more than BEP production levels that farm is in profit. This break even analysis can be illustrated with the help of following example:

Details:

1. Paddy production per hectare is 60 Q
2. Total fixed cost/ha is ₹ 4,000
3. Market price per quintal is ₹ 500
4. Per hectare variable cost is ₹ 300

Algebraically, break even point can be estimated by using the formula

$$BEP = \frac{F}{P - V}$$

Where,

BEP = Break even point in quintals

F = Per hectare fixed costs in ₹

P = Per quintal price of paddy in ₹

V = Per quintal variable cost in ₹

$$BEP = \frac{F}{P - V}$$

$$= \frac{4,000}{500 - 300}$$

$$= \frac{4,000}{200}$$

$$= 20 \text{ quintals}$$

Margin of Safety

After deducting break even point production from total per hectare production, remaining is the margin of safety.

Total per ha. production	–	60 Q.
BEP production	–	20 Q.
Margin of safety production	–	40 Q.

High margin of safety indicates that the enterprise will make profit. Small margin of safety will indicate that enterprise will make small profit.

26
Production Economics

Farm manager requires taking several decisions about production and hence, he must understand various techniques and principles of production economics.

Meaning and Scope

In farm production, economic logic is used. In agriculture production occurs on various farms, *i.e.*, crop production, dairy production. Agricultural production depends partly on nature and hence, it slightly varies from industrial production. Agriculture is modernizing year after year and use of production economics is becoming wide. Use of fertilizer, insecticide, pesticide is becoming popular. However, to what extent these inputs should be used in production process is to be answered by production economist. Production economics is not only used in crop production but also in dairy industry and in fisheries.

Objective of Production Economics

Production economics is used at two levels, one at farm level and another at region or at national level. At farm level, two kinds of problems required to be handled. First deciding optimum levels of inputs. Second, for maximizing total production from various enterprises which are taken on a farm, *i.e.*, combination of different enterprises.

At national level to judge which is significant factor of production as well as to judge its relative importance? Finally, production economist should be able to guide a production plan with country's limited resources. Dr. A.S. Kahlon and (Mrs.) H.K. Bal

have tried to provide a production function for a country as a whole.*
There are three main economic relationships exists, those are as follows:

1. Factor-product relationship,
2. Factor-factor relationship,
3. Product-product relationship.

1. Factor-product Relationship

Factor refers to input and product refers to output. Factor- product relationship also refers to law of diminishing returns. Crop production requires several inputs such as fertilizer, insecticides, irrigation water, seeds, etc. Here, important problem arises how much of particular input should be used and this problem can be solved by knowing factor-product relationship. This relationship can be illustrated with the help of following example. When fertilizer applied to crop, relationship between fertilizer applied and yield obtained can be expressed by three ways:

1. Tabular form, 2. Graphic form, 3. Algebraic form.

Tabular Form

Table 26.1: Input-output relationship

Sr. No.	Units of fertilizer	Total product	Average product	Marginal product	Profit in ₹ P_x = ₹10 P_y = ₹ 5
(1)	(2)	(3)	(4)	(5)	(6)
1.	1	2.5	2.5	2.5	2.5
2.	2	6	3.0	3.5	10
3.	3	10	3.3	4.0	20
4.	4	15	3.8	5	35
5.	5	20	4.0	5	50
6.	6	24	4.0	4	60
7.	7	27	3.9	3	65
8.	8	29	3.6	2	65
9.	9	30	3.3	1	60
10.	10	30	3.0	0	50
11.	11	29	2.6	-1	35
12.	12	27	2.3	-2	15

* Dr. A.S. Kahlon and H.K. Bal "Factor Share in Output Growth in Indian Agriculture: A Production Function Approach," *Issues in Indian Agriculture*, edited by Dr. K.R. Gupta, 1980, p. 191.

Total Product

In response to fertilizer application along with other factors of production crop yield is a outcome. As we will go on increasing use of input, total production is increasing as shown in column 3 of table 26.1.

Average Product

Average product is obtained by following formula:

$$\text{Average product} = \frac{\text{Total product}}{\text{Total units of input used}}$$

Average product figures for each input level are given in column 4 of the table 26.1.

Marginal Product

Marginal product means increase in output due to unit increase in input. Marginal product figures are given in column 5 of the table 26.1.

Graphic Form

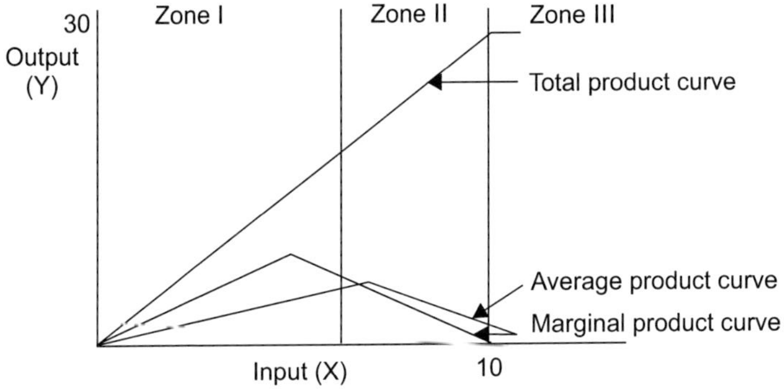

Fig. 26.1: Stages of production

Above curves (Fig. 26.1) can be obtained from the data given in table 26.1. Total product curve reaches to its maximum level at that time marginal product curve reaches to zero level of production. This indicates if additional doses of input are added, it will lead to negative return. Marginal product curve and average product curve cross each other before marginal product curve reaches to zero level.

Algebraic Form

Relationship between input and output can be expressed in algebraic form

$$Y = f(x)$$

where

Y is a dependent variable

X is an independent variable

Several mathematical relationships exist between input and output, however in this chapter cubic function is used for illustration.

Three Zones of Production Function

Production function is divided into three regions or zones depending upon characteristics of production behaviour.

Zone I: This zone starts from beginning, till marginal and average product curve cross each other. In this region, marginal product goes on increasing and hence average product also increases. Marginal product curve crosses the average product curve and here ends the first stage of production.

Zone II: This zone starts from crossing point of average product curve and marginal product curve till marginal product curve reaches to zero level. At the end of this stage, total product curve reaches to maximum level of production. In this zone marginal product goes on decreasing and average product curve is above marginal product curve. Average product also goes on decreasing.

Zone III: This zone is beyond the second zone, and in this zone marginal product is negative, total product goes on decreasing. This zone is called as irrational zone because; no producer will operate in this zone knowingly. In this zone, total product goes on decreasing with increase in in-put level. Any producer would not like to decrease his production with increase in cost and hence this zone is a irrational zone.

In the first zone, profit can be increased by adding inputs and no producer would like to continue production in first stage if the producer possesses sufficient capital. Hence, this zone is also called as irrational zone. Only second zone is a rational zone of production where profit can be maximized by equating marginal cost with marginal return. From table 26.1, it is observed that 8th unit of input which is in a second zone gives maximum profit. At this level marginal revenue is equal to marginal cost.

Elasticity of Production (E_p)

Elasticity of production refers to the percentage change in output in response to the percentage change input.

$$E_p = \frac{\varnothing Y / Y}{\varnothing X / X}$$

$$= \frac{\Delta Y}{Y} \cdot \frac{X}{\Delta X}$$

$$= \frac{\frac{\varnothing Y}{\varnothing X}}{\frac{Y}{X}}$$

$$= \frac{\text{Marginal physical product (MPP)}}{\text{Average physical product (APP)}}$$

Elasticity of production can be worked out at different input levels for the data given in table 26.1. It is as follows:

$$E_p \text{ at 5th unit of input} = \frac{5.0}{4.0} = \frac{\text{MPP}}{\text{APP}} = 1.25$$

$$E_p \text{ at 6th unit of input} = \frac{4.0}{4.0} = \frac{\text{MPP}}{\text{APP}} = 1.0$$

When elasticity of production is one, percentage change in input is equal to the percentage change in output. When elasticity of production is less than one, it is a diminishing return case and when elasticity of production is negative, it means total product goes on decreasing and it is a third stage of production.

2. Factor-factor Relationship

In above section, we analysed relationship between single input and single output. Particular output is produced by using more than one input and what quantities of various inputs should be used to produce particular output is a problem. For simplicity, two inputs and resulting output will be considered for following analysis:

Isoquant

Iso means equal and quant means quantity. Particular quantity of output can be produced by different combinations of two inputs, *e.g.*, 10 quintals of paddy can be produced by using different combinations of nitrogenous fertilizers and phosphatic fertilizers. Particular quantity of milk can be produced from a cow by feeding her different combinations of concentrates and green fodder.

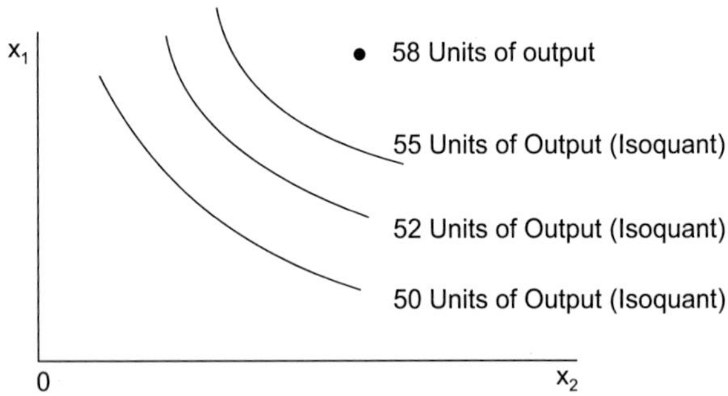

Fig. 26.2: Isoquants

In figure 26.2 different isoquants have been drawn. Particular (50 Units) output is obtained by following combination of inputs:

X_1	X_2
0	40
1	26
2	13
3	7
4	2
5	0

For higher level of output or for an isoquant of higher level, higher amount of input is required, for example for producing 52 units of output following combinations of inputs are required:

X_1	X_2
0	43
1	29
2	16
3	10
4	5
5	0

Thus, different isoquants are obtained till production reaches to maxima which are 58 units.

Isocost Line

Producer possesses a fixed amount of capital required for production and he can purchase various combinations of X_1 and X_2 required for producing Y. Suppose, producer is having ₹ 110 for purchasing quantities X_1 and X_2 required for producing Y. The price of X_2 is ₹ 1 and price of X_1 is ₹ 11 then if he spent all the amount on X_2 he can purchase 110 units of X_2 but if he spent all the amount on X_1 then he can purchase (110÷11) 10 units of X_1. Graphically, this can be shown in figure 26.3.

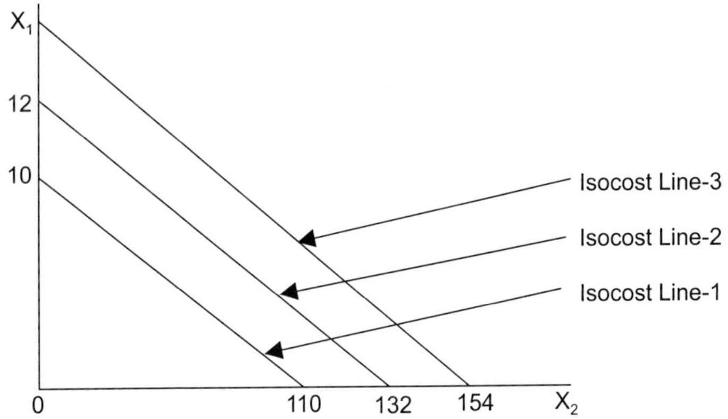

Fig. 26.3: Isocost lines

Isocost line indicates different combinations of X_1 and X_2 which can be purchased with the help of given amount. In Figure 26.3, isocost line-1 is for ₹ 110, isocost line-2 is for ₹ 132 and isocost line-3 is for ₹ 154. Price ratio indicates the slope of the isocost line.

$$\left(Px_1\ X_1 = Px_2\ X_2,\ \frac{X_1}{X_2} = \frac{Px_2}{Px_1} \right)$$

Profit Maximization or Cost Minimization

Level of input combination at maximum profit level can be found out by three ways.

1. *Arithmetic calculations*: With the help of simple arithmetic calculations profit level can be found out as shown in table 26.2.

It is observed that ₹ 35 is the least cost or minimum cost for producing 50 units of output. Two units of X_1 and 13 units of X_2 should be combined to obtain 50 units of output.

Table 26.2: Computation of minimum cost for producing 50 Units of output

Units of X_1	Units of X_2	Cost of X_1 @ ₹ 11	Cost of X_2 @ ₹ 1	Total cost
0	40	0	40	40
1	25	11	25	36
2	14	22	14	36
3	8	33	8	41
4	4	44	4	48
5	0	55	0	55

2. *Graphic method*: When slope of isocost line will be equal to slope of isoquant that particular combination of X_1 and X_2 will be profit maximizing level of inputs. Graphically, it is shown in figure 26.4.

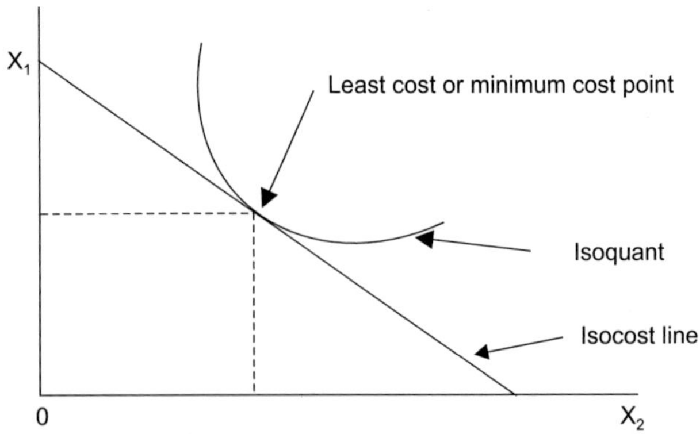

Fig. 26.4: Least cost combination

3. *Algebraic method*: In this method, first price ratio should be worked out, *i.e.*, $\frac{PX_1}{PX_2}$ and it should be equated to substitution ratio.

$$i.e., \frac{\Delta X_2}{\Delta X_1}, \left(PX_1 \times \Delta X_1 = PX_2 \times \Delta X_2\right)$$

Detail explanation of substitution ratio is given under, principle of substitution in chapter 21.

Expansion Path

Any firms acquire finance from outside sources and expand further. Now question arises, how it should expand? What should be the path of expansion of its business? Path should be such that all points on it should indicate maximum profit combinations. It can be graphically shown in figure 26.5.

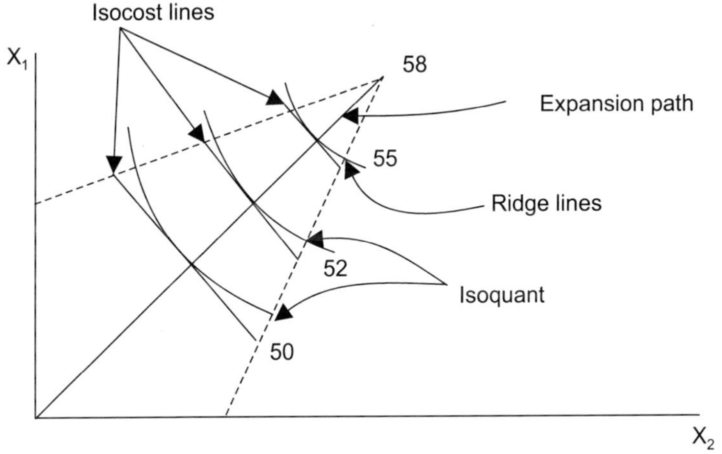

Fig. 26.5: Expansion path

If prices of inputs remain constant, then isocost lines drawn for higher financial outlays will be parallel to each other. These isocost lines are tangent to isoquants and when these tangency points are joined it will be a expansion path. When producer will possess sufficient finance, he should expand his business as per direction, provided by expansion path. When prices of X_1 and X_2 changes, slope of isocost line will change and there will be different set of tangency points. These tangency points are the least cost points. A line or curve connecting the least cost combinations of inputs for all output level is known as isocline. There can be as many isoclines as different set of prices; *Ridge lines* represent the points of maximum output from each input, given a fixed amount of other input. For example, in figure 26.5 dotted lines are ridge lines. Farm manager considers only one set of input prices, which he may think to be the most appropriate for the planning period and isocline which depend upon this set of prices called "expansion path".

3. Product-product Relationship

Until now, we have seen two types of relationships in this chapter, *i.e.*, factor-product and factor-factor. However, it is also necessary to know about product-product relationship. Farmer faces a problem, what should be the combination of different enterprises? At national level how much foodgrains should be produced and how much cotton should be produced? How much sugarcane or potatoes should be produced? Such problems can be handled with the help of product-product analysis. For simplicity, we will discuss two outputs Y_1 and Y_2 which can be produced by using input X. There can be one of the following relationships exist between two enterprises at a time, *i.e.*, joint, complementary, supplementary, competitive; these are discussed in chapter 21. Student should read through that portion as a pre-requisite for following analysis.

Production Possibility Curve

How much of two products can be produced from given input is indicated by production possibility curve. Production possibility curve is also called an iso-resource curve. For producing different quantity combinations of Y_1 and Y_2 equal amount of resource is required and it is indicated by this curve.

Drawing Production Possibility Curve

Production possibility curve can be drawn from production function. It can be explained with following example. Cultivator is having 6 hectares of land and he wants to grow two crops, *i.e.*, Bajra (Y_1) and Maize (Y_2). Hence, area under Bajra depends upon area under maize, *i.e.*, $Y_1 = f(Y_2)$. Yield of crops are as shown in Table 26.3.

Now land is only 6 hectares and question arises how 6 hectares should be distributed between two crops. If cultivator grows 6 hectares of Bajra, he cannot grow anything of maize. If he allotted 1 hectare for maize, he will get 8 quintals of maize

Table 26.3: Yield of two crops

Input (hectares)	Product Y_1 Amount of Bajra in Quintals	Product Y_2 Amount of Maize in Quintals
1	6	8
2	12	16
3	16.5	24
4	21	32
5	24	40
6	25	48

and he will be having only 5 hectares for Bajra where he will get 24 quintals of Bajra. Distribution of all land under two different crops will give rise to quantities of Bajra and Maize as shown in table 26.4.

Table 26.4: Yield of crops

Area in hectare (under maize) (1)	Maize in quintals (2)	Area in hectare (Bajra) (3)	Bajra in quintals (4)
6	48	0	0
5	40	1	6
4	32	2	12
3	24	3	16.5
2	16	4	21
1	8	5	24
0	0	6	25

If we plot figures from column two and four of table 26.4 we will get a curve which is called as production possibility curve. Graphically it is shown in figure 26.6.

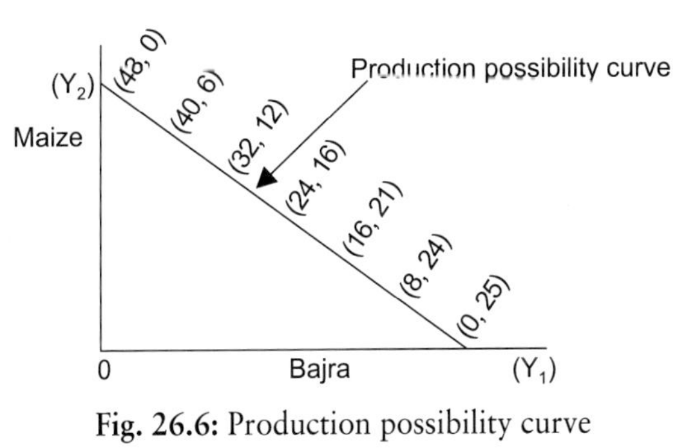

Fig. 26.6: Production possibility curve

Just like isoquants, there can be more production possibility curves at different input levels as showing in Figure 26.7.

Iso Revenue Line or Price Line

It is a line which defines all the possible combinations of two commodities which would yield an equal revenue or income. It can be illustrated by following example: Price of Bajra is ₹ 100 per quintal and price of maize is ₹ 50 per quintal. One thousand rupees income can be obtained by producing 10 quintals of Bajra or by producing 20 quintals of maize, graphically it will be shown in figure 26.8.

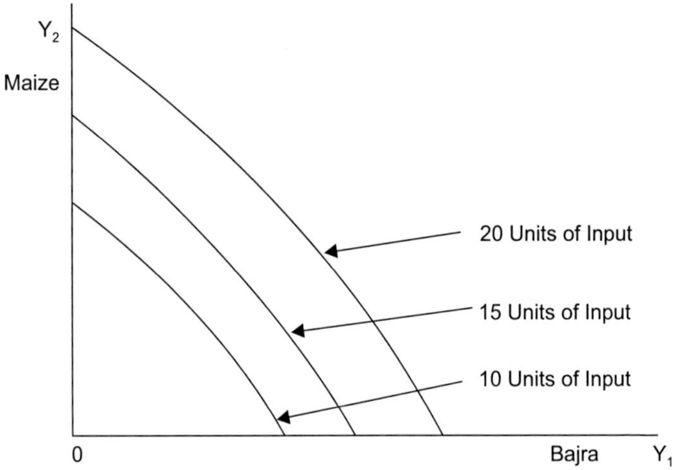

Fig. 26.7: Production possibility curves at different input levels

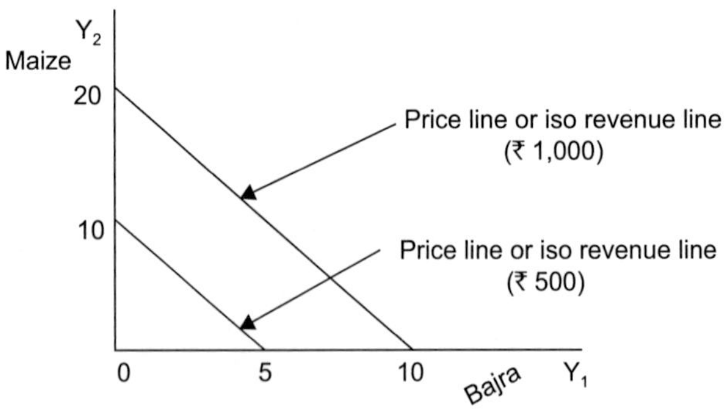

Fig. 26.8: Price line

For getting ₹ 500 revenue, 5 quintals of Bajra or 10 quintals of maize must be produced. Thus, prices of output remaining constant for different income levels there will be different iso revenue lines.

Revenue Maximization

For getting maximum revenue land should be distributed between two crops where price ratio $\left(\frac{Py_1}{Py_2}\right)$ will be equal to substitution ratio $\left(\frac{\Delta y_1}{\Delta y_2}\right)$. It will be clarified from table 26.5.

Table 26.5: Combination of area under Y_1 and Y_2 for maximum revenue

Y_2	Y_1	ΔY_2	ΔY_1	$\frac{\varnothing Y_2}{\varnothing Y_1}$	**Return from Maize @ ₹ 500/Q**	**Return from Bajra @ ₹ 1,000/Q**	**Total Return**
Q	Q				₹	₹	₹
48	0	—	—	—	24,000	0	24,000
40	6	8	6	1.33	20,000	6,000	26,000
32	12	8	6	1.33	16,000	12,000	28,000
24	16.5	8	4.5	1.8	12,000	16,500	28,500
16	21	8	4	2.0	8,000	21,000	29,000
8	24	8	3	2.67	4,000	24,000	28,000
0	25	8	1	8.0	0	25,000	25,000

It is observed from table 26.5 that cultivator will produce 16 quintals of maize and 21 quintals of Bajra, at that time he will get maximum total revenue. For producing 16 quintals of maize and 21 quintals of Bajra, he has to put 2 hectares under maize and 4 hectares under Bajra crop respectively. Thus, problem of distributing the input between two products or enterprises can be solved. Graphically it is shown in figure 26.9.

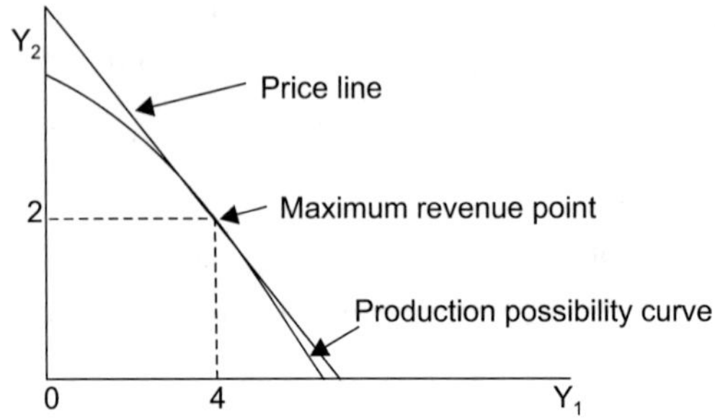

Fig. 26.9: Maximum revenue point

Expansion path

If prices of product Y_1 and Y_2 are assumed constant then slope of the price line will be constant and for getting higher income, cultivator should move along with the line AB which is called as expansion path which passes through each tangent point as shown in figure 26.10.

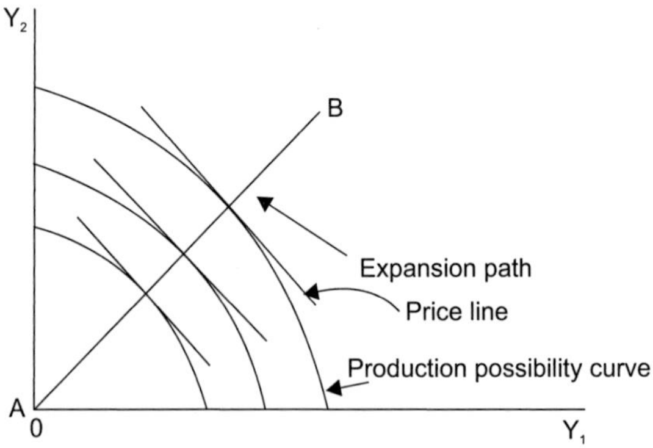

Fig. 26.10: Expansion path

27
Production Functions

We have seen in Chapter 26, about relationship between product and factors. It will be mathematically expressed as below:

$$Y = f(X_1, X_2, X_3, \ldots\ldots\ldots, X_n)$$

For maximizing profit it is necessary to use particular quantities of inputs. These quantities can be found out by using production function. Production functions are useful in making economic decisions. In above algebraic form Y stands for output such as crop and X_1 X_2 .... X_n refer to say fertilizer, irrigation..., etc. For our analysis, we have taken only one input variable but there are more than one input variables which are involved in the production process.

Form of Production Functions

There are different forms of production function exists. Nature of particular form depends upon its mathematical characteristics.

Selection of Production Function

While selecting particular form of a production function for particular input output data. Researcher should first plot the data on rough paper and should select the function which fits to nature of plotted curve. After initial selection of one or two production functions, final selection of a production function should be based on R^2 considering other characteristics of a production function as well as results obtained.

Following forms of production functions are frequently used in agriculture:

1. Linear
2. Cobb-Douglas or power function
3. Quadratic.

1. Linear production function

This is the simple production function. Its mathematical form is as below:

$$Y = a + b_1X_1 + b_2X_2 + \dots + b_nX_n$$

For simplicity, we will consider only one variable. Hence, the production function will be as below:

$$Y = a + bX$$

Where, Y = Dependent variable
a = Intercept
b = Regression coefficient
X = Independent variable

Interpretation of coefficients

When X will change by one unit Y will change by b units and when X is equal to zero then Y is equal to a (value of a).

In this function, rate of increase is constant and this is not a reality in several agricultural cases.

2. Cobb-Douglas production function

This function is used in several agril. production process. For single variable, it is expressed as follows:

$$Y = aX^b$$

Where,

Y = Dependent variable
X = Independent variable
a = Constant
b = Transformation ratio. When X is at different magnitudes, b is also caused as elasticity of production.

When there are *n* variables then function becomes as below:

$$Y = a X_1^{b1} X_2^{b2} X_3^{b3} \dots X_n^{bn}$$

Characteristics of C.D. function

1. This function allows either constant increasing or decreasing marginal productivity. It does not allow an input-output curve embracing all three.
2. This function assumes a constant elasticity of production, over the entire input-output curve. This is one of the limitation of a function because elasticity do not remain constant in several agril. productions.
3. Maximum production (maxima) is not defined in this function.
4. Because of multiplicative model, if any variable took a zero value, Y becomes zero and, in such cases, instead of zero very small figure, *i.e.*, (0.001) is taken for computational purpose.
5. When sum of b's is equal to one it is a constant return, when sum of b's is less than one it is a case of decreasing return and when sum of b's is more than one it is a case of increasing return to scale.

Estimation of C.D. function

For single variable it can be fitted with the help of calculating machine without any difficulty but when number of variables is more, function can be fitted with the help of electronic computer.

C.D. function is log linear and hence it should be converted in log form. Following example will make the estimation procedure clear. Yield of sugarcane is given for different levels of nitrogen.

Sr. No.	Yield of sugarcane in tonnes/ha. (X_1)	Nitrogen used in kg/ha. (X_2)
1.	125.69	150
2.	127.40	150
3.	115.00	150
4.	125.58	200
5.	129.88	200
6.	122.49	200
7.	129.46	250
8.	118.37	250
9.	125.63	250

Log values of these observations are given in table 27.1

Table 27.1: Computation of C.D. function

Sr. No.	X_1	X_1^2	X_2	X_2^2	X_1X_2
1.	2.0993	4.4071	2.1761	4.7354	4.5683
2.	2.1052	4.4319	2.1761	4.7354	4.5811
3.	2.0607	4.2465	2.1761	4.7354	4.4843
4.	2.0989	4.4054	2.3010	5.2946	4.8296
5.	2.1135	4.4669	2.3010	5.2946	4.8632
6.	2.0881	4.3602	2.3010	5.2946	4.8047
7.	2.1121	4.4610	2.3979	5.7499	5.0646
8.	2.0732	4.2982	2.3979	5.7499	4.9713
9.	2.0991	4.4062	2.3979	5.7499	5.0334
Total	18.8501	39.4834	20.6250	47.3397	43.2005
Mean	2.0945	4.3870	2.2917		
Antilog	124.30		195.70		

From data given in table 27.1, 'a' and 'b' coefficients are estimated as below:

$$\Sigma X_1X_2 = \Sigma X_1X_2 - \frac{\Sigma X_1 \times \Sigma X_2}{9}$$

$$= 43.2005 - \frac{18.8501 \times 20.6250}{9}$$

$$= 0.00235$$

$$\Sigma X_2^2 = \Sigma X_2^2 \frac{(\Sigma X_2)^2}{9}$$

$$= 47.3397 - \frac{(20.625)^2}{9}$$

$$= 0.07403$$

$$b = \frac{0.00235}{0.07403}$$

$$= 0.032$$

find out value of (a)

$$Y = a + b\bar{X}$$

$$a = Y - b\bar{X}$$

$$= 2.0045 - 0.032 \times 2.2917$$

$$= 2.0212$$

$$\text{Antilog} = 105$$

(1) Function will be as follows:

$$Y = 105\ X^{0.032}$$

Price of sugarcane is ₹ 1,000/tonne

Price of nitrogen is ₹ 10.87/kg.

Marginal production function is derived from total production function by finding out its first derivative and is equated to price ratio for finding out optimum quantity of nitrogen/ha.

$$Y = 105\ X^{0.032}$$

$$P_x = \text{Price of nitrogen/kg.}$$

$$P_y = \text{Price of sugarcane/tonne}$$

$$X^{0.968} = \frac{3.36 \times 1{,}000}{10.87}$$

$$x = 367.13 \text{ kg/ha.}$$

Yield at maximum profit level:

$$Y = 105\ X^{0.032}$$

$$Y = (105)\ (367.13)^{0.032}$$

$$= 126.84 \text{ tonnes/ha.}$$

(2) Thus, for obtaining maximum profit according to C.D. function, cultivator should use 367.13 kg of nitrogen per hectare.

(3) **Quadratic production function:** Quadratic function is also frequently used in agriculture. If we consider only one independent variable then function will be as follows:

$$Y = a + b_1X - b_2X$$

where, Y = Dependent variable

a = Intercept

X = Independent variable

b_1 & b_2 = transformation coefficients when X is at different magnitudes.

When there are two variables, function will be as follows:

$$Y = a + b_1 X_1 + b_2 X_2 - b_3 X_1^2 - b_4 X_2^2 + b_5 X_1 X_2$$

Thus, this function takes into account interaction effect or effect on Y due to interaction of independent variables. In above case $b_5 X_1 X_2$ is called as interaction term.

Characteristics of Quadratic Function

1. Elasticity of production is not constant over the entire input-output curve.
2. Maximum production (maxima) is defined or definite maximum production which can be attained can be shown in this function.
3. If any dependent variable assumed a zero value, production do not become zero.
4. Function can comprise two stages of production.
5. The isoquants are not asymptotic to the input axis as was true for the Cobb-Douglas function.

Estimation of Linear and Quadratic Production Function

Both the functions can be fitted from the table 27.2.

Table 27.2: Computation of linear and quadratic production function

Sr. No.	X_1	X_1^2	X_2	X_2^2	X_1X_2	$X_3(X_2^2)$	X_3^2	X_1X_3	X_2X_3
1.	0.4481	0.2008	0.50	0.25	0.2241	0.25	0.0625	0.1120	0.125
2.	0.3898	0.1519	0.50	0.25	0.1949	0.25	0.0625	0.0975	0.125
3.	0.4112	0.1691	0.50	0.25	0.2056	0.25	0.0625	0.1028	0.125
4.	0.5583	0.3117	1.00	1.00	0.5583	1.00	1.0000	0.5583	1.000
5.	0.5820	0.3387	1.00	1.00	0.5820	1.00	1.0000	0.5820	1.000
6.	0.5887	0.3466	1.00	1.00	0.5887	1.00	1.0000	0.5887	1.000
7.	0.5809	0.3374	1.50	2.25	0.8714	2.25	5.0625	1.3070	3.375
8.	0.6023	0.3628	1.50	2.25	0.9035	2.25	5.0625	1.3552	3.375
9.	0.6052	03663	1.50	2.25	0.9078	2.25	5.0625	1.3617	3.375
Total	4.7665	2.5853	9.00	10.50	5.0363	10.50	18.3750	6.0652	13.500
Mean	0.5296		1.00						

Example: The experimental data regarding nitrogen fertilizer application to paddy variety K-184. The three years' observations are condensed and are given in table 27.3.

Table 27.3

Sr. No.	Yield of K-184 variety (quintals/ha.) Y	Nitrogen dose (kg/ha.) X
1.	44.81	50
2.	38.98	50
3.	41.12	50
4.	55.83	100
5.	58.20	100
6.	58.87	100
7.	58.09	150
8.	60.23	150
9.	60.52	150

For computational easiness observations are divided by hundred.

$$\Sigma X_1^2 = \Sigma X_1^2 - \frac{(\Sigma X_1)^2}{N}$$

$$= 2.5853 - \frac{(4.7665)^2}{9}$$

$$= 0.0609$$

$$\Sigma X_2^2 = \Sigma X_2^2 - \frac{(\Sigma X_2)^2}{N}$$

$$= 10.5 - \frac{9 \times 9}{9} = 1.5$$

$$\Sigma X_3^2 = \Sigma X_3^2 - \frac{(\Sigma X_3)^2}{N}$$

$$= 18.375 - \frac{(10.5)^2}{9}$$

$$= 6.125$$

$$\Sigma X_1 X_2 = \Sigma X_1 X_2 - \frac{\Sigma X_1 \Sigma X_2}{N}$$

$$= 5.0363 - \frac{(4.7665)(9)}{9}$$

$$= 0.2698$$

$$\Sigma X_1X_3 = \Sigma X_1X_3 - \frac{\Sigma X_1 \cdot \Sigma X_3}{N}$$

$$= 6.0652 - \frac{4.7665 \times 10.5}{9}$$

$$= 0.5043$$

$$\Sigma X_2X_3 = \Sigma X_2X_3 - \frac{\Sigma X_2 \cdot \Sigma X_3}{N}$$

$$= 13.5 - \frac{9 \times 10.5}{9}$$

$$= 30$$

Linear Function

$$b = \frac{\Sigma X_1X_2}{\Sigma X_2{}^2}$$

$$= \frac{0.2698}{1.5}$$

$$= 0.18$$

$$y = a + bX$$

$$a = Y - bX$$

$$a = 0.5296 - 0.18 \times 1$$

$$= 0.3496$$

$Y = 34.96 + 0.18 \times$ (After adjusting for division by 100)

$$R^2 = \frac{b\Sigma X_1\Sigma X_2}{\Sigma X_1{}^2}$$

$$= \frac{(0.18)(0.2698)}{0.0609}$$

$$= 0.80$$

R^2 or square of multiple correlation coefficient = 0.80

Quadratic production function

$$b_1 = \frac{(0.2698 \times 6.125) - (0.5043 \times 3.0)}{(1.5 \times 6.125) - (3)^2}$$

$$= 0.7445$$

$$b_2 = \frac{(0.5043 \times 1.57) - (0.2698 \times 3)}{(1.5 \times 6.125) - (3)^2}$$

$= 0.2821$

$X_1 = a + b_1X_2 - b_2X_3$

$A = 0.5296 - (0.7445)(1) - (-0.2821)(1.1667)$

$= 0.1147$

$Y = 0.1147 + 0.7445\ X - 0.2821\ X^2$

Adjusting for division by 100

$$Y = 11.47 + 0.7445\ X - 0.0028\ X^2$$

R^2 or Square of multiple correlation coefficient = 1

$$R^2 = \frac{(0.7445 \times 0.2698) + (-0.2821 \times 0.5043)}{0.0609}$$

$$= \frac{0.2009 - 0.1423}{0.0609}$$

$= 0.96$

Hence, $Y = 11.47 + 0.7445\ X - 0.0028\ X^2$, $R^2 = 0.96$

Finding profit maximizing level of Nitrogen – Price of Nitrogen is taken as 10.87 ₹/kg. and per quintal paddy price is ₹ 550. Marginal productivity function is equated to price ratio.

$$0.7445 - 0.0056\ X = \frac{10.87}{550}$$

X = 129.38 kg of N per hectare for maximum profit. Yield at maximum profit level is found out by substituting value in production function.

$Y = 11.45 + 0.7445 \times 129.38 - 0.0028 \times (129.38)^2$

= 60.90 quintals of paddy per hectare

Total profit per hectare

$= 60.90 \times 550 - 129.38 \times 10.87$

= ₹ 32,089 profit per hectare

Thus, both the functions can be fitted.

Linear Programming

Budgeting approach of farm planning is not highly systematic method, it relies strongly on the judgement of the planner. Therefore, there is no guarantee that the most profitable combination of enterprises will be discovered through budgeting. Linear Programming is a more systematic and accurate method of determining mathematically the optimum combination of enterprises or inputs so as to maximise the income or minimise the cost within the limits of variable resources. The technique is being progressively utilized in finding solutions to various farm management problems and in planning the farm enterprises mix with a view to maximizing the given objective function. Farm planner requires to maximise his total profit. He has several alternative activities, and he has to select most profitable ones. Similarly, resources which he possesses are limited. Under such circumstances, Linear Programming a technique provides most profitable plan. Linear programming problem involves series of calculations and can be easily carried out with the help of electronic computer. Farm planner should take most care of accurate data.

Assumptions of Linear Programming

The basic assumptions of Linear Programming are linearity, divisibility, additivity, finiteness and single value expectations.

1. *Linearity*

The condition of linearity is met if every unit of input adds equal increments to the output, *i.e.*, Linear regression equation of the type (Y = bX) holds true. However, in some cases law of diminishing returns operates and non-linear rates of transformation holds good. In this case, various levels of input-output combinations are included as separate activities.

2. *Divisibility*

This assumption implies that it is possible to produce fractions of output and possible to use fractions of inputs. However, sometimes, linear programming might provide a solution of 9.6 cows, but the farmer cannot operate this enterprise in fractions, he can have only either 9 cows or 10 cows. Thus, wherever the answer should be in integers instead of fractions, linear programming can only approximate. In such cases, returns of the matrix are needed to see whether 9 or 10 cows are profitable.

3. Additivity

This is reciprocal of divisibility. This means, when two or more activities are followed, their total product must be equal to the sum of their individual products and total resources used equal to the sum of resources used by individual activity.

4. Finiteness

This means there should be limit to the number of alternative activities and to the resource restrictions. If activities and restrictions are infinite, planner will never complete his work.

5. Single value expectations

The entire coefficient in linear programming is assumed to be known with certainty. This is called as exact data and not the probable data is used. To take care of variations in some important variables, like prices, etc., techniques of variable programming are available.

Similarly, definite planning period is taken into consideration. Farm-firm is considered to operate within a static framework for the given period of planning.

Real Activities

Enterprises which are included in the programme are called as real activities, *e.g.*, if cultivator is considering how his land, labour and capital should be allotted in between maize and cotton then these two enterprises are called as two different real activities.

Disposal Activities

These are also known as slack variables or difference factors and are introduced one into each constraint equation to handle the problem of inequalities.

Thus, the excess availability of each resource over its use can be absorbed by the disposal activity.

An Illustration

For illustration data of particular farm situation is given in table 27.4.

Table 27.4: Resources available and input requirement for maize and cotton

Sr. No.	Item	Resource level	Per acre input Requirements	
			Maize (A_1)	Cotton (A_2)
1.	Land (A_3)	5 acres	1	1
2.	Labour(A_4) (man days)	64	8	16
3.	Cash (A_5) (in ₹)	1,600	400	200
	Return in ₹		200	400

Objective function is as follows:

$$Z = 200\ A_1 + 400\ A_2$$

A_1 and A_2 are real activities and A_3, A_4 and A_5 are disposal activities. This objective function should be maximised. Constraint inequality equations are as follows:

Land in acres	$5 \geq$	$1A_1 + 1A_2$
Labour in man days	$64 \geq$	$8A_1 + 16A_2$
Cash in ₹	$1{,}600 \geq$	$400A_1 + 200A_2$

Above information is written in matrix form as in table 27.5.

Table 27.5: Resource levels and input-output matrix

C			0	0	0	200	400	
Z	Resource constraints	B	A_3	A_4	A_5	A_1	A_2	Σ
0	land (A_3)	5 acres	1	0	0	1	1	8
0	labour (A_4) (man days)	64	0	1	0	8	16	89
0	(₹) (A_5)	1,600	0	0	1	400	200	2,201

In this matrix columns A_1 and A_2 are for real activities and columns A_3, A_4 and A_5 are disposal activities. A real activity column in this case indicates inputs of various resources per acre of a crop and returns from each activity are given at the top of the column in row 'C'. A disposal activity indicates the input of resources if a unit of a resource has to be kept idle or in disposal.

Suitable method for solving Linear Programming problem is the simplex method. Above-mentioned problem is solved by this method in table 27.6.

Following steps are involved in simplex method:

(Refer to table 27.6)

1. Multiply 'Z' values with corresponding column totals. This will give Zj row.
2. Deduct Cj from Zj and obtain Zj–Cj row.
3. Find the highest negative value in Zj-Cj row (–400 in this example). Column containing the highest negative value (A_2) will be the outgoing column.
4. Divide values of B column by corresponding values in A_2 column and this will give us R column.
5. Find the lowest R value (4). Row containing this lowest R value will be the outgoing row (A_4).
6. Find the value which is at intersection point of outgoing Row (A_4) and outgoing column (A_2), *i.e.*, 16.
7. Divide each value of outgoing row (A_4) by the value which is found out at intersection point of outgoing row and column, *i.e.*, 16.
8. Enter these values in the second iteration, replacing outgoing row (A_4).
9. All other rows of the second iteration can be calculated by deducting from each figure of the row, the product of the corresponding coefficient in the outgoing column of first iteration with the corresponding coefficient in the incoming row of the second iteration.

   i.e., 1 (First figure of B column of II iteration)

   = 5 (First figure of B column in 1st iteration) minus 1 (First figure of outgoing column of first iteration)

   multiplied by 4 (First figure of incoming row in B column of second iteration). (1 = 5 – 1 × 4).

Thus, second iteration can be derived from first iteration, observe values in Zj-Cj row, column with highest negative value will be outgoing column. Similarly, obtain values of R column, smallest value of R column of second iteration will indicate outgoing row and again all procedure is followed to obtain third iterations. Thus, different iterations are found out till we get all positive values in Zj-Cj row.

In this example, all values of Zj-Cj row of second iteration are positive and hence, second iteration provides final solution.

It is observed from the second iteration that cultivator should allocate 4 acres for cotton crop and should keep one acre idle as labour days are not available to him. Similarly, ₹ 800 also remains ideal. Farmer can find out still profitable plan by introducing labour hiring, capital borrowing and land renting activities in the programme. Thus, Linear Programming has tremendous potentialities in farm management research and extension.

Table 27.6: Simplex solution of the Linear Programming problem

		First Iteration								
C		0	0	0	0	200	400	600		
Z	Resource constraints	B	A_3	A_4	A_5	A_1	A_2	Σ	R
0	Land (A_3)	5 acres	1	0	0	1	1	8	5
0	Labour (A_4) (man days)	64	0	1	0	8	16	89	4
0	Cash in ₹ (A_5)	1600	0	0	1	400	200	2201	8
Zj		0	0	0	0	0	0	0	
Zj-Cj		0	0	0	0	-200	-400	-600	
		Second Iteration							
C			0	0	0	200	400	600	
Z	Resource constraints	B	A_3	A_4	A_5	A_1	A_2	Σ	
0	A_3	1	1	-0.06	0	0.5	0	2.44	
400	A_2	4	0	0.06	0	0.5	1	5.56	
0	A_5	800	0	-12	1	300	0	1089	
Zj.Cj		1600	0	24	0	0	0	1624	

Risk and Uncertainties

Farmer faces mainly three types of uncertainties:

1. **Yield uncertainty:** In agricultural production, there are certain factors which are beyond the capacity of farmer such as weather and other natural calamities. This introduces uncertainty in Agril. production.

2. **Price uncertainty:** It relates to variability in factor and product prices from year to year. However, recently, Government is declaring support prices of important agril. commodities without much year-to-year variation.
3. **Innovation uncertainty:** Due to research in Agril. Sciences, new varieties and new techniques are developed, and this introduces innovation uncertainty.

Thus, mainly variation in yield and prices introduces the variation in income. There are some modified Linear Programming models which take into account all such issues.

Decision Rules and Game Theory

Agricultural production depends upon several natural factors such as rainfall, temperature, insect/pest attacks, etc. These factors bring risk and uncertainty in the agricultural production. Decision rules and game theories help to take better decisions under conditions of risk and uncertainty. In the game theory, the choice problem which involve risk are analysed with the aid of utility theory. Game theory is applicable to situations which involve conflicting interests and in which outcome is controlled partly by one side and partly by the opposing side of the conflict. Game theory models are applied to several decision-making problems in the farming business, *e.g.*, what type of farming should be adopted, purchasing or renting of land, the amount to be borrowed, whether or not to use a new seed variety. Whether to store produce for late, Market, etc.

The ignorance of farmer regarding the manner of action of the other players introduces an element of uncertainty in the game. In agriculture, other players are represented by the outcomes in weather conditions, insect pest attack social and political situations market conditions, etc. All these players are treated as nature and then game problem in agriculture can be reduced to a simple two-person zero-sum game. Here only farmer gains or loses nature is passive in the sense of gains or losses.

Decision Rules

It is assumed that decision maker tries to maximise satisfaction. Similarly, ability and willingness for bearing risk varies from individual to individual. Hence, the appropriate decision criterion is most likely to vary from person to person and situation to situation. There are number of decision criteria, those can be used by different people in different situations.

Before we discuss different decision criteria, we will discuss "pay-off matrix". It is defined as the expected pay-offs from each strategy under different situations, *e.g.*, expected returns from different crops under three different situations such as good, normal and bad weather can be given in such a matrix.

Following hypothetical pay-off matrix involve five different strategies, *viz.* M, N, O, P, Q whose outcomes involve three different situations, *viz.* X, Y and Z.

Pay-off Matrix

Strategy	Situations		
	X	Y	Z
M	20	20	20
N	4	64	14
O	15	15	54
P	44	16	29
Q	19	39	29

Different decision-making criteria will be explained with the help of this pay-off matrix.

Different decision-making criteria are as follows:

The Maximum Criteria

This is also known as the Wald's criterion and is one of the most conservative of the decision rules. According to this criterion, the farmer will determine worst that can happen for each strategy, and he will select the strategy which is the least worst or which shows maximum of the minimum gains.

In the hypothetical example; minimum pay-off from strategy M, N, O, P and Q is 20, 4, 15, 44 and 19, strategy M gives highest worst pay-off. Hence, according to maximin criterion strategy M will be selected. However, here decision-maker is pessimistic, and it may be called as cowardice approach.

This criterion does not take into consideration all information given in pay-off matrix.

The Maximax Criterion

This decision rule is quite opposite to that maximin rule. This rule is suited to a person, who considers only the most, glittering values of a strategy and ignores the risk involved.

In the hypothetical example, maximum pay-off from strategy M, N, O, P and Q is 20, 64, 54, 44 and 39. Thus, the maximax criterion will select strategy N which shows the maximum of the maximum values. This rule also does not considers all information given in pay-off matrix.

The Minimax Regret (Savage) Criterion

In this method, a regret matrix is constructed. Regret means cost of mistake, cost of mistake or regret under particular situation is worked out by deducting the value of strategy under particular situation from highest value under that situation, *e.g.*, in our hypothetical example value of strategy M under situation X is 20 and highest value under situation X is 44 so difference is 24. Hence, cost of mistake (regret) is 24. Thus, other values of regret matrix are worked out and are given below:

Regret Matrix

	X	Y	Z
M	24	44	34
N	40	0	40
O	29	49	0
P	0	48	25
Q	25	25	25

Maximum regret value for strategy M, N, O, P and Q is 44, 40, 49, 48 and 25. Strategy Q shows minimum regret and hence, it is selected.

This criterion suffers from the limitation, *i.e.*, assumption of difference measures the regret may not be perfectly alright.

The Hurwicz Optimism-Pessimism Criterion

This is a compromise of the maximin and the maximax criteria. As per this criteria, weighted average of the minimum and the maximum pay-off of each strategy is used for selecting a particular strategy. Let ai and Ai be the minimum and maximum pay-offs for a strategy. Each strategy is considered as per optimism pessimism, index α which lies between 0 to 1. The index is worked out for each strategy as per following formula.

$$\underline{a}\ ai + (1 - \alpha)\ Ai$$

Strategy with highest α index is selected.

In our hypothetical example for strategy M, value of ai is 20 and value of Ai is also 20. Let us assume $\alpha = 0.75$, then an index for strategy M is worked out as follows:

$$75 \times 20 + (1 - 0.75)\ 20 = 20$$

Value of an index for strategy M, N, O, P and Q is 20, 19, 24, 75, 23, and 24. Strategy O is having highest an index and hence, it is selected. Although this rule considers both the maximum and the minimum values with certain specified weights attached to each of these strategies, the rule still does not consider the other values in the pay-off matrix.

The Laplace (Bayes) Criterion

When the state of nature is one of uncertainty, all the outcomes are given equal weightage. All situations are assigned equal probability and expected pay-offs are worked out. Strategy which shows highest pay-off is selected. Pay-off for strategy M is worked out as follows:

$$\frac{20 + 20 + 20}{3} = 20$$

Expected pay-off for strategy M, N, O, P and Q is 20, 27, 33, 28, 29, 67 and 29. Strategy 'P' gives highest expected pay-off and hence, it is selected.

This is oldest criterion and uses all values of pay-off matrix. It is more appealing than other criteria.

Mixed Strategies

All above-discussed rules refer to the selection of only pure strategies, but decision maker may prefer to choose mixed strategies. Decision maker can find out which mixed strategy yields the largest maximin value or the one which gives the lowest minimax regret figure, and such a mixed strategy is known as the optimal mixed strategy.

Criterion of benefit and Simon theory of satisfier is also sometimes used while making decisions.

Until now, game theory models are not much used in Agril. Economic research but it is one of the interesting and important fields to work.

Simulation Models

In simulation model-particular dynamic situation of farm production is simulated. Simulation model truly represents the particular situation of farm production. Simulation model can take into account different characteristics of agricultural production systems, are therefore, most relevant to the real world agricultural situation. Linear Programming aims at objective function to be optimized. Simulation does not require typically involve, an objective function to be optimized. It is an empirical technique used to evaluate, assess or predict the outcome of following different courses of action or policies. Simulation model builder first, prepare a simple diagram which illustrate the components of the system to be isolated and establishes their relationships with one another. This diagram will be further developed to express the dynamics of the system. Finally, a detailed diagram is constructed which is readily translated to a computer programme. Thus, final symbolic model will be expressed as a series of relationships and equations in a computer language, *e.g.*, sugar production model. In this case, mainly following components will be involved. Sowing of sugarcane crop—different input requirements—harvesting of sugarcane-transportation of sugarcane to sugar factory—crushing the sugarcane and production of sugar. Different components are related with each other and can be represented with the help of equations. The effect of change in one variable may be observed on other variables and finally right decision is taken.

Simulation model requires much computer time, *i.e.*, they are very costly. Hence, model can be developed for a average farm of the locality and effect of changes in various variables such as price policy, government policy, credit policy, management policy can be observed. This information is used for maximising returns and satisfaction.

28
Farm Records and Accounts

Farm records and accounts play an important role in farm business. Agriculture is modernizing, modern agriculture must be carried out like a business. If we observe, even a small shopkeeper, he keeps accounts properly and almost all the business houses maintain scientific records and accounts. Uptill now in India, this fact was not clearly recognized by our cultivators because mainly due to lack of education. However, recently this fact has been recognized by some of our cultivators and they are inclined towards maintaining proper records and accounts. Several cultivators make note of a transaction in their diaries. Some cultivators keep the sale receipts with them, but these efforts are inadequate. This will be useful only as a memory aid, but scientific records and accounts will provide more than this. We will see what the advantages of farm records and accounts are.

Advantages of Farm Records and Accounts

1. Farm records and accounts help in increasing income. This can be achieved by taking better decisions. Farm records and accounts help to understand following:
   (*a*) Farmer can know what the gains are and what the losses are.
   (*b*) Farmer can understand which the unproductive expenditure is.

2. Farmer can develop short-term and long-term plans for the farm, needed information is available from farm records and accounts.
3. Farm records and accounts will help to obtain credit; cultivator can repay in time and can increase his credit worthiness.
4. Farm records and accounts will be very useful in conducting research in agricultural economics.
5. Government can make useful policies using farm records and accounts.

Farm Book-keeping

Farm book-keeping can be defined as the art as well as science of recording in books, farm business transactions in the regular and systematic manner so that their nature and extent and financial effects can be readily ascertained at any time.

System of Book-keeping

There are two systems of book-keeping or accounting:

1. *Double Entry System*

Double entry system is a method of recording each transaction in the books of accounts in its two-fold aspects, *i.e.*, two entries are made for each transaction in the same set of books one being a debit entry and the other a credit entry. For example: (*i*) Suppose a farmer purchases an electric motor for ₹ 4,000. Here two accounts come into picture *i.e.*, machine accounts and second cash accounts. Machine account gets the money and cash account gives the money. Hence, machine account is debtor and cash account is creditor. Hence, entries should be made accordingly. Receiving account is a debtor and giving account is a creditor, (*ii*) Sold a cow to Prabhakar for ₹ 1,000 (on credit). Prabhakar receives the cow so Prabhakar's account is debtor and cow goes out so livestock account is creditor.

2. *Single Entry System*

The single entry system ignores the double effect of transactions. There are single entries. This is a simple system. When any income is received, entry is made to income side and when any expense occurs at that time it is recorded at expenditure side. At the end of the year, total of income and expenses is made. If income is more than expense, profit is a result and if expenses are more than income then loss will be the result. Majority of Indian farmers are small farmers and single entry system of accounting will be suitable to them. However, where there are many transactions on a big farm there is possibility of committing arithmetical mistakes, in those cases double entry system should be used to avoid writing and arithmetical mistakes. In double entry system, there is automatic check on mistakes committed, while making entries and on other arithmetical mistakes. Accuracy of single entry system cannot be tested by means of a trial balance which is possible under double entry system.

Finding Out Profit or Loss with the Help of Double Entry System

For understanding different steps involved in finding out profit or loss by double entry system, brief information is given below:

1. Diary

All transactions are first recorded in Diary. It is an initial record and entries in the journal and other books of original entry are made from this book. It should be written neatly and accurately. Following example will clarify the procedure. Mohan is a young farmer, he made following entries in his diary.

Mohan's Diary

1980	₹
1. January 1, bought two cows	15,000
2. February 1, sold two buffaloes	25,000

2. Journal

Journal means a daily record. Original entries in journal are written from diary. All the transactions are entered in it in a classified form of debits and credits, *i.e.*, in double entry form and strictly in the order of dates, so that they may be easily posted or transferred to the ledger.

Mohan's Journal

Sr. No.	Date	Particulars	Ledger Folio	Dr. (Debit) Amount ₹ P.	Cr. (Credit) Amount ₹ P.
1.	Jan. 1	Livestock account... To cash A/c for purchase of cows		15,000	15,000
2.	Feb. 1	Cash account... To Livestock account (For sale of two buffaloes)		25,000	25,000

Ledger

This is a main book of account. It is the book that contains a classified and summarised record of all transactions of the business, transferred or posted to it from the Journal or other books of original entry. There are separate accounts and all entries pertaining to particular account are found at one place. At the end of the year or at the end of given period, each account will contain the entire transactions relating to particular account in a condensed form. Ledger also serves as a permanent record for future references especially in regard to debtors and creditors. Every entry appearing in the debit column (Dr.) in journal is posted to debit side of the respective ledger account and every entry shown in the credit column in the journal is posted to the credit side of the respective ledger account. For example, our above-mentioned journal entries will be transferred to ledger in a separate account as follows:

Cash Account

		Dr.				Cr.
Date	Particulars	J/F Amount ₹ P.	Date	Particulars	J/F Amount ₹ P.
1980 Jan. 1	To livestock	25,000	1980 Feb.1	By livestock	15,000

Livestock Account

		Dr.			Cr.
Date	Particulars	J/F Amount ₹ P.	Date	Particulars	J/F Amount ₹ P.
1980 Feb. 1	To cash	15,000	1980 Jan. 1	By cash	25,000

Thus, entries are made in a separate account in a ledger. When cash entries are limited at that time cash account is opened in ledger but when cash transactions are many separate cash book is used.

Cash Book

If cash transactions are large in a business, it becomes inconvenient or rather impossible to journalise each of the; for saving time separate book is maintained to record all the transactions involving cash receipts and cash payments only. This book is called as cash book or the cash account book. Transactions are entered in the cash book directly from the diary.

Trial Balance

Before preparing profit and loss account or balance sheet, it is necessary to check arithmetical accuracy of the postings (entry or writing transaction in an account) in the ledger. So that errors in postings may be detected and necessary figures are collected for preparing the profit and loss account and the balance sheet. For this purpose, a statement or a list of total amounts or balances of the debit and credits of the ledger accounts including cash and bank balance from the cash book at a given date is prepared. This statement or list is called as trial balance. It is a test of accuracy.

Profit and Loss Account

At the end of the year, farmer is interested to know his total profit or loss and therefore profit and loss account is prepared. In preparing a profit and loss account, the balances of all the nominal accounts are carried to it as it is a nominal account. Nominal accounts are the accounts which record the gains or losses and the income or expenses of the business such as wage account, rent account, etc. Finally, totals of all debit and credit side are made, if the debit side is greater than the credit side, the difference is a net loss. If the credit side is greater than debit side the balance is a net profit, thus profit or loss is found out.

Balance Sheet

After the preparation of profit and loss account, the next step is to prepare a statement called balance sheet for finding out the accurate financial position of the farm business at the end of the year. In balance sheet, all assets and liabilities are given. Assets include all possession and liabilities are the total debts owed to others at any particular date. If the totals of the assets and liabilities are just equal that means capitals are just enough to discharge the liability. If assets exceed the liabilities that means capital is surplus or net worth of farm is positive and if liabilities are more than assets that means net worth of farm is negative and person is indebted. Thus, cultivator has to maintain various account books, if he followed double entry system of book-keeping.

There is no hard and fast rule about keeping particular record or account but main objective of keeping records and accounts is that farmer should be able to know his financial position at a particular point of time very easily. Similarly, keeping accounts and records should not be too difficult. Necessity of particular form for particular account and record books will be different. One farmer may keep one record other farmer may not have that activity and hence particular record may not be useful to him.

Following records are also useful to farmers:

1. Land utilization records,
2. Crop production and disposal records,
3. Livestock production records,
4. Labour records,
5. Machinery use records,
6. Feed records,
7. Store register, and
8. Farm inventory.

Selected References

Allen, R.G.D., *Mathematical Economics*, Second Edition, The Macmillan Press Ltd., London, 1973.

Chawdhari, T.P.S. and Others, *Resource Use and Productivity on Farms*, N.I.C.D., Hyderabad, 1969.

Cummings, J.T., "Crop Substitution and Market Influence: The Case of Wheat and Barley in Northwestern India," *Indian J. of Agril. Economics*, Vol. XXXII, No. 2, p. 1, April-June, 1977.

Dharm Narain, "Growth of Productivity in Indian Agriculture," *Indian*

Journal of Agril. Economics, Vol. XXXII, No. I, Jan.-March, 1977.

Folley, R.R.W., *Intensive Crop Economics*, Heinemann Educational Books Ltd., London, 1973.

Heariy, E.O., and Dillon, J.L., *Agricultural Production Function*, Kalyani Publishers, Ludhiana, 1961.

Henderson and Quant, *Micro Economic Theory*, Second Edition, McGraw Hill Kogakush Ltd., Tokyo, 1971.

Jain, C.S., *Farm Book Keeping*, New Delhi, 1964.

Johl, S.S., and Kapur, T.R., *Fundamentals of Farm Business Management*, Kalyani Publishers, Ludhiana, 1973.

Mehra, Sakuntala, "Some Aspects of Labour use in Indian Agriculture," *Indian J. of Agril. Econ.*, Vol. XXXI, No. 4, October-December, 1976.

Murray, W.G., *Farm Appraisal and Valuation*, The Iowa State University, Iowa, USA.

Nadkarni, M.V., and Despande, R.S., "Under Utilization of Land Climatic or Institutional Factors," *Indian Journal of Agricultural Economics*, Vol. XXXIV, No. 2, p. 1, April-June, 1979.

Naidu, R.T.R., "Trends in Farm Mechanization during the Post Green Revolution Period and Associated Variables," *An Inter State Analysis*, Vol. XXXII, No. 4, p. 107, October-December, 1977.

Rao, P., and Miller, R.L., *Applied Econometrics*, Prentice-Hall of India, New Delhi, 1972.

Singh, I.J., *Elements of Farm Management Economics*, Affiliated East West Press Pvt. Ltd., New Delhi, 1977.

Singh, Katar, *Some Alternative Strategies for Optimal use of Land and their Resources in the Hill Region of Uttar Pradesh*, Vol. XXXII, No. 3, p. 113, July-Sept. 1977.

Sridharan, B., and Radhakrishnan, S.A., *A Study on the Factors — Affecting Changes in the Cropping Pattern in Nilgiris District Tamil Nadu*, Vol. XXXIII, No. 4, p. 14, October-December, 1978.

Swaminathan, M.S., "Indian Agriculture at the Cross-Roads," *Indian Journal of Agril. Econ.*, Vol. XXXII, No. 4, p. 1, October-December, 1977.

Tandon, R.K., and Dhondyal, S.P., *Principles and Methods of Farm Management*, Published by A. Joshi, 3A/24, Azad Nagar, Kanpur-2, 1971.

Wale, M., and Osuji, L.O., "Incomes and Factor Productivity in Nigerian Peasant Agriculture," *Indian Journal of Agricultural Economics*, Vol. XXXIV, No. 3, p. 33, July-Sept., 1979.

PART V
Research Methodology

29
Science and Social Science

Before undertaking research project in social sciences, researcher must be aware of various concepts and aspects of social research. This will change the outlook of researcher, and he will go ahead in his research project with interest.

What is Science?

Meaning of science will be clear from following statements:

1. Science is knowledge not of things but of their relations.
2. Science is a process which makes knowledge. Knowledge is a power, and this power is increased with the help of science.
3. Science is the search of the reasons of things.
4. Science is that activity by which today we attain real bulk of our knowledge and control over the facts of nature.

Thus, science is a process which builds up the knowledge. If we compare a primitive man and modern man, we will find significant differences in their behaviour, because of process of knowledge building and utilising it for modernization, revolutionary changes have been taken place in a way of living of a man. Thus, science has increased happiness of human beings. Some scientists will take a clue or will concentrate their thinking on a particular issue which will lead to another discovery and thus, knowledge building is a continuous process. Publication also plays important role, it is the only means by which fellow scientist will come to know about recent development in the particular branch of knowledge.

Function of Science

Main function of science is to discover the truth. Scientists want to satisfy their curiosity and go on doing research works, discover various truths which can be best used for well-being of human beings. Sometimes, some problems are urgent. For example, demand for food grain is increasing, *i.e.*, total world population is increasing at faster rate than food grain production. Scientists continuously worked on this problem and found out varieties which can yield more food grains. Thus, various research projects are launched to solve practical human problems.

What is Social Science?

Science which deals with human behaviour and society is known as social science. Human being is the subject matter of social sciences. Man is not an isolated animal, he is gregarious and social. He lives in society. How individual behaves in a society as a member of the group. His different activities are studied in different social sciences. Economist will study behaviour of individual with reference to his unlimited wants and scarce means which have alternative uses. Psychology, history, sociology all deal with different aspects of human behaviour. Social sciences are compared with successive layers of onion. One social science is represented by a single layer.

Science is classified as below:

Science

Natural	Social
1. Physical	1. History
2. Biological	2. Economics
	3. Psychology
	4. Sociology
	5. Politics
	6. Ethics
	7. Anthropology

Limitations of Social Science Research

In physical sciences, exactness is observed. This is because physical sciences deal with non-living material, experimental material is passive. However, in social sciences we deal with human beings. Here, experimental material is not passive. Everybody has its own way of thinking and hence, behaviour of one varies from that of another. Base of the social science research is data. Researcher has to depend on others for the sake of data. If investigator is biased, he will not able to collect correct data as well as if the respondent is ignorant he may give unreliable information. This is a limitation of social science research.

Interdependence of Social Sciences

All social sciences depend on each other. Different social sciences aim to solve different problems of human beings. Psychology and economics are dependent on each other, economic forces may direct the individual to do the things which are rejected by an individual because of his personal psychological problems. Tribal people may not behave according to principles of economics. Politics and economics are also related. Politician must understand economics. He has to practically implement the things as advised by economists.

Theory and Fact

What is Theory?

To the scientist, theory refers to the relationship between facts or to the ordering of them in some meaningful way.

Different related facts are studied, and broad conclusions are drawn. When these conclusions are tested by various research workers, those conclusions are widely accepted. We call it as a theory.

Functions of Theory

1. Narrows the range of facts to be studied: With the help of existing studies, researcher will understand what facts must be studied for a particular objectives. Thus, it reduces the work.

2. Theory provides conceptual scheme by which the relevant phenomena are studied, classified and interrelated.
3. Theory summarizes facts: From the similar type of facts same conclusions are drawn, those conclusions after testing may be converted into theory. Thus, theory summarizes facts.
4. Theory predicts facts: Theory is established after testing the facts and based on theoretical information, certain facts can be predicted for future, *e.g.*, population specialist will predict population for future.
5. Theory points out gap in our knowledge: Knowledge of a person depends upon his experience and reading. Sometimes individual does not get opportunity to have a knowledge of particular thing and it remains as a gap in his knowledge.
6. Practical problems are solved with the help of theoretical knowledge, *e.g.*, J.M. Keynes' General Theory of Employment.

What is Fact?

Fact is an empirically verifiable observation. Population of a country, growth rate in food grain production, estimate for unemployed people, all these are facts.

Functions of Fact

1. Facts help to initiate theory: Studying various aspects of a particular fact one can come to final conclusion and establishes theory, *e.g.*, Malthusian Theory of Population.
2. Facts lead to reformulation of existing theory: As facts initiate theory in the same manner, with the help of recent facts one can reformulate existing theory, *e.g.*, like Malthusian Theory, Optimum Theory of Population also came into existence.
3. Facts charge the focus and orientation of theory: At a particular point of time, particular problem attracts the mind of the researchers, *e.g.*, employment problem has attracted minds of the researchers during recent years as it has become a serious problem in most of the countries.

4. Facts clarify and refine theory: Research is a continuous process hence, due to critical and advanced research, it has become necessary to refine the theory as well as recent facts better explain the theory.

Relationship between theory and fact: Theory is based on facts as well as refinements are also dependent on facts. Thus, theory depends on facts.

Research

What is Research?

The aim of research is to discover truth. (1) It is essentially a systematic enquiry, seeking facts through objectives, verifiable methods in order to discover the relationship among them and, to deduce from them broad principles or laws. (2) Research constitutes a method for the discovery of truth which is really a method of critical thinking and conducting experiment accordingly, till researcher comes to conclusion. (3) Research comprises defining and redefining problems, formulating hypothesis, collecting, organizing and evaluating data; making conclusions and at last carefully testing the conclusions to determine whether they fit the formulated hypothesis.

Types of Research

There are broadly three types of research:

1. Discovery of facts, *e.g.*, rural credit survey, debt and investment survey. In this case, data is collected with the help of schedule or questionnaire and these data were analysed; this leads to discovering the facts.
2. Here in this type, secondary data is analysed and interpretations are made. After rural credit survey report, several research workers used data given in those reports and wrote various research articles.
3. Purely theorizing type: After taking experience as well as after adequate reading one can build up a theoretical model for solving a particular problem, *e.g.*, J.M. Keynes' General Theory of Employment or Einstein's Theory of Relativity.

Categories of Research

There are two categories of research:

1. Basic Research
2. Applied Research.

1. Basic Research: Basic research is a search for broad principles and synthesis without any utilitarian object, *e.g.*, Franklin's Discovery of Electricity and Einstein's Theory of Relativity.

2. Applied Research: Application of principles, discovered in basic research to practical problems is called as applied research, *e.g.*, Thomas Alva Edison's work is an example of applied research.

Basic and applied research both are related and not quite different from each other. Even basic research is also undertaken with some objectives. Countries having sound resource base can undertake basic research to solve complicated problems of human beings. Developing countries should give priority to applied research and should make best use of their resources.

30
Concept and Hypothesis

Concept

Concept is a word or a phrase symbolizing the phenomena studied and helping to communicate the findings of the study, *e.g.*, land, rent, acceleration, multiplier, income elasticity, etc. Knowledge is continuously expanding and to summarise such a vast knowledge, concepts are necessary.

Uses of Concepts

1. Researcher can use concept as a tool of analysis, *e.g.*, multiplier, marginal efficiency of capital used by J.M. Keynes.
2. Because of concepts, it is easy to transfer knowledge from one place to another place and from one person to another person, *e.g.*, demand, supply, income, saving, credit, etc.
3. Because of concepts, it has become most easy to communicate knowledge which has given birth to publication. J.M. Keynes' single book made him world famous.
4. Because of concept lot of research worker's labour is saved. He can avoid mistakes carried out by others and will understand various things about the problem he is handling by reviewing literature. Development of literature becomes possible only because of concepts.

Following are some of the important things research worker should bear in mind:

1. Research worker should try to know all the concepts and way in which those have been used by previous research workers in his field of study. He should as far as possible maintain the similarity with previous research worker. Thus, it becomes easy for other research workers to understand what he wants to say. If it is necessary to form a new concept it should be fully defined and must be recognised by others.
2. Researchers should understand connotation of each concept clearly, precisely in the context of its use.
3. As far as possible concepts which are ambiguous should be avoided and if used one has to realize they are so.
4. Avoid highly general and vague concepts, *e.g.*, function; modern society.
5. Researcher should understand the concepts of related fields of study.
6. Researcher should first select the concepts and then define them precisely before their use.

Different research workers working in the same field comes together at the time of seminars, conferences and formally recognizes new concepts. Sometimes certain concepts become irrelevant and needs reconceptualization. Giving particular, operational definitions of a particular concept at the beginning of research report solves most of the problems.

Hypothesis

Beginning of the research project is made with hypothesis. It has been defined as a tentative solution posed on hasty or superficial observations of known and available data are used provisionally to explain certain events and to guide the investigation of others. When researcher starts any research project, he makes certain superficial observations as well as goes through the previous literature. Because of this, he gets the complete idea about the research work to be carried out and understand tentative solution to the problem. This is called as hypothesis.

Use of Hypothesis

Mainly, hypothesis guides the research. Researcher will understand what type of data will be required to test his hypothesis. Accordingly, he will construct the questionnaire to collect data. After analysis of data, hypothesis will be tested and conclusions will be drawn. Thus, hypothesis is very important.

Type of Hypothesis

1. Crude hypothesis
2. Refined hypothesis

Crude hypothesis mainly indicates kind of data to be gathered and does not lead to higher critical research. Whereas refined type of hypothesis indicates uniformity in social behaviour. They do not involve much of verification. When there are many variables involved it is rather difficult to provide tentative solution. However, refined hypothesis or careful statement may serve the purpose.

How Hypothesis Originate?

1. There are certain common beliefs, these common beliefs may originate hypothesis.
2. Particular science is another source of hypothesis. When research worker go through the concerned review of literature; he gets the idea of hypothesis for his study.
3. The casual observations and study of a sister science may suggest ideas for formulating hypothesis.
4. Personal experience and individual reaction give birth to hypothesis.

Researcher should bear following things in mind:

1. Conceptual clarity: Whatever concepts used in hypothesis should be cleared in their meanings.
2. Hypothesis must be specific and precise otherwise they are not much useful.
3. For testing hypothesis, particular technique of research is necessary to know. Hence, while formulating hypothesis one should give consideration for its testing and research technique to be used for this purpose.
4. Research worker should see that he is adding something to the existing theory and accordingly he should formulate hypothesis.

Testing of Hypothesis

Testing of hypothesis means one has to show that whether the hypothesis is accepted or rejected. It is examined with the help of data. For example: (*i*) Farm household income has positive relationship with farm household savings, (*ii*) Farm household savings have negative relationship with the size of the farm family.

The necessary data were used and following function is fitted to test the above hypothesis.

$$S = 209.57 \pm \underset{(0.12)}{\overset{***}{0.67}}\, Y - \underset{(101.93)}{\overset{***}{415.8}}\, M \qquad R^2 = 0.77$$

S = Saving of individual family

Y = Income of individual family

M = Man equivalent (size of each family)

R^2 = Square of multiple correlation co-efficient

* * * = Highly significant.

It is observed from the above regression equation, if income increased by one rupee, saving will increase by 67 paise, and if size of family increased by one-man equivalent saving will decrease by ₹ 415.80 and thus above-mentioned both the hypotheses are accepted.

31
Planning Research Project

There are mainly two ways of undertaking research work. First: Individual person undertakes research work; particularly post-graduate students undertake research work for their degrees. Here again two kinds, *i.e.*, research work for master and doctor degree. Both the research works are time-bound and students carry out their research work under the supervision of their research guide. Another kind of research work is a research project, sanctioned by particular research financing body, *i.e.*, Indian Council of Agricultural Research, University Grant Commission, etc. They grant the scheme, and provide finance. A team of scientist work in a project and finally research report is submitted to financing body.

What is Research Project ?

Research project can be defined as an investigation into a particular problem having different facts, carried out by a single technical research unit, *e.g.*, techno-economic survey is carried out by the group of experts, *i.e.*, economists, statisticians, sociologists, agronomists, etc.

Selection of a Research Problem

There are certain points one must consider while selecting a research problem:

1. Urgency,
2. Anticipation,
3. Resources,

(*i*) Available information,
(*ii*) Equipment,
(*iii*) Operational funds,
4. Specialization of expert.

Urgency

Some problems are important than others at a particular point of time and hence, research worker should give priority to urgent problems. For example, if government wants cost of cultivation of a particular crop and if this work is assigned to particular organization then that organization should give first priority to estimation of cost of cultivation of a particular crop.

Anticipation

Sometimes researcher has to anticipate which is the problem which needs solution, *e.g.*, if there is a dam site and government is likely to undertake its construction. Before construction starts, estimation of costs and benefits if readily available those can be useful to various government authorities. So that government will give priority to work.

Resources

While selecting a problem one must give full consideration to resources available for that particular research work.

(*i*) **Available Information:** While selecting a problem what kind of data will be required, what kind of data is available as well as what kind of data is to be collected, all these aspects should be considered.

(*ii*) **Equipments:** For analysis of data, computational facilities are necessary, while selecting a research problem these aspects must be considered otherwise this will create inconvenience.

(*iii*) **Operational Fund:** Operational fund is necessary for carrying out particular research work successfully, otherwise work will suffer due to lack of fund. Unless and until field investigators and other staff members are regularly paid, they cannot concentrate on the work. Administrator must see there will not be any difficulty for operational fund or concern institute should be able to manage it skillfully.

Specialization

Specialization of a person is also equally important while selecting or assigning a particular problem. If person who is going to handle a research project; is not a specialist in that particular branch of knowledge, he cannot give justice to the project, *e.g.*, if a person, who has not come across survey work is given a survey project, he will not able to handle that project successfully. Thus, problem must be assigned to a particular person taking into consideration his field of specialization.

Similarly, there should be sufficient supervisory and administrative staff so that there will not be any difficulty in carrying out research work successfully.

Difficulties in Planning a Research Project

While planning a research project various points require attention, and several points create difficulties in planning a research project. Those points must be considered well in advance.

(I) Selection of a Problem

(*i*) *Problem of equal importance*: Sometimes difficulty arises while selecting a problem. Both the problems are important. At this point, two research projects should be assigned to two different research organisations. So that both projects will be completed in time.

(*ii*) *Anticipation*: Sometime researcher assumes that government will not change its policies but his assumption may not be true and if government changed its policies it will affect conclusions of researcher. This point also be considered while selecting a problem.

(II) Resources

Sometimes secondary data is inadequate, for this purpose. Researcher should be able to do something either by seeking the information from other sources or by collecting primary data. Similarly, if equipments are being engaged in some other work or if funds are not available, it will badly hamper the work and hence, alternative must be found out for such difficulties well in advance.

(III) Specialization of Research Worker

If the institute is not having right person for handling the project, the person to which institute will assign work should be given orientation about problem. Thus, he will be capable or handling that research project.

Thus, various difficulties should be considered well in advance so that research work will not remain incomplete.

32
Data, Schedule and Questionnaire

Data

Data is very essential thing for research work. The success of results of research depends upon reliability of data. Hence, before starting analysis of data, researcher should be very critical in judging the reliability of the data. In India, most of the cultivators do not keep records and hence, it is difficult to obtain reliable data for research in farm economics. Most of the literature developed in India, pertaining to rural credit and rural problems were based on the data which is collected by survey method. Survey method has its own limitations regarding memory bias of the respondent. However, now central and state government has started to collect the data pertaining to agriculture and cultivator by cost accounting method; where investigator has to stay in villages and record the data of selected cultivators once in a three to four days. This data is more reliable, but the expenditure incurred for collecting this data is more as compared to survey method. Cost accounting data is more reliable and will increase the reliability of the estimates.

Classification of Data

For convenience mainly data classified according to its source:

1. Primary source or primary data,
2. Secondary source or secondary data, and
3. Tertiary source or tertiary data.

The various countries collect census data and those census documents are primary source. From this source, data about each country is obtained and demographic yearbook is prepared by the United Nations, it is called as secondary source. Some research workers will use data from United Nation's demographic yearbook for their book and that will be called as tertiary data or data from tertiary source. Thus, when compiling authority and purpose changes, class of data or type of data also changes.

Another example, if any banking company wanted to prepare report about its progress. Company will use its own publication such as annual reports, balance sheets, etc. It will be primary source for bank and may be called as primary data. However, data from RBI publication pertaining to same bank may be called as secondary source and when Research workers will use data in their books from RBI publication. The book data is called as tertiary source. If newspaper editor used data from RBI publication in his newspaper it may be called as tertiary data or tertiary source. Rural credit survey report is treated as secondary source. When authors will use data from this report in their books, those books will be tertiary source.

For research purpose which data should be used depends upon from where the data is available as well as who has compiled them. In case of national estimates or macro studies, RBI publication and certain all India reports are the main source and hence researcher should use them and must mention where from information is taken.

Another issue is about post-graduate students' approved theses. Various universities possess various theses, *i.e.*, detail information on different aspects of the same subject and may be termed as secondary source of information on the ground that purpose or objective for which data is being used is changing. However, permission of the author will be desirable thing in such cases.

In social science research, field data is also collected. Field data term is used to primary data which is directly collected by survey method, using schedule and questionnaires. This data is basically primary data from which secondary data is developed. In India most of the social information is collected by survey method. This information may be referred as primary data or field data.

The Schedule and Questionnaire

"The schedule is a detailed, planned, and classified and seriated list of items on which information is required for a particular research project." In India majority of population is illiterate and if data is to be collected from them with less expenditure, survey method is used. Hence, investigator or interviewer is essential for filling the schedule. If interviewers are trained, they can ask skillfully and collect the required information from respondents. Schedules were used in Rural Credit Survey, National Sample Survey and several post-graduate students of social sciences use schedules.

Schedules are slightly different from questionnaire. In questionnaire, information of various items is collected by asking several questions. Questionnaire is a list of questions and generally mailed. In case of questionnaire respondent should be literate and responsible one. So that they can answer the questions and send back the questionnaire to the researcher.

While constructing a schedule researcher has to consider some points which are explained below:

1. Schedule should not be very long, otherwise interest of the respondent will be lost as well as such schedule is inconvenient to handle.
2. The items in the schedule should be precisely and clearly worded. Otherwise, wrong information may be gathered.
3. For minimising space, tabular forms may be used.
4. Separate note may be given for clarification of different concepts used in schedule.
5. Some blank space may be provided, so that if there is any special information is to be recorded, it can be used.
6. As far as possible items listed in schedule should be in local language. Local terms and units may be used so that time will not be wasted in conversion and there will not be any chance for mistake.
7. Quantitative and objective information is important and effort must be made to obtain such information.

These points must be considered while constructing a schedule.

Construction of a Questionnaire

Following points one must consider while constructing a questionnaire.

1. Questions should cover all the aspects of the research project.
2. Questions must be easy to understand.
3. Questions should be such that their answers must be accurate, so that there will not be any confusion.
4. Questions should be few, limited to facts and of interest to the respondent.
5. Funnel approach should be followed, *i.e.*, initially general questions and later on specific questions should be asked.
6. Sequence should be such that one question should lead to other.
7. Vague questions must be discarded.
8. Wording should be such that questions will be easily understood.
9. Questions should be appropriate to respondent's level.
10. Questionnaire should demand respondent's minimum time.

While sending questionnaire to respondent, request must be made in forwarding letter, so that respondent will answer the questions immediately and will send it back.

Thus, questionnaire and schedule both are tools of collecting information.

Interview

Schedule is filled in by asking information to respondent by the interviewer or by investigator.

It is one of the research tools, superiority of this technique is the flexibility. Points may be explained well to respondent, so that he will give correct information. As well as some more personal data is also obtained. Particularly, in a country like

India where literacy percentage is low, interview technique is very useful in this technique information is obtained from the respondent by asking information about various points which are mentioned in schedule. Sometimes, misunderstanding of respondent is also removed.

Limitations of Interview

In this process, investigator or interviewer is very important. If the respondent is trained one, he will collect the correct information. If interviewer is not a trained person, he may not able to conduct a successful interview. Similarly, technique requires more expenditure, time and labour as compared to mailed questionnaire. Sometimes, there is tendency of respondent to exaggerate about information. However, at present this technique is widely used.

Case Study

This is another tool of social investigation. Case study refers to the intensive investigation of a particular unit. The data gathered may relate to some phase of the life history of the unit. In an underdeveloped country, this tool is very important. Generally, qualitative aspects are provided more attention. Here investigator plays important role. He remains in contact with respondent for a longer time and his remarks about respondent are valuable. Information collected is detail one and covers most of the aspects of a case under study.

Limitations

However, this technique requires more money, time and trained investigator. Similarly, sufficient numbers of records must be thoroughly studied. Thus, results require more time.

33
Research Reporting

Research reporting is the final stage of research work. First formulation of project, collection of data, analysis of data and final stage comes as reporting. Sometimes problem is also discussed with colleagues at the beginning and at intermediate stages. Research reporting is the oral or written presentation of the evidence and the findings in such detail and forms as to be readily understood and assessed by the reader, listener and as to enable them to verify the validity of the conclusions. Reporting is treated as a part of research. Reporting requires considerable thought, efforts, patience, skill, penetration and control over language.

Types of Reporting

(*i*) Oral reporting

(*ii*) Written reporting.

(*i*) **Oral Reporting:** While conducting a research, researcher wanted to know, ideas of other co-worker and hence he arranges seminar. Seminar on the research project may be arranged at the beginning of research work as well as at different stages of work. This is two-way communications. Researcher explains his research project and other colleagues express their views. Researcher may accept certain important suggestions and improve his work in future. Similarly, researcher has to explain about his project to his superior or to those, who are interested in the project. For better oral reporting researcher, should have command over language. He should explain and discuss important aspects in which he is having doubts as well as he wants suggestions from others. National Council of Applied Economic Research, New Delhi carry out techno-economic surveys and here in this case, it becomes necessary that all staff should exchange their ideas and discuss research topics. This improves the quality of work.

(*ii*) **Written Reporting:** The oral report has a limitation that one cannot study the topic afterwards. Written report overcomes those limitations. There are following types of written reports:

1. To the layman (popular report),
2. To the administrator,
3. To the technical expert (technical report).

1. Popular report: Popular report is meant for laymen, popular report should contain broad facts, findings and recommendations. However, over-simplification should be avoided. Newspaper articles are the examples of popular report. Here, in this case language should be such that laymen will follow easily. One should state why this popular article is written; in the first paragraph. Thus, readers will get idea of problem tackled in the article and they will be interested to read remaining part of the article. In agriculture, information of new technique tool, as well as certain suggestion for well-being of the farmer can be tackled in popular report. It has importance because those are the people, who use new techniques which are invented by research workers and hence, popular article should be convincing to them.

2. Report for administrator: Administrator is not much interested in methodology, but he is interested in findings. He would like to know about facts and some numerical information will also interest him. As well as such type of report should be brief one because administrator has to finish it within a limited time.

3. Technical report: This is most important type of report. Technical report should emphasize on technique used because reliability of the result also depends upon method used. Technical report is useful to another researcher, working in the same field.

Forms of technical report:

1. Monograph,
2. An article,
3. Full technical report.

The research article for publishing in a professional journal is prepared. It contains one or few aspects and is prepared skillfully. Reader should get complete idea from the article. Good research article is a credit to the researcher. Monographs are also prepared to report research findings.

Technical Report

Technical report is prepared by using technical language which is different from layman's language. Techno-economic surveys comprise different fields such as geology, transport, agriculture, fisheries, forest, etc. Expert of each field should submit his report to overall director, who is generally an economist; these are the technical reports. Director will use, all these reports for preparing his economic report.

Organization of Technical Report

Ordering the different parts of the report and planning the writing is called organization of technical report. Technical report for convenience is divided into following parts:

1. Introduction,
2. Stating the problems,
3. Methodology,
4. Findings,
5. Implications,
6. Conclusions,
7. Recommendations, and
8. Summary.

1. *Introduction*

Researcher should provide much attention on this part. Brief idea about the research work should be given in introduction. After reading the introduction, reader should get idea about what this report deals with, and they should be stimulated to read through the report. Researcher should explain importance of the problem in the introduction. Similarly, brief review of findings should be given in introduction.

2. *Stating the Problems*

Particular statement of the problem, objectives of the study, hypotheses of the study should be given in this part. Reader will get complete idea about study from this part.

3. *Methodology*

Methodology is very important in research. Findings will vary according to methodology. As well as methodology is very important on the point of view of other research worker for verification of the findings. Hence, accurate methodology should be given in this part.

4. *Findings*

This is also important part, all research is meant for findings. Findings may be directly used by policy makers and hence those should be clearly given in this part. Findings flow directly from the facts.

5. *Implications*

Implications pin-point the real significance of the facts and the findings. Implications are useful for assessing the value of the research. Here, one has to consider related issues and findings together. How the findings will affect related issues that one has to give in this part.

6. *Conclusions*

Conclusions are in fact the researcher's final assessment of what the data and findings mean. Because of personal element, the same data and findings may lead to different conclusions and more particularly to differing recommendations. The conclusions have to look forward to the application of these findings and implications.

7. *Recommendations*

Based on findings and conclusions, researcher can recommend for the benefit of the society and this is the last stage in research. Researcher at the most, recommends and can do more than that. Concerned politicians and people, they will implement the recommendations if they are satisfied.

8. *Summary*

Sometimes, people don't have much time to read through the whole report and hence, they will read summary and will know what it is. Hence, summary should deal in brief, each part and should be skillfully prepared. No new idea should be introduced in summary.

Outline

Before starting the research work, outline is prepared. In outline, skeleton of research work should be given. Single aspect is explained in a separate paragraph. Outline may be prepared twice, one for before starting research work and another before preparing the final draft.

Write-up of a Technical Report

After organization of a technical report, researcher has to prepare a final draft, and this is known as write-up. There are three steps each consisting of writing quite a few times.

First Draft

It brings all facts together; it concentrates on substance of the investigation. Language and form are of secondary importance in this draft.

Researcher has to bring all important facts together in this draft and hence it is important draft.

Second Draft

In second draft, researcher should give importance to language. Readability, clarity and lucidity become important in this draft.

Third Draft

This is the final draft; hence, researcher should concentrate on finish and final touches, *i.e.*, on documentation and polishing to make the report authoritative and attractive.

Documentation

The term documentation has two different meanings. One, on the point of view of librarians and another on the point of view of individual research worker. Librarians search for literature on a particular topic prepare the list and make it available to the reader. This is called as documentation.

For individual research worker, documentation indicates reference to the sources. Because of documentation, research report becomes more authoritative and complete. Good research paper also depends upon accurate and complete recording of the references.

Purposes Served by Documentation

1. It supports the fact presented.
2. It enables the investigator to acknowledge his debt to others.
3. Here some legal and moral aspects are involved.
4. Useful to point out differences of views, facts and findings.
5. It leads the reader to further information.
6. It is possible to provide additional or detailed information either in the footnotes or in the appendices to the main report.

Forms of Documentation

Documentation has following components:

1. Footnotes,
2. Bibliography,
3. Quotations,
4. Translations,
5. Tables,
6. Diagrams,
7. Appendices, and
8. Preface.

Sometimes these are mixed up with text.

Footnotes

Any important thing which is not relevant in main text can be given at the end of the page. It is called footnote. Footnote serves various purposes:

1. Footnote can be given for recognizing ideas borrowed.
2. To provide a reference to the sources which may be consulted for more details?
3. To clarify meaning of any term.
4. To explain meaning of any table heading.
5. To give cross reference to some other part of the report.
6. Distinguishing one's own contribution from that of all another person's contribution.

Bibliography

An essential of a research report is the bibliography. This contains information about books, reports, articles and other sources relevant to the investigation.

Quotations

Sometimes, researcher requires quoting certain writing of another research worker in support of his own writing. Here in this case, correct reference should be given in a footnote.

Tables, diagrams illustrate the issue correctly and those should be used in technical report.

Appendices

Too, detail things are not relevant in text but are important for other researchers for clear understanding. Hence, these things should be given in appendix at the end of report.

Preface

Preface by convention has become a part of the report. Researcher will very well explain about objectives of study and importance of study as well as he will acknowledge his indebtedness to his helpers of various types and for different services.

34
Sampling

In social sciences, oftenly researcher requires to study human behaviour or assets and liabilities of individuals. For this purpose, data from individuals is required. There are two ways of obtaining data, *i.e.*, by census enquiry and by sample enquiry. Census enquiry deals with the entire individual in population. This is expensive and time-consuming way. Sample study means studying representative part of the population. A sample consists of a small collection from some larger aggregate about which we wish information. We study sample and use those estimates or conclusions for population. That is why; whatever sample we will study must be representative of population. Here population refers to individuals for which we want certain estimate or for which we want to conclude.

Objective of Sampling

Most important aim of sampling studies is to obtain maximum information about the phenomena under study with the least sacrifice of money, time and energy.

Types of Sampling

1. Random sampling,
2. Purposive sampling,
3. Mixed sampling.
   (*a*) Stratified sampling,
   (*b*) Multistage sampling.

1. Random Sampling

In random sampling, selection of units in sample is on random basis. Random selection implies that every individual in the population has a known probability of appearing in the sample.

Population is that aggregate of which every member has a known probability of appearing in the sample.

Thus, individuals or items are taken in sample which will represent the whole population.

2. Purposive Sampling

When it is necessary to study particular trait in detail, one has to select purposive sample. Here selection is made according to choice of a selector. This helps in collection of an information regarding particular trait in detail. Here drawback is equal chance is not given for all those are in the population. While reporting we must make a mention that these conclusions are applicable only for that particular trait, *i.e.*, to those individuals having similar traits.

3. Mixed Sampling

(*a*) **In purposive sampling representativeness of a sample is destroyed:** But, sometimes, it is necessary to select purposively, *e.g.*, if we want to study about socio-economic changes in irrigated area, then one must purposively select villages where percentage irrigated area is maximum. Under such conditions partly purposive sampling and partly random sampling is done, *e.g.*, all the villages in a particular area are classified in two strata, *i.e.*, irrigated villages and unirrigated villages and from each strata cultivators are selected by random method. This type of sampling is called as stratified sampling.

(*b*) **Multi-stage sampling:** Here in this case random sampling is applied at different stages, *e.g.*, if few cultivators are to be studied then districts are selected randomly from a selected district talukas are randomly selected, from each selected taluka villages are selected and from each village cultivators are selected randomly. It is a multistage sampling.

Selected References

Bal, H.K., and Kahlon, A.S., "Methodological Issues on Measurement of Returns to Investment in Agricultural Research," *Indian Journal of Agril. Economics,* Vol. XXXII, No. 3, p. 181, July-Sept., 1977.

Bhatia, G.R., and Ram, G.S., "Marketing Efficiency in Retail Vegetable Markets in Delhi," *Agricultural Marketing,* January, 1977.

Bishnoi, R.N., "Problems and Possibilities of Co-operative Finance—A Case Study," *Financing Agriculture,* Vol. III, No. 3, p. 28, October, 1971.

Dahiya, C.N., "Impact of Optimum Agricultural Land Allocation Patterns on Farm Incomes—A Case Study of Transitional," *Agricultural Economy,* Vol. XXXI, No. 1, p. 23, Jan.-March, 1976.

Elhance, D.N., *Fundamentals of Statistics,* Fourteenth Edition, Kitab Mahal, Allahabad, 1973.

Goode and Hatt, *Methods in Social Research,* McGraw-Hill Book Company, Inc. Tokyo, Japan, 1952.

Gopal, M.H., *An Introduction to Research Procedure in Social Sciences,* Asia Publishing House, Second Edition, Bombay, 1970.

George, P.S., and Choukidar, V.V., "Marketing of Paddy in West Godavari District," *Agricultural Marketing,* January, 1972.

Gupta, K.R., *Issues of Indian Agriculture,* Atlantic Publishers and Distributors, New Delhi, 1980.

Hota, B.C., and Ramrao, "Price Spread in Tobacco," *Agricultural Marketing,* October, 1972.

Jha, Dayanath and Praduman Kumar, "Effect of Price Changes on Cost Structure and Factor Demand—A Case Study on Selected Farms in Delhi Territory," *Indian J. of Agril. Econ.,* Vol. XXXI, No. 3, p. 63, July-Sept., 1976.

Kahlon, A.S., "Impact of Mechanization on Punjab Agriculture with Special Reference to Tractorisation," *Indian Journal of Agril. Econ.,* Vol. XXXI, No. 4, p. 54, October-December, 1976.

Malya, M.M., "A Note on the Methodological Problems of Using the Employment Data from the Farm Management Studies," *Indian Journal of Agril. Economics,* Vol. XXXIV, No. 2, p. 83, April-June, 1979.

Pandey, H.K., "Institutional Credit and HYV Programme—A Case Study in Allahabad, Uttar Pradesh," *Financing Agriculture,* Vol. VI, No. 1, p. 23, April, 1974.

Prasad, Ayodhya, "Analysis of Price Variation of Fish in Allahabad," *Agricultural Marketing,* October, 1975.

Ranagacharyalu, S.V., and Pandurang Rao, J., "Small Farmer, Marginal Farmer and other Householders—An Estimation Procedure," *Rural Development Digest,* Vol. 3, No. 1, p. 57, January, 1980.

Singh, I.J., *Economics of Commercial Crops,* Vol. XXX, No. 1, p. 18, Jan.-March, 1975.

Singh, R.V., Patel, R.K., and Sirohi, A.S., "Economics of Mexican Wheat Cultivation in Western Uttar Pradesh," *Financing Agriculture*, Vol. VI, No. 1, p. 27, April, 1974.

Sirohi, A.S., Ram, G.S., and Singh, C.B., "Interstate Disparities in the Structural Distribution of Land Holdings in Rural India," *Indian Journal of Agril. Econ.*, Vol. XXXI, No. 3, p. 14, July-Sept., 1976.

Shukla, Tara, *Capital Formation in Indian Agriculture*, Vora and Co. Publishers Pvt. Ltd., Bombay, 1969.

PART VI
Economic Information about Indian Agriculture

35
Agricultural Resources in India

Importance of Agriculture in Indian Economy

Agriculture plays an important role in Indian economy. It forms the backbone of Indian economy. It is useful to Indian economy as follows:

First, Agriculture contributes nearly one-fourth of the national income, earlier its share was one-half, but it has declined during recent years, because service sector and industrial sector developed in a faster manner. In 2001-02, total net national product at factor cost with 1993-94 prices was ₹ 11,15,157 crores out of which agriculture contributed 24 per cent. Share of agriculture in total national income is declining, major reason is it depends upon natural endowments like water, land and climatic factors. However, in 1999 about 60 per cent economically active population was dependent on agriculture whereas in developed countries this proportion was 1.8 per cent in England, 2.2 per cent in USA, 4.7 per cent in Australia, 10.8 per cent in Russian Federation. This trend will lead India towards an industrialized and developed nation.

Second, about 16.7 per cent of the world population lives in India. However, India possesses only 2.4 per cent of world land. Now, Indian agriculture is able to satisfy country's requirement of food grains. India achieved a record food grains yield of 213.46 million tonnes in 2003-2004.

Third, agriculture supplies raw material to industrial sector such as cotton, jute, sugarcane, tobacco, etc., are supplied to different leading industries.

Fourth, agriculture provides large business to railways. Internal trade is mostly in agricultural products. Railway provides employment to several people.

Fifth, total export in India during 2002-03 was ₹ 2,55,138 crores, out of which agriculture and allied products contributed ₹ 33,691 crores, *i.e.*, 13.2 per cent. In 1970-71 it was 31.7%, in 1980-81 it was 30.6%, it indicates that share is decreasing this is because manufactured good's share is increasing very fast.

Because of these characteristics agriculture has acquired a great importance in Indian economy. It is the backbone of Indian economy and prosperity of agriculture can also largely be responsible for prosperity of the entire Indian economy.

Utilization of Land

Agricultural production can be increased by bringing more area under cultivation. Land is used for various purposes, according to priority, land is allocated for different purposes. At present land is classified as given in table 35.1.

The total geographical area of India is 328.05 million hectares, but land use statistics are available for 305.27 million hectares. The percentage net area sown increased from 41.8 per cent in 1950-51 to 46.1 per cent in 2000-01. This indicated slowly and slowly more land was brought under cultivation. However, the trend may not be infinite. However, by increasing irrigation facility area can be sown more than once and thus, total cropped area can be increased. In 1970-71, about 6.5 per cent land was fallow and it can be put under crops by improving it. Different concepts are used as follows:

1. **Geographical area:** The total area of the country as per boundaries of the country.
2. **Reporting area:** This is the total area for which statistics is available.
3. **Area under forests:** Area which is covered by forests.
4. Area not available for cultivation includes:
   (*i*) Area under non-agricultural uses: Includes land occupied by buildings, roads, railways, underwater, *e.g.*, rivers, canals and other lands put to uses other than agricultural.

Table 35.1: Classification of area in India (Percentages to the reporting area)
Land use classification in India (in million ha)

Classification	1950-51	1960-61	1970-71	1980-81	1990-91	1997-98#	1998-99#	1999-00#	2000-01#
I. Geographic area	328.73	328.73	328.73	328.73	328.73	328.73	328.73	328.73	328.73
II. Reporting area for land utilisation statistics (1 to 5)	284.32	298.46	303.76	304.15	304.86	305.79	306.05	306.01	306.25
1. Forests	40.48	54.05	63.91	67.47	67.80	69.01	68.98	68.97	69.41
	(14.2)	(18.1)	(21.00)	(22.2)	(22.2)	(22.6)	(22.5)	(22.5)	(22.7)
2. Not available for cultivation (a+b)	47.52	50.75	44.64	39.62	40.48	42.14	42.31	42.41	42.83
(a) Non-agricultural uses	9.36	14.84	16.48	19.66	21.09	22.70	22.80	23.27	23.57
	(3.3)	(5.0)	(5.4)	(6.4)	(6.9)	(7.4)	(7.5)	(7.6)	(7.7)
(b) Barren and uncultivable land	38.16 (13.4)	35.91 (12.0)	28.16 (9.3)	19.96 (6.6)	19.39 (6.4)	19.44 (6.4)	19.51 (6.4)	19.13 (6.2)	19.26 (6.30)
3. Other uncultivated land excluding fallow land (a+b+c)	49.45	37.64	35.06	32.31	30.22	28.55	28.66	28.49	27.93
(a) Permanent pastures and other grazing land	6.68 (2.3)	13.97 (4.7)	13.26 (4.4)	11.97 (3.9)	11.40 (3.7)	11.05 (3.6)	11.13 (3.6)	11.04 (3.6)	10.90 (3.6)
(b) Miscellaneous tree crops and groves	19.83 (7.0)	4.46 (1.5)	4.30 (91.4)	3.60 (1.2)	3.82 (1.3)	3.62 (1.2)	3.63 (1.2)	3.64 (1.2)	3.37 (1.1)

(Contd....)

Classification	1950-51	1960-61	1970-71	1980-81	1990-91	1997-98#	1998-99#	1999-00#	2000-01#
(c) Cultivable waste land	22.94	19.21	17.50	16.74	15.00	13.88	13.90	13.80	13.66
	(8.1)	(6.4)	(5.8)	(5.5)	(4.9)	(4.5)	(4.5)	(4.5)	(4.5)
4. Fallow land (a+b)	28.12	22.82	19.88	24.75	23.36	24.01	23.52	24.91	24.99
(a) Fallow land other than current fallow	17.44	11.18	8.76	9.92	9.66	9.75	9.93	10.08	10.19
	(6.1)	(3.8)	(2.9)	(3.3)	(3.2)	(3.2)	(3.2)	(3.3)	(3.3)
(b) Current fallow	10.68	11.64	11.12	14.83	13.70	14.26	13.59	14.99	14.80
	(3.8)	(3.9)	(3.5)	(4.9)	(4.5)	(4.7)	(4.4)	(4.9)	(4.8)
5. Net area sown	118.75	133.20	140.27	140.00	143.00	142.08	142.58	141.10	141.10
	(41.8)	(44.6)	(46.3)	(46.0)	(46.9)	(46.5)	(46.6)	(46.1)	(46.1)
6. Area sown more than once	13.14	19.57	25.52	32.63	42.74	48.49	50.45	49.22	46.84
7. Gross cropped area (5+6)	131.89	152.77	165.79	172.63	185.74	190.57	193.03	190.32	187.94
8. Cropping intensity*	111.1	114.7	118.2	123.3	129.9	134.1	135.4	134.9	133.20
III. Net irrigated area	20.85	24.66	31.10	38.72	47.78	54.98	56.50	56.76	54.68
IV. Gross irrigated area	22.56	27.98	38.19	49.78	62.47	73.01	77.64	77.99	75.14

Notes: 1. # Provisional

2. * Cropping intensity is percentage of the gross cropped area to the net area sown

3. Figures in parentheses indicate percentage to reported area.

Sources: 1. *Agricultural Statistics at a Glance, 2004*, Directorate of Economics and Statistics, Ministry of Agriculture, Govt. of India.

2. Agricultural Research Data Book-2005.

(*ii*) Barren land covers all barren and uncultivable lands like mountains, hills, deserts and hill-slopes. All land which can be brought under cultivation except at a high cost is classed as uncultivable land.

5. **Other uncultivated land:** This does not include fallow land. It includes area under permanent pastures, area under miscellaneous trees and culturable waste. Culturable waste land includes all lands available for cultivation but not taken up for cultivation or abandoned after a few years for one reason or the other. Such land may be fallow for more than five years and may be covered with shrubs and forests.
6. **Fallow land:** It includes current fallow and fallow land which is fallow more than one year and less than five years. Current fallows are those lands which are not cultivated for one year and are given rest so that fertility could be restored. Other fallow lands include those lands which are left fallow for one to five years due to inadequate water supply, unfavourable climate, poverty of the cultivator and unremunerative nature of farming.

Irrigation

Modern agriculture mainly depends upon irrigation facility. More crops can be taken once a year with the help of irrigation water. Gross irrigated area as percentage of gross cropped area during 1976-77 is given in table 35.2.

Table 35.2: State-wise area irrigated

State	Gross irrigated area as percentage of gross cropped area 1976-77	Gross irrigated area as percentage of gross cropped area 1999-2000
1. Uttar Pradesh	46	66.4
2. Bihar	33	48.2
3. Maharashtra	11	16.9
4. West Bengal	21	26.1
5. Andhra Pradesh	35	44.1
6. Madhya Pradesh	11	27.1

(Contd....)

State	Gross irrigated area as percentage of gross cropped area 1976-77	Gross irrigated area as percentage of gross cropped area 1999-2000
7. Tamil Nadu	47	55.0
8. Karnataka	16	26.1
9. Gujarat	18	37.8
10. Rajasthan	21	36.0
11. Orissa	21	29.05
12. Kerala	24	15.7
13. Assam	22	14.0
14. Punjab	86	90.9
15. Haryana	56	85.0
16. Jammu & Kashmir	42	40.7
17. Himachal Pradesh	17	18.7
18. Tripura	9	14.3
19. Manipur	40	37.9
20. Meghalaya	31	20.7
21. Nagaland	41	24.7
22. Sikkim	—	13.2
23. Goa	—	20.3
24. Mizoram	—	12.1
25. Arunachal Pradesh	—	13.6
ALL INDIA	**28**	**40.2**

Sources: 1. *Economic Indicators*, December 1978 Centre for Monitoring Indian Economy, Bombay.

2. Economic Survey of Maharashtra, 2003-04, Directorate of Economics and Statistics, Planning Department, M.S., Mumbai.

Only 28 per cent gross cropped area was irrigated in 1976-77. There is significant difference in per hectare yield of irrigated and unirrigated area. Total national agricultural production can be increased by increasing the irrigation facility. It is observed that progressive states like Punjab and Haryana are having largest irrigated area. In case of Maharashtra, irrigated area is only 16 per cent. Construction of multipurpose dams serve many purposes and priority for creating irrigation facility should be continued in future Five-Year Plans.

It is observed from table 35.3 that government canals and wells are the major source of irrigation and it can be increased still further.

Table 35.5, revealed that gross irrigated area of all the crop is increasing. However, it is only 40 per cent which indicate that still there is scope for increasing area under irrigation which will enhance total agricultural production.

Table 35.3: Percentage area irrigated by different sources in India

Source	1950-51	1960-61	1970-71
Government canals	34.3	37.2	37.1
Private canals	5.5	4.9	2.8
Tanks	17.3	18.5	14.5
Wells	28.7	29.6	37.7
Others	14.2	9.8	7.9
Total	100.0	100.0	100.0

Source: *Indian Agriculture in Brief*, Fourteenth Edition, 1975, p. 30.

Table 35.4: Percentage area irrigated by different sources in India.
Source-wise irrigated area

(in million ha)

Source	1980-81	1990-91	1995-96	1996-97	1997-98	1998-99	1999-00*	2000-01*
Govt. canals	14.45 (37.3)	16.97 (35.3)	16.56 (31.0)	16.87 (30.6)	17.11 (31.11)	17.20 (30.22)	16.37 (28.84)	15.79 (28.88)
Private canals	0.84 (2.2)	0.48 (1.0)	0.56 (1.0)	0.48 (0.8)	0.50 (0.91)	0.50 (0.88)	0.19 (0.34)	0.20 (0.37)
Tanks	3.20 (8.2)	3.25 (6.1)	3.11 (5.8)	3.34 (6.1)	2.74 (4.98)	2.94 (5.15)	2.57 (4.53)	2.52 (4.61)
Tube wells	9.53 (24.6)	14.21 (29.7)	17.91 (33.5)	18.43 (33.4)	18.91 (34.39)	20.40 (35.64)	21.81 (38.42)	21.73 (39.74)
Other wells	8.21 (21.1)	10.00 (21.7)	11.79 (22.2)	12.39 (22.5)	12.68 (23.06)	12.75 (22.38)	12.77 (22.50)	11.55 (21.12)
Other sources	2.58 (6.8)	3.08 (6.1)	3.46 (6.5)	3.62 (6.6)	3.05 (5.55)	3.27 (5.73)	3.05 (5.37)	2.89 (5.28)
Net irrigated area	38.81 (100.0)	47.99 (100.0)	53.39 (100.0)	55.13 (100.0)	54.99 (100.0)	57.05 (100.0)	56.76 (100.0)	54.68 (100.0)

Note: * Provisional, Figures in parentheses indicate percentage of the total area.

Source: *Fertiliser Statistics*, 2003-04, The Fertiliser Association of India, New Delhi.

Workers in Agriculture

Total workforce in agriculture as per 1971 census is given in table 35.6.

Table 35.5: Crop-wise irrigated area (in million ha)

Crops	1980-81	1990-91	1995-96	1997-98	1998-99*	1999-00*	2000-01*
Rice	16.34 (40.7)	19.42 (45.5)	21.46 (49.9)	22.12 (50.8)	23.42 (52.3)	24.34 (53.9)	23.96 (53.6)
Wheat	17.04 (76.5)	19.60 (81.1)	21.71 (85.8)	22.92 (85.8)	23.63 (85.8)	23.97 (87.2)	22.67 (88.1)
Coarse cereals	3.84 (9.2)	3.27 (9.0)	3.46 (11.0)	3.45 (11.0)	3.54 (12.0)	3.70 (12.6)	3.78 (12.5)
Total pulses	2.02 (9.0)	2.59 (10.5)	2.90 (12.9)	2.69 (11.3)	2.95 (12.1)	3.40 (16.1)	2.54 (12.5)
Total oil seeds	2.55 (14.5)	5.53 (22.9)	6.78 (26.6)	6.79 (24.3)	6.61 (23.2)	6.12 (25.2)	5.24 (23.0)
Total gross irrigated area	49.78 (28.8)	62.47 (33.6)	71.35 (38.4)	73.01 (38.3)	77.64 (40.2)	77.99 (41.4)	75.14 (40.2)

Note: Figures in parentheses indicate percentage of the total area, * Provisional.

Source: *Agricultural Statistics at a Glance*, 2004, Directorate of Economics and Statistics, Ministry of Agriculture, Govt. of India.

Table 35.6: Workers in agriculture according to 1971 census

(Thousands)

State/Union Territory	As cultivators	As agricultural labourers	Total
Andhra Pradesh	5,795	6,829	12,624
Assam	2,410	406	2,816
Bihar	7,580	6,806	14,386
Gujarat	3,620	1,888	5,508
Haryana	1,303	430	1,733
Himachal Pradesh	903	54	957
Jammu & Kashmir	890	42	932
Karnataka	4,073	2,717	6,790
Kerala	1,107	1,908	3,015
Madhya Pradesh	8,085	4,062	12,147
Maharashtra	6,537	5,393	11,930
Manipur	249	13	262
Meghalaya	309	44	353
Nagaland	203	4	207

(*Contd.*)

State/Union Territory	As cultivators	As agricultural labourers	Total
Orissa	3,368	1,938	5,306
Punjab	1,665	787	2,452
Rajasthan	5,225	749	5,974
Tamil Nadu	4,608	4,490	9,098
Tripura	235	86	321
Uttar Pradesh	15,698	5,454	21,152
West Bengal	3,955	3272	7,227
Union Territories	359	117	476
All India	78,177	47,489	1,25,666

Source: *Indian Agriculture in Brief*. Fourteenth Edition 1975, p.16.

It is observed from the table 35.6 that total workers in agriculture are 125.7 millions, 78.2 millions are cultivators and 47.5 millions are agricultural labourers. Andhra Pradesh was having maximum number of agricultural labourers. Similarly, maximum numbers of cultivators were in Uttar Pradesh. Yet, large percentage of workers depend upon agriculture as there is not any suitable alternative for them. When industrial sector will develop at that time more employment will be generated which will reduce pressure of workers on agricultural sector. However, better employment opportunities can also be developed in agricultural sector. This can be possible with modernization of agriculture and by using economic and business principles in farming. The recent information about agricultural workers is given in table 36.6 and in Table 36.7 in chapter 36.

Agricultural Holdings

The term 'Agricultural holding' implies the total area of land, which is used for cultivation as a single unit by an individual, joint family or by more than one farmer on a joint basis. Such land may either entirely be owned/taken on lease, or may be partly owned and partly rented.

An 'Operational holding' is one which includes all lands (*i.e.*, cultivated, fallow and even the land which is not under cultivation) used wholly partially for agricultural production operated as a single technical unit by a single household or a number of households operating jointly.

Economic Holding

Different authorities have defined it in different ways.

1. Dr. Keatinge says, Economic holding is the size of area of land sufficient to produce enough for a cultivator and his family to keep them in reasonable comforts.
2. Dr. Mann, It is that area of land which provides an average family of a farmer a minimum standard of life considered satisfactory for the farmer.
3. Dr. Stanley Jones, Professor in Madras University says, it is that size of a farm which gives farmer a high standard of living (high standard, he meant reasonably high, with fairly decent house, etc.).
4. Jathar and Berry. That area is economic which gives profitable employment to labour and capital engaged in agriculture.

Thus, different authorities expressed their different views in their definitions for our purpose we will define it as follows:

> It is that size of holding which can provide full employment to farm family members and gives income sufficient to live with reasonable standard of living.

Full employment refers to employment throughout the year and reasonable standard means, he should be able to satisfy his basic needs such as, food, clothes, education to children, medical facility etc., satisfactorily.

Economic size of holding will depend upon several things:

1. Nature of crops grown,
2. Irrigation facility,
3. Soil productivity,
4. Skill and efficiency of the cultivator, and
5. Marketing and transport facilities.

How to find out economic size of holding?

Suppose, annual expenditure of average size of family in a particular area is ₹ 6,000. The per hectare per year profit is achieved ₹ 2,000. Then for getting ₹ 6,000 cultivator should have three hectares of land. So economic size of holding will be three hectares in that area.

Sub-division and Fragmentation

The meaning of these terms is mixed up several times.

1. Sub-division: It is a continuous process of size of land becoming less and less whereas the total land remains the same. Due to increase in population in India, the land goes on dividing amongst their sons and it continued in every generation.

2. Fragmentation: Each sub-divided holding is scattered into a number of plots and is due to the reason that every son wanted equal share in quality and quantity of land.

Disadvantages of Sub-division and Fragmentation

1. Because of sub-division and fragmentation, holding becomes uneconomic for cultivation. It is not possible to have scientific agriculture on such small and scattered farms.
2. Since the holding is scattered all over the village, much of the energy is wasted in going from one plot to another.
3. There are many boundary disputes as boundaries of the field are not well-marked.
4. Cost of production is higher on such tiny plots.
5. Much land is wasted in boundaries.

Remedy over sub-division and fragmentation is consolidation. Conveniently, pieces of land are transferred to each other, and individual cultivator gets his holding at one place.

Advantages of Consolidation

1. Cultivators would be in a position to do intensive cultivation after consolidation and can try scientific method of agriculture.
2. Consolidation reduces litigations and crimes.
3. It has led to keen desire on the part of cultivators to improve their land.

Recent Poverty Status of India

The recent poverty status in India is given in tables, 35.7 and 35.8.

Table 35.7 showed that India has made a significant progress in removal of poverty at all India level only 26 per cent of population is below poverty line whereas in 1973, 55 per cent population in India was below poverty line.

Table 35.7: State-wise percentage of population below poverty line

States/Union Territories	1973-74	1977-78	1983-84	1987-88	1993-94	1999-00
Andhra Pradesh	48.86	39.31	28.91	25.86	22.19	15.77
Arunachal Pradesh	51.93	58.32	40.68	36.22	39.35	33.47
Assam	51.21	57.15	40.47	36.21	40.86	36.09
Bihar	61.91	61.55	62.22	52.13	54.96	42.60
Goa	44.26	37.23	18.90	24.52	14.92	4.40
Gujarat	48.15	41.23	32.79	31.54	24.21	14.07
Haryana	35.36	29.55	21.37	16.64	25.05	8.74
Himachal Pradesh	26.39	32.45	16.40	15.45	28.44	7.63
Jammu & Kashmir	40.83	38.97	24.24	23.82	25.17	3.48
Karnataka	54.47	48.78	38.24	37.53	33.16	20.04
Kerala	59.79	52.22	40.42	31.79	25.43	12.72
Madhya Pradesh	61.78	61.78	49.78	43.07	42.52	37.43
Maharashtra	53.24	55.88	43.44	40.41	36.86	25.03
Manipur	49.96	53.72	37.02	31.35	33.78	28.54
Meghalaya	50.20	55.19	38.81	33.92	37.92	33.87
Mizoram	50.32	54.38	36.00	27.52	25.66	19.47
Nagaland	50.81	56.04	39.25	34.43	37.92	32.67
Orissa	66.18	70.07	65.29	55.58	48.56	47.15
Punjab	28.15	19.27	16.18	13.20	11.77	6.16
Rajasthan	46.14	37.42	34.46	35.15	27.41	15.28
Sikkim	50.86	55.89	39.71	36.06	41.43	36.55
Tamil Nadu	54.94	54.79	51.66	43.39	35.03	21.12
Tripura	51.00	56.88	40.03	35.23	39.01	34.44
Uttar Pradesh	57.07	49.05	47.07	41.46	40.85	31.15
West Bengal	63.43	60.52	54.85	44.72	35.66	27.02
Delhi	49.61	33.23	26.22	12.41	14.69	8.23
A & N Islands	55.56	55.42	52.13	43.89	34.47	20.99
Chandigarh	27.96	27.32	23.79	14.67	11.35	5.75
Dadra & Nagar Haveli	46.55	37.20	26.22	67.11	50.84	17.14
Lakshadweep	59.68	52.79	42.36	34.95	25.04	15.60
Pondicherry	53.82	53.25	50.06	41.46	37.40	21.67
Daman & Diu	N.A.	N.A.	N.A.	N.A.	15.80	4.44
All-India	54.88	51.32	44.48	38.86	35.97	26.10

Notes: 1. Poverty ratio of Assam is used for Sikkim, Arunachal Pradesh, Meghalaya, Mizoram, Manipur, Nagaland and Tripura.
2. Poverty ratio of Tamil Nadu is used for Pondicherry & A & N Islands.
3. Poverty ratio of Kerala is used for Lakshadweep.
4. Poverty ratio of Goa is used for Daman & Diu.
5. Urban poverty ratio of Punjab used for both rural and urban poverty of Chandigarh.
6. Poverty line of Maharashtra and expenditure distribution of Goa is used to estimate poverty ratio of Goa.
7. Poverty line of Maharashtra and expenditure distribution of Dadra & Nagar Haveli is used to estimate poverty ratio of Dadra & Nagar Haveli.
8. Poverty ratio of Himachal Pradesh is used for Jammu & Kashmir for 1993-94.
9. N.A. Not available.

Source: *Agricultural Statistics at a Glance, 2004*, Directorate of Economics and Statistics, Ministry of Agriculture, Govt. of India.

Table 35.8: Percentage of population below poverty line

Year	Rural	Urban	Combined
1973-74	56.44	49.01	54.88
1977-78	53.09	45.24	51.32
1983-84	45.65	40.79	44.48
1987-88	39.69	38.20	38.86
1993-94	37.27	32.36	35.97
1999-2000	27.09	23.62	26.10

Sources: 1. Planning Commission Estimates.
2. *Compendium of Environment Statistics India,* 2002, Central Statistical Organisation, Ministry of Statistics and Programme Implementation, Govt. of India.
3. *Agricultural Statistics at a Glance*, 2004, Directorate of Economics and Statistics, Ministry of Agriculture, Govt. of India.

It is observed from table 35.8, that a greater number of poor people are in rural area than urban area and hence, priority should be given for removal of poverty in rural area.

Livestock and Poultry Position in India

The details about livestock and poultry position in India is given in table 35.9.

World Producers of vegetables and fruits

The detail information is given in tables 35.10 and 35.11.

Table 35.9: State-wise total number of livestock and poultry — 2003 (provisional)

States/Union Territories livestock	Cattle	Buffalo	Sheep	Goat	Pig	Horses and Mithun	Mule	Donkey	Camel	Yak and Ponies	Total	Total poultry
Andhra Pradesh	9300	10630	21376	6277	570	9	-	33	-	0	48195	102270
Arunachal Pradesh	462	12	17	231	325	6	-	0	0	208	1260	1177
Assam	8641	659	75	2783	1262	11	0	0	0	0	13431	17749
Bihar*	12913	5186	431	8415	873	148	10	17	0	0	27993	17798
Chhattisgarh	8882	1598	121	2336	546	4	-	-		0	13486	8178
Goa	76	37	0	11	87	-	-	0	-	0	212	566
Gujarat	7317	7006	2021	4368	321	17	1	64	53	0	21168	8135
Haryana	1539	6035	633	460	120	25	14	8	50	0	8884	13619
Himachal Pradesh	1953	847	1099	1232	8	14	18	8	0	3	5182	957
Jammu & Kashmir	3014	1046	3745	2097	2	177	165	27	1	71	10345	8055
Jharkhand	7553	1305	679	4843	1094	4	-	-	-	0	15478	14161
Karnataka	9539	3991	7256	4484	312	14	-	25	-	0	25621	25590
Kerala	2254	65	5	1222	81	1	-	1	-	0	3628	15046
Madhya Pradesh	18782	7549	546	8056	349	31	4	38	8	0	35363	11703
Maharashtra*	16072	5739	3122	10274	465	40	1	57	1	0	35771	34731
Manipur	418	77	6	33	415	2	0	0	0	20	971	2940
Meghalaya	767	18	18	327	420	2	0	0	0	0	1553	2821
Mizoram	36	6	1	17	218	2	-	0	0	2	281	1125
Nagaland	451	34	4	175	644	1	-	0	0	40	1349	2900

(*Contd.*)

States/Union Territories livestock	Cattle	Buffalo	Sheep	Goat	Pig	Horses and Mithun	Mule	Donkey	Camel	Yak and Ponies	Total	Total poultry
Orissa	13903	1413	1620	5803	662	-	-	9	-	0	23411	17587
Punjab	2039	5995	220	278	29	29	9	5	3	0	8607	10779
Rajasthan	10853	10446	10032	16808	338	25	3	143	498	7	49153	6134
Sikkim	248	2	6	124	38	2	0	0	0	0	419	208
Tamil Nadu	9046	2741	5259	6416	609	11	0	43	0	0	24125	36511
Tripura	759	21550	3	472	209	0	0	0	0	0	22993	3057
Uttar Pradesh*	19121	21550	1660	12416	2679	174	63	186	20	0	57870	11920
Uttarakhand	2188	1086	296	1158	33	17	22	1	0	0	4801	1984
West Bengal	18913	16	1525	18774	1301	18	-	-	0	0	40547	60656
A & N. Islands	63	23	0	78	50	0	0	0	0	0	214	924
Chandigarh	6	4	0	1	0	-	-	-	-	0	11	152
Dadra & Nagar Haveli	50	1	0	21	0	-	0	0	0	0	72	126
Daman & Diu	4	254	0	4	0	-	0	0	-	0	263	29
Delhi	135	0	11	9	29	1	0	0	0	0	184	359
Lakshadweep	4	4	0	46	51	0	0	0	0	0	105	146
Pondicherry	78	4	2	47	1	-	0	-	0	0	132	230
All-India	187382	96616	61789	120097	14142	788	310	665	635	352	482776	440696

Note: * Data from few districts are yet to be received from State Governments.

Source: *Basic Animal Husbandry Statistics*, 2004, Deptt. of Animal Husbandry & Dairying, Ministry of Agriculture, Govt. of India.

Table 35.10: Major world producers of vegetables (in 000'm t)

Country	Potato Production 2002	Country	Tomato Production 2002	Country	Onion Production 2002	Country	Brinjal Production 2002
World	320829	World	112995	World	51497	World	27974
China	75268	China	27151	China	16545	China	15433
Russian Fed	32871	USA	12238	India	4209	India	8001
India	23161	Turkey	9450	USA	3081	Turkey	970
USA	20856	India	7617	Turkey	2050	Egypt	703
Ukraine	16620	Egypt	6350	Iran	1525	Japan	432
Poland	15524	Italy	5748	Russian Fed	1402	Italy	332
Germany	11492	Iran	4109	Pakistan	1385	Indonesia	273
Belarus	7421	Spain	3878	Japan	1274	Sudan	230
Netherland	7363	Brazil	3653	Brazil	1222	Phillippines	180
U.K.	6967	Mexico	1990	Spain	1101	Spain	160

Note: N.A.: Not available.
Source: *Indian Horticulture Data Base*, 2004, National Horticulture Board, Ministry of Agriculture, Govt. of India.

Table 35.11: Major world producers of fruits (in 000't)

Country	Banana Production 2002	Country	Grapes Production 2002	Country	Orange Production 2002
World	67994	World	60463	World	26479
India	13304	Brazil	18530	India	12733
Brazil	6423	USA	11225	China	3513
China	5784	Mexico	3843	Thailand	1750
Ecuador	5528	Spain	2867	Mexico	1523
Philippines	5264	Iran	1880	Indonesia	1403
Indonesia	4384	Egypt	1725	Pakistan	1036
Mexico	1886	Italy	1723	Philippines	956
Thailand	1800	China	1643	Brazil	842
Costa Rica	1612	Pakistan	1400	Nigeria	730

(*Contd. ...*)

Country	Banana Production 2002	Country	Grapes Production 2002	Country	Orange Production 2002
Burundi	1603	India	1137	Egypt	326
World	56111	World	6191	World	15010
China	19251	India	2147	Thailand	1739
USA	3867	Brazil	1598	Philippines	1636
France	2478	Mexico	876	Brazil	1433
Iran	2334	Nigeria	755	China	1244
Turkey	2200	Indonesia	491	India	1172
Italy	2199	Ethiopia	226	Costa Rice	992
Poland	2168	Congo Dem	210	Nigeria	889
Russian Fed.	1900	Peru	173	Mexico	660
Germany	1471	China	163	Kenya	600
India	1348	Venezuela	153	Indonesia	556

Source: *Indian Horticulture Database*, 2004, National Horticulture Board, Ministry of Agriculture, Govt. of India.

36
Food Supply, Population and Economic Indicators

Food Supply

India was facing severe food problem few years back but due to green revolution, food production increased significantly. In 1978-79, country achieved a record level of food grains production, *i.e.*, 130.5 million, tonnes and about 23 million tonnes were in reserve stocks. Though the country succeeded in solving food problem quantitatively, qualitative aspects and distributional problems must be looked into.

Table 36.1: Production, consumption, imports and exports of cereals

(Million tonnes)

Year	Stock brought forward	Home production	Imports	Exports	Consumption	Stock carried over
1951	0.74	42.41	4.8	0.17	46.45	1.33
1961	2.8	69.31	3.49	—	72.96	2.64
1969	3.99	83.6	3.87	0.03	86.98	4.45
1971	5.57	96.6	2.05	0.03	96.05	8.14
1973	3.44	87.12	3.61	0.02	94.17	2.95

Source: *Indian Agriculture in Brief*, 14th edition, 1975, p. 121.

It is observed from the table 36.1 that food production is increasing significantly, and country do not require to import large quantities of cereals. The recent position of cereal production is still better.

Table 36.2: Total food grains production

Year	Total food grains (Million tonnes)
1951-52	52.0
1954-55	68.0
1959-60	76.7
1964-65	89.4
1969-70	99.5
1974-75	99.8
1978-79	130.5
1980-81	129.59
1990-91	176.3
1995-96	180.42
1998-99	203.61
2000-2001	195.92
2001-2002	211.17

It is observed from the table 36.2 that food grains production increased 2.5 times from 1951-52 to 1978-79.

Population

Population has got importance on two points of view, firstly it supplies labour force which is required for increasing production and secondly, government has to look after its subject, for providing necessaries of life.

Table 36.3: Total food grain production in India (in million tonnes)

Year	Rice	Wheat	Coarse cereals	Pulses	Total food-grains
1999-2000	89.68	76.37	30.34	13.41	209.8
2000-01	84.98	69.68	31.08	11.07	196.81
2001-02	93.34	72.77	33.94	13.37	212.85
2002-03	72.66	65.10	25.29	11.14	174.19
2003-04	87.00	72.06	33.72	15.23	212.05

Sources: 1. *Agricultural Research Data Book*, 2003, ICAR and IARS, New Delhi.

2. *Economic Survey of Maharashtra*, 2003-04.

It is observed from table 36.3 that food grains production in India has jumped from 130.5 million tonnes in 1978-79 to

212.05 million tonnes in 2003-04 and it is more or less more than 200 million tonnes since the year 2000 except 174.19 million tonnes in 2002-03.

Table 36.4: Net availability of food grains per day in India (gms/capita/day)

Year	Cereals	Pulses	Food grains
1951	334.2	60.7	394.9
1961	399.7	69.0	468.7
1971	417.6	51.2	468.8
1981	417.3	37.5	454.8
1991	468.5	41.6	510.1
2000	426.0	32.0	458.0

Source: *Agricultural Research Data Book*, 2003, ICAR and IARS, New Delhi.

It is observed from table 36.4 that per capita per day availability of cereals is increasing but that of pulses is decreasing. Hence, it is necessary to provide attention for increasing production of pulses.

Table 36.5: India's population, 1901-2001

Census year	Total population (million)	Rural population (million)	Urban population (million)	Annual compound growth rate (%)
1901	238.4 (100.00)	212.5 (89.1)	25.9 (10.9)	—
1911	252.1 (100.00)	226.2 (89.7)	25.9 (10.3)	0.56
1921	251.3 (100.00)	223.2 (88.8)	28.1 (11.2)	−0.03
1931	279.0 (100.00)	245.5 (88.0)	33.5 (12.0)	1.04
1941	318.7 (100.00)	274.5 (86.1)	44.2 (13.9)	1.33
1951	361.1 (100.00)	298.6 (82.7)	62.5 (17.3)	1.25
1961	439.2 (100.00)	360.3 (82.0)	78.9 (18.0)	1.96

(*Contd. ...*)

Census year	Total population (million)	Rural population (million)	Urban population (million)	Annual compound growth rate (%)
1971	547.9 (100.00)	438.8 (80.1)	109.1 (19.9)	2.2
1978-79	634.0 (estimated)	—	—	—
1981	683.3 (100.00)	523.9 (76.7)	159.4 (23.3)	2.22
1991	843.4 (100.00)	628.7 (74.3)	214.7 (25.7)	2.14
2001	1027 (100.00)	741.7 (72.2)	285.3 (27.8)	1.93
2006	1094.1 (100.00) (estimated)	—	—	1.55

Note: Figures in parentheses are percentages.
Source: *Data Book*, 2003, p. 24, ICAR and IARS, New Delhi.

It is observed from the table 36.5 that, population increased more than four times during 105 years (1901-2006). Decennial percentage growth rate is also increasing.

At present country is facing unemployment problem as well as some other problems due to excess population. Providing productive employment to unemployed people and strict family planning programme will solve the situation.

Country-wise Population Engaged in Agriculture

The details regarding economically active population in selected countries are given in table 36.6.

Table 36.6: Agricultural population and population economically active in agriculture as estimated during 2002 (in 000')

Country	Total population	Agricultural population	Economically active population		
			Total	Agriculture	Percentage agriculture
World	6224978	2588425	3036587	1333329	43.9
Algeria	31266	3740	11154	2660	23.8
Egypt	70507	24994	26338	8475	32.2

(*Contd. ...*)

Country	Total population	Agricultural population	Economically active population		
			Total	Agriculture	Percentage agriculture
Sudan	32878	19480	13063	7740	59.3
Canada	31271	747	16863	371	2.2
Mexico	101965	22709	42050	8510	20.2
USA	291038	6062	148537	2906	2.0
Argentina	37981	3671	15678	1460	9.3
Brazil	176257	27074	81406	12673	15.6
Afghanistan	22930	15201	9341	6192	66.3
Bangladesh	143809	77262	72931	39182	53.7
China	1302307	852330	780218	510950	65.5
India	1049549	553281	460252	270252	58.7
Indonesia	217131	92877	106275	49957	47.0
Japan	127478	4381	68275	2454	3.6
Myanmar	48852	33995	26495	18437	69.6
Nepal	24609	22864	11729	10897	92.9
Pakistan	149911	74841	55638	25669	46.1
France	59850	1816	26980	818	3.0
Italy	57482	2771	25318	1220	4.8
UK	59287	1017	29613	508	1.7
Australia	19544	865	9978	442	4.4
Russian Fed.	144082	14340	78100	7773	10.0

Source: *Fertilizer Statistics*, 2003-04, The Fertilizer Association of India, New Delhi.

Agricultural Workers in India

The details are given in table 36.7.

Table 36.7: Rural population and agricultural workers (All India level)

(Figures in crores)

Sr. No.	Class	1981	1991	2001
1.	Total population	68.3	86.60	102.70
2.	Rural population	52.39 (76.7)	62.87 (74.3)	74.17 (72.2)
3.	Cultivators	9.25 (37.8)	10.07 (35.2)	12.76 (31.7)
4.	Agricultural labourers	5.55 (22.7)	7.46 (23.8)	10.75 (26.7)

(*Contd. ...*)

Sr. No.	Class	1981	1991	2001
5.	Other workers	9.66 (39.5)	12.88 (41.0)	16.74 (41.6)
6 = 3+4+5	Total agricultural workers	24.46 (100.00)	31.41 (100.00)	40.25 (100.00)

Note: Figures in parentheses are percentages.

Source: *Agricultural Research Data Book*, 2003, ICAR and IARS, New Delhi.

It is observed from table 36.7 that population has crossed billion mark and it is necessary to control the population. Total agricultural workers have increased from 24.46 crores in 1981 to 40.25 crores in 2001, *i.e.*, 15.79 crores workers have been increased and hence it is necessary to generate employment for these youths in rural area. Fruit processing, dairy, poultry, repairs of tractors and various agril. implements these businesses have to be promoted.

Economic Indicators

Table 36.8: Annual indicators (India)

Item	Unit	1977-78	Growth rate between 1970-71 and 1977-78 (%)
GNP at market prices			
Aggregate	₹ crores	86500 (a)	11.5
Per capita	₹	1400 (a)	9.5
Food grains production	mil. tonnes	126	2.2
Edible oils imports	₹ crores	450	
Fertilizers (NPK)			
Consumption	mil. tonnes	4.2	10.2
Production	mil. tonnes	2.7	13.0
Imports	mil. tonnes	1.5	14.0
Energy			
Coal production	mil. tonnes	101.1	4.8
Crude oil production	mil tonnes	10.8	6.8
Imports of crude and products	mil. tonnes	17.5 (b)	4.8
Consumption of petroleum products	mil. tonnes	25.6 (b)	4.5 (*b*)
Electricity generation	Bil. Kwh	92.1	6.0
Public finance			

(*Contd. ...*)

Item	Unit	1977-78	Growth rate between 1970-71 and 1977-78 (%)
Government expenditure	₹ crores	25276	16.2
Money and prices			
Money supply (march end)	₹ crores	18052	13.8
Wholesale prices index			
Average for the year	1970 - 71 = 100	185.7	9.2
Consumer price index			
Average for the year	1960=100	324	8.2
External transactions			
Imports	₹ crores	6066	20.6
Exports	₹ crores	5374	19.6
Trade balance	₹ crores	-692	—
Net external assistance	₹ crores	467	—
Employment exchange	Lakhs	113.5	12.1
December data number of persons on live register			
Of which matriculates and above (a)	Lakhs	57.3	

Notes: (a) Estimated by the Centre for Monitoring Indian Economy.
(b) Figures relate to calendar year.

Source: *Economic Indicators*, December 1978, Centre for Monitoring Indian Economy, Bombay.

Table 36.9: National and per capita income at factor cost

Item	1993-94	1996-97	1999-2000
1. Net National Product			
At factor cost (₹ crores)			
At current prices	685912	1093961	1590301
	(100.00)	(159)	(232)
At 1993-94 prices	685912	852085	1011224
	(100.00)	(124)	(147)
2. Per capita Net National Product (₹)			
At current prices	7698	11601	16047
	(100.00)	(151)	(208)
At 1993-94 prices	7698	9036	10204
	(100.00)	(117)	(133)

(Contd. ...)

3. Gross National Product			
at factor cost (₹ crore)	769265	1230464	1771028
at current prices	(100)	(160)	(230)
at 1993-94 prices	769265	959360	1140389
	(100.00)	(125)	(148)

Notes: 1. Figures in parenthese indicates index numbers taking 1993-94 as base year.

2. Per capita income at current prices in 2003-04 was ₹ 20,989 which increased to ₹ 23,241 in 2004-05.

Source: *India 2002* (A reference annual) p. 297, Ministry of Information and Broadcasting, Government of India.

Table 36.10: India in the world

Item	India	World	Percentage share of India in the world	India's rank in the world
Area (1977)				
Area (mn.sq.km.)	3.3	133.9	2.4	7
Per capita geographical area (hectare)	0.6	3.4		
Population (1977)				
Population (mn.)	626	4124	15.2	2
Population growth rate (% per annum between 1967-77)	2.2	1.9	—	—
Persons per sq. km. of arable land	355	258	—	—
Gross National Product (1975)				
Total GNP (billion U.S. $)	86	6099	1.4	13
Per capita GNP (U.S. $)	140	1537	—	165
Agricultural Production (1977)				
Rice (mn. Tonne)	74	366.5	20.2	2
Wheat (mn. Tonne)	29	386.6	7.5	4
Cotton (mn. Tonne)	1.2	14.3	8.1	4
Milk Production (mn. Tonne)	26	448	5.7	4
Milk production per capita (kg)	41	109	—	94 (1971)
Industrial production (1977)				
Crude steel (mn.tn.)	10	665	1.4	15
Cement (mn.tn)	19	750	2.6	10

(*Contd.*)

Item	India	World	Percentage share of India in the world	India's rank in the world
Cane and beet sugar (mn.tn.)	5	91	5.7	5
Energy Sources (1977)				
Electricity generated (on. Kwh.)	91	6959	1.3	12
Crude petroleum production (mn.tn.)	10	3032	0.3	29
Coal production (mn.tn.)	100	2435	4.1	6

Source: *Economic Indicators*, December 1978, Centre for Monitoring Indian Economy, Bombay.

Table 36.11: India's position in world agriculture—2000

	Item	India	World	India's Share %	India's Rank	Next to
1.	Area**(million ha.)					
	Total area	329	13425	2.5	Seventh	Russian Federation, Canada, U.S.A., China, Brazil, Australia
	Land area	297	13062	2.3	Seventh	Russian Federation, China, Canada, U.S.A., Brazil, Australia
	Arable land	162 F	1364	11.9	Second	U.S.A.
	Irrigated area	55 F	272	20.2	First	
2.	Population (million)					
	Total	1025	6134	16.7	Second	China
	Agriculture	739	3211	23.0	Second	China
3.	Economically active population (million)					
	Total	451	2993	15.1	Second	China
	Agriculture	267	1327	20.1	Second	China

(*Contd. ...*)

	Item	India	World	India's Share %	India's Rank	Next to
4.	Crop production(million t)					
	Total Cereals	231	2086	11.1	Third	China, USA
	Wheat	68	583	11.7	Second	China
	Rice (Paddy)	132	593	22.3	Second	China
	Coarse grains	30	911	3.3	Fourth	China, Brazil, Russian Federation
	Total pulses	11	52	21.2	First	
	Groundnut	6*	35	17.1	Second	China
	Rapeseed	4	36	11.1	Fourth	China, Canada, Germany
5.	Fruits & Vegetables (million t)					
	Vegetables & Melons		68F	698	9.7	Second China
	Fruits excluding Melons		49F	466	10.5	Second China
	Potatoes	25F	308	8.1	Third	China, Russian Federation
	Onion (Dry)	5F	47	10.6	Second	China
6.	Commercial crop (million t)					
	Sugarcane	286	1255	22.8	Second	Brazil
	Tea	0.86*	3.06	28.1	First	
	Coffee (green)	0.30*	7.05	4.3	Sixth	Brazil, Vietnam, Colombia, Indonesia, Mexico
	Jute & allied fibre	1.88F	3.07	61.2	First	
	Cotton (lint)	1.75*	21.03	8.3	Fourth	China, USA, Pakistan
	Tobacco leaves	0.61F	6.35	9.6	Second	China
7.	Livestock (million head)					
	Cattle	220*	1352	16.3	First	
	Buffaloes	94*	166	56.6	First	

(Contd. ...)

	Item	India	World	India's Share %	India's Rank	Next to
	Camels	1.03F	19.33	6.3	Fifth	Somalia, Sudan, Mauritania, Ethiopia.
	Sheep	58*	1056	5.5	Third	China, Australia
	Goats	124F	738	16.8	Second	China
	Chicken	413F	14859	2.8	Sixth	China, USA, Brazil, Indonesia, Mexico
8.	Implements (000' numbers)**					
	Tractors-in-use	1525 F	26410	5.8	Fourth	USA, Japan, Italy
9.	Animal Products					
	Milk (000'Mt)	83970*	583339	14.4	First	
	Eggs (000'Mt)	1906*	56594	3.4	Fifth	China, U.S.A., Japan, Russian Federation
	Total meat					
	(000'Mt)	4917	236541	2.1	Seventh	China, U.S.A., Brazil, Germany, France, Spain

Note: F: FAO Estimates, *Unofficial Figures, **Figures relate to 2000.

Sources: 1. *Agricultural Statistics at a Glance*, 2004, Directorate of Economics and Statistics, Ministry of Agriculture, Govt. of India.

2. *Agricultural Research Data Book*, 2005.

It is observed from table 36.12 that in most of the crops India's share in world total production is less as compared to its share in total area under that particular crop in the world. This indicates India has to enhance productivity in different crops.

Table 36.12: Area and production of principal crops in the world and India's share (Area: in 000'ha, Production: in 000't)

Crops	Area			Production		
	2001	2002	2003	2001	2002	2003
Rice (paddy)	151679 (29.4)	147552 (27.2)	153522 (28.7)	598174 (23.4)	569527 (18.9)	589126 (22.4)
Wheat	214690 (12.0)	213716 (12.3)	208765 (11.9)	590520 (11.8)	573513 (12.7)	556349 (11.7)
Coarse grains	309925 (9.6)	300899 (8.8)	312051 (9.5)	919832 (3.6)	886015 (2.9)	929835 (3.8)
Total cereals	676293 (32.3)	662127 (30.9)	674338 (31.6)	2108526 (26.4)	2029055 (23.3)	2075309 (25.0)
Groundnut in shell	24041 (25.9)	24105 (24.7)	26463 (30.2)	36083 (19.5)	33303 (13.1)	35658 (21.0)
Cotton seed	34587 (26.3)	30725 (24.3)	32168 (26.1)	60674 (9.8)	52875 (9.0)	56097 (11.2)
Tea	2359 (18.7)	2406 (17.9)	2410 (18.4)	3068 (27.6)	3125 (27.1)	3207 (27.6)
Tobacco	3767 (7.7)	3790 (8.6)	3938 (11.0)	6192 (7.9)	6229 (6.2)	6195 (9.6)

Note: Figures* in parentheses denote India's share to World Area and Production of Principal Crops. * Unofficial figure

Source: *FAO Production Yearbook*, Vol. 57 – 2003. FAO of the United Nations, Rome, 2004.

Table 36.13: Economic indicators of some major countries

Sr. No.	Item	Unit	India	China	Japan	UK	USA	USSR
1.	Population: 1977	Million	626	866	114	56	217	259
2.	GNP at market prices: 1977							
	(*i*) Aggregate	U.S. $ billion	99	356	684	244	1887	733
	(*ii*) Per capita	U.S. $	158	412	6005	4378	8704	2831
3.	Real GNP Annual rate of growth 1971-77	%	3.9	NA	5.1	1.6	3.1	5.3 (*a*)
4.	Industrial Production Annual rate of growth 1971-77	%	4.9	8.6	3.4	0.3	2.4	6.6
5.	Consumer prices Annual rate of increase 1971-77	%	9.1	Neg.	11.5	14.7	7.0	Neg.

Note: Net Material Product.

Source: *Economic Indicators*, December, 1978, Centre for Monitoring Indian Economy, Bombay.

Table 36.14: Economic indicators of some major countries

Sr. No.	Item	Year	Unit	India	China	Japan	UK	USA	Russian Fed.	Pakistan
1.	Population	1999	Crores	99.80	126.68	12.65	5.89	27.62	14.72	15.23
2.	(*i*) Economically active population	1999	Crores	43.73	75.73	6.78	2.94	14.13	7.85	5.67
	(*ii*) Out of total, engaged in agriculture	1999	Crores	26.28	51.12	0.29	0.05	0.30	0.85	2.69
	(*iii*) Per cent (of *ii*) to total (*i*)	1999	Per cent	60.10	67.5	4.30	1.80	2.20	10.80	47.5
3.	GDP per capita	2001	PPP U.S.$	2840	4020	25134	24160	34320	7100	1890
4.	Life expectance at birth	2000	Years	63.3	70.6	81.3	77.9	76.9	66.6	60.4
5.	Contribution of agriculture in national income	2000	%	27	16	2	1	2	N.A.	N. A.
6.	Contribution of Industrial sector in national income	2000	%	27	49	36	25	26	N.A.	N.A.
7.	Contribution of service sector in national income	2000	%	46	34	62	74	72	N.A.	N.A.

Sources: 1. *Agricultural Research Data Book*, 2003, ICAR and IARS, New Delhi.
2. *Indian Economy*, Ruddar Datta and Sundharam, Golden Jubilee edition, Delhi.

Table 36.15: Some economic indicators of different states

Sr. No.	State	Area '000 sq. km.	Average normal rainfall (cm.)	Net sown area as % of reporting area 1974-75	Annual rate of increase in food grain output between 1961-62 and 1977-78	Villages electrified by March end 1978%	Per capita state income at current prices average of 1973-74 to 1975-76 in ₹	Per capita bank advances in ₹ December end 1977
1.	Uttar Pradesh	294(4)	127(8)	58(5)	2.3(9)	31(9)	768(11)	85(11)
2.	Bihar	174(8)	129(7)	48(8)	1.8(11)	28(13)	639(15)	55(13)
3.	Maharashtra	308(3)	132(6)	59(4)	2.5(7)	60(5)	1230(2)	585(1)
4.	West Bengal	88(11)	213(3)	73(3)	2.9(5)	31(10)	1020(5)	343(2)
5.	Andhra Pradesh	277(5)	87(11)	42(10)	1.5(12)	54(7)	921(6)	148(9)
6.	Madhya Pradesh	443(1)	124(9)	42(12)	1.0(15)	23(14)	786(10)	72(12)
7.	Tamil Nadu	130(10)	97(10)	43(9)	1.9(10)	99(3)	857(8)	299(3)
8.	Karnataka	192(7)	164(4)	54(7)	3.0(4)	57(6)	758(13)	283(4)
9.	Gujarat	196(6)	74(13)	42(11)	4.4(3)	44(8)	1105(4)	267(6)
10.	Rajasthan	342(2)	48(15)	40(13)	2.6(6)	30(11)	831(9)	92(10)
11.	Orissa	156(9)	153(5)	37(4)	1.4(13)	28(12)	731(14)	47(15)
12.	Kerala	39(15)	267(1)	57(6)	1.3(14)	97(4)	864(7)	191(7)
13.	Assam	79(12)	241(2)	32(15)	2.4(8)	10(15)	767(12)	54(14)
14.	Punjab	50(13)	64(14)	81(1)	6.2(1)	100(2)	1499(1)	282(5)
15.	Haryana	44(14)	76(12)	80(2)	4.9(2)	100(1)	1229(3)	185(8)
Other than major states								
16.	Jammu & Kashmir	222	102	15	3.2	60	—	125

(*Contd. ...*)

Sr. No.	State	Area '000 sq. km.	Average normal rainfall (cm.)	Net sown area as % of reporting area 1974-75	Annual rate of increase in food grain output between 1961-62 and 1977-78	Villages electrified by March end 1978%	Per capita state income at current prices average of 1973-74 to 1975-76 in ₹	Per capita bank advances in ₹ December end 1977
17.	Himachal Pradesh	56	184	19	7.2	46	1010	70
18.	Tripura	11	193	23	5.4	9	750	33
19.	Manipur	22	193	6	6.5	12	687	25
20.	Meghalaya	23	241	7	2.1	9	—	45
21.	Nagaland	17	193	7	1.6	25	—	33
22.	Sikkim	7	—	—	—	22	—	—
	All India	3288	121	46	2.5	38	963	247

Note: Figures in brackets indicate rank.

Source: Economic Indicators, December, 1978, Centre for Monitoring Indian Economy, Mumbai.

Table 36.16: Selected economic indicators of states in India

Sr. No. State	Geographical area (lakh sq. km.)	Population in lakh	Percentage of population to all India population	Percentage of Agricultural workers to total workers	Per capita income at current prices (₹) (P)	Per capita foodgrains production (kg.)	Number of banking offices per lakh of population (No.)	Deposits per capita (₹)
Reference year	2001	2001	2001	2001	2001-02	2001-02	31-3-03	31-3-03
1. Andhra Pradesh	2.75	757.28	7.37	62.30	17,642	194.0	6.8	9,470
2. Arunachal Pradesh	0.84	10.91	0.11	62.30	15,785	193.8	6.1	7,453
3. Assam	0.78	266.38	2.59	52.65	10,951	148.6	4.4	4,693
4. Bihar	0.94	828.79	8.07	77.35	5,445	138.9	4.1	3,548
5. Jharkhand	0.80	269.09	2.62	66.85	N.A.	73.0	5.2	6,773
6. Delhi	0.01	137.83	1.34	1.11	N.A.	3.0	10.0	95,853
7. Goa	0.04	13.44	0.13	16.61	49,673	88.8	21.0	59,733
8. Gujarat	1.96	505.97	4.93	52.04	21,276	94.6	6.9	13,572
9. Haryana	0.44	210.83	2.05	51.56	24,575	614.0	7.1	12,316
10. Himachal Pradesh	0.56	60.77	0.59	68.65	21,368	254.4	12.5	15,833
11. Jammu & Kashmir	2.22	100.70	0.98	50.10	N.A.	128.2	7.8	12,485
12. Karnataka	1.92	527.34	5.13	55.89	18,324	163.6	8.8	13,841
13. Kerala	0.39	318.39	3.10	23.26	22,668	22.7	10.3	18,362

(Contd. ...)

Sr. No.	State	Geo-graphical area (lakh sq. km.)	Population in lakh	Percentage of population to all India population	Percentage of Agricultural workers to total workers	Per capita income at current prices (₹) (P)	Per capita foodgrains production (kg.)	Number of banking offices per lakh of population (No.)	Deposits per capita (₹)
14.	Madhya Pradesh	3.08	603.85	5.88	71.59	11,718	211.4	5.5	5,993
15.	Chhattisgarh	1.35	207.96	2.02	76.46	N.A.	275.5	4.8	5,341
16.	Maharashtra	3.08	968.79	9.42	55.41	24,248	113.3	6.2	25,166
17.	Manipur	0.22	23.89	0.23	57.38	13,213	163.1	3.0	2,533
18.	Meghalaya	0.22	23.06	0.22	65.89	15,070	92.0	7.4	8,897
19.	Mizoram	0.21	8.91	0.09	59.77	N.A.	137.9	8.3	7,132
20.	Nagaland	0.17	19.89	0.19	68.03	N.A.	168.9	3.1	5,571
21.	Orissa	1.56	367.07	3.57	64.73	10,234	202.9	5.9	5,292
22.	Punjab	0.50	242.89	2.37	39.36	25,652	1004.7	10.3	22,587
23.	Rajasthan	3.42	564.73	5.50	66.0	13,151	240.9	5.6	5,863
24.	Sikkim	0.07	5.40	0.05	56.34	17,506	176.7	8.3	17,903
25.	Tamil Nadu	1.30	621.11	6.05	49.55	21,239	135.0	7.5	13,523
26.	Tripura	0.10	31.91	0.31	50.92	17,459	197.0	5.5	6,443
27.	Uttar Pradesh	2.41	1660.53	16.17	66.03	9,749	253.7	4.7	6249
28.	Uttarakhand	0.53	84.80	0.83	58.03	N.A.	197.9	9.7	17,678
29.	West Bengal	0.89	802.21	7.81	43.04	17,769	202.7	5.4	10,449
30.	India*	32.87	10,270.15	@100.00	@58.68	17,947	202.7	6.2	11,970

Note: Economic Survey of Maharashtra, 2003-04.

*Includes Union Territories @ Excluding Jammu and Kashmir (P) = Provisional N.A. = Not Available

Table 36.17: Some indicators for Maharashtra's comparison with India

Item	Unit	Maharashtra	India	Comparison with India (%)
Population (2001)				
Total population	In thousand	96,879	10,27,015*	9.4
(i) Males	In thousand	50,401	5,31,277*	9.5
(ii) Females	In thousand	46,478	4,95,738	9.4
(a) Rural population	In thousand	55,778	7,41,660*	7.5
(b) Percentage of rural population to total population	Per cent	57.60	72.22	—
(a) Urban population	In thousand	41,101	2,85,355	14.4
(b) Percentage of Urban population to total population	Per cent	42.40	27.78	—
Sex ratio	Females per thousand males	922	933	—
Literacy rate	Per cent	76.88	65.38	—
Agriculture (1999-2000)				
Net area sown	In thousand ha	17,691	1,41,231	12.5
Gross cropped area	In thousand ha	21,897	1,89,740	11.8
Gross irrigated area	In thousand ha	3,374	7,63,636	4.9
Percentage of gross irrigated area to gross cropped area	Per cent	15.4	40.2	—
Area under principle crops				
(i) Rice	In thousand ha	1,515	44,382	3.4
(ii) Wheat	In thousand ha	860	26,380	3.3
(iii) Gram	In thousand ha	5,141	10,011	51.4
(iv) Bajra	In thousand ha	1,645	9,425	17.5
(v) All cereals	In thousand ha	9,755	1,00,981	9.7
(vi) All food grains	In thousand ha	13,274	1,22,021	10.9
(vii) Sugarcane	In thousand ha	679	—	—
(viii) Cotton	In thousand ha	3,145	8,781	35.8
(ix) Groundnut	In thousand ha	486	6,680	7.3
Livestock census (1992)				
Total livestock	In thousand	36,393	4,70,830	7.7
Tractors	In thousand	46	1,222	3.8

(*Contd.*)

Item	Unit	Maharashtra	India	Comparison with India (%)
Oil engines with pumps	In thousand	1,189	11,393	10.4
Forests				
Total forest area* (1999)	Sq.km.	63,842	7,65,254	8.3
Industry*				
Factories-(2001)				
(*a*) working factories	Number	28,399	2,39,627	11.9
(*b*) average daily employment	In thousand	1,249	10,885	11.5
Electricity* (2001-02)				
Total generation	Million kwh.	64,430	5,15,300	12.5
Total consumption	Million kwh.	46,338	3,74,672	12.4
(*a*) industrial consumption	Million kwh.	17,435	1,07,293	16.2
(*b*) Percentage of industrial consumption to total consumption	Per cent	37.6	28.6	9.5
Banking				
Banking offices (scheduled commercial) (Dec. 2003)	Number	6,337	66,857	7.3
Towns and Villages having banking offices (Scheduled commercial) (March) 1993)	Number	2,750	37,724	13
State/National Income	(2002-03)			
Income at current prices	Crores ₹	2,63,225@	19,95,229**	13
Per capital income at current prices	₹	26,386 @	18,912**	—
Gross domestic product (GDP) at factor cost	Crore ₹	2,95,191@	22,49,493**	—
Per capita GDP	₹	29,590 @	21,322**	—

* Provisional @ Preliminary estimates, ** Quick estimates

Source: *Economic Survey of Maharashtra*, 2003-04.

Table 36.18: Fertilizer consumption per hectare of agricultural land in selected countries, 2000-01.

(kgs/ha)

Sr. No.	Country	Fertilizers per hectare				Yield per hectare			
		N	P	K	Total	Paddy	Wheat	Maize	Potato
1.	U.S.A.	57.3	21.3	24.8	103.4	7206	2706	8672	40161
2.	China	166.9	62.4	24.9	254.2	6361	3832	4933	15238
3.	India	64.4	24.8	9.2	98.4	2964	2742	1807	18643
4.	Japan	100.8	120.9	79.3	301.0	6659	3684	2400	29897
5.	Pakistan	103.2	30.9	1.0	135.1	3000	2333	1720	17104
6.	U.K.	173.8	47.9	64.1	285.8	—	7077	—	40028
7.	Ukraine	10.4	1.9	0.8	13.1	5262	3101	2773	8459
8.	World	54.5	21.8	14.8	91.1	3912	2725	4427	15968

Source: *Agricultural Research Data Book*, 2003, p. 189, ICAR and IARS, New Delhi.

Selected References

Anonymous, *Fertiliser Statistics,* Fertiliser Association of India, New Delhi, 1977-78.

Anonymous, *Indian Agriculture in Brief,* Fourteenth Edition, 1975.

Anonymous, *Economic Indicators,* Centre for Monitoring Indian Economy, Bombay, 1979.

Anonymous, *The Gazetteer of India,* Vol. III, Economic Structure and Activities, Ministry of Education and Social Welfare, p. 197, New Delhi, 1975.

Anonymous, *Report of the All India Rural Credit Review Committee,* Agricultural Credit Department, RBI, Bombay, 1969.

Anonymous, *All India Rural Credit Survey Committee Report*, Vol. I, Part II, Bombay, 1957.

Anonymous, *Data India, New* Delhi, 1979-80.

Bansil, P.C., *Agricultural Problems of India,* Second Edition, Vikas Publication, Delhi, 1975.

Dasgupta, A.K., *Agriculture and Economic Development in India,* Associated Publishing House, New Delhi, 1973.

Jain, S.C., *Agricultural Policy in India*, Second Edition, Allied Publishers, Pvt. Ltd., Bombay, 1967.

Khusro, A.M., *Economic of Land Reform and Farm Size in India*, The Macmillan Company of India Ltd., Madras, 1973.

Mamoria, C.B., *Agricultural Problems of India,* Eighth Edition, Kitab Mahal, Allahabad, 1976.

Pai, G.A., "Productivity in Agriculture," *Sahkari Viswa,* Special Issue, 1979.

Patel, D.P., *Indian Field Crops*, Atul Prakashan, Vasnabuzarg (Matar), Distt. Kaira, Gujarat, 1968.

Rane, A.A., "Application of Lorenz Curve and Gini Ratio in Concentration Studies in Agriculture," *Issues in Indian Agriculture,* Atlantic Publishers and Distributors (P) Ltd., New Delhi, 1980.

Schulz, T.W., *The Economic Organization of Agriculture*, McGraw Hill Book Company, INC., 1953.

Snodgrass, M.M., and Wallace, L.T., *Agriculture Economics and Resource Management*, Prentice-Hall, New Jersey, USA, 1970.

Soltani, G.R., *Small Farm versus Large Farm Development in Iran*, Vol. XXXIII, No. 3. p. 94, July-Sept., 1978.

PART VII
Agricultural Growth and Economic Development

37
Agricultural Growth and Economic Development

Agricultural development is a process of mobilizing a vast quantity of already existing resources and raising their productivity. This process should result in increase in total agricultural production which is termed as agricultural growth.

In most of the developing economies, agriculture contributes significantly in their national income. Hence, development of agriculture leads to economic development.

Economic development is a process whereby the real national income of an economy increases over a long period of time. If rate of economic development is greater than the rate of population growth, then the per capita real income will increase. The general result of this process is growth in the national product of an economy. In other words, economic development essentially consists in the growth of output per head of population. Thus, economic development means increase in per capita income. Economic development should result in improvement in social welfare. No any community in the economy be worse off than it was before the development occurred.

Countries are classified as poor and rich by comparing the per capita real income. The poor countries are usually referred to as underdeveloped countries, which are low in real per capita income by the standards of North America, Western Europe and Australia. Economic development of poor countries heavily depends upon their own will, commitment to progress and upon their own policies and programmes. In most low-income countries, an essential condition of economic development is a major increase in domestic production of farm products. Rural welfare as well as overall economic growth demands a transformation of the economic structure involving relative decline of the agricultural sector and large absolute and relative growth in the industrial sector of the economy. Policies which facilitate increase in agriculture's contribution to the economic transformation are in the long run are of the interest to agriculturists as well as to country as a whole.

Inter-relationships between Agricultural and Non-agricultural Development

In a rather fundamental sense, agricultural progress is normally a pre-requisite for industrial development. Increasing agricultural productivity supports and sustains non-agricultural, *i.e.*, industrial development in several ways. First, agricultural development raises agricultural incomes thereby increases purchasing power of rural community. This helps to buy the new industrial goods. Rural savings are also directly or indirectly mobilized to finance industrial development. Second, agricultural development permits agriculture to release part of its labour force for industrial employment. Third, agricultural development enables agriculture to supply the raw material in sufficient quantity to industrial sector. Finally, it provides variety of agricultural commodities to satisfy food need of industrial worker.

Similarly, development of industrial sector also helps for agricultural development by different ways. First, industrialization creates more productive non-agricultural employment opportunities to farm community. This helps in reducing the burden on agricultural sector. Second, industrialization increases the demand for agricultural commodities. This results in more favourable market for agricultural products which enable to break down the relatively stagnant subsistence sector of agriculture. Thereby, production of cash crops is stimulated. Third, industrialization also makes available to agricultural workers a wider range of consumption goods, encourages their level of want and increases their efficiency.

The Economic Nature of Traditional Agriculture

In most of the underdeveloped countries, agriculture is traditional type. This agriculture is characterised by low level of capital use. Land, labour, simple tools, irrigation facilities are important factors of production. The level of agricultural production in traditional agriculture is, therefore, limited by the amount and quality of land. Most of the farms are family or peasant farms. Production decisions are taken by individual cultivator. Savings and investment rates are low in traditional agriculture. Hence, returns are also low. Backward technology greatly reduces the productivity of capital. Mainly, subsistence type of farming is followed.

Modern Agriculture

Due to research in agricultural sciences, agriculture is modernizing day-by-day. Technological change is taking place in agriculture. Technological change is one of the more important forces which alters the structure of agricultural production process. Due to technological change capital and labour become more productive when applied to agriculture. The low productivity of traditional input is due to the lack of input of technological change which is needed to complement them. Agriculture is modernised by using improved seeds, fertilizers, undertaking plant protection measures, etc. Credit requirements of modern agriculture are high. Rate of investment and returns are also high in case of modern agriculture as compared to traditional agriculture. The effect of technological change in raising the returns to investment from water and fertilizer inputs are particularly striking. Modernization makes possible the substitution of inputs which have relatively elastic supply schedules for those with relatively inelastic supply schedules, *i.e.*, inorganic fertilizers are substituted for organic. Pesticides and weedicides may substitute for labour. Modernization both raises the productivity of inputs and promotes the use of inputs with more elastic supply schedules. Following points are important for achieving agricultural development.

1. **Incentives:** One of the preconditions for development is that cultivators should get enough incentives for higher agricultural production.

2. Availability of improved inputs: Agricultural production can be achieved by using improved farm inputs such as new crop varieties, inorganic fertilizers, insecticides, weedicides, improved breeds of livestock, etc. These inputs must be easily available at reasonable prices.

3. Research in agricultural sciences: Research must be continued in agricultural sciences so as to find out suitable production techniques, thereby to obtain more and more agricultural production from the existing resources.

4. Institution to provide better services: Needs of the modern agriculture are increasing, those must be satisfied by various institutions. Hence, attention must be paid for establishment of necessary co-operative and other institutions.

5. Extension service: Cultivators must be trained in modern techniques of agricultural production. Similarly, cultivators must be well-informed about prices of inputs and outputs, so that he can take better decisions which will help for increasing agricultural production.

38
Comparison of Growth Experiences

Agricultural development of any economy depends upon several factors such as its resources endowment, technological advancement, infrastructure, institutional facilities, skill, enthusiasm, hard work of people and government policies. Difference in development occur due to level of these factors employed for development.

Japan achieved spectacular development during recent years. Comparison of Japanese rice farm and Indian rice farm will reveal some of the important issues.

Table 38.1: Comparison between Indian and Japanese rice farm

Region	Average size of holding (acres)	Labour available per acre	Labour utilization per acre	Operating expenses per acre	Value of fertilizer per acre	Gross output per acre
India (West Bengal rice farm)	2.9	8	1.9	\$17.3	\$2.7	\$45.8
Japan	3.0	12	7.2	\$132.0	\$34.90	\$448.3

Source: Dan M. Etherington, *Structural Changes in Peasant Agriculture, A Comparative Study of Indian and Japanese Farm Data*.

It is observed from table 38.1 that size of holding is more or less same but Japanese cultivator uses four times more labour, eight times more capital and 13 times more fertilizer than Indian cultivator. Due to these differences in input levels, gross output and net profit obtained by Japanese cultivator is about 10 times more than his counterpart in India. Thus, performance of Japanese farm is remarkable.

Incentives, to cultivator also plays important role in agricultural development.

Table 38.2: Fertilizer consumption in different countries (2002-03) (kg per hectare)

Country	Nitrogen	Phosphorus	Potash	Total
India	57.8	22.1	9.1	89.0
Japan	89.2	92.9	65.3	247.4
USA	26.4	9.4	11.0	46.9
China	45.5	17.8	7.5	70.9

Sources: 1. *Fertilizers Statistics*, 2003-04, The Fertilizer Associations of India, New Delhi.
2. *Agricultural Research Data Book*, 2005.

Comparison of Growth Experiences between States

Level of different factors of production varies from state to state and hence growth rate of agricultural production varies from state to state.

Table 38.3: Compound growth rates of yield (Y) and output (O) in some Indian states (1956-1975).

State/Crop	Rice		Wheat		Sugarcane		Total food grain	
	Y	O	Y	O	Y	O	Y	O
Maharashtra	0.4	1.4	1.4	2.5	1.3	5.7	1.2	3.9
Punjab	4.0	9.6	4.1	7.8	2.0	4.4	4.0	5.2
Andhra Pradesh	1.7	3.4	...	...	0.8	4.8	1.8	...
Rajasthan	...	...	1.9	5.3	...	...	1.3	4.0
UP	1.6	2.7	2.9	4.4	...	2.9	1.3	1.8
Bihar	2.0	2.3	4.7	9.5	3.5	3.3	2.5	2.8

Source: *Indian Journal of Agricultural Economics*, April–June 1980 issue, p. 78.

It is observed from table 38.3, that Punjab is having highest growth rate of yield and output of total food grains. This is because application of fertilizer, water and skill in technical know-how. Punjab is having highest percentage of area irrigated in country. Bihar is also having impressive performance.

Compared to Punjab, Rajasthan has only 19 per cent area irrigated in 1974-75, fertility of the soil is poor and hence performance is also poor. In case of UP, though percentage area irrigated is 45 per cent, water is inadequate to grow more than one crop in a year. As climatic conditions are conducive to grow sugarcane in Maharashtra, it has registered highest growth rate in Sugarcane output.

Thus, growth in agricultural production depends upon level of technical know-how, irrigation facilities, availability of fertilizers and better credit and marketing facilities.

Table 38.4: Yield per hectare of different crops in selected countries—2003

(kg/ha)

Continent/ Country	Paddy	Wheat	Maize	Total cereals	Total pulses	Potato	Soy-bean	Coffee (Green)
Africa								
Egypt	9431	6150	7711	7249	2960	23750	2833	-
Morocco	3522	1722	562	1433	621	22302	1000	-
South Africa	2286	1778	2900	2631	1239	27392	1370	-
North & Central America								
Canada	-	2250	7819	2744	1506	29499	2167	-
Cuba	3499	-	2722	3189	1189	23971	-	208
Mexico	3793	4788	2526	2830	825	25212	1186	418
USA	7448	2974	8924	6033	1803	41152	2248	1653
South America								
Brazil	3238	2371	3696	3365	802	20481	2790	819
Asia								
Bangladesh	3429	1992	2000	3315	772	13807	-	-
Bhutan	2111	1136	1591	1585	800	7875	650	-
China	6074	3907	4854	4849	1507	14842	1737	1313
India	3000	2617	2114	2356	552	17321	1054	851
Indonesia	4538	-	3252	4247	963	13550	1277	701
Iran	-	-	8571	2418	497	19722	1386	-
Israel	-	2267	12000	2942	1970	32917	-	-
Japan	5850	4030	2462	5451	1494	33333	1525	-
Korea Dem. Rep.	3849	2500	3485	3350	857	10761	1143	-
Korea Rep.	5990	3048	4118	5756	1110	27000	1424	-
Nepal	2681	1977	1729	2166	801	10571	937	233
Pakistan	3055	2381	1457	2302	465	16406	1250	-

(Contd. ...)

Continent/ Country	Paddy	Wheat	Maize	Total cereals	Total pulses	Potato	Soy-bean	Coffee (Green)
Philippines	3427	-	1802	2813	723	12115	1000	815
Sri Lanka	3370	-	1098	3283	927	11369	1124	675
Syria	-	2736	4000	-	-	-	-	-
Thailand	2455	615	3913	2584	900	12125	1217	809
Europe								
Denmark	-	7832	-	5857	3536	42446	-	-
France	5611	6235	7137	6134	4146	39971	1838	-
Germany	-	6503	7225	5759	2893	34599	1429	-
Italy	6181	2754	7744	4370	1496	21920	2788	-
Netherlands	-	9119	8000	8196	4691	40725	-	-
Russian Fed.	3175	1707	3262	1787	1325	11585	985	-
UK	-	7778	-	7030	3638	40814	-	-
Ukraine	3500	1371	3533	1752	1277	11563	1100	-
Australia	10290	1999	5267	2072	1209	30238	1905	-
New Zealand	-	7419	10535	6465	3044	44248	-	-
World	3837	2665	4472	3078	793	13182	2261	747

Note: Data pertain to the Calendar Year in which the entire harvest or the bulk of it took place.

Sources: 1. *Fertilizer Statistics*, 2003-04, The Fertilizer Association of India, New Delhi.
2. *Agricultural Research Data Book*, 2005.

Table 38.4, revealed that per hectare paddy yield of India is 3,000 kg per hectare which shows significant increase over period of time, however Japan obtains 5,850 kg per hectare, which is about double than India's per hectare paddy yield.

Consequences of Growth

Growth in agricultural production has several consequences, those are as under:

Employment generation

For achieving growth in agricultural production, farmer has to grow more number of crops in a year, *i.e.*, cropping intensity increases and this leads to generation of employment in agricultural sector. Modern agriculture requires inputs such as credit, fertilizers, pesticides, etc. Due to which employment is generated in this sectors also. Due to voluminous agricultural production more transport facilities are required which leads to generation of employment in transport business. Thus, due to agricultural development employment increases.

Income level and income distribution

Due to modern technology, agricultural production increases and automatically income of the concerned cultivators also increases. In case of India, significant improvement took place in wheat production and automatically, income of the concerned cultivator increased. However, imbalance in income of the cultivators growing wheat and other cultivators took place which lead to regional disparities in income. Cultivators those afford to spend more for their agricultural production benefited more than others, *i.e.*, small cultivators were not able to spend more for their agricultural production and hence benefited less than large cultivators. Similarly, irrigation is a pre-requisite for modern agriculture and hence, income of areas where irrigation is available was several times more than cultivators from unirrigated areas. Study undertaken in villages near Delhi in 1972-73 showed that income of irrigated village cultivator is three times more than income of unirrigated village cultivator. Thus, disparity also increases along with development and Government should take corrective measures for developing egalitarian society.

Table 38.5: Selected indicators of agriculture development in India, Asia-Pacific region and the World

Indicator	Year	India	Asia-Pacific region			World
			Developing Countries	Developed Countries	Total	
Agriculture land ('000 ha)	1989	169485	447069	56989	504058	1499667
	1999	159000	443546	56375	499931	1490752
Agriculture land as % of total land	1989	57.0	20.6	6.9	16.8	11.5
	1999	53.5	20.5	6.8	16.7	11.4
Agriculture population ('000)	1989	500601	1764117	10470	1774587	243567
	1999	553227	1877007	6583	1883590	2575456
Agriculture population as % of total population	1989	60.0	63.7	7.3	61.0	47.0
	1999	55.4	58.3	4.4	55.9	43.1

(Contd. ...)

Indicator	Year	India	Asia-Pacific region			World
			Developing Countries	Developed Countries	Total	
Ratio of agriculture land to agriculture population (ha/person)	1989	0.34	0.25	5.44	0.28	0.62
	1999	0.29	0.24	8.56	0.27	0.58
Irrigated land as % of agricultural land	1989	26.5	30.3	8.7	27.8	15.9
	1999	37.1	36.7	9.2	33.6	18.4
No. of agricultural tractors in use	1989	925365	2507709	2444120	4951829	26415750
	1999	1520000	3632968	2511000	6143968	26424260

Sources: 1. *Selected Indicators of Food and Agriculture Development in Asia-Pacific Region*, 1999-2000, FAO Regional Office for Asia and the Pacific, Bangkok, October, 2001.

2. *Agricultural Statistics at a Glance*, 2003, Directorate of Economics and Statistics, Ministry of Agriculture, Govt. of India.

3. *Agricultural Research Data Book*, 2005.

It is observed from table 38.5, that only 7.3 per cent population of developed countries depends upon agriculture, however, in India 60 per cent population depends upon agriculture. Efforts are needed to generate employment in other sectors of economy.

39
Organisation of Indian Agriculture for Development

For achieving development in agriculture, several concerned factors must be reorganised.

1. Land Holding

Land holding plays important role in agricultural production. Professor Minhas and K.N. Raj are of the opinion that redistribution of land would not affect adversely either agricultural production or volume of savings from agricultural incomes. Farm management studies indicated that output per acre generally declined with increase in size of holding. Hence, land reform plays important role in development of Indian economy.

Table 39.1: Distribution of land holding (per cent)

Category of farmer	Per cent with respect to total holdings	Cumulative total percentage
Marginal (below 1 ha.)	51	51
Small (1 ha. to 2 ha.)	19	70
Medium (2 ha. to 10 ha.)	26	96
Large (above 10 ha.)	4	100

Source: All India Report on Agricultural Census, 1970-71.

It is observed from table 39.1 that 70 per cent of holdings belong to small and marginal categories. Thus, in India small holders are large in number and they possess negligible share of total cultivated land. These small farms are uneconomic unit of cultivation. These small holdings are divided in small plots and scattered over different places. Similarly, division occurs for every new generation. So as to achieve development, it is necessary to bring out land reforms. Here, in this case economic holding should be taken into consideration. Economic holding is that size of holding which can provide full employment to farm family members and should provide income sufficient to live with reasonable standard of living. Thus, ceiling on land holding must be considered effectively implemented in India. This will lead to agricultural development in the country.

Table 39.2 (*a*): Number and area of operational holdings by type of holding in India (Number in thousand, area in thousand hectares)

Sr. No.	Major size classes	Number 1995-96	Average size of holding in ha.	Area 1995-96
1.	Marginal (below 1 ha.)	71179 (61.6)	0.40	28121 (17.2)
2.	Small (1 to 2 ha.)	21643 (18.7)	1.42	30722 (18.8)
3.	Semi Medium (2 to 4 ha.)	142611 (12.3)	2.73	36953 (23.8)
4.	Medium (4 to 10 ha.)	7092 (6.1)	5.84	41398 (25.3)
5.	Large (10 ha. and above)	1404 (1.2)	17.21	24163 (14.8)
6.	All size classes	115580 (100.0)	1.41	3357 (100.0)

Note: Figures within parentheses indicate per cent contribution.

Source: *Agricultural Statistics at a Glance*, 2003 Directorate of Economics and Statistics, Ministry of Agriculture, Govt. of India.

It is observed form table 39.2 (*a*) that about 61.6 per cent of the holdings belong to marginal farmer category. The 18.8 per cent of the holdings belong to small farmer category. About 18.4 per cent farmers are medium farmers and only 1.2 per cent farmers are large farmers. There are total 11.56 crore holdings in India and possess 163.36 million hectares of land. Out of 328.7 million hectares of geographical area of a country 50 per cent land comes under operational holding.

2. Agricultural Credit

Agricultural credit plays important role in modern agriculture and hence cultivators should be motivated to make use of credit. Credit agencies must be directed to provide credit facilities on priority basis to this vital sector of Indian economy.

Table 39.2 (*b*): Number and area of operational holdings by type of holding in Maharashtra (Number in thousand, area in thousand hectares)

Sr. No.	Major size classes	Number 1995-96	Average size of holding in ha.	Area 1995-96
1.	Marginal (below 1 ha.)	4266 (40.0)	0.49	2087 (10.5)
2.	Small (1 to 2 ha.)	3176 (30.0)	1.45	4606 (23.2)
3.	Semi Medium (2 to 4 ha.)	2152 (20.0)	2.73	5872 (29.5)
4.	Medium (4 to 10 ha.)	943 (9.0)	5.76	5436 (27.3)
5.	Large (10 ha. and above)	116 (1.0)	16.2	1879 (9.5)
6.	All size classes	10653 (100.0)	1.87	19880 (100.0)

Note: Figures within parentheses indicate per cent contribution.
Source: *Agricultural Statistics at a Glance*, 2003 Directorate of Economics and Statistics, Ministry of Agriculture, Govt. of India.

During ancient period, cultivators were dependent on money-lenders, who were taking advantage of their misery and ignorance. Cultivators were exploited by these money-lenders. However, development of co-operative credit societies and nationalization of commercial banks made the credit availability easy. Now, cultivators are able to obtain short, medium and long-term credit on suitable terms and conditions. However, some issues pertaining to credit need considerations. Some cultivators are not taking advantage of credit due to their ignorance. Cultivators face difficulties in completing formalities for obtaining loans. As size of holding of majority of cultivators is too small that they are not in a position to go for mechanization and for digging of wells, etc. Government should find out some solution for the problems of these small cultivators. Similarly, procedure for obtaining credit must be simplified. Agricultural Finance officers should help these cultivators sincerely.

3. Marketing Organization

Efficient marketing is important in modern agriculture. Produce is produced in one part of the country and is spread all over the country; some of the produce is also exported. All this is done by Marketing Organization. Mere production of commodity is not of much use, unless it is marketed. For increasing the agricultural production, it is necessary to have better marketing system which will give remunerative and stable prices to agril. produce. Similarly, adequate marketing channels and marketing facilities should be provided. Marketing plays important role in stimulating and maintaining development. It is as follows:

1. There should not be big gap between producer and consumer.
2. Detail knowledge about prices. Where, when and how much products can be sold is essential in determining which crop and which crop variety may be grown.
3. Inputs required for agricultural production should be readily available at reasonable prices, so that production may not be hampered.
4. Improved marketing facilities are essential to take full advantage of production opportunities. Owing to poor transport, high market margins, high risk allowances; production for marketing becomes uneconomic. Producer should get lion's share in price paid by consumer. There should be proper grading system, storing facilities etc.
5. Market research is also necessary for better marketing.
6. Repairing of vehicles required for transport should be easily carried out, for that purpose necessary workshops should be established.
7. Regulated markets must be established wherever possible.

4. Five-Year Plans

Economic situation was unfavourable at the beginning of First Plan. Whatever improvements were made in respect of roads, railways, ports, etc., during British Regime were in accordance with its colonial policy, *viz.*, exploiting the economic and natural resources for raw materials and then to consider the economy as an assured market for manufactured goods from Great Britain. The levels of income and consumption had been very low.

As India become independent, Government of India launched first plan. The main objective of this plan was defined by Planning Commission as follows:

> To initiate a process of development which will raise living standard and open out opportunities to the people for richer and more varied life. Hence, human and material resources may be utilised in effective manner to obtain increased production of goods and services.

During First Plan, priority was given to agriculture. Out of total outlay 31 per cent was allocated to agriculture, community development and irrigation. At the end of First Plan, total food grain production increased from 51.2 million tonnes in 1951-52 to 65.8 million tonnes in 1955-56.

However, more emphasis was given to Industrial sector during Second Plan. Agriculture, community development and to irrigation accounted for about 20 per cent of the total outlay as against 31 per cent in First Plan. Total food grain production increased from 68.8 million tonnes in 1956-57 to 79.3 million tonnes in 1960-61. Second Plan sought to rebuild rural India to lay the foundation of industrial progress and to secure to the greatest extent feasible opportunities for weaker and under privileged sections of the people, and to bring out balanced development of all parts of the country.

Twin objectives of Third Plan were to produce enough food grain to be self-sufficient and to produce enough commercial crops to meet the needs of export and industry. Foodgrain production decreased from 82.71 million tonnes in 1961-62 to 72.3 million tonnes in 1965-66. This is because 1965-66 was a drought year. This shortage resulted in import of foodgrains worth ₹ 1,100 crores.

Due to famine and wars during 1962 and 1965, Government of India postponed Fourth Plan and annual plans started. Due to use of high yielding varieties and application of chemical fertilizers, food grain production increased to 95 million tonnes in 1967-68. During this plan minor irrigation received high priority.

Main objective of Fourth Plan in agricultural sector was to achieve growth of 5 per cent per annum and help small, marginal cultivators and agricultural labourers. Production of food grain increased from 94 million tonnes in 1968-69 to 104.6 million tonnes in 1973-74. However, targeted level for 1973-74 as 129 million tonnes.

The main objective of Fifth Plan was removal of poverty and attainment of economic self-reliance. Total food grain production increased from 104.6 million tonnes in 1973-74 to 131.5 million tonnes in 1978-79, whereas target was 140 million tonnes.

The main approach in Sixth Five-Year Plan (1980-85) was growth with social justice achievement of full employment and removal of poverty. Stress was laid on tackling inter-related problems through a systematic approach with greater management, efficiency and intensive monitoring in all sectors and active involvement of people in formulating specific schemes of development at the local level and securing their speedy and effective implementation. The actual expenditure in Sixth Plan stood at ₹ 1,09,291.7 crores at current prices.

The Seventh Plan (1985-90) emphasized policies and programmes, which aimed at rapid growth in food grain production, increased employment opportunities and productivity within the famework of basic tenets of planning namely growth, modernization, self-reliance and social justice. Foodgrain production during 7th Plan increased by 3.23 per cent as compared to a long-term growth rate of 2.68 per cent between 1967-68 and 1988-89. For reducing unemployment, "Jawahar Rozgar Yojna" was launched in addition to existing programmes. The total expenditure during the entire 7th plan stood at ₹ 2,18,729.62 crores at current prices. Gross GDP grew at an average rate of 5.8 per cent.

Annual Plans

The new government, which assumed power at the Center in June 1991, decided that the 8th Five-Year Plan would start from 1st April, 1992 and that 1990-91 and 1991-92 should be treated as separate Annual Plans. The basic thrust of these Annual plans was on maximization of employment and social transformation.

Eighth Plan

The Eighth Five-Year Plan (1992-97) was launched immediately after the initiation of structural adjustment policies and macro stabilization policies which were necessitated by the worsening Balance of Payments position and inflation position during 1990-91. The various structural adjustment policies were introduced gradually so that the economy could be pushed to a higher growth path and improve its strength and thus prevent Balance of Payments and inflation crisis in future. The eighth plan envisaged an annual average growth rate of 5.6 per cent. Against this an average annual growth rate of 6.5 per cent was achieved during this plan period. The total expenditure during the entire 8th Plan stood at ₹ 4,95,669 crores at current prices.

Ninth Plan

The Ninth Plan (1997-2002) was launched in the fiftieth year of India's Independence. The targeted GDP growth rate of 7 per cent per annum for the Ninth Plan period was decided. Importance was given to double the food production and making India hunger free within 10 years. Rapid improvement in physical infrastructure, national water policy, rural housing, urban housing, health care services, education, urban water supply and sanitation, rural water supply and sanitation, Information Technology. The growth rate realized in first, second and third year of 9th Plan was 4.8%, 6.6% and 6.4%, respectively. The public sector outlay is proposed at ₹ 8,59,200 crore, out of which the central plan outlay would be ₹ 4,89,361 crore.

During the 50 years (1950-51 to 2000-01) since India became a Republic, the National Income, Net National Product (NNP) has increased eight times from ₹ 1,33,499 crores to ₹ 10,72,906 crores (at 1993-94 prices) implying a compound growth rate of 4.2 per cent per annum. The per capita income has increased 2.87 times from ₹ 3,718 to ₹ 10,654 (at 1993-94 prices) registering a compound growth rate of 2.1 per cent. All the aggregates measured at factor cost at 1993-94 prices.

Tenth Plan

Tenth Five-Year Plan (2002 to 2007) aims at higher growth rate and common minimum programme. To achieve 7.5 per cent growth, investment has to be increased from 26.3% of GDP to 31.13% by 2008-09. At present, inflation is in control. Finance Minister recently mentioned that ₹ 9,81,113 crore investments is projected in the 10th plan but only ₹ 4,55,837 crores has been invested in the first three years (2002-05), *i.e.*, about 50% of total outlay yet to be spent and that work has to be completed in next two years, *i.e.*, 2005-06 and 2006-07. To achieve 8 per cent growth rate this is a set target for the 10th five year plan. At present, 26.1% population is below poverty line this percentage has to be reduced to 19.7 per cent during 10th Plan. Similarly total 50 million jobs are to be generated during 10th Plan.

Common Minimum Programme

Congress and its alliance parties DMK, PMK, NCP, RJD, Lokjanshakti party, PDP, JMM, IUML, CPI (M), CPI, and Forward Block, formed a Govt. of India and this group is known as UPA, *i.e.*, United Progressive Alliance. Mrs. Sonia Gandhi is a Chairperson for UPA. UPA released a final draft of Common Minimum Programme (CMP) on 27th May, 2004. This CMP is approved by UPA members. The economic content of CMP is:

1. Employment: To enact a Nation Employment Guarantee Act to provide for at least 100 days of employment to begin with an asset creating public works programme every year at minimum wages for at least one able-bodied person in every rural, urban poor and lower middle class households. In the interim, a massive food for work programme will be started.

2. Agriculture: In agriculture, irrigation will receive highest priority and all on-going projects will be completed according to a strict time schedule. Flow of rural credit will be doubled in next three years, small and marginal farmers will be paid more attention for institutional finance. Similarly, Government will introduce a special programme for dry land farming in the arid and semi-arid regions of the country. Watershed and wasteland development programmes will be taken up on a massive scale.

3. Education and health: The UPA Government decides to raise public expenditure in education to at least 6% of GDP with at least half of this amount being spent on primary and secondary schools. Nobody will be denied professional education because, he or she is poor. Similarly, at least 2-3% of GDP over the next five years will be spent.

4. Schedule caste and schedule tribe: The UPA Government will initiate a dialogue with all political parties and industry and all other organizations to see how best the private sector can be persuaded to provide reservations for SCs/STs in the private sector.

Providing drinking water to all people, efforts will be made on priority basis as well as top priority will be given for infrastructure development. Foreign Direct Investment (FDI) will continue to be encouraged and actively sought particularly in areas of infrastructure high technology and export and where local assets and employment are created on large scale. The FDI will be tripled. UPA Govt. will be making efforts for rural prosperity and improving quality of public services.

In India, planning plays crucial role for development of the agriculture. However, some difficulties are faced while implementing the plans, *i.e.*, peasants are illiterate, their participation is poor, similarly, lack of efficient and honest officials.

Japanese Government first provided full attention to agricultural sector, development of agricultural sector helped Japan to finance their industrial sector. Thus, now both the sectors are well-developed. India should capitalize experience of Japanese government for its economic development. Accordingly, priorities may be fixed in five year plans. These will lead to development of agricultural sector as well as economic development of the country as a whole.

5. International trade in agricultural products: In most of the less developed countries, agriculture plays important role for determining its national income. Governments of such countries should follow modern techniques in agricultural production and should try to export the agricultural commodities which will help them to earn foreign exchange and this will help them to import sophisticated machinery, required for development of industrial sector. Hence, in their planning priority should be given to agricultural sector. In India, second plan gave more emphasis on industrial development, for that purpose country required to import sophisticated machinery, similarly, due to less attention on agriculture sector, forced the country to import food grains for feeding their growing millions. This lead to exceed Import Bill than Export Bill. It is also stated by several economists that agricultural surplus is a pre-requisite for economic development. Hence, agricultural production must be increased by making use of modern technology and by injecting required capital.

Theory of comparative advantage plays important role in specialising and for international trade. For example, if India's climate is suitable for sugarcane production, *i.e.*, per unit cost of production is lower in India than in some of other countries, under such circumstances, India should specialise in sugarcane production. It is profitable to other countries to import sugar from India and produce profitable crop in their countries. Thus, law of comparative advantage plays important role in international trade in agricultural products. Thus, for economic development international trade in agricultural products plays important role.

Selected References

Anonymous, *Agricultural Development in Developing Countries—Comparative Experience*, Indian Society of Agricultural Economics, Bombay, 1971.

Anonymous, *Economic Development of Agriculture,* Thacker & Co. Ltd., Bombay, 1970.

Anonymous, *Indian Journal of Agricultural Economics (1940-1964)—Selected Readings*, Indian Society of Agricultural Economics, Bombay, 1965.

Anonymous, *Indian Journal of Agricultural Economics Issues from 1974 to 1982,* Indian Society of Agricultural Economics, Bombay, 1982.

Echer Car and Witt Lawrence, *Agriculture in Economic Development,* Vora & Co. Publishers Pvt. Ltd., Bombay, 1970.

Heady, E.O., *Economics of Agricultural Production and Resource Use,* Prentice-Hall, INC Englewood Cliffs, N.J. USA, 1960.

Heady, E.O. & Jensen, H.R., *Farm Management Economics*, Prentice-Hall of India Pvt. Ltd., Delhi, 1964.

Kulkarni, R.G., *Deficit Financing and Economic Development*, Asia Publishing House, Bombay, 1966.

Kuznets Simon, *Economic Growth Structure,* Oxford & IBH Publishing Co., Bombay, 1974.

Misra, R.P., Sundaram, K.V., *Multilevel Planning and Integrated Rural Development in India,* Heritage Publishers, New Delhi, 1980.

Nadkarni, M.V., *Agricultural Prices and Development with Stability,* National Publishing House, Delhi, 1973.

Rane, A.A., *Poverty and Irrigation,* Productivity, July–September Issue, Delhi, 1981.

Schultz, T.W., *Economic Organization of Agriculture,* Tata McGraw-Hill Publishing Company, Bombay, 1953.

Shah, S.M., *Rural Development Planning and Reforms,* Abhinav Publications, New Delhi, 1977.

Shukla, Tara, *Economics of Underdeveloped Agriculture,* Vora & Co. Publishers, Bombay, 1969.

Shukla, Tara, *Capital Formation in Indian Agriculture,* Vora & Co. Publishers Pvt. Ltd., Bombay, 1965.

Southworth, H.M., & Johnston, B.F., *Agricultural Development and Economic Growth,* Cornell University Press, Ithaca, New York, 1968.

PART VIII
Agricultural Business Management

40 Agricultural Business Management

Agricultural business management is also mentioned as Agri-business management. Broadway has mentioned Agri-business comprises two different but inter-related exercises firstly, the organization and management of production, right from the use of farm resources to harvesting. Secondly, processing and marketing of the agricultural produce. Snodgrass has mentioned in his book, *Agricultural Economics and Resource use* that Agri-business is an off farm activity namely processing and marketing. It will be better if we consider activities related to farm production, processing of produce and marketing of farm produce under agri-business management. Agri-business includes supply of inputs like seed, compost, fertilizers, plant protection products, etc.

Management

Management is defined in different ways as follows:

1. In economic terms, management is one of the factors of production together with land, labour and capital.
2. According to specialists in administration and organization, management is a system of authority.
3. According to Newman and Summer, management is considered to be a process consisting of organizing, planning, leading and controlling.
4. Management is conceived as a group effort towards a common goal in which team behaviour plays the important role.

5. Management process is that it is the art of getting things done through others.

Managerial Economics

Managerial Economics is defined as application of principles of Economics to the problems of management/decision-making process. For becoming a good manager, knowledge of economics is very much essential.

Characteristics of Good Manager

Good manager should possess:

1. Knowledge of business in which he is employed. Technical knowledge of agriculture, processing helps in taking better decisions.
2. Decision making power: Manager should able to take decision at appropriate time.
3. Self-reliance: Manager should be a self-reliant person, he should not depend upon employees for his private issues.
4. Self-assertion: Manager should able to give his definite opinion about particular thing.
5. Regard for others and social sensitivity.
6. Emotional stability: Manager should function scientifically and his decision should not be affected by emotions.

Scope of Agri-business Management

Agri-business management has a vast scope. Prime Minister, Dr. Manmohan Singh, then finance minister of Government of India had proclaimed the government's decision to set up an agri-business consortium and pronounced that it would be a "Second agricultural revolution". Agri-business consortium had determined tasks in different areas like—1. Horticulture 2. Aquaculture 3. Sericulture 4. Oil seeds 5. Dairy 6. Foodgrains 7. Sugar 8. Cotton 9. Fodder forest and wasteland reclamation. This indicates Government of India had decided higher level of production, generation of employment and through this process removal of rural poverty.

In future, it is necessary to pay greater attention on intensive agriculture, production in green houses, use of biotechnology and use of genetic engineering. Knowledge of agri-business management will help the farmer in increasing his personal income.

Types of Business management:

1. Production management,
2. Material management,
3. Farm management: For details refer part IV of this book.
4. Personal management,
5. Financial management: For details refer part I of this book.
6. Purchase management,
7. Marketing management: For details refer part III of this book.
8. Wholesale and retail management,
9. Office management,
10. Export and import management,
11. Agricultural tourism management.

Principles of Business Management

Fayol, a management philosopher distinguished fourteen principles of management which are now widely accepted. Those are as follows:

1. Division of work is the principle of specialization through which higher norms of efficiency are attained.
2. Authority and Accountability clearly defines the rights of manager and his expected performance.
3. Discipline is the soul of teamwork and the basis of organized industry.
4. Unity of command: Each manager must be clear whom he should command and from whom he shall receive the command.
5. Unity of direction is a guarantee of well-aimed progress. Uncertain, shifting and ill-defined aim is the surest killer of initiative.

6. Superiority and priority of the general interest leads to cohesion and elimination of individual or group interests within a concern firm.
7. Adequate remuneration secures required workers and sustain employee's interest and participation.
8. Centralization is the cementing force in an organization which brings about concentrated efforts towards achievement of the highest common enterprise objective.
9. Scalar chain is the principle of the observance of the chain of command, *i.e.*, hierarchy. Hierarchy helps in proper decision-making which discourages level jumping unless peculiar situation occurs in the interest of organization.
10. Order is the quality of systematic and methodical conduct. A place for everything and everything in its place.
11. Equity is the law of social world which alone secures loyalty of employees and their co-operation.
12. Stability and security of job is a basic motivation for attention to work, ensures hard work from the employees.
13. Initiative is the willing exercise of thinking imaginative and creative faculty in employees which leads towards satisfying the objective of concern organization.
14. Co-operation and fellow-feeling is the cohesive force in the organization in which everybody helps everybody else in a close spirit of team work.

These 14 management principles are applicable for any business organization.

Principles Applied in Farm Business Management

1. Laws of returns, *i.e.*, increasing returns, constant returns and diminishing returns.
2. Principle of least cost combination or law of substitution.
3. Principle of equimarginal returns or opportunity cost.
4. Enterprise combination.
5. Principle of comparative advantage.
6. Time decisions in making investments.

Above mentioned principles are discussed in chapter 21 "Principles Applied to Farm Management" of this book.

Tools of Agri-business Management

Various records and accounts, business diary, Journal, Ledger, Cash book, Trial balance, Profit and Loss account, Balance Sheet — These are the tools of Agri-business management and are discussed in chapter 28 of this book.

Uptill now more attention was given for increasing agril. production, henceforth in addition to efforts in increasing agril. production, the attention on processing of agril. commodities is needed. This will add to the original value of agril. commodities and will generate employment to job seekers. Agricultural business includes farm products, poultry, fishery, dairy, supply of inputs and therefore has a high potential in generating employment. Similarly, present era is an era of globalization, liberalization and privatization more processed products can be exported to other countries and more profit can be earned. India is a second largest country in population and thousands young men need employment, agri-business can provide jobs to millions. Uptill now our farmers were illiterate but slowly and slowly educated young generation is taking over the management of farm business, which will lead towards modern type of farming which will enhance production, processing and marketing. NABARD will be financing knowledge centers these will provide recent knowledge of hybrid and high yielding seeds, prevailing prices at different markets, chances for exporting our agril. produce.

Selected References

A.C. Broadway, *A Textbook of Agribusiness Management*, Kalyani Publishers, Ludhiana.

Shyamlal Banerjee (1995), *Principles and Practice of Management*, Oxford and IBH Publishing Company, New Delhi.

Snodgrass, M.M., and Walace, E.T., *Agricultural Economics and Resource Use*, Prentice-Hall India Ltd., p. 17.

Abbreviations and Contractions

Agricultural Finance

1.	ADB	Agricultural Development Branch
2.	AFC	Agricultural Finance Corporation
3.	AIRCRC	All India Rural Credit Review Committee
4.	AIRCSC	All India Rural Credit Survey Committee
5.	AIRDISC	All India Rural Debt and Investment Survey Committee
6.	BIRD	Bankers Institute for Rural Development
7.	CALCOB	Committee on Agricultural Loans through Commercial Banks
8.	CCA	Capital Consumption Allowance
9.	CIRRs	Commercial Interest Reference Rates
10.	CR	Current Ratio
11.	CRAFICARD	Committee to Review Arrangements for Institutional Credit for Agricultural and Rural Development
12.	CRR	Cash Reserve Ratio
13.	DBOD	Department of Banking Operations and Development
14.	DCCB	District Central Co-operative Bank
15.	DCP	District Credit Plan
16.	DICGC	Deposit Insurance and Credit Guarantee Corporation
17.	DIRS	Differential Interest Rate Scheme
18.	LMBP	Individual Maximum Borrowing Power
19.	IMF	International Monetary Fund
20.	IOU	I Owe You

21. IRDP	Integrated Rural Development Programme
22. IRR	Internal Rate of Return
23. LAMPS	Large Sized Aadivasi Multipurpose Co-operative Societies
24. MPCCS	Multipurpose Co-operative Credit Society
25. NABARD	National Bank for Agricultural and Rural Development
26. NAFED	National Agricultural Co-operative Marketing Federation
27. NIBM	National Institute of Bank Management
28. NPW	Net Present Worth
29. PACS	Primary Agricultural Co-operative Credit Societies
30. PCARDBs	Primary Co-operative Agricultural and Rural Development Banks
31. PR	Price Ratio
32. RBI	Reserve Bank of India
33. SBI	State Bank of India
34. SCARDBs	State Co-operative Agricultural and Rural Development Banks
35. SLBC	State Level Bankers Committee
36. SLR	Statutory Liquidity Ratio
37. UPOV	Union for the Protection of New Varieties
38. WR	Working Ratio

Farm Management

39. AFC	Average Fixed Cost
40. APP	Average Physical Product
41. AR	Average Revenue
42. ATC	Average Total Cost
43. AVC	Average Variable Cost
44. AVP	Average Value Product
45. BCR	Benefit Cost Ratio
46. BEP	Break Even Point
47. BoP	Balance of Payment
48. CYI	Crop Yield Index
49. Ep	Elasticity of Production
50. FCR	Fixed Cost Ratio
51. FSS	Farmers Service Society

52. LP Linear Programming
53. MC Marginal Cost
54. MFC Marginal Factor Cost
55. MPP Marginal Physical Product
56. MR Marginal Revenue
57. MRS Marginal Rate of Substitution
58. MRTS Marginal Rate of Technical Substitution
59. MVP Marginal Value Product
60. TC Total Cost
61. TFC Total Fixed Cost
62. TPP Total Physical Product
63. TR Total Revenue
64. TVC Total Variable Cost
65. TVP Total Value Product

Agricultural Marketing

66. AGMARK Agricultural Produce Grading and Marketing Act
67. AoA Agreement on Agriculture
68. BIS Bureau of Indian Standards
69. DMI Directorate of Marketing and Inspection
70. DSB Dispute Settlement Body
71. DTA Domestic Tariff Area
72. WTO World Trade Organization

General

73. BPL Below Poverty Line
74. CACP Commission on Agricultural Costs and Prices
75. CADA Command Area Development Authority
76. CWC Central Warehousing Corporation
77. DCC District Consultative Committee
78. DI Disposable Income
79. DWCRA Development of Women and Children in Rural Area
80. ECGC Export Credit Guarantee Corporation
81. EPZ Export Promotion Zones
82. EXIM Export Import Bank of India
83. FAO Food and Agricultural Organization
84. FCI Fertilizer Corporation of India

85. FCI	Food Corporation of India
86. GATT	General Agreement on Tariff and Trade
87. GDP	Gross Domestic Product
88. GI	Gross Income
89. GNP	Gross National Product
90. HADP	Hilly Area Development Projects
91. HIPC	Heavily Indebted Poor Countries
92. IBRD	International Bank for Reconstruction and Development
93. IDA	International Development Association
94. IDADA	Integrated Dryland Agricultural Development Agency
95. IDBI	Industrial Development Bank of India
96. IFC	International Finance Corporation
97. ISI	Indian Standards Institute
98. IT	Income Tax
99. IT	Information Technology
100. ITO	International Trade Organization
101. KVIC	Khadi and Village Industries Commission
102. MFALDA	Marginal Farmers and Agricultural Labourers Development Agency
103. MFNs	Most Favoured Nations
104. MIGA	Multilateral Investment Guarantee Agency
105. NCA	National Commission on Agriculture
106. NCCF	National Consumers' Co-operative Federation
107. NCDC	National Co-operative Development Corporation
108. NDDB	National Dairy Development Board
109. NI	National Income
110. NNP	Net National Product
111. NREP	National Rural Employment Programme
112. NRY	Nehru Rojgar Yojana
113. NSS	National Sample Survey
114. NTB	Non-Tariff Barriers
115. NWDB	National Wasteland Development Board
116. OCR	Operational Cost Ratio
117. OECD	Organization for Economic Co-operation and Development

118. OGL	Open General License
119. PBR	Plant Breeders Rights
120. PBRS	Patents and Plant Breeders Rights
121. PDS	Public Distribution System
122. PI	Personal Income
123. QRs	Quantitative Restrictions
124. REC	Rural Electrification Corporation
125. SDR	Special Drawing Rights
126. SFDA	Small Farmers Development Agency
127. SHG	Self-Help Group
128. SPS	Sanitary and Phytosanitary Measures
129. SWC	State Warehousing Corporation
130. TADP	Tribal Area Development Programme
131. TR	Tariff Barriers
132. TPRM	Trade Policy Review Mechanism
133. TRIFED	Tribal Co-operative Marketing Development Federation
134. TRIMs	Trade Related Investment Measures
135. TRIPs	Trade Related Intellectual Property Rights
136. TRYSEM	Training of Rural Youth for Self-Employment
137. APL	Above Poverty Line
138. BSE	Bombay Stock Exchange
139. CAG	Comptroller and Auditor General
140. CAGR	Compound Average Growth Rate
141. CMP	Common Minimum Programme
142. COFEPOSA	Conservation of Foreign Exchange and Prevention of Smuggling Activities
143. CPI	Consumer Price Index
144. CSIR	Council of Scientific and Industrial Research
145. CSO	Central Statistical Organisation
146. CWC	Central Warehousing Corporation
147. DIC	District Industries Centre
148. DRDAs	District Rural Development Agencies
149. EEC	European Economic Community
150. EGS	Employment Guarantee Scheme
151. EPF	Employees Provident Fund
152. EWS	Economically Weaker Sections

153. FDI	Foreign Direct Investment
154. IADP	Intensive Agricultural District Programme
155. ICAR	Indian Council of Agricultural Research
156. ICICI	Industrial Credit and Investment Corporation of India
157. IFFCO	Indian Farmers Fertilizers Co-operative Ltd.
158. ILO	International Labour Organisation
159. IMF	International Monetary Fund
160. IRDP	Integrated Rural Development Programme
161. NAFED	National Agricultural Co-operative Marketing Federation
162. NCA	National Commission on Agriculture
163. NCAER	National Council of Applied Economic Research
164. NIRD	National Institute of Rural Development
165. NPC	National Planning Commission
166. NSC	National Seeds Corporation
167. PSU	Public Sector Undertakings
168. SSEs	Small Scale Enterprises
169. VAT	Value Added Taxation
170. WPI	Wholesale Price Index

Questions

PART I
AGRICULTURAL FINANCE

Multiple Choice Questions

Q. Select Correct Answer

1. Agricultural finance includes:
   (a) Credit
   (b) Keynesian theory
   (c) Econometric models
2. Agricultural finance is that part of:
   (a) Credit
   (b) Farm management
   (c) Econometrics
3. Future scope of agricultural finance is:
   (a) Vast
   (b) Narrow
   (c) Little
4. Credit refers to:
   (a) Amount saved
   (b) Amount earned
   (c) Amount borrowed
5. Credit worthiness also depend upon:
   (a) Height of a person
   (b) Character of a person
   (c) Weight of a person
6. Because of credit burden on metallic money is:
   (a) Reduced

(b) Increased
(c) Normal

7. Credit may encourage:
(a) Stealing
(b) Saving
(c) Extravagance
8. As per 1991 data share of commercial bank credit in total borrowing by Indian cultivator is:
(a) Increasing
(b) Decreasing
(c) Constant
9. As per 1991 data share of private credit in total borrowing by cultivator is:
(a) Increasing
(b) Decreasing
(c) Constant
10. NABARD came into existence in:
(a) 1982
(b) 1972
(c) 1992
11. World Trade Organization came into force in:
(a) 1985
(b) 1995
(c) 2005
12. Major proportion of advances by RRBs is to:
(a) Weaker section
(b) Rich section
(c) Only to agril. labourers
13. Agricultural Finance Corporation was established in:
(a) 1969
(b) 1963
(c) 1968
14. Agricultural Refinance and Development Corporation was established in:
(a) 1969

(b) 1963
(c) 1968

15. Credit makes capital:
(a) Productive
(b) Unproductive
(c) None of the above
16. Reserve Bank of India was set up in:
(a) 1930
(b) 1935
(c) 1934
17. Rural Credit Survey Committee was set up in:
(a) 1951
(b) 1954
(c) 1955
18. SFDA and MFAL agencies were suggested by:
(a) Rural Credit Survey Committee
(b) Rural Credit Review Committee
(c) Debt and Investment Survey Committee
19. SFDA has covered only:
(a) All the districts
(b) Selected districts
(c) Randomly selected districts
20. Marginal farmer is a farmer having size of holding less than:
(a) One acre
(b) One hectare
(c) One bigha
21. Small farmer is a farmer having size of holding less than:
(a) Five acres
(b) Five hectares
(c) Five gunthas
22. Returns, Repayment capacity, Risk-bearing ability:
(a) Can be quantified
(b) Cannot be quantified
(c) Cannot be understood

23. Family expenditure is taken into consideration while estimating:
    (a) Returns
    (b) Repayment capacity
    (c) Risk-bearing ability
24. Equity can be a:
    (a) Difference between total assets and total liabilities
    (b) Differences between saving and income
    (c) Difference between returns and repayment capacity
25. In even repayment plan installments are:
    (a) Even
    (b) Uneven
    (c) Unequal

ANSWERS

1. *a*	2. *b*	3. *a*	4. *c*
5. *b*	6. *a*	7. *c*	8. *a*
9. *b*	10. *a*	11. *b*	12. *a*
13. *c*	14. *b*	15. *a*	16. *b*
17. *a*	18. *b*	19. *b*	20. *b*
21. *a*	22. *a*	23. *b*	24. *a*
25. *a*			

Statements

Q. State whether the following statements are true or false, if false correct them and rewrite.

1. Credit means trust in borrower's ability to pay and his willingness to pay.

   Ans. False. Credit means trust in borrower's ability to repay and his willingness to repay.
2. Credit never refers to amount borrowed.

   Ans. False. Credit refers to amount borrowed.
3. Because of credit burden on metallic money is increased.

   Ans. False. Because of credit burden on metallic money is reduced.

4. Credit makes capital unproductive.
   Ans. False. Credit makes capital productive.
5. Credit discourages extravagance and waste.
   Ans. False. Credit encourages extravagance and waste.
6. Credit is sometimes needed for repayment of old debt.
   Ans. True.
7. Crop loan is a long-term credit.
   Ans. False. Crop loan is a short-term credit.
8. Credit required for purchasing land is called short-term.
   Ans. False. Credit required for purchasing land is called long-term credit.
9. Percentage share of commercial bank in total borrowing by Indian cultivators is increasing during recent years.
   Ans. True
10. Percentage share of professional money-lenders in total borrowing by Indian cultivators is also increasing during recent years.
    Ans. False. Percentage share of professional money-lenders in total borrowing by Indian cultivators is decreasing during recent years.
11. Because of crop loan cultivators are encouraged for cultivating commercial crops.
    Ans. True.
12. Better the asset position worse is the credit worthiness.
    Ans. False. Better the asset position better is the credit worthiness.
13. Credit may discourage productive investment.
    Ans. False. Credit encourages productive investment.
14. Loan for purchasing buffalo is called short-term loan.
    Ans. False. Loan for purchasing buffalo is called medium-term loan.
15. Higher the equity lowers the repayment capacity.
    Ans. False. Higher the equity, higher the repayment capacity.
16. Taccavi loans are not granted to all farmers.
    Ans. False. Taccavi loans are granted to all farmers.

17. Institutional credit agencies charge low interest rate than private credit agencies.

    Ans. True.

18. Repayment capacity also depends upon family expenses.

    Ans. True.

19. It is always true that large cultivators have higher repayment capacity than medium cultivators.

    Ans. False. It is sometimes true that large cultivators have higher repayment capacity than medium cultivators.

20. Imbalance in resource availability always helps in improving repayment capacity.

    Ans. False. Imbalance in resource availability decreases repayment capacity.

21. Nationalization of major 14 commercial banks took place in 1970.

    Ans. False. Nationalization of major 14 commercial banks took place in 1969.

22. According to Dantewala committee report (regarding regional rural banks) expansion of regional rural bank must be encouraged.

    Ans. True.

23. Social control came in force before nationalization of commercial banks.

    Ans. True.

24. In amortized decreasing repayment plan amount of capital per instalment goes on increasing.

    Ans. False. In amortized decreasing repayment plan amount of capital per installment remains constant.

25. Crop insurance helps for improving the risk-bearing ability of the cultivator but diversification of production does not.

    Ans. False. Crop insurance and diversification of production help for improving risk-bearing ability of the cultivator.

26. By adjusting the time-period of loan repayment, borrower can strengthen his repayment capacity.

    Ans. True.

27. Credit required for purchasing production equipment, furniture's, transport equipment is classified under the heading "Non-farm business purpose".

    Ans. True.

28. Government purchase of shares of co-operative organization is termed as direct finance by the Government.

    Ans. False. Government purchase of share of co-operative organization is termed as indirect finance by the Government.

29. The one of the objectives of NABARD is to provide guidance to State Governments.

    Ans. True.

30. By 2004, about 10 lakh self-help groups (SHGs) have started functioning in India.

    Ans. True.

31. By the end of May 1980, total numbers of nationalized banks were more than 14.

    Ans. True.

Short Notes

Q. Write short notes on following:

1. Commercial Bank finance,
2. RRBs,
3. RBI,
4. Crop loan system,
5. Advantages of institutional credit agency,
6. Rural Credit Survey,
7. Follow up Survey,
8. Self-Help Groups,
9. Credit and credit worthiness,
10. Amortized even repayment plan,
11. Repayment schedule,
12. Margin fund,
13. Income and expenditure statement,

14. Procedure for obtaining crop loan,
15. Regional Rural Bank
16. Agricultural development branches of State Bank of India
17. Farmer's service societies
18. Financing primary credit co-operatives by commercial banks
19. NABARD
20. Importance of agricultural credit
21. Improved agricultural technology and credit requirement
22. Agricultural credit policy
23. SFDA & MFAL
24. Agricultural money-lender
25. Indirect finance by Government
26. Long-term credit
27. Private credit agencies
28. Quasi variable repayment plan
29. Loan procedure for obtaining a crop loan from commercial banks
30. Defaulters of multipurpose co-operative society.

Full Questions

1. Define credit and give detail classification of credit with examples.
2. Enumerate different credit agencies supplying agricultural credit. What is percentage share of individual credit agency in total borrowing by Indian cultivator in 1991?
3. Give in brief advantages and disadvantages of private and institutional credit agencies.
4. Explain principles of agricultural finance.
5. What do you mean by three R's of credit? How these are useful in determining credit worthiness of the borrower?
6. Write an essay on "Role of commercial banks in financing agriculture".

7. How returns, repayment capacity and risk-bearing ability concepts are useful to the lender?
8. What is the role of RBI in supplying agricultural credit?
9. What different measures will be adopted by progressive cultivator for strengthening his risk-bearing ability?
10. What is the role of NABARD in agril. development of the country?
11. What were the objectives of Rural Credit Survey? How it was undertaken? In what way it is useful?
12. How did nationalization of major commercial banks help for development of agriculture?
13. Write an essay on "Role of RRBs in financing agriculture".
14. Explain the following concepts and also explain the importance of each concept from the point of view of borrower and lender.
    (*a*) Repayment capacity.
    (*b*) Risk-bearing ability.
15. What are the different measures, cultivator can undertake for strengthening his repayment capacity?
16. Explain in brief various repayment plans.
17. What do you mean by agricultural finance? Discuss in brief the importance of micro and macro finance in agricultural development in India.
18. What is meant by overdues and recovery? Enlist the causes of overdues in agricultural credit and suggest the measures to improve the recovery performance.
19. What is meant by three 'Cs' of credit? Explain each of them in detail.

Problems

1. Cultivator wanted to obtain a medium-term loan from commercial bank for poultry of 500 birds. Give the details regarding following points:
    1. Total amount of loan required.
    2. Margin fund.

3. Income and expenditure statement.
4. Repayment schedule and net income.

Information

(*a*) Cost of one-day-old chick is ₹ 16
(*b*) Cost of feed ₹ 10 per kg.
(*c*) Cost of medicine, labour charges, electricity, etc., per annum
₹ 2/chick
₹ 4/bird
(*d*) Price of eggs ₹ 170 per 100 eggs
(*e*) Brooder's and layer's house ₹ 150/sq.ft.

2. Cultivator wanted to obtain a long-term loan from commercial bank for two acre alphonso mango orchard give the details regarding following points:
   1. Total amount of loan required.
   2. Margin fund.
   3. Income and expenditure statement.
   4. Repayment schedule.
3. What are the problems of multipurpose co-operative society of your own village? Suggest suitable solutions.
4. What is total credit requirement of cultivator, who grows five hectare of paddy and five hectare of sugarcane crop?
5. Prepare a loan scheme for starting a dairy (five buffaloes).
6. Prepare a loan scheme for purchasing a tractor (35-HP).

PART II
CO-OPERATION

Multiple Choice Questions

Q. Select Correct Answer

1. Co-operation originated in:
   (*a*) Europe
   (*b*) Asia
   (*c*) North America

2. "Co-operation is a voluntary organization of people meant for satisfying their economic interests", defined by:
   (*a*) A.A. Rane
   (*b*) C.R. Fay
   (*c*) Calvert
3. Principles of co-operation approved by:
   (*a*) United Nations
   (*b*) ICA
   (*c*) USA
4. International Co-operative Alliance (ICA) appointed a commission in 1964 under the chairmanship of Prof. D.G. Karve of:
   (*a*) Nepal
   (*b*) UK
   (*c*) India
5. State co-operative bank is called as:
   (*a*) Commercial bank
   (*b*) First bank
   (*c*) Apex bank
6. State Co-operative Agricultural and Rural Development bank is at:
   (*a*) State level
   (*b*) District level
   (*c*) For a particular region
7. In 1993-94, total number of primary co-operative societies in India was:
   (*a*) 15.5 lakh
   (*b*) 0.66 lakh
   (*c*) 155 lakh
8. In 2001-02 total number of central co-operative banks in India was:
   (*a*) 5000
   (*b*) 3410
   (*c*) 369

9. In 2001-02 total number of apex banks in India was:
   (*a*) 30
   (*b*) 22
   (*c*) 31
10. In 2001-02 total number of SCARDBs (central land development banks) in India was:
    (*a*) 22
    (*b*) 20
    (*c*) 31
11. In 2001-02 total number of PCARDBs (primary land development banks) in India was:
    (*a*) 87200
    (*b*) 8720
    (*c*) 739
12. The loan advanced by PCARDBs during 2001-02 were rupees:
    (*a*) 1930 crores
    (*b*) 1500 crores
    (*c*) 200 crores
13. District central co-operative bank is a connecting link between apex bank and:
    (*a*) PACS
    (*b*) PCARDBs
    (*c*) SCARDBs
14. In which year Fredric Nicholson was deputed for studying land banks in Europe:
    (*a*) 1792
    (*b*) 1892
    (*c*) 1829
15. Which is the instrument of planned economic action in democracy?
    (*a*) Communism
    (*b*) Co-operation
    (*c*) Capitalism

16. Which is the birth place of co-operative movement in world:
    (*a*) U.S.A.
    (*b*) England
    (*c*) Germany
17. Robert Owen was from:
    (*a*) Canada
    (*b*) England
    (*c*) Germany
18. Co-operative movement was introduced in Denmark by:
    (*a*) Robert Owen
    (*b*) Calvert
    (*c*) H.C. Sonne
19. Long-term credit in Agriculture is provided by:
    (*a*) PCARDBs
    (*b*) PACS
    (*c*) RBI
20. The first co-operative societies act was passed in the year:

(*a*) 1919
(*b*) 1912
(*c*) 1904

ANSWERS

1. *a*	2. *a*	3. *b*	4. *c*
5. *c*	6. *a*	7. *b*	8. *c*
9. *a*	10. *b*	11. *c*	12. *a*
13. *a*	14. *b*	15. *b*	16. *c*
17. *b*	18. *c*	19. *a*	20. *c*

Statements

Q. State whether the following statements are true or false, if false correct them and rewrite.

1. There is not any scope for land reclamation societies in Konkan region.

   Ans. False. There is wide scope for land reclamation societies in Konkan region.

2. PACS is a district level co-operative institution.
   Ans. False. PACS is a base level institution.
3. Co-operative farming achieved a grand success in India. **Ans.** False. Co-operative farming did not achieve a grand success in India.
4. Assistant registrar is a superior authority to deputy registrar in co-operation department.
   Ans. False. Deputy registrar is a superior authority to assistant registrar in co-operation department.
5. Registrar for co-operatives is Brahma, Vishnu, Mahesh of the co-operative department.
   Ans. True.
6. State Board of supervision carry out audit work also.
   Ans. False. State Board of supervision is engaged in supervisory duties.
7. 'Co-operation has failed but co-operation must succeed,' stated by Maclagan Committee.
   Ans. False. 'Co-operation has failed but co-operation must succeed' is stated by Rural Credit Survey Committee.
8. Primary credit co-operatives borrow from commercial banks in certain states.
   Ans. True.
9. Integrated scheme of rural credit is recommended by Rural Credit Survey Committee.
   Ans. True.
10. All India Rural Credit Review Committee Report was published in 1969.
    Ans. True.
11. In 2003-04, it is estimated that total institutional credit provided to agriculture was ₹ 80,000 crores.
    Ans. True.
12. Exemption from payment of taxes, stamp duty, registration fees is a fiscal form of state aid to co-operatives.
    Ans. True.
13. Agricultural credit department of RBI looks after the problems of agril. credit.

Ans. False. NABARD looks after the problems of agril. credit.

14. Work of the co-operative department is general administration, supervision, inspection and audit of co-operatives.

    Ans. True.

15. 'B' class co-operative society is better than 'A' class society.

    Ans. False. 'A' class co-operative society is better than 'B' class co-operative society.

16. Growth with stability and growth with social justice are national objectives.

    Ans. True.

17. Germany is the birthplace of co-operative credit movement in the world.

    Ans. True.

18. There is no difference between Raiffeisen societies and Schulze Banks.

    Ans. False. There is difference between Raiffeisen societies and Schulze Banks.

19. Rochdale Pioneers are from Germany.

    Ans. False. Rochdale Pioneers are from England.

20. Canada is the world's second largest country in size.

    Ans. True.

21. In this big world, this small country is called as 'The Co-operative Denmark'.

    Ans. True.

22. Kibbutz is famous in Japan.

    Ans. False. Kibbutz is famous in Israel.

23. Co-operative training college was established at Poona in 1947.

    Ans. True.

24. Members of co-operative societies are trained in principles of co-operation.

    Ans. True.

25. In June 1973, the Government of India constituted an Informal Expert Group on Co-operative Education under the Chairmanship of Dr. M.S. Swaminathan.

    Ans. True.

26. Co-operation and Community Development are not related.

    Ans. False. Co-operation and community development are related.

27. Dr. C.R. Fay has defined 'community development'.

    Ans. False. Dr. C.R. Fay has defined co-operation.

28. Co-operation and socialism are same things.

    Ans. False. Co-operation and socialism are different things.

29. At least ten members are necessary for forming a co-operative society.

    Ans. True.

30. The minimum number of members in Joint Stock Company is two, but there is no limit to maximum number.

    Ans. True.

31. In partnership, minimum number of members is two and maximum number has been limited to 10 in a banking business and 20 in other business.

    Ans. True.

32. Co-operative society is registered by Registrar of Co-operative under the Co-operative Society Act of 1904.

    Ans. True.

33. Joint stock company is registered under the Indian Companies Act, 1956.

    Ans. True.

34. Partnership is registered under the Indian Partnership Act, 1932.

    Ans. True.

35. Partners of a firm have unlimited liability.

    Ans. True.

36. Principles of co-operation once again reformulated by a commission appointed by the ICA in 1964 under the Chairmanship of Prof. D.G. Karve of India.

    Ans. True.

37. Follow up surveys completed before rural credit survey.

    Ans. False. Follow up surveys were undertaken after rural credit survey.

38. Majority of the co-operative societies have limited liability.

    Ans. True.

39. Central co-operative bank is not needed in co-operative credit structure.

    Ans. False. Central bank is needed in co-operative credit structure.

40. State co-operative bank is called as apex bank.

    Ans. True.

41. For long-term co-operative loan, two-tier system exists in India.

    Ans. True.

Short Notes

Q. Write Short Notes on Following:

1. Co-operative credit structure,
2. Supervision of co-operative societies in Maharashtra,
3. Integrated scheme of rural credit,
4. Schulze banks,
5. Act of 1912,
6. Economic depression of 1930 and co-operative development,
7. Committee on co-operative administration,
8. Raiffeisen societies,
9. Limited liability,
10. Unlimited liability,
11. Processing co-operatives,
12. Capitalism and co-operation,
13. Socialism and co-operation,

14. Communism and co-operation,
15. Co-operative better farming societies,
16. Co-operative joint farming society,
17. Co-operative sugar factory,
18. Co-operative rice mill,
19. Legislative state aid,
20. State partnership in credit and non-credit societies,
21. RBI and co-operative development,
22. Supervision of co-operatives,
23. Inspection of co-operatives,
24. Auditing of co-operatives,
25. Raiffeisen Bank societies,
26. Rochdale Pioneers,
27. Dairy co-operatives in Denmark,
28. Kibbutz,
29. Moshav Ovdim,
30. Moshvan Shitufi,
31. Co-operative Training College, Pune,
32. Community development and co-operation,
33. Philosophy of co-operation,
34. Open membership,
35. Each for all and all for each,
36. Self-help and mutual help,
37. Co-operative Societies Act of 1904,
38. Maclagan Committee,
39. Primary agricultural credit society,
40. Central co-operative bank,
41. State co-operative bank,
42. Land development bank.

Full Questions

1. Define co-operation and explain principles of co-operation in brief.
2. Explain in brief the principles of co-operation formulated by a commission appointed by the International Co-operative Alliance.

3. What are the problems of multipurpose co-operative society of your own village? Suggest suitable solutions.
4. Write detail information regarding multipurpose co-operative society.
5. What different steps you will take to start multipurpose co-operative society in a village where there is no co-operative society?
6. What do you mean by co-operative farming? Explain in brief different categories of co-operative farming.
7. What do you mean by government aid to co-operatives? Explain in brief different forms of state aid.
8. What is the role played by Reserve Bank in development of co-operative movement?
9. Write in brief about co-operative movement in Germany/England/Canada/Israel/Denmark/Japan.
10. Write in brief about co-operative education and training in India.
11. How community development and co-operation is related?
12. Write in brief about development of co-operative movement before independence.
13. Write in brief about development of co-operative movement after independence.
14. What do you mean by primary agricultural credit societies? Write in detail about the same.
15. What do you mean by PCARDBs and SCARDBs (land development bank)? Write in detail about them.

PART III
AGRICULTURAL MARKETING

Multiple Choice Questions

Q. Select Correct Answer

1. Agricultural marketing is one of the important branch of:
   (*a*) Economics
   (*b*) Agriculture

(*c*) Agricultural Economics

2. Market means an open place or a large building where actual:
   (*a*) Buying and selling take place
   (*b*) Buying take place
   (*c*) Selling take place
3. Marketing is that part of economics which deals with the creation of:
   (*a*) Time utility
   (*b*) Place utility
   (*c*) Time, place of possession utilities
4. Markets for agricultural produce may broadly be divided into:
   (*a*) Two categories
   (*b*) Three categories
   (*c*) Four categories
5. Terminal markets are those in which the producer is either finally disposed of direct to consumers or to processor or assembled for:
   (*a*) Distribution
   (*b*) Shipment to foreign countries
   (*c*) Consumption
6. Fruits and vegetables are:
   (*a*) Sweet
   (*b*) Butter
   (*c*) Perishable
7. Wheat is substituted by:
   (*a*) Vegetables
   (*b*) Jowar
   (*c*) Fruits
8. Assembling is a:
   (*a*) Dispersing marketing function
   (*b*) Concentrating marketing function
   (*c*) Neither (*a*) nor (*b*)
9. In India transportation means are:

(*a*) Well-developed
(*b*) Not well-developed
(*c*) Neither (*a*) nor (*b*)

10. What are the types of buying?
(*a*) Buying for consumption
(*b*) Buying for resale
(*c*) Both mentioned in (*a*) and (*b*)

11. Open auction method of selling is followed in:
(*a*) Regulated market
(*b*) Unregulated market
(*c*) Neither (*a*) nor (*b*)

12. How many channels of distribution exist for a commodity?
(*a*) Several
(*b*) One
(*c*) Two

13. Vegetables and fruits must be distributed through:
(*a*) Shorter channels
(*b*) Longer channels
(*c*) Broader channels

14. Channel of distribution can be controlled by:
(*a*) Retailer
(*b*) Consumer
(*c*) Producer or by their co-operatives

15. Paddy miller is included to:
(*a*) Few channels of distribution of paddy
(*b*) Every channel of distribution of paddy
(*c*) First and last channel of distribution of paddy only

16. Superfluous middlemen:
(*a*) Increase market cost
(*b*) Decrease market cost
(*c*) Neither (*a*) nor (*b*)

17. Multiplicity of weights and measures is observed in:
(*a*) English market
(*b*) American market
(*c*) Indian market

18. Forced sale is more prominent in:
    (*a*) Medium cultivator
    (*b*) Small cultivator
    (*c*) Large cultivator
19. Co-operative marketing can:
    (*a*) Reduce some of the marketing defects
    (*b*) Increase some of the marketing defects
    (*c*) Neither (*a*) nor (*b*)
20. Market committee consists more than:
    (*a*) Fifty per cent middlemen
    (*b*) Fifty per cent cultivators
    (*c*) Fifty per cent government nominees
21. Settlement of disputes in regulated market is done by:
    (*a*) Court of law
    (*b*) Dispute committee
    (*c*) Market committee
22. Large cultivators contribute:
    (*a*) Significant quantity towards marketable surplus
    (*b*) Non-significant quantity
    (*c*) Neither (*a*) nor (*b*)
23. Creation of adequate agricultural surplus would lead to:
    (*a*) Prosperity
    (*b*) Misery
    (*c*) Starvation
24. Lengthy distribution channel will require:
    (*a*) Little marketing cost
    (*b*) Less marketing cost
    (*c*) More marketing cost
25. More the marketing cost:
    (*a*) More the producer's share is consumer's rupee
    (*b*) Less the producer's share in consumer's rupee
    (*c*) Neither (*a*) nor (*b*)
26. Marketing efficiency is of:
    (*a*) Three kinds
    (*b*) Two kinds
    (*c*) Four kinds

27. When price will be more than equilibrium price then there will be:
    (*a*) No pressure on price
    (*b*) Upward pressure on price
    (*c*) Downward pressure on price
28. Price should be:
    (*a*) Stable
    (*b*) Too high
    (*c*) Too low
29. Main role of Commission on Agricultural Costs and Prices is to:
    (*a*) Purchasing of agril. commodities
    (*b*) Fixing prices
    (*c*) Advise government on fixing prices
30. During recent years the trends in prices of agril. commodities is:
    (*a*) Decreasing
    (*b*) Constant
    (*c*) Increasing

ANSWERS

1. *c*	2. *a*	3. *c*	4. *b*
5. *b*	6. *c*	7. *b*	8. *b*
9. *b*	10. *c*	11. *a*	12. *a*
13. *a*	14. *c*	15. *b*	16. *a*
17. *c*	18. *b*	19. *a*	20. *b*
21. *b*	22. *a*	23. *a*	24. *c*
25. *b*	26. *b*	27. *c*	28. *a*
29. *c*	30. *c*		

Statements

Q. State whether the following statements are true or false, if false correct them and rewrite.

1. Risk-bearing is not a dispersing function.
   Ans. False. Risk-bearing is also a dispersing function.
2. In auction sale tenders are invited.
   Ans. False. In auction sale tenders are not invited.

3. Transportation is not a marketing function.

   Ans. False. Transportation is a marketing function.

4. In Dara sale system, the heaps of grain of different quantities are sold at a flat rate.

   Ans. True.

5. Processing sugarcane or cotton is one of the marketing functions.

   Ans. True.

6. Risk-bearing is not important marketing function.

   Ans. False. Risk-bearing is an important marketing function

7. Commodities are exported from terminal market.

   Ans. True.

8. Market intelligence is one of the marketing functions.

   Ans. True.

9. A marketing function is an act, operation or service by which the original producer and final consumer are linked together.

   Ans. True.

10. Market research is a part of market intelligence.

    Ans. True.

11. Cotton is not sold by open auction method in a regulated market.

    Ans. False. Cotton is sold by open auction method.

12. Rice mill owners purchase paddy on large scale.

    Ans. True.

13. Terminal markets are not important in marketing of agricultural commodities.

    Ans. False. Terminal markets are important in marketing of agricultural commodities.

14. Food Corporation of India is helpful in stabilization of domestic prices.

    Ans. True.

15. Only milch animals are sold at animal markets.

    Ans. False. All type of animals are sold at animal markets.

16. Demand for all agricultural commodities is inelastic.

    Ans. True.

17. Higher the market cost, higher the market efficiency.

    Ans. False. Higher the market cost lower the market efficiency.

18. Forced sales cannot be called as a defect of agriculture marketing.

    Ans. False. Forced sales are a defect of agricultural marketing.

19. The market may extend to a locality, village, town, region or a country according to the demand for a commodity.

    Ans. True.

20. Marketing includes all activities, which are concerned with effecting changes in the ownership and possession of goods and services.

    Ans. True.

21. Mandis at district places are called as primary wholesale markets.

    Ans. False. Mandis at district places are called as secondary wholesale markets.

22. Consumers do not purchase anything from secondary wholesale markets.

    Ans. False. Consumers can purchase from secondary wholesale markets.

23. Marketing is as important as production.

    Ans. True.

24. Prices are fixed by Agricultural Price Commission.

    Ans. False. Prices are fixed by government but recommended by Agricultural Price Commission.

25. Procurement price of wheat is decreasing year-after-year.

    Ans. False. Procurement price of wheat is increasing year-after-year.

26. There are two equilibrium prices in a perfect competitive market.

    Ans. False. There is only one equilibrium price exists in a perfect competitive market.

27. Monopoly is a market form in which only one seller controls the supply of a commodity.

    Ans. True.

28. Prices are stabilized automatically.

    Ans. False. Prices are stabilized through certain measures.

29. Lower market efficiency indicator means that market is comparatively inefficient.

    Ans. True.

30. Market margin is greater than consumer's price.

    Ans. False. Market margin is a part of consumer's price.

Short Notes

Q. Write short notes on following:

1. Open auction,
2. Characteristics of farm produce,
3. Marketable surplus,
4. Grading,
5. Regulated market,
6. Market,
7. Types of market,
8. Pyle's classification of marketing function,
9. Method of selling,
10. Transportation,
11. Channel of distribution of paddy/wheat,
12. Co-operative marketing,
13. Marketed surplus,
14. Market cost,
15. Price spread,
16. Market efficiency,
17. Market intelligence,
18. Agricultural Price Commission,
19. Market committee,
20. Dispute committee,
21. WTO.

Full Questions

1. What is market? What is marketing? Write in brief importance of agril. marketing in India.
2. Define marketing functions and explain in brief various marketing functions.
3. Explain price spread and total market cost in brief.
4. Explain in brief any two distribution channels of mango/paddy/cotton/vegetables.
5. What are the defects in present system of agricultural marketing? Suggest solutions to overcome them.
6. Classify markets and give brief description about them.
7. What do you mean by co-operative marketing society? Explain in brief organization and functions of co-operative society.
8. What is regulated market? Explain in brief advantages of regulated market.
9. What do you mean by channel of distribution? Explain in brief factors affecting the choice of distribution channel.
10. Explain in brief marketable and marketed surplus.
11. How price is determined in perfect competitive market and in a monopoly market?
12. What do you mean by stabilization of prices? Why it is needed? How it is achieved?
13. What is the impact of WTO on export of agricultural commodities from India?

PART IV
FARM MANAGEMENT AND PRODUCTION ECONOMICS

Multiple Choice Questions

Q. Select Correct Answer

1. The main objective of modern farmer is to maximize:
   (*a*) Net profit
   (*b*) Grain production
   (*c*) Employment opportunity to family members

2. "As the science which considers the organization and operation of the farm from point of view of efficiency and continuous profit", defined by:
   (*a*) Warren
   (*b*) Karl Marx
   (*c*) Efferson
3. Which is the rational stage of production?
   (*a*) Third
   (*b*) First
   (*c*) Second
4. At least cost combination point, substitution ratio and price ratio are:
   (*a*) Equal
   (*b*) Unequal
   (*c*) Not comparable
5. Principle of equimarginal return and opportunity cost principle leads to:
   (*a*) Dissimilar decisions
   (*b*) Similar decisions
   (*c*) Different decisions
6. Cost C includes cost B plus:
   (*a*) Imputed value of family labour
   (*b*) Interest on fixed capital
   (*c*) Rental value of land
7. At the end of the first stage of production average cost curve and marginal cost curve:
   (*a*) Originate
   (*b*) Ends
   (*c*) Crosses each other
8. Several Indian farmers follow:
   (*a*) Cost concepts
   (*b*) Minimum loss principle
   (*c*) Production concept
9. Land is evaluated by:
   (*a*) Income capitalization method

(*b*) Straight line method
(*c*) Contract method

10. Depreciation can be calculated by:
    (*a*) Straight line method
    (*b*) Rent capitalization method
    (*c*) Contract method
11. Intensity of cropping is a:
    (*a*) Land efficiency indicator
    (*b*) Labour efficiency indicator
    (*c*) Capital efficiency indicator
12. Land efficiency indicators and production efficiency indicators are:
    (*a*) Same
    (*b*) Different
    (*c*) Neither (*a*) nor (*b*)
13. In case of C.D. function elasticity of production is:
    (*a*) Varying
    (*b*) Constant
    (*c*) Unity
14. Maximum production in C.D. function is:
    (*a*) Defined
    (*b*) Not defined
    (*c*) Varying
15. Quadratic function comprises:
    (*a*) Only one stage
    (*b*) Four stages
    (*c*) Two stages of production
16. All transactions are first recorded in:
    (*a*) Diary
    (*b*) Journal
    (*c*) Ledger
17. Isoquants are asymptotic in case of:
    (*a*) C.D. function
    (*b*) Quadratic function
    (*c*) Neither (*a*) nor (*b*)

18. Arithmetical accuracy is tested with the help of:
    (*a*) Trial balance
    (*b*) Ledger
    (*c*) Balance sheet
19. Profit is known from:
    (*a*) Diary
    (*b*) Journal
    (*c*) Profit and loss account
20. Small cultivators should follow:
    (*a*) Single entry system
    (*b*) Double entry system
    (*c*) Neither (*a*) nor (*b*)

ANSWERS

1. *a*	2. *c*	3. *c*	4. *a*
5. *b*	6. *a*	7. *c*	8. *b*
9. *a*	10. *a*	11. *a*	12. *a*
13. *b*	14. *b*	15. *c*	16. *a*
17. *a*	18. *a*	19. *c*	20. *a*

Statements

Q. State whether the following statements are true or false, if false correct them and rewrite.

1. Complementary relationship is useful for both the enterprises.
   Ans. True.
2. At maximum revenue combination slope of production possibility curve and slope of iso-revenue line are equal.
   Ans. True.
3. Marginal cost curve and average variable cost curve do not cross each other at the end of first stage of production.
   Ans. False. Marginal cost curve and average variable cost curve cross each other at the end of first stage of production.

4. $\frac{\Delta X_2}{\Delta X_1} = \frac{Px_2}{Px_1}$

   Ans. False. $\frac{\Delta X_2}{\Delta X_1} = \frac{Px_1}{Px_2}$

5. Average cost is the change in total cost in response to a unit increase in output.

   Ans. False. Marginal cost is the change in total cost in response to a unit increase in output.

6. Fixed costs are same for all output levels.

   Ans. True.

7. Farm planning does not require any information.

   Ans. False. Farm planning requires various types of information.

8. Double entry system of book-keeping is easier than single entry system.

   Ans. False. Single entry system of book-keeping is easier than double entry system of book-keeping.

9. At least cost combination point isoquant and iso-cost line are tangent to each other.

   Ans. True.

10. There are different iso-cost lines for different money outlays.

    Ans. True.

11. From the product-product analysis, we come to know that this analysis is also useful for allocation of limited resources.

    Ans. True.

12. USA is a pioneer country in the field of scientific farm management.

    Ans. True.

13. Farm management is not related with any other agricultural sciences.

    Ans. False. Farm management is related with all other agril. sciences.

14. At the end of the first stage, marginal product curve and average product curve crosses each other.

    Ans. True.

15. Supplementary enterprises compete for resources available.

    Ans. False. Competitive enterprises compete for resources available.

16. Net returns at cost C level is greater than net returns at cost A level.

    Ans. False. Net returns at cost A level is greater than net returns at cost C level.

17. During short run, size of the plant or size of the farm cannot be altered.

    Ans. True.

18. Plan should take into account available marketing facilities.

    Ans. True.

19. Value of animals initially appreciates and later on their value is depreciated.

    Ans. True.

20. Slow turnover is a good sign of farm business.

    Ans. False. Faster turnover is a good sign of farm business.

21. Analysis of factor-product relationship helps us to decide optimum level of input for maximum profit.

    Ans. True.

22. Iso-cost line and iso-resource line are same.

    Ans. False. Iso-cost line and iso-resource line are different.

23. Balance sheet is prepared after preparing a profit and loss account.

    Ans. True.

Short Notes

Q. Write short notes on following:

1. Complementarity,
2. Iso-revenue line,
3. Variable cost,
4. Marginal cost,

5. Average fixed cost,
6. Expansion path in product-product analysis,
7. Joint product,
8. Iso-cost line,
9. Minimum loss principle,
10. Opportunity cost,
11. Elasticity of production,
12. Comparative advantage,
13. Farm budgeting,
14. Diminishing return,
15. Constant return,
16. Increasing return,
17. Straight line method of depreciation,
18. Cost A,
19. Collective farming,
20. Farm planning,
21. Iso-quant,
22. Ridge line,
23. Scope of farm management,
24. Principle of combining enterprises,
25. Short-run planning period,
26. Variable cost,
27. Complete budgeting,
28. Partial budgeting,
29. Intensity of cropping,
30. Crop yield index,
31. Operating ratio,
32. Cobb-Douglas production function,
33. Quadratic production function,
34. Single entry system of book-keeping,
35. Double entry system of book-keeping,
36. Trial balance.

Full Questions

1. Name three zones of cost function. Explain with suitable diagram relationship between average variable cost curve and marginal cost curve in different zones.
2. What is production possibility curve? How to draw it? What is its purpose?
3. How to draw iso-cost line or price line?
4. Explain the principle of equimarginal returns with the help of hypothetical data.
5. Explain with suitable diagram 'the least cost combination of inputs'.
6. Write in brief about principles of farm management.
7. What is meant by partial budgeting?
8. Explain the law of diminishing returns with the help of suitable example.
9. Define farm management and explain its objectives.
10. What do you mean by types of farming? Explain in brief various types of farming.
11. What do you mean by system of farming? Explain in brief various systems of farming.
12. Explain in brief various methods of evaluation.
13. What do you mean by expansion path? Draw suitable diagram and explain.
14. What is farm management? Explain in brief objectives of farm management.
15. What is farm planning? Explain in brief, characteristics of good farm plan.
16. What do you mean by labour efficiency? How you will measure it? How it can be increased?
17. What do you mean by production function? Explain characteristics of Cobb-Douglas production function.
18. Explain characteristics of quadratic production function.
19. Explain advantages of farm records and accounts.
20. What do you mean by short-term and long-term farm planning? Explain in detail.

Problems

1. Determine least cost combination of two inputs X_1 and X_2 which substitute at diminishing rate for producing 90 units of output. Find out substitution ratio and price ratio at least cost combination point.

   Data Px_1 = ₹ 2
   Px_2 = ₹ 1

X_1 Input	X_2 Input
1	9.50
2	7.50
3	6.00
4	5.00
5	4.50
6	4.25
7	4.15
8	4.00
9	4.50
10	5.25

2. Fill in the blanks of columns of the table given below:

Input units	Total output units	Total fixed cost ₹	Total variable cost at ₹4 per units	Total cost	Average total cost	Marginal cost
0	0	20				
1	2	20				
2	5	20				
3	9	20				
4	14	20				
5	19	20				
6	23	20				
7	26	20				
8	28	20				
9	29	20				
10	29	20				

3. Find out the maximum revenue combination of products. Given the following information what is the substitution ratio and price ratio at maximum revenue combination?

   Units of input = 7 acres
   Py_1 = ₹ 2/unit
   Py_2 = ₹ 1/unit

Production possibilities

Y_2	Y_1
33	0
32	2
30	8
26	13
20	17
12	20
2	22
0	23

4. Find out marginal rate of increase in following production and mention the nature of marginal returns:

Wheat seed rate (kg)	Total Production of wheat (kg)	ΔX	ΔY	ΔY/ΔX
10	1000			
20	1025			
30	1075			
40	1150			
50	1250			
60	1375			

5. Cultivator is having ₹ 2,500 with him, how he should spend the amount on different enterprises so that he will get maximum profit? What is the amount of profit?

₹	Crop (₹)	Dairy (₹)	Poultry (₹)
500	700	750	600
500	600	600	550
500	500	450	450
500	300	300	300
500	200	200	275

6. Fill in the blank columns and find out least cost combinations.

Units of X_1	Units of X_2	Cost of X_1 @ ₹ 4	Cost of X_2 @ ₹ 5	Total, Outlay for X_1 & X_2
8	1			
6	2			
5	3			
4.5	4			
3.5	5			

PART V
RESEARCH METHODOLOGY

Multiple Choice Questions

Q. Select correct answer

1. Science is a:
   (*a*) Knowledge
   (*b*) Knowledge not of things but of their relations
   (*c*) Power
2. Science is a process:
   (*a*) Which build up the knowledge
   (*b*) Which degenerate the knowledge
   (*c*) Which increase sadness
3. Main function of science is to:
   (*a*) Carry-out research
   (*b*) Discover the truth
   (*c*) Discover the problem
4. Ethics is a:
   (*a*) Social science
   (*b*) Science
   (*c*) Commerce subject
5. Politics and economics are:
   (*a*) Distantly related
   (*b*) Not related
   (*c*) Closely related
6. In physical sciences exactness:
   (*a*) Is not observed
   (*b*) Is observed
   (*c*) Is not possible
7. Social sciences are compared with:
   (*a*) Paddy crop
   (*b*) Fruit crop
   (*c*) Successive layers of onion
8. Conceptual scheme is provided:
   (*a*) By fact

(*b*) By theory
(*c*) By book

9. Facts are predicted by:
   (*a*) Theory
   (*b*) Fact
   (*c*) Fortune teller
10. Thomas Alva Edison's work is a:
    (*a*) Theoretical research
    (*b*) Basic research
    (*c*) Applied research
11. Researcher can use concept as:
    (*a*) Procedure of analysis
    (*b*) A tool of analysis
    (*c*) A weapon
12. Multiplier is a:
    (*a*) Procedure
    (*b*) Model
    (*c*) Concept
13. Hypothesis is a:
    (*a*) Tentative solution to the problem
    (*b*) Concept
    (*c*) Mechanism
14. Hypothesis must be specific and precise otherwise they are:
    (*a*) Useful
    (*b*) Much useful
    (*c*) Not much useful
15. Which point is considered, while selecting a research problem:
    (*a*) Cleverness of a research worker
    (*b*) Boldness of a research worker
    (*c*) Urgency of a problem
16. Researcher assume that government policies will:
    (*a*) Change
    (*b*) Not change and should plan his research work
    (*c*) Likely to change

17. If funds are not available in time it will:
    (*a*) Hamper the progress of work
    (*b*) Results of research will be wrong
    (*c*) Give good results
18. Field data is a:
    (*a*) Secondary data
    (*b*) Tertiary data
    (*c*) Primary data
19. Which is the most reliable data:
    (*a*) Tertiary data
    (*b*) Primary data
    (*c*) Newspaper data
20. For research generally:
    (*a*) Tertiary data should not be used
    (*b*) Primary data should not be used
    (*c*) Secondary data should not be used
21. Which is lengthy?
    (*a*) Schedule
    (*b*) Questionnaire
    (*c*) Tables
22. Words used in schedule should be:
    (*a*) Unknown
    (*b*) Difficult
    (*c*) Easy to understand
23. Initially general questions and then specific question, it is called as:
    (*a*) Way of answering
    (*b*) Plan of answering
    (*c*) Funnel approach
24. Personal relation is developed, while filling the:
    (*a*) Schedule
    (*b*) Questionnaire
    (*c*) Tables
25. Interview of respondent is undertaken:
    (*a*) While filling the schedule

(*b*) While selecting the candidate
(*c*) Only by employer

26. Case study refers to the intensive investigation of a particular:
(*a*) Field
(*b*) Unit
(*c*) Person

27. Seminar on a particular problem is called as:
(*a*) Oral reporting
(*b*) Written reporting
(*c*) As a detail investigation

28. Outline is prepared before starting the research work and before:
(*a*) Starting the writing of a technical report
(*b*) Printing the report
(*c*) Analysing of the problem

29. Popular reports are linked to:
(*a*) Laymen
(*b*) Scientist
(*c*) Doctors

30. Because of documentation, research report becomes more:
(*a*) Authoritative
(*b*) Easy
(*c*) Difficult

ANSWERS

1. *b*	2. *a*	3. *b*	4. *a*
5. *c*	6. *b*	7. *c*	8. *b*
9. *a*	10. *c*	11. *b*	12. *c*
13. *a*	14. *c*	15. *c*	16. *b*
17. *a*	18. *c*	19. *b*	20. *a*
21. *a*	22. *c*	23. *c*	24. *a*
25. *a*	26. *b*	27. *a*	28. *a*
29. *a*	30. *a*		

Statements

Q. State whether the following statements are true or false, if false correct them and rewrite.

1. Cost accounting method is costlier than survey method.
   Ans. True.
2. Social sciences are independent.
   Ans. False. Social sciences are dependent on each other.
3. There is no relationship between theory and fact.
   Ans. False. Theory and fact are related.
4. Science is a knowledge not of things but of their relationship.
   Ans. True.
5. Ethics is a social science.
   Ans. True.
6. Applied research depends upon basic research.
   Ans. True.
7. Scientists want to satisfy their need and that is why they do research.
   Ans. False. Scientists want to satisfy their curiosity and that is why they do research.
8. Anthropology is a natural science.
   Ans. False. Anthropology is a social science.
9. All social sciences depend on each other.
   Ans. True.
10. Theory summarises facts.
    Ans. True.
11. Facts do not help to initiate theory.
    Ans. False. Facts help to initiate theory.
12. Poor countries should spend more on applied research.
    Ans. True.
13. Because of concept, it is easy to transfer knowledge.
    Ans. True.
14. One should use highly general and vague concepts.
    Ans. False. One should avoid use of highly general and vague concepts.

15. Hypothesis misguides the research.

    Ans. False. Hypothesis guides the research.

16. Personal experience and individual reaction give origin to hypothesis.

    Ans. True.

17. Urgent problem is selected first.

    Ans. True.

18. Sometimes government changes its policies which have a negative effect on conclusions of research worker.

    Ans. True.

19. Most of the newspaper articles are technical articles.

    Ans. False. Most of the newspaper articles are popular articles.

20. Field data is a secondary data.

    Ans. False. Field data is a primary data.

21. Mailed questionnaires are filled up by investigators.

    Ans. False. Mailed questionnaires are filled up by respondents.

22. Schedule must be in English.

    Ans. False. As far as possible schedule should be in local language.

23. Oral reporting is only for laymen.

    Ans. False. Oral reporting is for any type of participant.

24. In popular report detail data must be given.

    Ans. False. In popular report detail data is not needed.

25. Researcher should concentrate on finish and final touches in second draft.

    Ans. False. Researcher should concentrate on finish and final touches in third draft.

26. Librarian search for literature, prepare the list and make it available to the reader is called as documentation.

    Ans. True.

27. Documentation leads the reader to further information.

    Ans. True.

28. Tables and charts do not come under documentation.

Ans. False. Tables and charts are also components of documentation.

29. Stratified sampling is a mixed sampling.

    Ans. True.

30. Fact is an empirically verifiable observation.

    Ans. True.

Short Notes

Q. Write short notes on following:

1. Theory,
2. Fact,
3. Research,
4. Basic research,
5. Concept,
6. Applied research,
7. Science,
8. Interview,
9. Case study,
10. Primary data,
11. Secondary data,
12. Field data,
13. Bibliography,
14. Survey method,
15. Cost accounting method,
16. Schedule,
17. Questionnaire,
18. Interdependence of social sciences,
19. Footnote,
20. Outline,
21. Write-up,
22. Stratified random sampling,
23. Social science,
24. Tertiary data,
25. Multi-stage sampling,

26. Purposive sampling,
27. Thesis writing,
28. Documentation,
29. Oral reporting,
30. Preface.

Full Questions

1. What do you mean by the term concept? State the role of concept in social science research.
2. What is hypothesis? State the significance of hypothesis in research.
3. What aspects will you consider while planning a research programme?
4. What is schedule? What points you will consider while constructing a schedule?
5. What are the difficulties in planning a research programme?
6. What is questionnaire? What points you will consider while constructing a questionnaire?
7. What is documentation? What are the purposes served by documentation?
8. What do you mean by research? Explain in brief types of research.
9. What is hypothesis? What are the steps involved in testing the hypothesis?
10. What are the different types of data? Write in brief about reliability of each type for using them for research.
11. What do you mean by sampling? Explain in brief different sampling methods.
12. What do you mean by technical reports? What are the different parts of technical report?
13. What are the objectives of first draft, second draft and third draft?

PART VI
ECONOMIC INFORMATION ABOUT INDIAN AGRICULTURE

Multiple Choice Questions

Students require to prepare themselves for university examinations as well as some candidates prepare for Bank Recruitment Board's tests for recruitment of Agricultural Finance Officers. These test papers contain objective type of questions and emphasis is laid mainly on the test of technical agriculture. In agriculture, the questions are wide ranging and cover Agronomy, Dairy, Animal Husbandry, Plant Protection and Agricultural Financing. Following questions will help students for preparing themselves for such recruitment tests as well as for university examinations.

1. In 2001-02, the contribution of agriculture towards national income is about:
   (*a*) 30%
   (*b*) 24%
   (*c*) 80%
2. In 1999, what percentage of economically active population was dependent on agriculture?
   (*a*) 90%
   (*b*) 40%
   (*c*) 60%
3. In 2001-02, the highest per capita income was in:
   (*a*) Goa
   (*b*) Tamil Nadu
   (*c*) Maharashtra
4. The major source of financing to the farmers is:
   (*a*) Private agencies
   (*b*) Co-operative banks
   (*c*) Commercial banks
5. What is percentage of net sown area to geographical area in India?
   (*a*) 80

(*b*) 43
(*c*) 20

6. In 2000, approximate contribution of agriculture in national income in UK was:
   (*a*) 1%
   (*b*) 10%
   (*c*) 15%
7. Total geographical area of India in million hectares is:
   (*a*) 328
   (*b*) 428
   (*c*) 228
8. In 2000, contribution of service sector in national income in India was?
   (*a*) 46%
   (*b*) 56%
   (*c*) 66%
9. Small farmers are those whose holdings are:
   (*a*) Not more than 4 hectares
   (*b*) Not more than 2 hectares
   (*c*) Not more than 3 hectares
10. Marginal farmers are those whose holdings are:
    (*a*) Not more than 1 hectare
    (*b*) Not more than 2.5 hectare
    (*c*) More than 1 hectare
11. Agricultural labourers are the persons, whose wage earnings mainly from agriculture should be about:
    (*a*) 50 per cent of total income
    (*b*) 80 per cent of total income
    (*c*) 10 per cent of total income
12. The use of tractor is considered economic, when it is utilized on the farms for minimum of:
    (*a*) 1000 hours per year
    (*b*) 300 hours per year
    (*c*) 800 hours per year

13. What is the main function of NABARD?
    (*a*) Financing directly to the farmers
    (*b*) Providing refinance to the banks
    (*c*) Helping in recovery
14. Loan for crop production is:
    (*a*) Medium-term
    (*b*) Short-term
    (*c*) Long-term
15. Medium-term loans are repayable:
    (*a*) Up to 5 years
    (*b*) Beyond 8 years
    (*c*) Up to 9 years
16. What per cent subsidies are provided by SFDA/MFAL to beneficiaries?
    (*a*) 60%
    (*b*) 25% to 33%
    (*c*) 15%
17. Primary revenue records are maintained by:
    (*a*) BDO
    (*b*) Tehsildar
    (*c*) Talathi or Patwari
18. The water lost in seepage through channels is estimated to be:
    (*a*) 60%
    (*b*) 20%
    (*c*) 45%
19. Which of the following tractors is air-cooled?
    (*a*) Eicher
    (*b*) International
    (*c*) Hindustan
20. Large white Yorkshire is an improved breed of:
    (*a*) Cow
    (*b*) Pigs
    (*c*) Poultry
21. Jersey is an improved breed of:
    (*a*) Cow

(*b*) Sheep
(*c*) Buffalo

22. The average lactation period of a cow is:
(*a*) 350 days
(*b*) 550 days
(*c*) 150 days

23. The average lactation period of buffalo is:
(*a*) 462 days
(*b*) 662 days
(*c*) 200 days

24. What is the annual average milk yields of a cross-breed cow?
(*a*) 2182 litres
(*b*) 6000 litres
(*c*) 1000 litres

25. Multiple cropping means taking:
(*a*) More than 2 crops
(*b*) 3 crops at a time
(*c*) 2 crops at a time

26. Double cropping means taking:
(*a*) Two crops
(*b*) More than two crops
(*c*) Many crops at a time

27. Ranikhet disease is commonly found in:
(*a*) Poultry birds
(*b*) Sugarcane
(*c*) Buffalo

28. A layer requires a space of:
(*a*) 2 sq. ft.
(*b*) 15 sq. ft.
(*c*) 12 sq. ft.

29. A layer may lay eggs up to:
(*a*) 360
(*b*) 600
(*c*) 150

30. A broiler may lay eggs up to:
    (*a*) 300
    (*b*) None
    (*c*) 400
31. In 2001, total cultivators in India were:
    (*a*) 40 crores
    (*b*) 12.76 crores
    (*c*) 5 crores
32. Nitrogen percentage in Ammonium Sulphate is:
    (*a*) 20.5%
    (*b*) 60%
    (*c*) 10%
33. Nitrogen percentage in Urea is:
    (*a*) 46%
    (*b*) 20%
    (*c*) 80%
34. P_2O_5 percentage in Super Phosphate (single) is:
    (*a*) 48%
    (*b*) 16%
    (*c*) 8%
35. P_2O_5 percentage in Ammonium Phosphate is:
    (*a*) 28%
    (*b*) 20%
    (*c*) 56%
36. K_2O percentage in Sulphate of Potash is:
    (*a*) 70%
    (*b*) 25%
    (*c*) 50%
37. K_2O percentage in Muriate of Potash is:
    (*a*) 60%
    (*b*) 80%
    (*c*) 20%
38. What does the term CADA indicate?
    (*a*) Comprehensive Area Development Agency
    (*b*) Command Area Development Agency
    (*c*) Canal Area Development Agency

39. What does the term ICDP mean?
    (*a*) Intensive Centres for Development Programme
    (*b*) Intensive Cattle Development Programme
    (*c*) Intensive Care of Development Projects
40. What is canker?
    (*a*) Fruit
    (*b*) A disease
    (*c*) A pest
41. The approximate height of Kalyan sona plant is:
    (*a*) 95 cm.
    (*b*) 60 cm.
    (*c*) 140 cm.
42. The mortality percentage on well-managed poultry farm is approximately:
    (*a*) 1%
    (*b*) 10%
    (*c*) 40%
43. A hen starts laying when it is:
    (*a*) 12 months old
    (*b*) 5 to 6 months old
    (*c*) 15 months old
44. NDRI is situated at:
    (*a*) Karnal
    (*b*) Shimla
    (*c*) Ludhiana
45. IARI is situated at:
    (*a*) Bombay
    (*b*) New Delhi
    (*c*) Patna
46. Where is IVRI?
    (*a*) Izatnagar
    (*b*) Poona
    (*c*) Trivendrum
47. In 2000, the per capita availability of food grains in India was:

(*a*) 458 gm/day
(*b*) 300 gm/day
(*c*) 900 gm/day

48. Which animal is the most prolific breeder?
(*a*) Pig
(*b*) Cow
(*c*) Goat

49. How much area is sufficient to feed 5 to 6 cattle around the year?
(*a*) 1 acre
(*b*) 5 acres
(*c*) 6 acres

50. The ordinary compost contains Nitrogen approximately:
(*a*) 5%
(*b*) 0.5%
(*c*) 4%

51. Which is the ideal time for purchasing a buffalo/cow:
(*a*) Just before calving
(*b*) Before conception
(*c*) Just after calving

52. What is a cockerel?
(*a*) Male poultry bird
(*b*) He buffalo
(*c*) Bullock

53. What is a pullet?
(*a*) Female poultry bird
(*b*) Breed of pig
(*c*) Cross-breed buffalo

54. How many shearing's are done to a sheep in a year?
(*a*) Two
(*b*) Three
(*c*) One

55. The term ewe refers to:
(*a*) Female goat
(*b*) Female sheep
(*c*) Male sheep

56. What is WTO?
    (*a*) World Trade Organization
    (*b*) World Tobacco Organization
    (*c*) World Timber Organization
57. What is the normal life of a tractor?
    (*a*) 20 years
    (*b*) 10 years
    (*c*) 5 years
58. Which of the fertilzers can be sprayed?
    (*a*) Super phosphate (double)
    (*b*) Urea
    (*c*) Ammonium sulphate
59. In 1999, India was first in world in production of:
    (*a*) Milk
    (*b*) Eggs
    (*c*) Meat
60. How many total districts in India?
    (*a*) 576
    (*b*) 356
    (*c*) 446
61. What was total food grains production in 2001-02?
    (*a*) 211.17 million tonnes
    (*b*) 110 million tonnes
    (*c*) 120 million tonnes
62. 'Alphonso' is a variety of:
    (*a*) Coconut
    (*b*) Mango
    (*c*) Banana
63. 'Sugar baby' is a name of:
    (*a*) Onion variety
    (*b*) Watermelon variety
    (*c*) Sugarcane variety
64. Co. 740 is a variety of:
    (*a*) Sugarcane
    (*b*) Jowar
    (*c*) Maize

65. Per hectare seed requirement of hybrid jowar is:
    (*a*) About 10 kg
    (*b*) More than 20 kg
    (*c*) Less than 5 kg
66. Approximate per quintal cost of production of jowar is ₹:
    (*a*) 300
    (*b*) 180
    (*c*) 60
67. In 2000, contribution of agriculture in national income in USA was:
    (*a*) 2%
    (*b*) 20%
    (*c*) 40%
68. In 2003-04, approximate per quintal cost of groundnut was:
    (*a*) 1453 ₹
    (*b*) 1700 ₹
    (*c*) 500 ₹
69. Approximate per acre seed rate of transplanted paddy is:
    (*a*) 6 kg
    (*b*) 20 kg
    (*c*) 30 kg
70. Approximate per acre seed rate of spreading type groundnut is:
    (*a*) 70 kg kernels
    (*b*) 35 kg kernels
    (*c*) 100 kg kernels
71. Approximate per acre seed rate of irrigated wheat is:
    (*a*) 25 to 40 kg
    (*b*) 80 kg
    (*c*) 100 kg
72. Duration of safflower crop is:
    (*a*) 5 months

(*b*) 10 months
(*c*) 9 months

73. Per acre seed rate of gram is:
    (*a*) 30 kg
    (*b*) 60 kg
    (*c*) 90 kg
74. Per acre seed rate of Berseem is:
    (*a*) 25 kg
    (*b*) 50 kg
    (*c*) 5 kg
75. Kali Sahebi is a variety of:
    (*a*) Onion
    (*b*) Paddy
    (*c*) Grape
76. Kew is a variety of:
    (*a*) Grape
    (*b*) Bhindi
    (*c*) Pineapple
77. 2, 4-D is a:
    (*a*) Insecticide
    (*b*) Weedicide
    (*c*) Variety of crop
78. Sahyadri hybrid is a variety of:
    (*a*) Jowar
    (*b*) Paddy
    (*c*) Sugarcane
79. Nitrogen content of groundnut cake is:
    (*a*) 6%
    (*b*) 12%
    (*c*) 1%
80. Nitrogen content of Sanhemp is:
    (*a*) 2%
    (*b*) 0.75%
    (*c*) 10%

81. Paclobutrazol chemical is used in production of:
    (*a*) Mango
    (*b*) Jowar
    (*c*) Sugarcane

ANSWERS

1. *b*	2. *c*	3. *a*	4. *c*
5. *b*	6. *a*	7. *a*	8. *a*
9. *b*	10. *a*	11. *a*	12. *a*
13. *b*	14. *b*	15. *a*	16. *b*
17. *c*	18. *c*	19. *a*	20. *b*
21. *a*	22. *a*	23. *a*	24. *a*
25. *a*	26. *a*	27. *a*	28. *a*
29. *a*	30. *b*	31. *b*	32. *a*
33. *a*	34. *b*	35. *a*	36. *b*
37. *a*	38. *b*	39. *b*	40. *b*
41. *a*	42. *b*	43. *b*	44. *a*
45. *b*	46. *a*	47. *a*	48. *a*
49. *a*	50. *b*	51. *c*	52. *a*
53. *a*	54. *a*	55. *b*	56. *a*
57. *b*	58. *b*	59. *a*	60. *a*
61. *a*	62. *b*	63. *b*	64. *a*
65. *a*	66. *a*	67. *a*	68. *a*
69. *a*	70. *a*	71. *b*	72. *a*
73. *a*	74. *a*	75. *c*	76. *c*
77. *b*	78. *b*	79. *a*	80. *b*
81. *a*			

PART VII
AGRICULTURAL GROWTH AND ECONOMIC DEVELOPMENT

Multiple Choice Questions

Q. Select Correct Answer

1. When economic development takes place, per capita income:
    (*a*) Decreases
    (*b*) Increases
    (*c*) Do not change

2. When income increases, purchasing power also:
   (*a*) Increases
   (*b*) Decreases
   (*c*) Do not change
3. The stock of capital and the proportion of income invested are:
   (*a*) High in traditional agriculture
   (*b*) Low in traditional agriculture
   (*c*) Normal in traditional agriculture
4. Due to technological change productivity of existing resources:
   (*a*) Increases
   (*b*) Decreases
   (*c*) Do not change
5. For agricultural development, incentives to cultivators:
   (*a*) Do not play any role
   (*b*) Are absurd
   (*c*) Play important role
6. In 2000, per capita GDP (PPP) in India was higher than:
   (*a*) USA
   (*b*) Pakistan
   (*c*) UK
7. In Second Plan more attention was paid to:
   (*a*) Agriculture
   (*b*) Industry
   (*c*) None of the above
8. In international trade, law:
   (*a*) Of comparative advantage plays important role
   (*b*) Of diminishing return plays important role
   (*c*) None of the above
9. Due to development employment is:
   (*a*) Increases
   (*b*) Decreases
   (*c*) Not affected

10. Modern agriculture requires:
    (*a*) Higher amount of credit
    (*b*) Lower amount of credit
    (*c*) No credit

ANSWERS

1. *b*	2. *a*	3. *b*	4. *a*
5. *c*	6. *b*	7. *b*	8. *a*
9. *a*	10. *a*		

Statements

Q. State whether the following statements are true or false, if false correct them and rewrite.

1. Agricultural development leads to economic development of a country.

   Ans. True
2. In underdeveloped countries, there is no large scale application of the fruits of scientific and technological advance to agriculture and industry.

   Ans. True
3. Agricultural and non-agricultural development is not inter-related.

   Ans. False. Agricultural and non-agricultural development is inter-related.
4. Land, labour, simple tools and water system are important factors of production in traditional agriculture.

   Ans. True
5. Research in agricultural sciences plays important role in modern agriculture.

   Ans. True
6. In 2000, Maharashtra was having highest percentage area under irrigation in the country.

   Ans. False. Punjab was having highest percentage area under irrigation in the country.
7. Removal of poverty and attainment of economic self-reliance was the main objective of first plan.

Ans. False. Removal of poverty and attainment of economic self-reliance was the main objective of fifth plan.

8. Agricultural surplus is a pre-requisites to economic development of a country.

   Ans. True.

9. Due to modern technology, agricultural production increases and if cultivator received reasonable prices, income of the cultivator also increases.

   Ans. True

10. One of the preconditions for development is that cultivators should get enough incentives for higher agril. production.

    Ans. True

Short Notes

Q. Write short notes on following:

1. Agricultural development,
2. Economic development,
3. Modern agriculture,
4. Land holding,
5. Credit facilities,
6. Marketing organization,
7. Five-Year Plans,
8. International trade in agril. products,
9. Technological change,
10. Consequences of economic development.

Full Questions

1. Define economic development and explain role of agriculture in economic development.
2. Explain relationship between agricultural and non-agricultural development.
3. Compare agricultural development in Japan and in India.
4. How you will organize Indian agriculture for development?

5. What is the role played by Five-Year Plans in development of India's agricultural sector?

PART VIII
AGRICULTURAL BUSINESS MANAGEMENT

Full Questions

1. What do you mean by agricultural business management? State its scope and importance in India.
2. What do you mean by management? Explain the term managerial economics.
3. What are the characteristics of good manager?
4. State and explain fourteen principles of management.

Agricultural Scientists Recruitment Board Syllabus and Questions

AGRICULTURAL ECONOMICS

Section 1: Economic Theory

Microeconomics: Definition and scope of microeconomics. Theory of consumer behaviour—marginal utility, indifference curve maximization of utility, substitution and income effects, price and income consumption curves. Theory of revealed preference. The theory of the firm-concept of production function, optimizing behaviour, constrained cost minimization and constrained revenue maximization, elasticity of supply. Market classification—pure and perfect competition, behaviour of the firm and industry. Supply-demand functions. Imperfect competition, monopolistic competition, monopoly, duopoly and oligopoly. Price discrimination. Theory of factor pricing. Effects of taxation and subsidies on prices and output supply.

Macroeconomics: Definition and scope of macroeconomics. National income accounting. Price level, employment, unemployment and output in the economy. Theories of income determination. Theory of employment—classical, Keynesian and post-Keynesian. IS-LM curves. Saving and investments. Theory of income distribution and factor shares. Inflation deflation, inflationary gap. Business cycle. Monetary and fiscal policies. Public borrowing—internal and external aid, deficit financing, development financing.

Section 2: Agricultural Econometrics

Analysis of economic time, series components and their interpretation. Growth curves and their estimation: Index numbers, their characteristics and construction of price and quantity index numbers. Econometric model and types of data. Classical linear regression model. Ordinary least squares estimation of simple and multiple regression models: The BLUE properties of least squares estimate, tests of significance and confidence intervals. Problems of multicollinearity, auto-correlation and heteroscedasticity. Use of dummy variables, Factor analysis, Principal component analysis. Generalised Aitken's least-squares methods of estimation. Random coefficient models. Durbin-Watson test. Specification errors. Mixed estimation. Instrumental variables. Autoregressive and distributed lag models—partial adjustment, adaptive expectations model and partial adjustment-cum-adaptive expectations models. Estimation from grouped data: Pooling of time series and cross section data.

Simultaneous equation systems—basic rationale, identification problems, indirect least squares, two-stage least squares and K-class estimators, three state least squares. Recursive models. Seemingly unrelated regression model and its estimates.

Section 3: Economics of Agricultural Development and Policies

Concept, meaning of development, characteristics of developing and developed economies. Theories of development and underdevelopment. Role of economic, technological, social and cultural factors and constraints in development savings and economic development. Interdependence between agricultural and industrial development. Role of agriculture in economic development. Economic growth with equity and social justice. Growth models—Harrod Domar, Neo-classical, Von-Neumann. Special target programmes for backward area/regional/ community development.

Agricultural growth analysis—determinant of agricultural growth and its measurements. Planning models, features of planning in capitalist, socialist, neo-socialist and mixed economics. Types of planning—micro level, regional, sectoral, agro-eco regional planning, etc. Developmental needs of rural women and their participation in agricultural development. People's self-action for development. Role of NGOs in agricultural development case studies.

Agricultural policy analysis—Policies for energy, water, fertilizer, land, labour, technology, rural infrastructure. Institutional development policies. Marketing policies—market liberalization policies agricultural market reforms.

Food security and nutrition policy-analysis-concepts and definition of food security and malnutrition, impact analysis of production-oriented policies, food price policies, food subsidies, food safety net, food for work programme, and food quality, Measurement of poverty. Poverty alleviation and development strategies.

Section 4: Economics of Natural Resource, Environment and Sustainability

Natural resources—definition, characteristics and classification of natural resources. Historical development of natural resource economics, major natural resource issues role of economics in natural resource planning, policy formulation and management. Time and space analysis in use of renewable and non-renewable natural resources. Natural resource scarcity, measures of scarcity approach to mitigate resource scarcity, individual utility and the social welfare function. Allocation of renewable and non-renewable resources under various market structures citing examples of fisheries, forests, water resources and land resources. Natural resource planning and management.

Environmental concerns concept of environmental degradation, estimation of economic losses due to environmental degradation and adjustment measures, comparative advantage/disadvantage of alternative technologies on environment and sustainability, environmental policy analysis. Global environmental issues.

Sustainability concerns—definitions and concept of sustainability, conditions for sustainable development, indicators of sustainability, measurement of sustainability, agro-forestry.

Section 5: Project Appraisal, Agricultural Research Evaluation and Impact Assessment of Agricultural Technology

Project appraisal: Definition of project in agriculture. Need for project appraisal. Methods for project appraisal and case studies.

Agricultural research evaluation: Agricultural research system—national and international, structure of research system, linkages between research systems. Agricultural research investment—investment indicator, trends in investment: public and private, determinants of public and private investment. Need for research evaluation, extant and ex-post evaluation, data needs for research evaluation. Agricultural research prioritization and resource allocation meaning, dimensions and need for research prioritization. Research prioritization models—economic surplus, scoring approach, mathematical programming, simulation. Trade-off between research objective, price and technology spillover effects. Scientific productivity—meaning, measurement and factors affecting scientific productivity. Agricultural research and technology development policy.

Impact assessment of agricultural technology: Identification of impact indicators, technological change concept and its measurement. Parametric and non-parametric approaches for impact assessment— economic surplus, total factor productivity and its sources of growth, returns to investment in research, extension, infrastructure, human resource development, etc.

Section 6: Farm Management Economics

Farm management—nature, scope and objectives. Characteristics of modern farming. Basic principles of farm management—principles of marginal returns, costs substitution in choice of practices, equimarginal returns, combining enterprises and time comparison, law of comparative advantage. Measurement of management input, farm efficiency. Methods of evaluating farm assets, outputs and inputs. Methods of working depreciation. Cost concepts. Farm planning and budgeting—sources of data and illustration. Process of decision-making under different knowledge situations. Essentials of farm planning and budgeting, farm surveys, questionnaire preparation and pre-testing, data collection and analysis, enterprise budgets, partial and complete budgets and whole farm planning. Elements of risk and uncertainty in agriculture, measurement of risk and adjustments of risk. Resource management—input use efficiency, allocation of resources, farm planning, risk management. Diversification of agriculture. Agri-business development.

Section 7: Agricultural Production and Resource Economics

Production concepts. Historical background and characteristics of different forms of production functions—linear, quadratic, square root, Spillman, cubic, semi-log, Cobb-Douglas, transcendental, CES, VES and Leontief. Static and dynamic production function and their application. Frontier production functions.

Dualities between production, cost and profit functions. Derivation of supply and factor demand functions from production and profit functions. Optimisation and resource allocation. Multiple product relationships. Production possibility curves. Choice between products and resource use. Spatial and temporal allocation of resources. Resource-use efficiency; size, productivity and returns to scale, allocative efficiency, analysis of factor shares in agriculture and their implications on income distribution. Risk attitudes in agriculture, optimization under risk and uncertainty. Measurement of technological change—decomposition analysis, total factor productivity. Technology and supply forecasting concepts and issues.

Programming Techniques—formulation of LP problems and its solution in agricultural sector, parametric programming, integer programming.

Section 8: Agricultural Finance and Co-operation

Definition and scope of agricultural finance. Financial accounting system. Rural credit structure, role of credit in agricultural and rural development. Classification of capital and its sources. Classification of agricultural credit, methods for estimation of credit requirement. Credit supply and gap, credit cost. 3Rs of credit, 3Cs of credit and their relation to 3Rs of credit. Credit worthiness and methods for assessing repayment capacity. Agricultural credit policy. Review of various committee reports on rural credit and investment. Role of public and private sector banks and co-operatives in financing. Role and functioning of international financial institutions. Principles of agricultural finance and financial management. Principles and practices of co-operation. Successes and failures of co-operative sector in India. Role of co-operatives under changed economic policy.

Section 9: Agricultural Marketing, Price Analysis and International Trade

Agricultural marketing: Nature and scope of marketing in a developing economy. Classification of markets structure—conduct-performance analysis. Problems of marketing agricultural produce. Marketable and marketed surplus. Functions of marketing, Regulated markets and other state interventions. Channels of marketing agricultural produce, price spread, market efficiency. Application of quantitative techniques to marketing problems—markow chain analysis, decision theory and decision tree analysis, transportation model, network, analysis, queuing theory. Buffer stock operations. Co-operative marketing. Processing, transportation, storage and warehousing. Forward trading, speculation, future markets. Emerging markets for new products.

Price analysis: Demand for and supply of farm products. Demand supply models. Estimation of elasticities. Demand supply projections. Marketed surplus model—Raj Krishna, Behraman, Janvrey and Kumar. Demand for and supply of factor inputs in agriculture; Cobweb model, price policy models for inputs and output. Agricultural price policy. Market integration, storage, buffer stocks and price stabilization measures and policies. Leontif input-output analysis. Vertical integration.

International trade: Basic concepts, theory of international trade, absolute and comparative advantage. International trade equilibrium. Trade policy-protection, tariff and non-tariff measures, trade liberalization, WTO/GATT.

Section 10: Problems of Indian Agriculture

Characteristics of Indian agriculture. Importance of agricultural sector. Agricultural and non-agriculture linkages-backward and forward linkages in agricultural sector, Five-Year Plans and agriculture. Rainbow (Green, White, Yellow, Blue, etc.) revolution. Agricultural labour in India—problems and remedies. Agricultural inputs—seeds, fertilizer, plant protection, irrigation, mechanization, cattle feeds and fodder. Agricultural output—crops, livestock, poultry, fish forestry, etc. Productivity and performance of Indian Agriculture, Characterising agricultural growth—changes in cropping pattern, decomposition analysis and sources of output growth, analysis of instability. Capital formation, crop livestock insurance, infrastructure. Transfer of technology—constraints to technology adoption, yield gap analysis and research planning, agricultural information system. Storage problem. Post-harvest losses. Agricultural exports—problems and prospects. Past experiences and future strategies for the growth of export.

YEAR 1991
QUESTION PAPER I
ADVANCED ECONOMICS THEORY WITH APPLICATION TO AGRICULTURE

Time Allowed: 3 hours *Maximum Marks*: 200

1. Attempt any Eight Questions.
2. All questions carry equal marks.
3. Answers must be written in the medium specified in the admission certificate issued to the candidate.

1. Distinguish between the Classical and Keynesian Theories of Investment. Does the rate of interest really determine the level of investment in Indian agriculture? (10+15)
2. Explain the theory of production. What are the assumptions of Cobb-Douglas production function? (15+10)
3. What is 'Price discrimination'? In which type of market price discrimination is practiced? Explain the basis on which the price discrimination is done. (5+5+15)
4. How do you measure 'Economic development'? Justify. How the Integrated Rural Development Programme has been able to help the economic growth with equity in agriculture and rural development in India? (10+15)
5. Land reform measures were considered to help in increasing agricultural production in India. Discuss whether or not the land reform policies have been helpful in increasing agricultural production in India. (25)
6. It is believed that Fiscal and Monetary policies are the only two options opened to planners to set right the Indian economy. Which of these two policies is more appropriate to Indian economy? Justify your answer with the help of a diagram. (25)
7. Illustrate clearly the differences between short-run and long-run optimality in production. (25)
8. Explain 'Swan' model and indicate graphically how it incorporates the capital embodied technological change to promote the growth rate in income. (10+15)

9. What is inflation? Can there be an inflation without rise in price? Explain the anti-inflationary policy measures best suited at present for the Indian economy. (5+5+15)

10. Write short notes on any five of the following:
    (*a*) Isoquants and their properties.
    (*b*) Advantages of Rupee Devaluation.
    (*c*) Liquidity trap.
    (*d*) Euler's Theorem.
    (*e*) Keynesian Transactionary demand for money.
    (*f*) Cash-balance approach to quantity theory of money.
    (*g*) Rural unemployment.
    (*h*) Tax-multiplier.

PAPER II
PRODUCTION ECONOMICS AND FARM MANAGEMENT AND AGRICULTURAL FINANCE, CO-OPERATION AND MARKETING

Time Allowed: 3 hours *Maximum Marks*: 200

1. Attempt any Eight Questions.
2. All questions carry equal marks.
3. Answers must be written in the medium specified in the admission certificate issued to the candidate.

---

1. The different tools or methods of analysis commonly employed to achieve one or more of the stated objectives of agricultural production economics include budgeting, production function and mathematical programming. Explain the methodological framework of each one of these methods. Discuss the merits and demerits of these methods particularly keeping in mind the nature of decision-making environment and data availability in agriculture. (25)
2. What are different types of risks in agriculture? Describe at least one statistical method and one programming approach to incorporate risk in farm planning. (25)
3. One of the reasons for low adoption of farm technology in India is stated to be lack of understanding of whole farm framework. How farming system approach can help planners for better understanding of what is happening on the farms and develop technologies best suited to a farming system. (25)
4. Explain with the help of neat diagrams different types of production relationships in agriculture. How product-product problems are important to a farmer and the Nation? Do we have to promote the practice of farm record keeping by our farmers? (25)
5. Describe different kinds of farm records that are to be kept by our farmers. Discuss the importance of farm accounting for managerial analysis. Write a note on how to promote the practice of farm record keeping by our farmers. (25)
6. The problem of agricultural credit in India in recent years had to do with utilization than availability. How do these

two have varied over the years? Discuss measures for efficient utilization of available credit by farmers. (25)

7. Multiplicity of credit sources in rural areas in the absence of effective co-ordination and control has added to the problem of repayment of agricultural credit. Discuss with illustrations wherever necessary. (25)
8. The success of co-operatives in limited spheres is attributed to managerial input. What are the problems and prospects of introducing this input on a wider scale in Indian co-operative institution? (25)
9. It is often complained that in general, the real producer (farmer) will not receive the price, he deserves for his output. How can the producer's share in consumer's price in the marketing of agricultural products be increased?(25)
10. Discuss the price policy of oilseeds and pulses *vis-a-vis* other crops. Has it achieved its objectives? If not, outline a policy strategy for increasing oilseeds and pulses production in India. (25)

YEAR 1992
PAPER II

Time Allowed: 3 hours *Maximum Marks*: 200

1. Attempt any Eight Questions.
2. All questions carry equal marks.
3. Answers must be written in the medium specified in the admission certificate issued to the candidate.

1. Distinguish between static and dynamic economics. Do you think that static equilibrium indicates the equilibrium of a stagnant economy and a dynamic equilibrium relates to a progressive economy? (15+10)
2. 'Cost curves and production curves are dual of each other', discuss. With the help of suitable illustrations, explain the relationship between various cost concepts. (10+15)
3. Distinguish between pure monopoly and discriminating monopoly. How equilibrium is attained in these situations? (10+15)
4. Explain Herred-Domar model. How this model is more suitable for the developing countries? (15+10)
5. What do you mean by monetary and fiscal policy? What are the limitations of fiscal policies? Discuss the significance of the fiscal policies in the context of recent changes in economic policy regime. (5+10+10)
6. What do you understand by the term economic development and growth? Explain economic, technological, social and cultural factors affecting development of the country. (10+15)
7. What do you understand by instability in agriculture? What measures are commonly used to measure instability in agriculture? How it affects the farmers? (5+10+10)
8. Discuss the nature and scope of agricultural policy. Do you think agricultural policies so far followed by the Government of India were congenial and conducive for the development of Indian agriculture? Give reasons in support of your answer. (10+15)
9. Explain in brief the important methods and techniques of planning. Which one has been adopted by the Indian

planners in the preparation of Five-Year Plans? Do you agree with this approach? Give reasons in support of your answer. (15+10).

10. Write short notes on any five of the following:
    (*a*) Social accounting.
    (*b*) Keynesian Transactionary demand for money.
    (*c*) Cash-balance approach to quantity theory of money.
    (*d*) Foreign trade payments of developing countries.
    (*e*) Oligopoly.
    (*f*) Role of Voluntary Organizations in Rural Development.
    (*g*) Poverty line and its application.
    (*h*) Problems of international monetary system. (5×5)

YEAR 1994
PAPER II

Time Allowed: 3 hours	*Maximum Marks*: 200

1. Attempt any Eight Questions.
2. All questions carry equal marks.
3. Answers must be written in the medium specified in the admission certificate issued to the candidate.

1. Given the information on a portion of an individual's demand curve for good X, when the price of good Y is ₹ 2 and income is ₹ 100:

Price of X in ₹ per unit	10	8	6
Quantity of X in units	4	6	10

Using the above information (10+5+10 = 25)

(*a*) Determine the utility maximizing combination of X and Y at each Px.

(*b*) Graphically illustrate your answer to part (*a*). Draw the price consumption curve.

(*c*) Are goods X and Y normal or inferior—Explain.

2. Explain the behaviour of the oligopolistic market for price determination; discuss the phenomenon of price leadership. (15+10 = 25)

3. What is meant by dualism in economic development? Explain with reference to India's development experience during the era of planned development. Suggest ways and means of ensuring equity in economic development. (5+10+10 = 25)

4. What are structural features of Indian agriculture? Explain the needed structural changes and the scope for such transformation in the context of recent liberalization policies of economic development in the country. (10+15 = 25)

5. The twin problems of poverty and unemployment in rural sector needs multi-sectoral approach. Evaluate how these problems are effectively handled through Integrated Rural Development Programme in India.

6. Comment on the terms of trade for agriculture in India. Suggest needed changes in policies and strategies to ensure sustained growth of agriculture. (10+15 = 25)

7. What are the salient features of agricultural price policy in India? Evaluate its role in increasing agricultural production in the country. (15+10 = 25)
8. What are the problems faced by the co-operative credit institutions in meeting the credit needs of the farmers? Highlight the role played by the NABARD in the agricultural and rural development in India. (15+10 = 25)
9. What is meant by marketing efficiency? What are the alternative approaches to evaluate the efficiency of the market for a farm product? (10+15 = 25)
10. Write brief notes on any five of the following:
    (*a*) Shadow prices.
    (*b*) Opportunity cost.
    (*c*) Net worth of a farm.
    (*d*) Internal rate of return.
    (*e*) Marketing Margins and Price-spread.
    (*f*) Food security.
    (*g*) Agro-climatic Regional Planning.
    (*h*) Linear Programming. $(5 \times 5 = 25)$

YEAR 2003
PAPER II

Time Allowed: 3 hours *Maximum Marks*: 200

1. All questions are compulsory and carry equal marks.
2. Answers must be written in Ball Pen/Ink in the medium specified in the admission certificate issued to the candidate.
3. Instructions given in the admission certificate should be followed strictly.

1. What is project appraisal?
   (*a*) Describe different types of project appraisal with illustrations.
   (*b*) How project appraisal differs between agricultural projects and non-agricultural projects?
   (*c*) What peculiarities are to be handled agricultural project analysis under different contexts?
   (*d*) What methodological improvements are required to handle the peculiarities of agricultural projects?
2. In the wake of the WTO, what are the institutional innovations required for helping farmers in facing challenges in realizing their margin?
   (*a*) Which existing marketing regulations constrain the marketing functions in helping farmers to face the challenges of WTO?
   (*b*) What steps are required to be taken to facilitate farmers to achieve remunerative returns in the framework of WTO?
3. What is marketing efficiency?
   (*a*) How marketing efficiency is measured?
   (*b*) What is market integration?
   (*c*) Does market integration alone result in market efficiency?
   (*d*) What policies promote market integration?
4. Discuss the features of Cobb-Douglas and Quadratic production functions:
   (*a*) Find MP, AP, EP, MRS, Isoquant, Ridgelines, PPC.

(*b*) Interpret MP, AP, EP, MRS, Isoquant, Ridgelines, PPC.

(*c*) Highlight similarities and contrasts in the two production functions with potential applications to agriculture.

5. What is input-output analysis? For the following input-output table:

(*a*) Derive the Leontief inverse

(*b*) Interpret the technical coefficients

(*c*) Interpret the elements of the Leontief inverse.

Sectors	Agriculture	Manufacturing	Final demand	Total output
Agriculture	20	60	20	100
Manufacturing	30	20	50	100
Primary input	50	20	30	100
Total output	100	100	100	100

6. (*a*) What are the basic assumptions of production function analysis?

(*b*) Calculate the maximum profit when Total Cost function (TC) and Total Revenue functions (TR) are given where Q is Quantity

$TR = 1400G - 7.5Q^{v}$

$TC = Q^3 - 6Q^{v} + 14Q + 750$

7. (*a*) Explain what do you understand about producers surplus of Agricultural Commodities?

(*b*) Enumerate the factors affecting the marketable surplus.

(*c*) Is there any relation between marketed surplus and marketable surplus? Briefly explain.

8. (*a*) Differentiate between types and systems of farming. Enumerate different types of farming with suitable examples.

(*b*) Distinguish between Discounting and Compounding. List out different discounted and undiscounted measures. Write a note on internal rate of return.

9. (*a*) What is NAFED? Explain in brief its functions. How it helps in solDving the problems of agricultural marketing?

(*b*) What do you understand by 'GATE' and 'Dunkle Proposal'? Explain how Indian Economy is affected by them?

10. Explain with an example that how will you determine the risk-bearing capacity of a cultivator. If he decides to borrow
    (*a*) for meeting working costs, such as fertilizers, pesticides, seeds, etc.
    (*b*) for purchasing a tractor.

YEAR 2005
PAPER II

1. What is consumption theory? Analyse the consumer equilibrium through utility and indifference curves techniques.

OR

What is national income? Discuss different methods of computing national income of India along with difficulties and solutions.

2. Explain elasticity of demand. Discuss various degrees of elasticity of demand along with their practical uses.
3. Differentiate risk and uncertainty in agriculture. Discuss their role and effects in resource allocation of Indian agriculture.

OR

What is price spread? Discuss different methods of calculating marketing margins along with their significance and limitations.

4. Discuss appropriate marketing and price policy related measures to address the paradoxical situation of existence of hunger and food surpluses in India.
5. What is inflation? Describe effects of inflation and measures to combat it.

OR

Discuss the conceptual framework of optimal utilization of renewable natural resources along with underlying assumptions.

6. What is linear programming? Explain the role of linear programming in decision-making in farming along with assumptions and limitations.

OR

Discuss the process of adjustment of savings and investment in an economy with suitable examples.

7. Explain 3Rs and 3Cs of credit. Discuss the farm credit scenario in India.

8. What is production function? Describe characteristics, merits and demerits of different production functions commonly used for analyzing the farm data.
9. What is multicollinearity and how to detect it? Describe the consequences of multicollinearity and their solutions.

OR

Explain economic development. Discuss the role of agriculture in India's economic development.

10. Differentiate between farm planning and budgeting. Explain their role, importance and significance in Indian agriculture.

Index

L

M

N

O

P